UNCHARTED STRAIT

UNCHARTED STRAIT

The Future of China-Taiwan Relations

RICHARD C. BUSH

BROOKINGS INSTITUTION PRESS
Washington, D.C.

Library of Congress Cataloging-in-Publication data

Bush, Richard C., 1947-
  Uncharted strait : the future of China-Taiwan relations / Richard C. Bush.
    pages   cm
  Includes bibliographical references and index.
  Summary: "Focuses on cross-Strait relations during Ma Ying-jeou's first term,
assessing the impact of stabilization on economics, politics, and security and the
implications for resolution of Taiwan and China's fundamental dispute. Examines
how Taiwan can strengthen itself; how China can promote a mutually acceptable
outcome; and how Washington can protect its interests in South Asia"--Provided by
publisher.
  ISBN 978-0-8157-2384-4 (hardcover : alk. paper)
  1. Taiwan--Relations--China. 2. China--Relations--Taiwan. I. Title.
DS799.63.C6B86 2013
327.51051249--dc23   2012045085

2 4 6 8 9 7 5 3 1

Printed on acid-free paper

Typeset in Minion

Composition by Oakland Street Publishing
Arlington, Virginia

Printed by R. R. Donnelley
Harrisonburg, Virginia

For my grandchildren

SEBASTIAN BUSH

MACALLISTER "CAL" KOLLET

VIVIAN BUSH

Contents

Acknowledgments

As I put the final touches on *Uncharted Strait*, I was reminded once again of how much a solitary author depends on the generous assistance of others. In my case, that help has come in many different forms, and I am grateful for it all.

The first objects of my gratitude are those who provided the financial support for this project: the Smith Richardson Foundation; the Taiwan Semiconductor Manufacturing Corporation Foundation; the Government of Norway; and an anonymous donor. Each has supported me in the past and I am pleased that they have done so again.

I could not have asked for a better intellectual home than the Brookings Institution. Strobe Talbott and Martin Indyk have been unstinting in their encouragement of my work, as have the staff of the Foreign Policy program. My own staff—Kevin Scott, Jennifer Mason, and Aileen Chang—have assumed much of the responsibility for managing of the Center for Northeast Asian Policy Studies, which frees me to do my scholarly work. In addition, Jennifer again served admirably as my research assistant, saving me much time and correcting a great number of mistakes. My colleagues in Brookings's Foreign Policy program have been consistently supportive, and none more so than those in the John L. Thornton China Center: Ken Lieberthal, Jeff Bader, Cheng Li, Jonathan Pollack, and Erica Downs. Cheng kindly clarified bits of Chinese language that I did not understand. Michael O'Hanlon offered a number of helpful comments. The Brookings Press—and especially my editor, Eileen Hughes—was instrumental in turning a rough manuscript into a presentable book.

Outside of Brookings, countless friends have been generous in their support. Most broadly, I have always benefited from the stimulating intellectual exchange that takes place among China and Taiwan specialists, whether in the United States, Taiwan, China, Hong Kong, or Europe. At the risk of drawing invidious distinctions, there are specific individuals whose help I cannot but acknowledge. Tom Christensen of Princeton and Steve Goldstein each reviewed the manuscript and made a number of valuable suggestions. Alan Romberg, Shelley Rigger, Robert Sutter, Su Chi, Ho Szu-yin, Chu Yun-han, and Lin Bih-jaw have been a constant and multifaceted source of guidance. Larry Diamond, Jacques deLisle, and Jean-Pierre Cabestan gave me opportunities to field test some of the ideas that I have incorporated into this book. Phillip Saunders, Dafydd Fell, Gary and Ming-yeh Rawnsley, Lin Zhengyi, Chang Ya-chung, and Sun Zhe were helpful in specific and important ways. Several scholars in China were generous with their time when I made visits to China in April 2011. The faculty and staff of the Department of Politics and Administration of the University of Hong Kong—particularly John Burns and Richard Hu—provided an ideal setting for my work when I was in residence in January and April 2011. All of these friends, colleagues, and institutions have helped me make *Uncharted Strait* a better book. I alone am responsible for the errors that inevitably but regrettably remain.

Sadly, I must note the tragic and untimely passing in 2012 of two giants in the field of Taiwan studies. Alan Wachman of Tufts University left us in June and Nancy Bernkopf Tucker in December. Each contributed seminal ideas to our understanding of Taiwan and its relations with China and the United States, and both were good friends and a source of inspiration.

Finally, I owe a debt of gratitude to my family for providing a loving environment in which I could go off on my own to read, think, and write. This book is dedicated to the clan's newest members, who have brought us great joy.

UNCHARTED STRAIT

1 | *Introduction*

May 20, 2008, was a brilliant day in Taipei, Taiwan's capital city. A cold front had blown away the clouds and pollution, and the sky was crystal clear. Fine weather was uncommon at that time of year in northern Taiwan, but it fit the political calendar well. For May 20 was the day that Ma Ying-jeou took office as the president of the Republic of China after winning a decisive victory in the election. His party, the Kuomintang (KMT), thus resumed control of Taiwan's executive branch. Ma and the KMT promised to end the problems that had beset Taiwan during the eight years under his predecessor, Chen Shui-bian, leader of the Democratic Progressive Party (DPP). In particular, Ma promised a new path for Taiwan's future. Concerning China, he would replace Chen's edgy and sometimes provocative approach with reassurance and cooperation. That was, he believed, the best way to preserve the island's prosperity, freedom, dignity, and security. The public seemed to believe that turning the political page offered hope for a new start.

China welcomed the KMT's return to power as a "major and positive change" that created a hard-to-come-by "major opportunity." It declared its expectation that negotiation channels, which had been largely suspended for the previous nine years, would reopen and expand the areas of cross-Strait cooperation. A senior official asserted: "The future of the peaceful development of cross-Strait relations is in the hands of the compatriots on both sides of the Strait. . . . We believe compatriots on the two sides of the Strait have enough wisdom and ability to jointly open up a new phase in the peaceful development of cross-Strait relations, and jointly herald in a prosperous and thriving tomorrow of the Chinese nation."[1]

1

The United States also was pleased with Ma's ascension to power. The State Department spokesman congratulated Ma Ying-jeou on his inauguration and said that Washington looked forward "to working with Taiwan's new leaders and maintaining the vibrancy" of the bilateral relationship. Most of all, the Bush administration welcomed Ma's initiatives to reduce tension in the Taiwan Strait, believing that his election provided "a fresh opportunity for Taiwan and China to reach out and engage one another in peacefully resolving their differences."[2] Senator Barack Obama conveyed a letter of congratulations in which he said that Ma's inauguration "holds promise for more peaceful and stable relations between the two sides of the Taiwan Straits, in no small measure because you have extended the hand of peace and cooperation to Beijing."[3]

That Beijing and Washington saw promise in Ma Ying-jeou was a function, in large part, of their attitude toward the Chen Shui-bian administration. The Beijing leadership had believed since the mid-1990s that trends on Taiwan were building momentum in favor of de jure independence for the island, negating its position (and the traditional position of the KMT) that the territory of Taiwan was a part of the state called China. The island's democratization after 1986 had given Taiwan independence advocates a place in the political debate, and the DPP had made independence one of its goals. Chen Shui-bian and Lee Teng-hui, the KMT president who preceded him, had, in Beijing's eyes, taken steps that reflected a covert separatist agenda. In response, the modernization of the People's Liberation Army was accelerated, focusing in particular on Taiwan.

The PRC (People's Republic of China) had worked even harder than before to constrain Taiwan's participation in the international community. For its part, the United States had grown increasingly worried that political initiatives taken by Taiwan's leaders might provoke a violent reaction from China. Even if those initiatives were not in fact designed to promote de jure independence, what mattered was how Beijing interpreted them and what actions it took in response. Washington feared also that should conflict erupt through miscalculation, it might have to intervene on Taiwan's behalf against China, with which the United States shares economic and foreign policy interests. Now, the election of Ma Ying-jeou promised a change for the better. He had pledged that independence would not be an issue during his administration and offered other reassurances to both Beijing and Washington. The prospects of unwanted conflict declined.[4]

In the wake of Ma's inauguration, Taiwan and China moved quickly to end the stalemate between them, which had persisted for over a decade. The two governments agreed to resume semi-official negotiations on the basis of something called the "1992 consensus."[5] They did so and quickly reached agreements to expand charter flights between the two sides of the Taiwan Strait (especially important for Taiwan business people working in China) and to increase the number of Mainland tourists coming to Taiwan.[6] Those were followed over the next two years by agreements that established regular air transportation and opened direct sea transport and mail services as well as agreements on food safety, financial cooperation, Mainland investment in Taiwan, agricultural inspection, industrial standards, and fishing. Then, in June 2010, Beijing and Taipei signed the Economic Cooperation Framework Agreement (ECFA), which was the first step toward creating a free trade area, and an agreement on the protection of intellectual property.

A sample of news items during the week before and after May 20, 2010—the precise midpoint of Ma's first term—gives some sense of the pace of activities. Delegations of PRC officials were regular visitors at the offices of Taiwan officials, businesses, and nongovernmental organizations (thereby also boosting hotel occupancy rates). In mid-May alone, a vice minister of agriculture, the governor of Fujian, the vice governor of Shandong, provincial secretaries from Shanxi and Sichuan, and the vice mayor of Nanjing were visiting the island. The Mainland delegations sought investment opportunities on Taiwan and concluded agreements to purchase agricultural and industrial goods, in part to foster goodwill among the island's farmers, workers, and business people, while Taiwan officials promoted their particular agendas. Meanwhile, Chinese business executives were exploring the feasibility of investing in Taiwan banks and real estate, and Taiwan business executives actively explored new investment opportunities in China—in Fujian, Zhejiang, Jiangsu, and Hebei in the east, in Hubei in the center, and in Yunnan and Guizhou in the southwest. The two sides signed cooperation agreements at the provincial and municipal levels and between nongovernmental organizations. Taiwan entities held trade fairs in Chinese provinces. An association of Taiwan-owned companies in China, whose main purpose was to lobby PRC agencies for improvements in the business environment, held its annual meeting in Beijing. Moreover, military issues were not ignored. Xiamen University in Fujian convened an academic conference on measures that the armed forces of the two sides might take to increase mutual trust and minimize problems, and retired generals of the two armies participated in a golf tournament in Nanjing.[7]

Not everyone was happy with the positive developments in cross-Strait relations. The opposition DPP warned repeatedly that Ma's policies were selling out the island's interests by increasing economic dependence on China and failing to protect Taiwan's claim that it was a sovereign entity; Taiwan was thus becoming more vulnerable to Beijing's demands for unification on its terms.[8] For example, Lu Hsiu-lien, Taiwan's vice president during the 2000–08 DPP administration, warned that an agreement that the Ma administration had signed with Beijing to liberalize economic relations "has laid the foundation for China's attempt to use economic integration to reach its ultimate goal of political unification."[9] Lurking beneath those policy critiques was a political subtext: Ma Ying-jeou's family were Mainlanders who had come to Taiwan in the late 1940s with Chiang Kai-shek's KMT. The KMT regime had ruled Taiwan harshly for forty years thereafter, repressing the political aspirations of island residents whose ancestors had arrived decades or even centuries before. Therefore, according to this subtext, the native Taiwanese could not trust Mainlander Ma's intentions or those of his party. At worst, he might try to transfer Taiwan to PRC rule.[10]

Concerns were voiced elsewhere too. In China, there were growing calls for rapid movement toward talks on political and security issues within a year of Ma's inauguration. Chinese officials and scholars argued, moreover, that China had made most of the concessions on economic issues and that therefore it was time for Taiwan to satisfy Beijing by addressing the political direction of their interaction.[11] Japanese observers assumed that the reduction of cross-Strait tensions would lead ineluctably to unification and deployment of People's Liberation Army units to Taiwan, which in turn would threaten Japan's unfettered access to sea lanes of communication with markets in Europe and oil fields in the Persian Gulf. Some in the United States also worried about where Taiwan was heading. In March 2010, the U.S.-China Economic and Security Review Commission, a body established by Congress to monitor China's policies and behavior, held a hearing to assess, among other things, whether the economic integration that it believed was occurring was leading toward political integration between the two sides of the Strait.[12] Still, the predominant response in all three capitals was to welcome the reconciliation that occurred after mid-2008, with its attendant reduction of tensions.

Four years later, Ma Ying-jeou faced the Taiwan electorate again. Having clearly enunciated his policy agenda in 2008, he ran on his record of cross-Strait rapprochement in 2012. Tsai Ing-wen, the leader of the Democratic Progressive Party, campaigned on the narrative that Ma's policies, among other things, had benefited only the rich and had undermined Taiwan's sovereignty. The weather on election day, Saturday, January 14, seemed ominous for Ma and his party. There were cloudy skies and intermittent showers over the northern half of the island, where KMT support was substantial. Down south, in the DPP's stronghold, it was partly sunny. In the event, weather and politics did not align. Ma won by 5 percentage points over Tsai, a victory that was not as sweeping as his victory in 2008 but still comfortable. The Kuomintang lost seats in the legislature but still retained control. Both Beijing and Washington were relieved at the outcome, but more important than their views was the positive verdict that the Taiwan public rendered concerning Ma's political stewardship.

Questions on Ma's Policy Course

The policy direction taken by Ma in his first term and the public's apparent affirmation of it in the 2012 election do raise questions. First of all, will China and Taiwan steadily continue to address points of friction and expand areas of cooperation? Will they move successfully from the "easy," principally economic, issues with which they began to harder issues in the areas of politics and security? Or will the difficulty inherent in addressing the latter at some point cause the whole process to stall? If so, what happens next?

Those questions focus on the short and medium term, but the longer term is more important. Where will cross-Strait interaction lead? Will the two sides find a way to resolve the fundamental dispute that has existed between them since 1949? After all, China's ultimate goal is not just to have stable, cooperative relations with Taiwan; it is to end what it regards as a state of national division. If dispute resolution is in the cross-Strait future, what form will it take? Will it be the form that China used in Hong Kong and Macau, as China proposes? Or will it be a looser association? If resolution does not occur, what will happen? Will cross-Strait relations continue in their current mode or revert to the conflicted coexistence of the Chen Shui-bian era?

What are the implications of all of this for the United States? Is the current convergence between Beijing and Taipei a good thing? If so, should Washington seek to encourage it? If not, what, if anything, should the United States do to stop the trend? Some American scholars have warned that the cross-Strait equation is changing in ways that are detrimental to U.S. interests and that it is time to prepare for those changes. Others say that it is good for the United States that Taiwan is moving steadily into China's orbit. Still others argue that Taiwan has become a strategic liability for Washington that should be jettisoned. And some worry that neither Taipei nor Washington sees the downside of current trends.

This book addresses these complex questions. The Chinese Communist Party (CCP) has defined "territorial integrity and national reunification" as one of its "core interests" and a fundamental regime goal.[13] Chinese in the PRC support that objective without hesitation. In contrast, as some people on Taiwan contemplate the idea of Taiwan's incorporation into China, they recall the poor treatment that they or their forebears received at the hands of rulers from outside. All are conscious of the nature of the Chinese communist system. The postwar relationship between Taiwan and the United States, despite much change and some lingering ambiguity, has been a fixture of East Asian security, and a change in Taiwan's relationship with China would certainly alter the regional architecture.

The Taiwan conundrum is intellectually interesting. At the heart of the problem is a question of definition. Does the dispute stem from the protracted division of the Chinese state after World War II, or does the Republic of China on Taiwan in some sense constitute a successor state of the old Republic of China (ROC), one on a par with the People's Republic of China on the Chinese mainland?[14] Whether and how the unification of the two entities might occur hinges on the answer. Indeed, I have argued that the core of the dispute between the two sides has been their disagreement over whether the Republic of China—or Taiwan—is a sovereign entity for purposes of cross-Strait relations.[15] It follows that if unification is a real option, the two sides must form a political union that bridges the disagreement over the island's legal status. Is that possible?

Then there is the question of the role that the people of Taiwan would have in any decisions about the island's future. Members of the Taiwan public, who were previously denied a say in decisions about their fate (including decisions by the United States), would have to live with the consequences. The island's democratic system gives the people a check on misguided decisions by their leaders, and in principle, that is a good thing. Yet the fact that Taiwan voters now get to pick some of their leaders through open elections raises the deeper question of how well any democratic system makes choices. Here there are no easy answers. Both representative democracy and direct democracy have their limits and create distortion of the popular will. Moreover, democracies that have yet to be fully institutionalized, such as Taiwan's, are subject to even greater distortions.[16] As a result, the Taiwan public might be denied options that represent an optimal response to the challenges that the island faces.

Finally, the interaction between Taiwan and China is occurring as China's power is rapidly growing. Hypothetically, that increases the chances that China might try to achieve its ultimate objective of unification not through negotiations in which Taiwan truly voluntarily agrees to a resolution but through intimidation, using its growing power to exert leverage on Taiwan decisionmakers and restrict their choices to the one that Beijing prefers. Or does Taiwan have ways to defend its interests despite China's power? More broadly, how does the outcome of the Taiwan Strait issue affect the rise—or more accurately, the revival—of China as a great power and the position of the United States as guardian of the international system?[17]

Today the future of the Taiwan Strait is open-ended, more so than at any other time in recent decades. The current engagement between Beijing and Taipei creates the *possibility* that they can find a solution to their six-decade-long dispute. Whether, when, and how that might happen is shrouded in uncertainty. Metaphorically speaking, the waters of the Strait are uncharted, and each of the actors worries about shoals beneath the surface. China fears the island's permanent separation, whether it makes an overt move to de jure independence or simply refuses unification. Taiwan fears subordination to an authoritarian regime that does not have its best interests at heart. The United States worries about the stability of the East Asian region.

Design of the Book

To gauge the prospects for the future, this book focuses on the course of cross-Strait relations during Ma Ying-jeou's first term. But this work is more analysis than chronicle. I begin by setting the historical and political context and laying out my conceptual framework. Particularly important analytically is the idea that the hallmark of the 2008–12 period was an effort to stabilize and improve the cross-Strait status quo through negotiations. I then assess what stabilization accomplished (or did not accomplish) in the areas of economics, politics, and security and evaluate the implications for resolution of the fundamental dispute. In brief, China and Taiwan made more progress on economic stabilization than in the political and security arenas. The course of Taiwan's 2012 presidential election, described next, suggests that the island's voters approved of the progress made to that point.

The effort to improve the status quo occurred in what I call the paradigm of mutual persuasion, wherein the two sides seek mutually beneficial outcomes by engaging in some degree of reciprocal accommodation. But there is another possibility. Their interaction could occur in the "paradigm of power asymmetry," wherein Beijing, losing patience with negotiations, exploits its greater power by seeking its ultimate goal (unification) through pressure and intimidation. Although the probability of this more coercive scenario seems low, the growth of China's economy and military power makes it plausible. In that context, I assess the prospects for the medium-term future. In turn, I examine what Taiwan might do to strengthen itself and make PRC pressure less likely; what China might do to enhance the prospects for a mutually acceptable outcome; the implications of the evolution of cross-Strait relations for the United States; and what Washington should do to protect its interests.

2

Historical and Political Context

The story of Taiwan's historical development and relationship with China is a complicated tale, one that has been told before. Others have provided their own fine treatments, and I offered mine in *Untying the Knot*.[1] The discussion that follows lightly covers what transpired in cross-Strait relations before 1988 and then summarizes in more detail what happened in the three decades that preceded Ma Ying-jeou's election.

Taiwan, which first came into the Chinese cultural orbit in the sixteenth century, became a unit within the imperial administrative system in 1689. An unruly frontier area for more than a century thereafter, it was ruled with a light hand. It was only in the latter part of the nineteenth century that the Qing government decided to strengthen its position there, to keep the island out of the covetous hands of countries like France and Japan. But when a rising Japan defeated a declining China in the war of 1894–95, Taiwan was part of the spoils of war, and it became Japan's first colony. Japanese rule was harsh at times, but it also brought civil order and economic and social development to the island. Although Taiwan was spared the internal strife that plagued Mainland China during the first half of the twentieth century, it was a target of repeated American bombing raids during World War II. Toward the end of that conflict, the Allies decided that Taiwan should be returned to China, then ruled by Chiang Kai-shek's Kuomintang, and it was his military units that took control of the island from the Japanese in 1945.

The KMT's initial rule of the native Taiwanese population was exploitative and abusive, and the people erupted in rebellion in February 1947. When Chiang sent troops to suppress the uprising, they did so with indiscriminate violence. Within two years, however, Chiang's regime, facing military defeat at the hands of Mao Zedong's communist army, came to regard Taiwan as its only refuge and moved there in late 1949. To secure its control, it imposed harsh political constraints on the native people, many of whom had only hatred for their new rulers.

It was only North Korea's invasion of South Korea in 1950 that saved Taiwan from a communist takeover. Occupied with the Korean War, Mao put off plans to take the island, and the United States gradually committed itself to ensuring its security. Taiwan soon became a link in the U.S. chain of containment in East Asia; it also became the principal obstacle to any improvement in relations between Washington and Beijing. Mao's People's Republic of China and Chiang's Republic of China remained bitter ideological rivals. The only thing that they agreed on was that Taiwan was a part of the state called China. They disagreed on which was the legal government of that China, and each wished to end their rivalry by defeating the other.

This deadlock continued for two decades; it changed only when Richard Nixon decided that perhaps the United States could use China as a counterweight to the Soviet Union. Mao, who had his own disputes with Moscow, came to the same conclusion. The two began a gradual rapprochement that culminated in the establishment of diplomatic relations in 1979—at Taiwan's great expense. The United Nations replaced the ROC with the PRC as the holder of China's seat, as did most other international organizations. In 1979, Washington terminated diplomatic relations with Taipei and voided their mutual defense treaty of 1955.

Yet Taiwan was able to survive as a separate and autonomous actor. One reason was the continued political commitment of the United States, exemplified by the Taiwan Relations Act and a stream of weapons systems that flowed from the United States, growing in quality and quantity over time. A second reason, just as important, was the determination of the island's government and people to achieve Taiwan's economic and social development. They succeeded: in 1990 it was approximately the twentieth-largest economy in the world, depending on the method of measurement used. A third reason was that China had long lacked the ability to take Taiwan militarily or persuade it to submit politically. Beijing had some hope in the early 1980s that Taipei, weakened after losing the battle for international recognition, would come around to agreeing to unification on the PRC's terms. But the proposal that it rolled out in 1981, the "one-country, two-systems" formulation, was dead on arrival in Taipei—and remains so to this day.

Economic developments gave China new hope in the mid-to-late 1980s. Although there had been little business interaction between the two sides of the Strait since 1949, each now had incentives to pursue mutually beneficial business relations. Taiwan companies were becoming less competitive globally because of rising domestic labor costs and the appreciation of Taiwan's currency. China, under the reformist leadership of Deng Xiaoping, who wished to regain political legitimacy through economic growth, was prepared to allow firms from capitalist economies to invest and set up operations. Beijing favored Taiwan companies for such investment, in part because it hoped that economic cooperation would foster political reconciliation.

Cross-Strait Relations, 1988–2004

Three developments at the end of the cold war shook the PRC's confidence. The first stemmed from the violent way in which the PRC regime ended the protest movement of 1989, particularly in and around Tiananmen Square, which destroyed the passive consensus that had existed in the United States about policy toward China. As a result, some Americans saw less reason for Washington to accommodate Beijing in conducting U.S. relations with Taipei, and they pushed to improve relations.

The second development was the decline and fall of the Soviet Union. Strategically, that tectonic shift in world politics eliminated the original reason for the U.S.-China rapprochement and any justification for Washington to give Beijing exceptional treatment. A more concrete consequence was the collapse of the world arms market, and China seized the opportunity to purchase more advanced equipment at bargain prices, particularly fighter aircraft. Taiwan tried to exploit the distress of Western defense contractors in order to get their governments to ignore PRC objections and approve sales to Taiwan that they had previously rejected. Thus, France sold Taiwan *Lafayette* frigates and *Mirage* fighters. To compete, the United States brooked Beijing's anger and provided F-16 aircraft and other systems. From then on, China's military buildup and U.S. arms sales to Taiwan were a chronic irritant in U.S.-China relations.

China objected to U.S. arms sales in part because it had always believed that Taiwan would be more compliant in any political negotiations if it was militarily weak; moreover, the early 1990s was a time when such talks were growing more likely.[2] Deeper economic ties created the need for interaction between the two governments on basic matters like the authentication of documents, but the Taiwan government refused to move into political issues or even to have direct official contacts. Beijing and Taipei therefore created official organizations within their executive branches as the focal point for cross-Strait policy and then established nominally private bodies to conduct actual contacts on behalf of the governments; those bodies allowed the two sides to avoid questions about their political relationship and status with respect to the other. The official government organizations were the Taiwan Affairs Office, for the PRC, and the Mainland Affairs Council, for Taiwan; the semi-official, nominally private, bodies were the Association for Relations across the Taiwan Strait (ARATS), in China, and the Straits Exchange Foundation (SEF), in Taiwan.

In 1992, Beijing and Taipei reached an agreement in principle to advance cross-Strait relations through a meeting between Koo Chen-fu, the head of SEF, and Wang Daohan, the head of ARATS, in which the two would sign certain technical agreements. But before a meeting could occur, the two sides had to address a threshold issue: what the political basis of their interaction was and whether it should be cited in the text of the agreements. China wanted the one-China principle to be mentioned in the texts; for policy and political reasons, Taiwan preferred that it not be. To bridge the gap, Beijing and Taipei reached a compromise in which each "orally" expressed its views on the subject of one China in a way that allowed the other to preserve its position. ARATS said, "Both sides of the Taiwan Strait uphold that One-China principle and strive to seek national unification. However, in routine cross-Strait consultations, the political meaning of 'One China' will not be touched upon." SEF said, "Although the two sides uphold the one-China principle in the process of striving for cross-strait national unification, each side has its own understanding of the meaning of one-China." This bit of creative ambiguity became known as the "1992 consensus," and it made possible a meeting between Ku and Wang in April 1993 in Singapore.

Note that the parallel statements did not reflect a full coincidence of views of the sort that two governments formalize in the text of a bilateral treaty or executive agreement. Differences coexisted with points of overlap. The two sides stated that they upheld the one-China principle—a factual statement at the time—but they disagreed on how to talk about the goal of unification and on whether their differences on the one-China principle were procedural or substantive. The Taiwan formulation stressed the extent of disagreement: it defined the goal less clearly and focused more on process than substance. Indeed, Taiwan officials have defined the "consensus" as "one China, different interpretations," a phrase that China has opposed. Taipei took this stance in part to protect the principle that the Republic of China still exists as a sovereign entity; China took the view that the ROC disappeared in 1949 with the end of the civil war on the Mainland. The lack of agreement on the 1992 consensus has continued to this day.

If Beijing had high hopes that political talks would occur quickly, they were soon dashed because of the third development that shook the PRC's confidence after the end of the cold war: democratization on Taiwan. That had a variety of consequences:

—It gave a large boost to Taiwan's international image, at the very time that China suffered opprobrium for the suppression of the Tiananmen demonstrations.

—It created the possibility that native Taiwanese might assume positions of power. Indeed, Chiang Ching-kuo's selection of the Taiwanese Lee Teng-hui as his vice president in 1984 ensured that that would happen, to Beijing's consternation.[3]

—It broadly liberalized political participation, thus legitimizing individuals and groups whose views had hitherto been taboo. Most important in this regard was the Democratic Progressive Party, which was founded in 1986. It was a native-Taiwanese party born of KMT repression. As early as 1991, the DPP announced its fundamental goals:

> In accordance with Taiwan's actual sovereignty, an independent country [to be called the Republic of Taiwan] should be established and a new constitution promulgated [through a national referendum] in order to create a legal and political system appropriate to the realities of Taiwan society.[4]

Beijing would later take that declaration into account as it evaluated the DPP's intentions.

—Political liberalization also gave currency to new ideas. One was the claim, put forward by some DPP politicians, that the people on Taiwan might be Chinese ethnically but not in terms of nationality or citizenship. Identity soon became a key lever in Taiwan politics. Another was that negotiations between the Kuomintang and the Chinese Communist Party governments might betray the interests of the Taiwanese. That quickly constrained negotiators on the Taiwan side.[5] A third idea was that Taiwan had a right to participate in international society, the PRC's views to the contrary notwithstanding. None of the three ideas sat well in Beijing, and some created problems for Washington.

It was on the boulder of "international space" for Taiwan that incipient cross-Strait political reconciliation ran aground. As Lee Teng-hui probed the accepted limits for third countries' relations with Taiwan, Beijing began to worry that his goals were fundamentally antithetical to China's.[6] Jiang Zemin, China's paramount leader, tried in January 1995 to encourage Lee to steer in a more PRC-friendly direction, but Lee demurred.[7] He wanted to visit the United States, in part to gain voters' support in Taiwan's first popular election, scheduled for March 1996, and in part because he thought that China should not determine his diplomacy. Through a sophisticated lobbying effort, he was able to get the Clinton administration's grudging acceptance of his visit, which occurred in June 1995. At his alma mater, Cornell University, Lee gave a speech whose content was more political than either China or the United States had expected.[8]

It was at that point that a political dispute became a military one. Beijing had already concluded that Taiwan trends might require a coercive response. In the overhaul of China's national strategy that began in 1993, "containing Taiwan independence" and "preventing Taiwan from fomenting any great 'Taiwan independence' incidents" had become the "main strategic direction" for Chinese defense planning.[9] Lee Teng-hui's U.S. trip therefore led senior party and military leaders in Beijing to agree that a tough response was necessary. Among the measures taken were military exercises, including missile tests, conducted in the Taiwan area in the summer and fall of 1995 and right before the March 1996 Taiwan presidential election.

Militarization aside, there was more going on than an argument over Lee Teng-hui's freedom to travel abroad or the ROC's right to rejoin the United Nations (another Taiwan project). That was a more fundamental debate over Taiwan's legal character and whether it was a sovereign entity. If it was, as Taipei consistently argued, then it deserved to participate in the international system. If it was not, as Beijing asserted, it should remain in diplomatic quarantine.

But the sovereignty debate had another dimension, and that concerned Taiwan's legal identity for purposes of any resolution of the underlying cross-Strait dispute. Under China's one-country, two-systems formula for unification, the "second system" had a lot of autonomy but no sovereignty. Taiwan's view was that the ROC was a sovereign state and any discussion of unification would have to take that as a premise. Beijing interpreted Taiwan's sovereignty claims at both the international and cross-Strait levels not as a political disagreement but as Taipei's intention to permanently separate Taiwan from China.

That difference of opinion undermined any efforts to mitigate conflict and expand cooperation. If Beijing insisted that any interaction had to be based on the one-China principle, as it tended to do, and if Beijing defined that principle in a way that Taipei interpreted as denying its claim of sovereignty, then no interaction would occur.[10] If Taipei insisted that negotiations could occur only if Beijing in some way acknowledged its sovereign status and if Beijing interpreted Taiwan's claim as separatist, then negotiations would never begin. Mutual suspicion and caution effectively stalled any efforts to narrow the gap during the 1990s.

The two sides' political differences reinforced Beijing's incentives to build modern military capabilities. In July 1999, Taiwan president Lee Teng-hui announced that cross-Strait relations were a "special state-to-state relationship." He did so because Beijing and Taipei were moving toward some level of political dialogue, and he believed that it was necessary to stake out a position on Taiwan's sovereignty in advance and to preempt what he believed to be a looming PRC effort to gain a rhetorical advantage.[11] China interpreted his statement as a stealthy move toward independence and mounted strong opposition, which included more aggressive patrolling of the Taiwan Strait by the air force of the People's Liberation Army (PLA). The mini-crisis dissipated after an earthquake on Taiwan, but the lesson that PRC leaders drew was that they needed a much stronger PLA to deter Taiwan independence (or what they interpreted as separatism) and to punish Taiwan if deterrence failed. The PLA was only too happy to see its budget and capabilities grow, and Russia was only too willing to provide more advanced equipment. Moreover, the mission of deterring Taiwan independence gave Chinese military modernization a focus that it did not have before and spurred the improvement of China's defense industry, making it less dependent on external suppliers.

Militarization of the cross-Strait dispute had profound consequences. Taiwan became the only conceivable issue on which China and the United States might end up going to war, despite their compelling reasons to avoid conflict.[12] The anxiety already present in the U.S.-Taiwan relationship deepened. Washington worried that the political initiatives of Taiwan leaders might prompt a PRC overreaction and demand U.S. intervention in an unnecessary conflict. For its part, Taipei feared that the United States might take China's side and abandon Taiwan.

Other drivers were at work here. On the PRC side was a misunderstanding of why Lee Teng-hui was making such a point of Taiwan's sovereignty. Beijing inferred that his claim was prima facie evidence that he was a separatist, but it had more to do with *how* Taiwan might fit in a unified China rather than whether it should. Moreover, although Lee certainly was not the compliant interlocutor that Beijing might have wanted, there is a good case that his actions were in fact his *response* to Beijing's rigid approach to cross-Strait relations concerning unification formulas, Taiwan's international space, and so forth.[13] The secondary driver was domestic politics on Taiwan. Neither Lee

Teng-hui nor his successor, Chen Shui-bian of the opposition Democratic Progressive Party, wanted to alienate the parts of the electorate that were most suspicious of China's intentions, including those that did in fact favor de jure independence.[14]

Lee Teng-hui was certainly a Taiwanese nationalist, but his dissent was not a rejection of Taiwan's unification with China. Indeed, he often referred to "one divided China [that] must be reunified." His focus was on the terms and conditions for the incorporation of Taiwan rather than on whether it should be incorporated. For him, Taiwan's sovereign status was not a bar to unification; there are, after all, political unions made up of sovereign entities. Beijing misread what Lee was saying. At a minimum, it saw Lee's position as incompatible with the PRC political system, with the central government as the unitary sovereign. At worst, it thought Lee's claim of sovereignty for Taiwan reflected a desire to pursue de jure independence.

Beijing regarded Chen Shui-bian, who succeeded Lee in May 2000, as a more serious challenge. As noted, the DPP was already associated with the goal of de jure independence. And China was not assuaged by Chen's effort in 1999 to tone down the DPP's independence image by passing a party resolution that accepted "Republic of China" as the current name of the state that the party preferred to call Taiwan. In addition, the resolution emphasized a democratic process for determining Taiwan's future but was silent on what that future should be.[15] Early in his presidency, Chen used similar rhetorical formulations, such as his inaugural address, to try to assure Beijing that he was not the threat that it assumed. But he also said other things that reinforced existing suspicions, mainly the result of his inexperience and the resistance that he encountered from hard-core, pro-independence forces within the DPP.

From 2002, Chen decided to move toward those "fundamentalist" forces, in part because the PRC had not responded to what he regarded as Taipei's moderation and goodwill. China had hoped that it could simply wait him out. He had received 40 percent of the votes in a three-way election. If the KMT fielded only one candidate in the 2004 election, Beijing assumed, Chen would lose and the KMT would be returned to power. So Beijing temporized and declined to cooperate with him, much less allow him to achieve anything with respect to cross-Strait relations that would enhance his and the DPP's political stature within Taiwan.

In partial response, Chen unveiled initiatives that evoked the nation creation and popular sovereignty themes of the 1991 party charter. For example, in August 2002, he announced that there were "two countries [one] on each side" of the Taiwan Strait.[16] In September 2003, he proposed creation of a new constitution, to be ratified by referendum. He took those steps to encourage a large turnout of DPP supporters to increase the chances that he would win reelection in 2004. The result was a surprising, razor-thin victory over Lien Chan, the sole KMT candidate. He used the same mobilization playbook four years later as the de facto campaign manager for his putative successor. For example, prior to the 2008 legislative and presidential elections, Chen sought to mobilize support for his Democratic Progressive Party by proposing that on election day there be a referendum on whether Taiwan should join the United Nations and do so under the name of Taiwan rather than its official name, the Republic of China. China, regarding that as a highly provocative act and a way to creep toward legal independence, declared that this was a "period of high danger." Beijing, of course, believed that Chen's initiatives were incremental, covert steps toward independence, and the Bush administration opposed them as well. In addition to their domestic political purpose, they allowed Chen to test the degree of PRC tolerance. Getting away with one step created the possibility of getting away with more.

Chen's approach to the question of Taiwan's sovereignty and Chinese unification also differed from that of Lee Teng-hui. Like Lee, he believed that Taiwan was a sovereign, independent state, and he preferred to use the name "Taiwan" rather than "Republic of China." He once used the term "political integration" to suggest that some sort of amalgamation was possible, but whereas Lee had talked about a divided China that would again be a unified state, Chen saw Taiwan as an entity outside of China that might choose to combine with it. Thus, they agreed on the possibility of union and on Taiwan's status within that union. But they disagreed on the starting point. Beijing was unhappy with both.

The end result was a downward spiral of deepening mutual suspicion. Each side feared that the other was preparing to challenge its fundamental interests. China, fearing that Taiwan's leaders were going to take some action that would have the effect of frustrating its goal of unification and permanently separating Taiwan from China—the functional equivalent of a declaration of independence—increased its military power to deter such an eventuality. Taiwan feared that China wished to use its military power and other means to intimidate Taiwan into submission, to the point that it would give up what it claimed was its sovereign character. Taiwan's deepening fears only led it to strengthen and reassert its claim of sovereignty. This corrosive political dynamic, which began under Lee Teng-hui and became more serious under Chen Shui-bian, happened in spite of the two sides' complementary economic relationship.

The Role of the United States

The United States came to play a special role in the deteriorating cross-Strait situation. Although Washington deliberately avoided taking sides in the fundamental dispute, each side interpreted U.S. evenhandedness as siding with its rival. The Chinese believed that the United States was obstructing the unification that Beijing sought, even as they acknowledged occasional U.S. efforts to block Taiwan from pursuing de jure independence. Some in Taiwan believed that Washington had sold out its democratic values for the sake of commercial and foreign policy benefits from China, even as they admitted that U.S. security support kept the island safe. Sometimes in diplomacy, the best a country can do is to make everyone else equally unhappy.

Washington's point of departure was its underlying and long-standing goal of preserving peace and security in the Taiwan Strait and East Asia more broadly. The downward spiral of cross-Strait relations that began in the mid-1990s put that objective at some degree of risk. First the Clinton and then the George W. Bush administration worried that the two sides might inadvertently slip into a military conflict through accident or miscalculation. In that case, Washington would, unhappily, have to choose sides. So each administration employed the "dual deterrence" approach. Each warned Beijing not to use force against Taiwan, even as it offered reassurance that it did not support Taiwan independence. Each warned Taipei not to take political actions that might provoke China to use force, even as it conveyed reassurance that it would not sell out Taiwan's interests for the sake of the U.S.-China relationship.[17]

The exercise of dual deterrence was governed by the circumstances of each particular case. In deciding the mix of warnings and reassurances that it would convey to Beijing or Taipei, Washington would take account of which party was more responsible for the tensions of the day. In 1995, after Lee Teng-hui's visit to the United States, the Clinton administration was modest in its warnings regarding Chinese exercises related to Taiwan. When in March 1996 the PLA conducted missile tests toward areas closer to Taiwan, the United States sent two carrier battle groups to the Taiwan area. In 1999, after Lee Teng-hui's "special state-to-state" announcement, the administration leaned more on Taipei than Beijing. Then, when it appeared that China might overreact to the election of DPP candidate Chen Shui-bian, China was the target of U.S. warnings. When Chen took his provocative steps during the 2004 and 2008 presidential campaigns, Taipei was again on the receiving end of U.S. warnings.[18]

Reversing the Spiral

Leadership change on both sides of the Strait brought a reversal of the downward spiral, but only through an extended and gradual process. The first stage occurred between 2002 and 2004 as Hu Jintao replaced Jiang Zemin as the PRC's paramount leader, taking the positions of president, general secretary of the Chinese Communist Party, and chairman of the Central Military Commission. Gradually, Hu took steps to adjust and moderate the Taiwan policy of his predecessor, creating the possibility of improving relations if Taiwan reciprocated.

Particularly after Chen Shui-bian's unexpected reelection, China decided on a more focused, articulated, and political approach, all the while continuing its military buildup. The focus shifted from promoting longer-term objectives like unification to the more near-term goal of blocking Taiwan independence. Articulation came in the form of a series of statements on what Taiwan had to gain by rejecting the DPP. The political approach was to link up more overtly with the KMT.

The policy statements began three days before Chen Shui-bian's 2004 swearing-in. On May 17, 2004, the Taiwan Affairs Office, the key PRC organization for implementing Taiwan policy, issued a statement that gave "Taiwan leaders" a choice between two roads. One was to reaffirm the "one-China principle" and to end "separatist activities"; in return, dialogue and exchanges would resume, economic cooperation would deepen, and Taiwan could have a greater sense of security and some possibility for participating in the international community. There was a specific reference to "jointly building a *framework* for peaceful, stable, and growing cross-Strait relations." If, on the other hand, Chen Shui-bian clung to his "independence position" and "separatist stance," none of that would happen. The statement stressed that "[t]o put a resolute check on the 'Taiwan independence' activities aimed at dismembering China and safeguard peace and stability in the Taiwan Straits is *the most pressing task* before the compatriots on both sides of the Straits."[19]

Next, Beijing enacted its newly articulated policy in the anti-secession law passed by the National People's Congress in March 2005, which restated China's opposition to Taiwan independence and the essential importance of the one-China principle. It identified a number of ways in which economic, cultural, and other forms of interaction would occur and defined the basic security and political issues that the two sides would discuss in a phased and flexible way to achieve peaceful reunification. Yet it also set forth a warning:

In the event that the "Taiwan independence" secessionist forces should act under any name or by any means to cause the fact of Taiwan's secession from China, or that major incidents entailing Taiwan's secession from China should occur, or that possibilities for a peaceful reunification should be completely exhausted, the state shall employ nonpeaceful means and other necessary measures to protect China's sovereignty and territorial integrity.[20]

The promised cooperation sounded good, but there was an emphasis on the one-China principle. Further, the warning was striking in its vagueness and the discretion that Beijing reserved to interpret Taiwan's actions as it pleased.

In April 2005, one month later, Lien Chan journeyed to Beijing, the first time that a chairman of the KMT had been on the Mainland since the party's defeat in 1949. He and Hu Jintao, in his capacity as general secretary of the Chinese Communist Party, issued a press communiqué on April 29. The two parties agreed to uphold the 1992 consensus, oppose Taiwan independence, pursue peace and stability in the Taiwan Strait, and promote the development of cross-Strait relations. On that basis—and if the KMT regained power—they proposed to resume cross-Strait negotiations (suspended since 1999) on issues of common concern, work toward an end to the state of hostilities, and conclude a peace accord. They also agreed to develop economic exchanges leading to an economic cooperation mechanism, discuss Taiwan's role in the international community (which China had consistently blocked), and establish a platform for future party-to-party contact.[21]

The KMT's initiative was not without political risk. It exposed the party to charges on Taiwan that it was plotting with "the enemy" and selling out the interests of the island's people. The fear of "traitors in our midst" was a staple of Taiwan political culture. In addition, there was the sensitive question of the basis on which the government or a political party agreed to engage with Beijing. Both the one-China principle and the 1992 consensus were controversial on Taiwan.

Beijing's preference has been the one-China principle, the long-standing core of its approach to the Taiwan Strait issue. The prevailing definition had been enunciated in January 2002 by Vice Premier Qian Qichen: there is one China in the world; the Mainland and Taiwan both belong to one China; China's sovereignty and territorial integrity brook no separation.[22] For the DPP, the idea that Taiwan was a part of China was a nonstarter (for many DPP members, there was one China and Taiwan was *not* part of it). For a much broader group in Taiwan, the "brook no separation" clause seemed to rule out the concept, to which they held strongly, that Taiwan was a sovereign entity.[23] The 1992 consensus posed similar issues, since each side associated itself with "one China" but disagreed on how to interpret the term.

In Taiwan's legislative and presidential elections of 2008, voters rendered their verdict on eight years of DPP rule and, apparently, on whether and how to respond to the offers that the PRC had made since 2005. Ma Ying-jeou, the KMT's presidential candidate, ran on the premise that Taiwan could better guarantee its prosperity, security, freedom, and international dignity by reassuring and cooperating with Beijing than by provoking it. He won a convincing 58 percent of the vote, and his party's candidates for the Legislative Yuan got three-quarters of the seats.

Ma's inaugural address, delivered on May 20, addressed three issues: identity, intentions, and the terms of reengagement with China.[24] His treatment of identity began with his use of terms. He referred to both the Republic of China and Taiwan and did so, it seemed, interchangeably, yet the two were not identical. "[T]he Republic of China [ROC] was reborn on Taiwan," he said. "The destinies of the ROC and Taiwan have been closely intertwined." The difference, it seemed, was that the ROC was a political entity, a "democratic republic" (on other occasions he would call it a sovereign state). It was established in 1912, and only part of its history was associated with Taiwan.[25] Taiwan, on the other hand, was more a geographical entity that was home to an ethnic Chinese society; its people were part of the Chinese race (*huaren*). What he called its "core values" were Confucian: benevolence, righteousness, and so forth. It was also an immigrant society, with different ethnic or subethnic groups that together had created, as he put it, "our homeland." Voters in the 2008 election had chosen "ethnic harmony" after several years of DPP leaders' attempts to build political power by fanning ethnic divisions. Interestingly, Ma stated that the geographic scope of that homeland was only the territory controlled and administered by the ROC government: the islands of Taiwan, Penghu, Jinmen, and Mazu, but his government still took the position that the sovereign territory of the ROC was all of China.

When talking about the PRC, Ma referred only to "mainland China" (*Zhongguo dalu*)—again, a geographic entity, whose people were also part of the Chinese race. He did not mention the PRC government in any way, and he used the title "Mr." to refer to China's paramount leader, Hu Jintao.[26]

Ma conveyed reassurances in two directions: to Beijing and to the people of Taiwan. He pledged that during his term he would maintain the status quo, which was and is the strong preference of the Taiwan public. In the process he ruled out not only de jure independence (which China feared) but also unification and the use of force (which Taiwan's people feared) and said that the ROC constitution would be his working framework. His fundamental orientation was to shelve differences and expand areas of cooperation, which, he said, overlapped with Hu Jintao's view. Ma made clear that, as a matter of dignity, the ROC would act in the international community—something that the Taiwan public wanted. The ROC would not be a troublemaker, but the two sides should jointly contribute to international society. Ma pledged to "protect Taiwan with all my heart" and vowed that his goal was "putting Taiwan first for the benefit of the people." He did not repeat a standard promise that the Taiwan people would decide the island's ultimate future, but that was implicit in his stress on democracy.

When it came to cross-Strait reengagement, Ma called for a resumption of negotiations and offered the 1992 consensus as the basis for them. He defined the consensus as "one China, different interpretations." Beijing did not accept that definition because Ma on previous occasion had said that his "interpretation" was that China was the ROC, but China could take comfort in the affirmation of one China. Moreover, Beijing knew that a point of agreement in the 1992 understanding had been the goal of unification, something that Ma was now eschewing while he was in office. In effect, Ma made a bet that China would accept his 1992 consensus pledge as long as the two sides did not dwell on what the consensus meant.[27]

Concerning the substance of negotiations, Ma's first priority was the "normalization of economic and cultural relations." He also called for consultations on Taiwan's international space and on a "possible" peace accord. As noted, his emphasis was on reducing mutual mistrust and broadening cooperation in order to "attain peace and co-prosperity." He made the intriguing remark that "in resolving cross-Strait issues, what matters is not sovereignty but core values and way of life." Long-term "peaceful development" (the term used by Beijing) would occur if "mainland China" continued to move toward "freedom, democracy, and prosperity for all the people" (these were the Three Principles of the People enunciated by Sun Yat-sen, the KMT's founder).

Taiwan Domestic Politics

With leadership change in both Beijing and Taipei and the exchange of reciprocal statements, a virtuous circle replaced a vicious circle. What happened next and where it might lead is the subject of this book. Yet it is obvious from the historical summary presented here that domestic politics have been an important factor in limiting leaders' choices and shaping cross-Strait outcomes. Lee Teng-hui hardened his cross-Strait policy in the mid-1990s in part to discourage left-of-center Taiwanese voters from supporting the DPP in the 1996 direct presidential election—the first in Taiwan's history. As leader of the DPP, Chen Shui-bian employed two different electoral strategies over three election cycles: tacking to the center in 2000 by taking a moderate stance on China policy and then mobilizing his base in 2004 and 2008 by proposing initiatives that fit their more radical agenda. Although China lacks Taiwan's lively democratic system, its unique mix of populism and authoritarianism means that leaders there are not immune to opposition either. Because bringing Taiwan "into the embrace of the motherland" remains a fundamental goal of the PRC, leaders who somehow "fail" in advancing that objective may become vulnerable to political attack from within the regime or without. To the extent that domestic sentiment constrains leaders as they formulate policy, cross-Strait relations become more complicated.

Political Groups

Taiwan has used colors to represent the political groups that contend for voters at election time, for dominance in the Legislative Yuan, and for the attention of the media. On the one hand, there is the "Blue" camp, which is made up of the KMT and a couple of small parties or groups that share its relatively conservative ideology and favor improving relations with China. On the other side is the "Green" camp, which is made up of the DPP and the Taiwan Solidarity Union, a party that Lee Teng-hui founded after he left office in 2000.[28]

Yet Taiwan's political color spectrum is more sophisticated than that of the United States, with its simple distinction between blue and red. Within each Taiwan camp are significant shades of difference, known as Deep Green, Light Green, Deep Blue, and Light Blue. A variety of factors define this spectrum: preference for independence, the status quo, or unification; fear versus greater trust and confidence regarding China's intentions; stress on a separate Taiwan identity versus a mixed identity or exclusively Chinese one; and emphasis on social welfare and the environment versus economic growth.[29] The Deep Greens are most committed to independence and most afraid of China; they stress Taiwan identity and emphasize social welfare goals most. The Deep Blues are more likely to have a relatively positive view of China.

In terms of party identification, Deep Greens are most likely to be strong supporters of the DPP and the Taiwan Solidarity Union. Deep Blues are loyal to the KMT or the small People First Party (PFP). Swing voters are more likely to fall in the "Light" camps. In terms of "ethnic" background, Deep Blues tend to be Mainlanders, whose families came after World War II. Native Taiwanese from Fujian tend be Deep or Light Greens or Light Blue. Hakka people generally fall in the Light Blue camp. A very rough estimate of the size of the four color groups is 10 to 12 percent for the Deep Blues; around 30 percent for the Light Blues; about 20 percent for the Light Greens; and about 25 percent for the Deep Greens; the affiliation of 10 percent or so is unclear.[30]

Taiwan does have voters who lack a strong loyalty to either of the two major political parties, but how many is debated. Therefore, according to one polling organization, for most of Ma Ying-jeou's presidency those who identified with the Blue camp fluctuated between 33 and 40 percent; DPP voters accounted for about 20 to 25 percent; and swing voters constituted around 35 percent.[31] Yet poll respondents who say that they are swing or "independent" voters may actually have a mild preference for one camp, and they usually vote for a party within that camp, though not always. Ho Szu-yin of National Chengchi University believes that the share of truly independent voters is around 17 percent of the electorate. Of those, around 40 percent are highly informed on policy issues and mark their ballots after serious thought. The remaining 60 percent of the 17 percent are not well informed, but they may not vote at all. So whether strong or weak, party identification remains a significant factor.[32]

But the island's citizens differ on more than party loyalty and party programs. They also argue over fundamental factors of political and national identity. History is the reason. When the KMT began its rule in the late 1940s, it believed that the island's longtime residents had become less "Chinese" after living under Japanese rule for fifty years. So after the regime imposed its rather harsh control, it proceeded to "re-sinify" its new subjects through a variety of policies. By doing so and by denying the populace any political participation, it created popular alienation and a focus by the Taiwanese on the "sadness" of their lot. Some Taiwanese even translated their experience into the claim that their homeland was a separate country and culture, that the ROC was an illegitimate regime, and that outsiders could not be trusted. They reached that conclusion even though they and almost all the other people on Taiwan were ethnically Chinese. It was dangerous to express such ideas under martial law, but with the democratization of the 1990s they were aired widely. More and more, people saw themselves as Taiwanese rather than Chinese or as a combination of the two.[33]

Increasingly, Taiwan identity—and national identity at that—became an organizing principle of Taiwan politics. In 1996, Lee Teng-hui placed it at the center of his campaign, in part to tap public pride in Taiwan but also to play on the underlying fear of outsiders, whether it was KMT Mainlanders or PRC

Communists. Winning reelection had a higher priority than preserving cross-Strait relations, at least temporarily, and the People's Liberation Army helped him by conducting missile tests right before the election. As noted, Chen Shui-bian chose a centrist course in 2000, but he reverted to identity politics in 2004 after, in his view, he got no benefit from Beijing in return for his moderation. The temptation to win reelection by appealing to the identity of his political base was overwhelming, and he increased his vote total by 1.5 million votes. By 2008, however, identity was declining as the most salient political issue. Ma Ying-jeou was able to win because the broad majority of voters were tired of economic uncertainty and DPP provocations of Beijing.

Yet it is worth noting that nationalism can have different dimensions, each of which can offer a different basis for solidarity or differentiation. "The nation" can have a racial, geographic, ethno-cultural, civic, or policy focus—or any combination thereof.[34] About a quarter of the Taiwan population takes the geographic and ethno-cultural view that the island is its own nation and should have its own state. The PRC, arguing from a similar perspective and from its definition of history, maintains that "Taiwan is a part of China." Perhaps a majority of the Taiwan population might be prepared to accept the idea that Taiwan is geographically and culturally a part of the Chinese nation, but for them the focus of their identity and loyalty is the Republic of China and its democratic political system. Theirs is a civic nationalism, not an ethno-cultural one.[35]

Voter Sentiment on Cross-Strait Relations

For a number of years, the Taiwan government's Mainland Affairs Council has sponsored polls assessing the public's evaluation of the pace of cross-Strait policy. A plurality has usually said that the pace is "just right," and that share has ranged between 40 and 47 percent during the years of the Ma administration. The share that thought that progress was too slow peaked at the time of Ma's inauguration at 35 percent and then dropped quickly to the teens. The percentage that felt that the pace was "too fast" rose from 19 percent in May 2008 into the 30 percent range for the rest of his term. A poll taken toward the end of his first term was consistent with these levels.[36] The recent trend, therefore, is that only a third of those surveyed believe that cross-Strait relations are developing too quickly, while over half are satisfied or impatient with the stabilization that has occurred. Still, there is ambivalence. In a late 2009 poll by *CommonWealth* (*Tien Hsia*) magazine, 55 percent thought that the government's top priority should be improving the economy, while 61 percent worried that the island's economy was "over-reliant" on the Mainland. A majority preferred not to work in China and did not want their children to go to school there. A significant majority was unhappy with Ma Ying-jeou's performance (a majority inflated by the government's poor response to a typhoon in August), but no other leader or political institution got high marks. Only 19 percent said that they supported the KMT, and 12 percent said that they supported the DPP; 61 percent would not align with any party.[37]

Another staple of Taiwan polling concerns the long-term outcomes that people prefer. The Election Studies Center of National Chengchi University has conducted a series of polls on this issue. In November 2011, for example, it found that 4.1 percent of those polled wanted Taiwan independence as soon as possible; 1.3 percent wanted unification as soon as possible; 17.3 percent wanted to preserve the status quo now and then move toward independence; 8.6 percent wanted to preserve the status quo now and then move toward unification; 26.5 wanted to preserve the status quo indefinitely; and 34.2 percent wanted to preserve the status quo now and make a decision later but did not express a preference on what the decision should be. Thus 60.7 percent wished to avoid choosing a long-term outcome; 10.9 had some preference for unification; and 21.4 percent had some preference for independence.[38]

To make matters even more complex, Shelley Rigger's careful analysis revealed that the strength of Taiwan nationalism (desire for independence, hatred of China, and so forth) is very much a function of when Taiwanese individuals came to political consciousness. Those who lived as adults under Japanese colonialism and KMT repression expressed much stronger Taiwanese nationalism (as Rigger defines it) than those who became politically conscious around and after 1985. That transition point is important because that was when cross-Strait economic relations began and just before KMT leaders started to dismantle the apparatus of repression and move toward democracy. As Rigger writes: "The attitudes that are most destructive to cross-strait ties are held by older Taiwanese, whose political influence will wane in the coming years. Younger Taiwanese tend to be pragmatic and flexible in their views; they lack the passionate emotion that drives many [of their elders]. This is not to say that younger Taiwanese do not feel a strong connection to Taiwan as their homeland; they do. But for them, loving Taiwan does not mean hating China."[39] At least some PRC Taiwan specialists understand this trend and its positive implications for Chinese interests.[40]

There are obviously tensions at play here—between committed and swing voters; between young adults and their elders; and between those who say that they prefer the status quo and those who seek unification or independence. Among the pragmatic majority that prefers some version of an undefined status quo, there still is a diversity of views. Furthermore, Taiwan citizens understand that although they want the status quo, Beijing ultimately wants something different: unification on its terms.

These tensions create dilemmas for the island's two political parties as each seeks to gain an advantage over the other. The KMT can argue that it can bring about a beneficial status quo through a policy of stabilization, which includes expanding areas of cross-Strait cooperation and reassuring Beijing that its intentions are benign. It can also assert that a DPP government would put the benefits of cooperation at risk because the DPP's basic approach and past behavior would unnecessarily put Beijing on its guard.[41] The DPP, on the other hand, can argue that KMT policies have placed Taiwan on a slippery slope to integration with China and that the DPP's more skeptical approach to China can better protect Taiwan's best interests. It can also play on the public's knowledge that the PRC's long-term intention is definitely not preservation of the current status quo as well as on the hardy perennials about "traitors in our midst" that complicate the politics of cross-Strait policy, thereby putting the KMT on the defensive and gaining some advantage for itself.

The tensions among points of view plus the thrust and parry between the two major political parties mean that the politics of cross-Strait policy is highly contested. Each party seeks to put the other on the defensive and has its ways of doing so. Each seeks to consolidate its base voters while appealing to swing voters. Ma Ying-jeou has sustained support for a policy of stabilization, at least in the economic area, but even that has met with difficulties.

Legislature

Taiwan's Legislative Yuan (LY) is composed of seventy-three seats selected on the basis of votes cast in single-member geographical districts. Thirty-four seats are allocated proportionately among the parties and caucuses based on a separate ballot that voters cast for their favorite organization, and six seats are reserved for people classified as aborigines. The KMT has usually held a majority of seats—as many as three-fourths after the 2008 elections. Because Taiwan's system is more presidential than parliamentary, divided government is possible: from 2000 to 2008 the DPP controlled the executive branch while the KMT held the legislature. Local elections are by definition local in their focus, but their outcome is often treated as a barometer of how well the ruling party is doing on national issues.

Domestic Politics and China

Since Taiwan began direct elections in 1996, China has struggled to find the right way to encourage Taiwan political outcomes that support its objectives or at least mitigate its fears. It has learned since then that intimidating Taiwan voters through words and actions can increase their support for candidates that Beijing does not like. Still, the complexity of Taiwan public opinion creates a dilemma for Beijing as it tries to "game" the Taiwan system. For example, during Ma Ying-jeou's first term, China understood that it could foster domestic support for his policies by making concessions to his government (something that Taiwan encouraged). But it also recognized that if Ma lost the 2012 election, his DPP successors would benefit from many of those concessions, even though they would not offer the sort of reassurances that Ma had extended. If the DPP had won in 2012, in part by criticizing KMT policies toward China, Beijing would have feared a pro-independence challenge to its fundamental interests, based solely on past experience and its evaluation of DPP goals. But if Beijing were to act on its fears by not cooperating with the DPP government, it would run the risk of alienating the Taiwan public, whom it wishes to win over.

Over the long run, China faces a more formidable obstacle. Despite the gradual and generational moderation of political attitudes on the island, the "sadness" of native Taiwanese, born of their encounter with Chinese "outsiders" after 1945, still lingers. As a fairly young Taiwan friend of mine noted, "If China wants to win the hearts and minds of Taiwanese, it has to address the 'sadness' history of Taiwanese by showing some true respect."[42] However, the Communist Party's record of rule on the Mainland only reinforces fears of what unification would be like. In its declared objective of winning the hearts and minds of the Taiwan people, the PRC is a victim of Taiwan's past and its own present-day domestic policies.

Chinese Domestic Politics

Even though China is a one-party authoritarian state, it still has competition over power and policy—that is, politics. It just occurs in ways that differ from those in Taiwan and other pluralistic systems. Four arenas in particular are important.

The first is the struggle within the leadership of the Chinese Communist Party itself. Approximately three dozen individuals—Politburo members, senior generals, vice premiers, state councilors, party department heads, and the first party secretaries of the most important provincial units—dominate the political system. Subgroups within this leadership collective take responsibility for specific policy issues. If individual leaders somehow fail in carrying out their responsibilities, they can be subject to criticism from their colleagues and end up in a weakened position.[43] Because the ultimate unification of China has always been a fundamental priority of the party, any leader who mishandles it is especially vulnerable to attack. For example, in 1995 colleagues of President Jiang Zemin and Foreign Minister Qian Qichen placed them on the political defensive for not blocking Lee Teng-hui's visit to the United States.[44]

The second arena concerns the Chinese Communist Party regime more broadly. As China's external relations, including the external dimension of Taiwan policy, have expanded and grown more complex, the number of actors within the regime who seek to influence policy toward Taiwan has grown.[45] In the late 1980s, only officials responsible for foreign affairs, intelligence, national security, and united front activity were part of the relevant policy team. By 2008, it also included individuals from the party secretariat, the party propaganda department, and the foreign trade sector.[46]More actors increase the difficulty of policy coordination and the task of forging consensus because different agencies have conflicting views on how to respond to policy challenges.[47]

The third arena concerns scholars who work for government research institutes or universities, part of an expanding cadre of public intellectuals who have the freedom to comment publicly on external policy in general and on Taiwan policy in particular. They are not the policy elite, and their role differs from that of high-level officials in the CCP regime. They "take part in public discourse and try to influence informed public opinion and government policy on a range of issues." Their audiences are varied: the government, each other, and the broader public.[48] Their opinions, conveyed through television, radio, newspapers, and journals, can have an impact on the broader viewing, listening, and reading public and thereby affect policy indirectly.[49]

The fourth arena involves the public at large, or at least the members of the public that pay some attention to external affairs. They have relatively modest knowledge of the world at large and Taiwan in particular. They have no direct impact on external policy, including Taiwan policy, but they still have views. The opinions expressed in Internet chat rooms and on bulletin boards tend to come from the more nationalistic segment of the public. Indeed, what the entire Chinese public really wants when it comes to Taiwan is completely unclear. The regime knows exactly what it wants (unification), and it has shaped public views to support that objective over a long period of time, to the exclusion of any alternative approach. So any serious effort to measure Chinese opinion regarding Taiwan would likely only confirm official orthodoxy. For the most part, the top leadership dominates policy. It is when regime policy appears to have had a setback that at least some parts of the public express themselves, sometimes in a vociferous and xenophobic fashion.

Politics PRC-syle can put the country's leadership in a dilemma. Those in charge of Taiwan policy understand that achieving unification is a long-term process, one that must patiently take account of divided public opinion in Taiwan's democratic system. Consequently, the PRC leadership has, in effect, set aside resolution of the fundamental dispute for the medium term and concentrated on the stabilization of relations. Yet the regime has sought to enhance its legitimacy by casting itself as the embodiment of Chinese nationalism and as the agent for fulfilling goals such as ending the long-standing division of the county.[50] The more the regime accommodates Taiwan public opinion by pursuing a measured and cautious policy toward the island, it runs some risk of alienating some members of the Chinese public and the elite.

3

Setting the Analytical Stage

After Ma Ying-jeou's inauguration as Taiwan's president in May 2008, Taipei and Beijing were able to reverse the downward spiral of the previous fifteen years and put their relations on a more normal footing. This chapter and the two that follow present an analytical assessment of what happened and what did not happen during Ma's first term and what that means. The question to be addressed is how far the upward spiral has spun and how much further it can go. That progress occurred in Ma's first term does not mean that it will continue in the second. That the two sides successfully addressed "easy," mainly economic, issues does not mean that they will be able to tackle harder ones. For this assessment, two distinctions are critical:

The first concerns the character of the 2008–12 period, which has not seen the continuation of the conflicted coexistence that existed from 1995 to 2008. It can be defined as one of two alternatives: one is as a prelude to the resolution of the fundamental China-Taiwan dispute; the other is as a conceptually distinct, intermediate state, which I call stabilization. I argue that the 2008–12 period has been the latter.

The second distinction concerns the ways in which stabilization might move toward resolution, if in fact it does. Analytically, two ways seem possible. One is through a process of mutual persuasion, in which Taiwan and China make concessions to each other on the key issues that divide them. The other stems from the asymmetry of power between the People's Republic of China and the Republic of China, which creates the potential for the PRC to use its greater power to shape Taiwan's decisions through leverage and even coercive diplomacy. If it did, an increasingly weak Taiwan might abandon the hope of changing Beijing's policies through persuasion and judge that it had no choice but to involuntarily accept some version of China's terms.

Resolution versus Stabilization

In a May 2009 poll, people in both Taiwan and China were asked what the future held for cross-Strait relations (the time frame was undefined). Of Mainland respondents, 64.2 percent predicted the unification of the island with China. In contrast, 60 percent of those surveyed on Taiwan believed that the status quo would continue.[1] Methodologically, that poll may not have been the best done on cross-Strait relations, but it was enough to demonstrate that the two publics have very different expectations for the future. They also appear to understand that there is a difference between the current situation and some final outcome. That is the distinction between resolution of the fundamental dispute (for example, by Taiwan's unification with the PRC system) and what I term stabilization.[2]

Resolution of the Fundamental Dispute

The fundamental dispute has existed since the Chinese Communist victory on the Mainland in 1949, but it has taken different forms. For at least three decades after 1949, the core of the disagreement was the question of which government—the Republic of China on Taiwan or the People's Republic of China—represented the state called China in the international community. Of course, it was not just a political competition. In 1954 and 1958, Beijing also engaged in coercive diplomacy to probe the state of Taiwan's military defenses and the U.S. commitment to the island's Kuomintang regime. But the fight was mainly over which government represented China, and Beijing won that round. It gained entry into most international organizations and established diplomatic relations with most other countries, including the United States.

Since the early 1980s, the core of the dispute has been over whether the geographic territory of Taiwan will be part of the Chinese state—and, if so, with what political status. China believes that Taiwan is a part of China. The Democratic Progressive Party has said that Taiwan should be a separate state; the Kuomintang has generally said that Taiwan is a part of China but has worried more about its legal identity should unification occur. China believes that Taiwan's reunification should occur on basically the same terms as reunification of Hong Kong and of Macau. In contrast, the KMT has held that it is a sovereign entity, a claim that China has rejected. Both the KMT and the DPP have sought to expand Taiwan's limited international role.

There are significant substantive and political obstacles to resolving the fundamental cross-Strait dispute in the near term. Substantively, the gap between the two sides is wide. On Taiwan, the DPP, the KMT, and the public have opposed Beijing's one-country, two-systems unification formula because it would deny Taiwan's claim of sovereignty. Hence, Ma Ying-jeou has declared that during his term of office, unification is off the agenda. And, as noted in chapter 2, only around 10 percent of those surveyed in polls support unification in either the near or long term. For its part, the Beijing government appears to understand that resolution is a long-term proposition, but it would strongly oppose both a DPP government that actively sought de jure independence and a serious KMT effort to foster a two-Chinas solution.

At its core, the fundamental dispute is about two issues that have divided Taiwan and China since the early 1990s: security and sovereignty. The root of the security issue is the fear that each side feels about the intentions of the other: Beijing fears that Taiwan might maintain its de facto independence permanently, and Taipei fears that China's leaders might, despite their pledge of "peaceful unification," someday use their superior military power to coerce Taiwan to end the fundamental dispute on their terms. The previous chapter outlined the deepening of their mutual fear in the late 1990s and early 2000s; chapter 5 of *Untying the Knot* provides a more comprehensive and analytical treatment of the problem.[3]

The sovereignty issue has been at the heart of Taiwan's multifaceted resistance to Beijing's one-country, two-systems formula (see the detailed discussion in chapter 4 of *Untying the Knot*).[4] Taipei has argued that because Taiwan is a sovereign entity it should not be treated in the same way as Hong Kong and Macau, which, as colonial territories, lacked sovereignty before unification with China and have only autonomy under the Beijing sovereign. Following the definition of types of sovereignty presented by Stanford University's Stephen Krasner, Taipei's claim of sovereignty would be the basis for Taiwan's

—participation in the international community—for example, in UN organizations

—absolute right to rule the territory under its jurisdiction, free of any PRC interference (Westphalian sovereignty)

—unrestricted operation of its political system, particularly in terms of which parties may compete and which leaders may be selected.[5]

Stabilization

The stabilization of cross-Strait relations is conceptually different from resolution of the fundamental dispute. It is a process that is an improvement over the conflicted coexistence and tense status quo that has prevailed, but it is not a transformation so profound that it leads ineluctably to resolution. Stabilization is what has taken place since May 2008, turning the negative spiral of the years before 2008 into a positive one and allowing the two sides to suppress their reflexive mistrust of each other in order to gain the benefits of working together. Stabilization may create a better environment for resolution and may ultimately lead to it, as the Chinese hope and some on Taiwan fear, but there is no automatic connection between the two.

The stabilization of cross-Strait relations has included several elements. First, it was facilitated through a series of formal negotiations. During Ma Ying-jeou's 2008–12 term, teams of officials from each side discussed and concluded sixteen formal agreements in areas in which they believed that mutual benefit was possible. Those agreements were designed to define the scope of cross-Strait cooperation, giving it greater predictability and setting standards against which performance can be measured. Although the negotiations were conducted under the aegis of the semi-official Straits Exchange Foundation and the Associations for Relations across the Taiwan Strait, they were in fact discussions between government officials of the two sides.

Second, the negotiations required a basis on which the two sides could confidently engage each other. Beijing and Taipei used the 1992 consensus, in which each side expressed its view on the matter of one China in its own way. Each side knew that the other defined the consensus in a way that was somewhat contrary to its own view, and Ma stated that the "one China" was the ROC. But neither made an issue of their differences in order to break the long-standing suspension of dialogue.

Third, to fulfill the purpose of the negotiations—which was to expand areas of China-Taiwan cooperation in various fields—the two sides removed obstacles to normal economic intercourse during Ma Ying-jeou's first term and began to liberalize trade and investment . Cooperation also broadened in areas like law enforcement. Assuming that the potential of cooperation is realized, it can build constituencies and political support on each side of the Strait and increase the costs of tension and conflict.

Fourth, stabilization took an institutionalized form. Institutionalization implies establishment of organizations on each side to manage affairs on a regular basis; mutual acceptance of certain basic principles, norms, and practices; creation of mechanisms to address problems; insulation from politics; and therefore greater certainty that tomorrow will be more or less like today. The Economic Cooperation Framework Agreement (ECFA), concluded in June 2010, created a cross-Strait economic cooperation committee composed of officials who were given the tasks of supervising and assessing ECFA's execution, interpreting its regulations, circulating relevant information, and settling disputes concerning interpretation and implementation. Leaders also floated the idea of agreements in security and political affairs that might promote further institutionalization.

The process through which stabilization occurs—and it is a process, not an end state—is an important factor in the success of stabilization efforts. Stabilization might happen through a "grand bargain," in which all issues are on the table. That sort of all-or-nothing solution requires a sudden boost in mutual trust and in confidence in the benefits of cooperation, but it faces two problems. First, it may not command broad support in an open political system, and Taiwan is quite divided on China policy. Second, if the bargain lacks momentum, mistrust quickly returns. A more sustainable approach is to set general goals and then take incremental and reciprocal steps toward reaching those goals. Reciprocity builds trust between the two parties and the domestic constituencies to which they must answer. A step-by-step pace ensures that any deviations from the path do not sink the whole enterprise. Yet incrementalism can stall if the parties concerned lose confidence about where cooperation is going. Therefore, China must retain hope that at the end of the process it will achieve its ultimate goal, unification. Taiwan must have the assurance that what it most values will not be put at risk.

What is the relationship between stabilization and "the status quo," which Taiwan polls say that the island's people wish to maintain? That question is hard to evaluate because polls on the question do not clearly define the status quo that a majority of the Taiwan people say that they wish to preserve. What is probably meant is Taiwan's de facto independence and nonsubordination to the PRC. Today, "status quo" probably does not mean the dysfunctional and conflicted cross-Strait coexistence that characterized the mid-1990s to 2008. Compared with that, what happened after 2008 appears more promising.

How the Two Sides Talk about Stabilization

Neither the PRC nor Taiwan governments use the term "stabilization" to describe their approach to cross-Strait relations, even though they would agree that stabilization is occurring. It is my analytical construct for making sense of recent and current developments. But each side talks about its policies in terms that allude to what I describe as stabilization, with respect to both purpose and effect.

The most authoritative statement of Beijing's position was Hu Jintao's speech on December 31, 2008, some seven months after Ma Ying-jeou took office.[6] Hu certainly did not ignore the question of ultimate resolution; for policy and political reasons, it was impossible to not mention Beijing's final goal. "What is central to the settlement of the Taiwan question," he stressed, "is the reunification of the motherland." And he made clear that peaceful means and the one-country, two-systems proposal remained China's approach to that settlement. But his speech was also a justification and elaboration of "peaceful development," which was something different. That was the formulation that Hu, in the spring of 2005, had established as the theme of China's policy prior to unification. "Safeguarding peace" and "developing cross-Strait relations" serve as the foundation for realizing unification.

In his 2008 speech, Hu stressed in various ways that peaceful development was a long-term process. China needed to take "the long view from an elevated vantage point." The elements of peaceful development—emotional harmony, mutual trust, shared prosperity, and rejuvenation of the Chinese nation— almost by definition required gradualism. Consequently, Hu said, "we should, *for a long time to come*, continue to adhere to and comprehensively implement these general policies and guiding principles that have proven to be correct in practice." The two sides should "*gradually* solve the legacy issues in cross-Strait relations and any new issues that arise." To the extent that people on Taiwan misunderstand the Mainland or are skeptical of its policies, Beijing should "undo such sentiments and counsel them with *the greatest tolerance and patience*" (emphasis added in each case).[7]

Moreover, under Hu's policy, peaceful development should be based on formal agreements that include some degree of institutionalization. For business and trade, the two sides should conclude an "economic cooperation agreement" and create "a mechanism of economic cooperation." They should negotiate an agreement on cultural and educational exchange. They should conclude a formal end to the state of hostilities through a peace agreement and consider military confidence-building measures, but, in keeping with the principle of gradualism, those issues should first be addressed in an "exploratory" way.

Some Chinese scholars have supported and elaborated on the idea of peaceful development as an incremental and institutionalized process. Huang Jiashu of People's University in Beijing argues that peaceful development requires a "breaking-in" stage, in which "both sides should have patience and lower expectations and not presume that all problems can be solved in a short time." He recognizes that reconciliation has just begun and will face structural conflicts that cannot be "eliminated overnight." Instead, peaceful development "means institutionally tying the two sides" through a process of trial and error.[8] Similarly, Zhang Nianchi, the director of the Shanghai Institute of East Asian Studies, argues that "the 'phase of peaceful development' is a long, long historical transition period prior to the 'phase of peaceful reunification.'" Some in China may not like certain Taiwan policies during the transition, but that cannot be avoided, and "blindness and impatience are of no help to the matter."[9] Li Peng, of the School of Taiwan Studies at Xiamen University, asserts that "the peaceful development of cross-Strait relations is . . . a long-lasting, complicated, and arduous undertaking," in which peace and development should interact in a mutually reinforcing and dialectical way. In this process, "institutionalization is a must." Only through institutionalization "can the channels and arrangements for the communication between the two sides be secured, the consistent and continuous cooperation be established, the contingent and accidental events in handling affairs . . . be processed effectively and, in time, a stable and long-standing framework for peaceful development of cross-Strait relations be safeguarded."[10]

Ma Ying-jeou is equally clear on the nature of the current era. First of all, he has repeatedly said that during his presidency he would preserve the status quo of "no unification, no independence, and no use of force." As he told the *China Times* in September 2010, "the conditions are not in place and the timing is not right to discuss unification. There is no way for Taiwan to discuss such matters. Haste makes waste, and if we proceed too hastily, things could backfire." Instead, his policy was that the two sides would "engage in deep interactions and exchanges" over a long period of time.[11] Cross-strait differences, he noted in his 2009 National Day speech, "are rooted in historical factors that cannot be overcome all at once." The two sides must "remain patient, face up to practical realities, and move forward in a gradual, orderly manner."[12] Moreover, Ma spurned the idea that he should undertake symbolically significant initiatives, such as meeting with Hu Jintao. "The most important thing is to lay the groundwork for institutionalized infrastructure between Taiwan and the Mainland"—a hallmark of stabilization.[13]

Some influential Taiwan scholars have the same incrementalist mind-set, although those who support the DPP believe that the Ma administration is already moving too quickly. Chu Yun-han of Academia Sinica notes that a number of "political reefs" could cause cross-Strait progress to founder if Beijing and Taipei are not careful, including conflicting perspectives on Taiwan's role in the international community and U.S. arms sales to the island's military, plus Ma's need to maintain a balance between Taiwan's international ambitions and cross-Strait economic integration. Finally, he observes, integration has been "driven more by sheer economic pragmatism than blood-thicker-than-water cultural identity"; therefore, in order to prevent a political backlash, Ma must both spread the benefits of economic interaction with China more broadly within Taiwan society and reassure the Taiwan public that any political costs—concerning Taiwan's sovereignty, for example—are minor.[14] Lin Bih-jaw of National Chengchi University argues that Taiwan "simply wants to stabilize relations with the mainland and seek further institutionalization," particularly in economic relations. Gradualism is required because that is the only way to reduce mutual mistrust, and "any hasty opening will meet with resistance from society."[15] The implication of Chu's and Lin's analysis is that any premature attempt to resolve the fundamental dispute would not only fail but also undermine whatever stability the two sides had already achieved.

From Stabilization to Resolution

How should we understand the relationship between the reality of stabilization on one hand and the possibility of resolution on the other? Even if the two are analytically distinct and the former does not lead ineluctably to the latter, how might a transition from stabilization to resolution occur? What factors make a particular kind of transition more or less likely? On the one hand, stabilization can create a far better environment for resolution, since positive and incremental reciprocal steps may foster an environment of mutual trust in which it is easier to address the tough conceptual issues that are at the heart of the dispute. On the other hand, steps taken during the stabilization phase may end up creating a long-term advantage for one side and so undermine the negotiating position of the other when it comes to resolution of the fundamental dispute. To draw an analogy, the working assumption in the Israel-Palestine dispute is that the West Bank is the principal territory available for establishment of a Palestinian state and so is a key to a final settlement. However, the building of Jewish settlements on the West Bank (or, more precisely, the Palestinians' failure to secure a stop to such settlements in negotiations) has complicated the task of drawing the territorial boundaries for the Palestinian state. To reach an agreement, the Israelis will have to accept removal of some or all of the settlements or the Palestinians will have to accept that there will be less land for a Palestinian state.[16]

To answer these questions, it is useful to draw a second distinction, between two different ways that transition might occur. The first is what I call the "mutual persuasion paradigm." Here, the two sides reduce their differences and expand cooperation through a process of mutual accommodation, beginning with stabilization and, perhaps, moving toward resolution of their differences on more fundamental issues. In the process, they also gain greater confidence in the intentions of the other. The second way is what I call the "power asymmetry paradigm," in which Beijing might use its growing power to get Taiwan to accept its demands, not because Taipei finds them acceptable but because it is too weak to resist. This dynamic reinforces rather than reduces Taiwan's fear of Beijing's intentions. Clearly, this distinction is for the purpose of analysis; any political interaction can involve both persuasion and pressure. But it is still a useful distinction.[17]

Returning to the dynamics of the transition process, the first paradigm involves incremental change, while the second brings qualitative change in which China gains a significant advantage over Taiwan. The persuasion paradigm is akin to a war of attrition while the asymmetry paradigm is like a war of maneuver. In the last four years, the two sides have been in the paradigm of mutual persuasion. But China's growing power and the communist regime's rather tough-minded approach to statecraft means that the paradigm of power asymmetry cannot be ruled out.

The Mutual Persuasion Paradigm

The mutual persuasion paradigm deals, of course, with substantive issues, first concerning stabilization and later, perhaps, resolution of the long-standing disagreements over security and sovereignty. Yet the heart of mutual persuasion is how it occurs as a process. There are six "keys for success."

First, each side must know its goals, what it wishes to achieve or preserve. Here, China knows exactly what it wants: to prevent Taiwan independence in the near term and bring about unification in the long term. It has certainly succeeded in achieving the first goal. By offering Taiwan carrots and holding sticks in reserve, it has enlarged Taiwan's stake in the status quo to the point that the Taiwan public would be taking a risk if it elected a DPP administration that pledged to pursue de jure independence. Regarding the second goal (unification), it continues to propose terms that apparently have not changed in essence since Deng Xiaoping formulated them more than thirty years ago. One might argue that Beijing should update its ideas of what a unified Taiwan would look like to take account of changes over the last three decades, but there is little pressure to do so now because both Hu Jintao and Ma Ying-jeou have decreed that resolving the fundamental dispute is a long-term proposition. In the near term, it is Taiwan that needs to clarify what it wishes to protect. Ma Ying-jeou proclaimed on the night of his 2012 election victory that he would "safeguard the sovereignty of the Republic of China with my life."[18] Yet to carry out that objective requires knowing specifically what is to be safeguarded.

Second, mutual persuasion requires each side to communicate clearly what it needs from its interaction with the other. If Taipei believes that it must protect the sovereignty of the ROC during the period of stabilization for reasons of both substance and domestic politics, it must be prepared to explain why in detail. If Beijing believes that it needs a Taiwan stance on one China that is less ambiguous than the 1992 consensus, it should be prepared to say why.

Third, mutual persuasion requires each side to have a clear understanding of the other's goals to avoid misunderstanding. The Ma administration has sought to foster the PRC's confidence that someday it will achieve its fundamental objectives, thereby encouraging China to accept the incrementalism of a stabilization process. Beijing has emphasized that Taiwan has nothing to fear from peaceful development and further negotiations. Yet each side has a history of misinterpreting the actions of the other and reading the worst into them. In the current period, probably the greater danger is that Beijing would misinterpret Ma's pledge to "safeguard the sovereignty of the ROC" as a clever way to create a two-China solution. One danger, of course, is that deploying this "keep hope alive" tactic in the medium term might require Taipei to make concessions that have negative strategic consequences for the long term.

Fourth, mutual persuasion requires each side to have a coherent and relatively unified formulation of its position. That requires, to the extent possible, the forging of a political consensus on cross-Strait policy. Here, authoritarian China is at an advantage over democratic Taiwan, since Taiwan's political system is both open and still fairly divided on China policy. Taiwan observers regard the absence of policy consensus as a source of weakness, but there are ways that such "weakness" can provide a negotiating advantage.

Fifth, mutual persuasion involves exploring points of substantive overlap and convergence. Beijing and Taipei acted on this principle in Ma's first term by focusing on economic interests, which offered mutual benefits.[19] Each side's definition of the benefit may have been different (economic growth for Taiwan and political conditioning in China's case), as may its expectations for Ma's second term. China may be eager to discuss points of difference on political issues, and it may be in Taiwan's interest to engage Beijing in a controlled discussion of points of convergence. Doing so will reassure China that incrementalism does not preclude its desired outcome while perhaps demonstrating in more depth the gulf between China and Taiwan that still exists in the political domain. Before having that discussion, Taipei would, of course, need to know its own position on those political issues.

Sixth, mutual persuasion requires each side to protect its political flanks at home and to coordinate politics and negotiations. It is not in the interest of either to make commitments for which domestic political support is lacking. Obviously, Taipei has the bigger challenge here.

The interactions between PRC and Taiwan officials right after Ma Ying-jeou's election in 2008 reveal an effort to define the norms of the mutual persuasion process that would characterize Ma's first term. At that time, Vice President-elect Vincent Siew attended a PRC-sponsored regional economic forum at Boao on the island of Hainan. While there, he met with China's president, Hu Jintao, and he made a sixteen-character declaration composed of four four-character phrases that conveyed Taiwan's view of how to improve cross-Strait relations: "Squarely face reality, open up to the future, shelve disputes, and pursue a win-win situation." Hu met with KMT honorary chairman Lien Chan a couple of weeks later in Beijing and offered his own sixteen-character formulation: "Establish mutual trust, shelve disputes, seek common ground while reserving differences, and together create a win-win situation."

In this typically Chinese way of articulating policy on very complex subjects, Siew and Hu conveyed their respective approaches on the process of mutual persuasion. They agreed that mutually beneficial outcomes ("win-win situations") were desirable—but note the difference in verbs, with Siew more tentative ("pursue") than Hu ("create"). They agreed on the need to set aside disputes temporarily, which was sensible since those disputes had roiled cross-Strait relations since the early 1990s. Elliptically, each side called on the other to provide reassurance that the other would not challenge its fundamental interests. Hu's appeal for mutual trust likely referred to the mistrust toward China that had built up during the Lee Teng-hui and Chen Shui-bian eras, and the "reality" that Siew wanted China to face was that of the Republic of China. The only four-character phrases that differed were Siew's "face the future" and Hu's "seek common ground while reserving differences," which is a staple of PRC negotiating rhetoric.[20]

The next two chapters discuss how Beijing and Taipei pursued stabilization through mutual persuasion in Ma Ying-jeou's first term—that is, they avoided any discussion of fundamental resolution. Stabilization progressed mostly in the economic arena, where the mutual benefit was the greatest. In the process, I argue, Taiwan did not make concessions that undermined its negotiating position on sovereignty in any future discussions of the basic disagreement. Little or no progress occurred on stabilization in the political and security areas, precisely because Taiwan's concerns for sovereignty and security were too great—and the island's public was not ready.

The Power-Asymmetry Paradigm

It cannot be assumed that the current paradigm of negotiation, persuasion, incrementalism, and mutual adjustment will continue and so govern the possibility and shape of any resolution of the fundamental Taiwan-China dispute. Beijing could undertake a political campaign to pressure Taipei to capitulate to unification on its terms. That reflects the Athenian attitude that Thucydides reported in the Melian Dialogue: "The strong do what they can, and the weak suffer what they must." The power imbalance between the two sides could create an opportunity for Beijing to pressure Taipei to accept outcomes that it would resist within the persuasion paradigm.[21] Robert Sutter of George Washington University argues that the Ma administration's conciliatory approach to cross-Strait relations has actually exacerbated Taiwan's problem because it "reinforces ever-growing and deepening Chinese influence over Taiwan," economically, diplomatically, and militarily.[22]

So even if the Taipei government did a good job of protecting its substantive interests in specific negotiations, Beijing would be able to use its growing power and influence to manipulate the environment in which Taipei makes its calculations concerning a fundamental solution. One influential PRC scholar put it quite bluntly: "The severe asymmetrical balance of power between mainland China and Taiwan is a fact that no one can change. Moreover, this problem . . . will continue to increase, a situation that Taiwan needs to handle pragmatically and calmly"—that is, accommodate China even though it may not want to.[23] Thus, a war of attrition would become a war of maneuver.

There is no question that China's power is growing. By one method of calculation, it became the world's second-largest economy in 2010. Increasingly, China is the site for the production and assembly of manufactured goods in a globalized world. It has steadily modernized its military, and the U.S. Department of Defense judged in 2010 that the China-Taiwan military balance continued to shift in the PLA's favor.[24] Diplomatically, Beijing is becoming a key actor on any important international issue. Taiwan's trajectory is more gradual, and it faces some of the challenges of a post-industrial society. The sensible assumption is that the gap will continue to widen, which might enhance Beijing's confidence that China could use its new power to dictate its preferred solution—and the sense in Taipei that Taiwan is increasingly vulnerable to such an outcome. At least one observer suggests that China's fundamental strategy takes a page from the movie *The Godfather*: to bend an adversary to one's will by creating a set of circumstances so constraining that the adversary faces "an offer that he can't refuse."[25]

There are several dimensions on which China's growing power might significantly limit Taipei's options, expand Beijing's advantage (or create the impression of one), and so transform the cross-Strait situation. One is economic. That is, the economic interdependence that has grown between the two sides of the Strait evolves into Taiwan's dependence on the Mainland as its principal source of economic prosperity. Second, China might seek to manipulate that dependence to "encourage" Taiwan to accept a political settlement on its terms. Another is security. That is, if China were to acquire the ability to defeat Taiwan militarily, that would serve as a "force multiplier" to any political effort to pressure the island's leaders to capitulate. That the People's Liberation Army could prevail in a conflict does not, of course, mean that it would initiate one. But the threat to resort to violent coercion, whether explicit or implicit, would certainly affect Taiwan's calculus on whether to bend to China's will and negotiate on its terms.

A number of questions arise with respect to how China might exploit power asymmetry. First of all, would Beijing ever seriously consider exploiting its power advantage to extort the outcome that it prefers if Taipei would not voluntarily accept it? After all, the current conventional wisdom is that it sees no need to resort to coercion of any kind because it is confident that time is on its side and that "peaceful development" will bring Taiwan around. Second, is there anything that Taiwan can do to strengthen itself—economically, politically, and militarily—in order to reduce both the power imbalance and the risk of pressure tactics? Or is it inevitable that at some point China will abandon the paradigm of persuasion and move to the paradigm of power asymmetry? If so, should Taipei reassess its demands within the paradigm of persuasion in order to reduce the risk of pressure? How should the United States, which faces its own challenges in responding to the revival of China as a great power, craft its policy on cross-Strait relations? I return to these questions in chapters 7, 8, and 10.

To sum up the discussion so far, three variables are at play in determining the long-term outcome of cross-Strait relations and of any negotiations on resolving the fundamental dispute. The first is the dominant paradigm of interaction: mutual persuasion or power asymmetry. Second is Taiwan's performance: whether it negotiates well and whether it takes significant steps to strengthen itself. If it does, it is in a better position in any negotiations to resolve the fundamental dispute, particularly if interaction remains within the mutual persuasion paradigm. If it negotiates well but does not self-strengthen, it is in good shape only if mutual persuasion persists. If Taiwan neither negotiates well nor self-strengthens, its position is poor to dire, particularly if the power asymmetry paradigm prevails. The third variable is the domestic political climate in each country. If a broad and sustained consensus on Taiwan supports the current policy of stabilization and strengthening the island economically, militarily, politically, psychologically, and so on, the island's leadership will be better able to position Taiwan well for any negotiations on resolution of the fundamental dispute. Political division and failure to recognize and act on the need for self-strengthening will weaken Taiwan's position. On the PRC side, those responsible for Taiwan policy will have greater flexibility to pursue a policy of gradualism and some accommodation of popular sentiment on the island if they can sustain the tolerance of senior leaders not responsible for the Taiwan issue, of scholars, and of the nationalistic segment of the public.

4

Economic Stabilization

In the summer of 2008, Taiwan and China began the task of stabilizing their relationship through negotiations. Their focus on the economic sphere made eminently good sense. The two sides understood that success was more likely if they tackled easy issues first and difficult ones later. Economic issues had their own complexity, to be sure, but mutually satisfactory business relations were already quite advanced, and broad constituencies on each side favored removing policy obstacles and creating new business opportunities. The benefits of expanded economic cooperation appeared to outweigh the costs, which was not the case for political and security issues. Trying to resolve those issues at the outset would have been the kiss of death for negotiations, because understanding and trust were so low. That was one of the lessons of the Lee Teng-hui era.

The decision of the officials of the two governments to tend to the economic agenda after Ma Ying-Jeou's inauguration soon bore significant fruit. They concluded sixteen major agreements from June 2008 through June 2012: five in 2008, seven in 2009, three in 2010, and one in 2011. While some did not concern economics and trade (for example, cooperation in law enforcement and medicine and health), most did. Most significant was the Economic Cooperation Framework Agreement (ECFA), concluded in June 2010, which laid the basis for a free trade agreement between the two sides of the Strait.

Yet those achievements raise significant questions. Does the approach that Beijing and Taipei have adopted for their economic relationship actually foster positive stabilization? Or does it produce more problems than it solves? Specifically, have cross-Strait economic agreements in fact benefited Taiwan economically? What are the political ramifications, particularly on Taiwan? Have the two sides conducted the economic negotiations in ways that bias the parameters for political negotiations if and when they occur? Will the intensified economic interdependence that the agreements foster create broader political dynamics on Taiwan that render it vulnerable to PRC pressure? If Taiwan is vulnerable, what should it do to compensate?

Taiwan-China Economic Relations

Prior to the mid-1980s, economic intercourse across the Taiwan Strait was miniscule. On the Taiwan side, the reason was ideological: the KMT regime did not wish to make life easier for the PRC. But by the 1980s, Taiwan business people faced rising labor costs and stricter environmental laws on Taiwan and growing U.S. pressure to appreciate the value of the Taiwan currency, which would make goods produced on the island more expensive. They concluded that trade with and investment in China was the best way to adapt to those trends. President Chiang Ching-kuo understood that Deng Xiaoping's economic reforms represented a new policy departure, so he was prepared to accommodate his business community. Because he wished to stimulate political change on the Mainland also, he accelerated Taiwan's own nascent democratization.[1]

So Taiwan industrialists moved their production facilities across the Strait, often creating wholly owned subsidiaries of the Taiwan parent company. Both the central government in Beijing and local governments welcomed the investment because it promoted China's economic development, boosted employment, and fostered social stability. Beijing also hoped that the stake that Taiwan business people were gaining in China would improve the climate for reunification.

The movement of production across the Strait occurred in several waves. The first, in the late 1980s, was dominated by labor-intensive small and medium-size enterprises (SMEs) that turned out products like garments, shoes, and basic consumer electronics. The second wave occurred in the mid-1990s, as larger Taiwan firms in sectors such as petrochemicals and food processing joined the SMEs. The third wave surged in the late 1990s, when information technology (IT) firms, which had become Taiwan's dominant economic sector, moved to the Mainland to maintain the competitiveness of their low-end products. The recession that began in 2000, which hit the global IT industry especially hard, only accelerated the trend. By the end of 2009, around 70,000 Taiwan companies had investments in the PRC.[2] Investment drove trade.

Figure 4-1. *Taiwan Two-Way Trade with China, 1997–2011*

U.S. dollars, millions

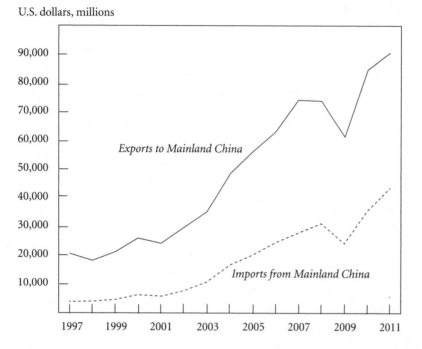

Source: "Major Indicators of Taiwan Economy," *Taiwan Economic Forum*, vol. 10 (April 2012), pp. 102–03.

The bulk of the products that Taiwan shipped to the Mainland were components for the assembly of almost-finished goods that were returned to Taiwan for final finishing or for finished goods for the international market (other products were produced in China for the Chinese market). Thus Taiwan companies positioned themselves in the middle of global supply chains, providing critical functions from their Taiwan base while other functions were performed wherever it was most feasible. For a laptop computer, for example, production of the most advanced components might occur in the United States, along with branding and marketing, while low-end production and assembly occurred in China. In short, Taiwan companies mastered the imperatives of economic globalization.[3] Figure 4-1 shows the trend in two-way trade since 1994. Figure 4-2 shows the trend for Taiwan investment in Mainland operations, using two different indicators.

The migration of operations was complex because major Taiwan companies chose not to do every task in house. Instead, they contracted out elements of

Figure 4-2. *Trends in Taiwan Investment in China, 1991–2011*

U.S. dollars, millions

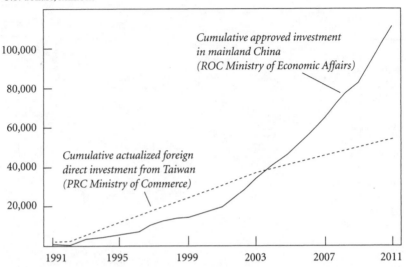

Sources: Investment Commission, Ministry of Economic Affairs, Taiwan; Ministry of Commerce, People's Republic of China.

their business operations to other, smaller companies that could perform them more cheaply.[4] The result was a number of coalitions of companies that were able, with skillful management, to produce quality goods, often under the brands of multinational corporations, at low cost and in a timely manner while responding to changing tastes in the international markets. Shoes for upscale markets and laptop computers are just two examples.

When the predominant company in a coalition moved operations (assembly of laptop computers, for example) to China, some elements of the network had incentives to move as well, in order to ensure that distance did not increase delivery times or diminish quality. In most major product areas, there emerged a complex and shifting geographic division of labor, determined by where each task could be performed most efficiently and effectively. Some Taiwan companies chose to preserve a predominantly Taiwan footprint—producers of semiconductors, for example—but most chose migration to the Mainland to ensure their survival.[5]

There was, therefore, a natural complementarity between the Taiwan and Chinese economies. Each side contributed assets to the enterprise: Chinese localities made available cheap land and labor and ignored environmental regulations; Taiwan companies provided capital, technology, management expertise, and participation in global supply chains. And despite the "great migration" of Taiwan-invested operations to China, the island's economy did not "hollow out." Manufacturing as a share of Taiwan's GDP was 25.2 percent in 1991, as the migration began; it was 24.8 percent two decades later.[6] Yet politics soon intruded, in the late 1990s and the first years of the 2000s. It was not just restrictive Taiwan government policies, such as limits on how much of its capital a Taiwan firm could invest in a Mainland operation or the inconvenience to executives of spending extra hours on flights from one side of the Strait to the other because the Taiwan government required those flights to transit through Hong Kong or Macau. It was also the growing uncertainty that the China policies of Lee Teng-hui and especially Chen Shui-bian created and how Beijing might respond. Taiwan companies continued to operate in that climate, but they would have preferred to do so without dark political clouds on the horizon. The election of Ma Ying-jeou created an opportunity to clear away obstacles and create a more stable business environment.

The Cross-Strait Economic Agenda

After Ma Ying-jeou took office in the summer of 2008, Taiwan and China changed their economic relationship in three ways. They partially *normalized* it by removing past policy and ideological barriers. They began to *liberalize* it by removing barriers to market entry. And they started to *institutionalize* it by creating mechanisms for policy implementation and management. Specifically, Taiwan's Straits Exchange Foundation (SEF) and China's Association for Relations across the Taiwan Strait (ARATS), the semi-official organizations that the two governments authorized to conduct negotiations, concluded a series of agreements on economic and other issues (see table 4-1).

Some of the agreements normalized economic relations by addressing the legacy issues of direct trade, postal service, and air and sea transport. The ROC government had banned the three activities after its retreat to Taiwan in 1949 and allowed them on only an indirect basis from the mid-1980s. Allowing the "three direct links" removed inconveniences that had raised the cost of doing business for Taiwan companies. Normalization was also the result of agreements that facilitated government regulation and supervision in various fields (financial services; the quarantine and inspection of agricultural products; inspection and certification of industrial standards; and food safety). A couple of accords were responses to unanticipated but politically sensitive

Table 4-1. *Cross-Strait Agreements, 2008 through Summer 2012*

Mainland Tourists (6/13/08) (also memo on weekend charter flights)
Postal Services (11/4/08)
Sea Transport (11/4/08)
Air Transport (11/4/08)
Food Safety (11/4/08)
Joint Crime-Fighting and Mutual Judicial Assistance (4/26/09)
Financial Cooperation (4/26/09)
Normalizing Air Transport (4/26/09)
Joint Investment (Consensus) (4/26/09)
Quarantine and Inspection of Agricultural Products (12/18/09)
Fishery Labor Cooperation (12/18/09)
Inspection, Measurement, and Certification of Industrial Standards (12/18/09)
Economic Cooperation Framework (6/29/10)
Protection of Intellectual Property (6/29/10)
Medical and Health Cooperation (12/21/10)
Nuclear Safety Cooperation (10/21/11)

---

issues: food safety, prompted by revelations about additives in Chinese milk products, and nuclear safety, after the massive earthquake in Japan in March 2011.

Going beyond legacy and regulation issues were agreements that promoted the liberalization of economic relations by reducing or removing barriers to market access. The first of them opened Taiwan to Mainland tourists. More significant was the Economic Cooperation Framework Agreement, which stemmed from the proposal of Vincent Siew Wan-chang for a cross-Strait common market. (Siew had served as premier in the late 1990s and became Taiwan's vice president when Ma Ying-jeou became president.) The ECFA, which was signed on June 29, 2010, did two things. First, the two sides specified a number of goods for which there would be an "early harvest" of tariff reduction. Second, they pledged to conclude agreements further liberalizing trade in goods, liberalizing trade in services, and establishing mechanisms for protection of investments and settlement of disputes.

In pursuing ECFA, Taipei was trying to catch up with liberalization trends in the East Asian region. The free trade agreement (FTA) between China and the countries in the Association of Southeast Asian Nations (ASEAN), which went into effect on New Year's Day 2011, put Taiwan firms at a competitive disadvantage. ECFA's early harvest would preserve a relatively level playing

field for a range of agricultural and industrial products (for example, petrochemicals, machinery, auto parts, textiles, electronics, metallurgical products,
medical equipment, instruments, and gauges) and some services like health
care and banking.[7] Taipei, moreover, had concluded that signing the ECFA
would make it easier for Beijing to tolerate Taiwan's pursuit of similar liberalization measures with other countries.

The most obvious example of institutionalization was ECFA's creation of
the Cross-Straits Economic Cooperation Committee to provide a venue for
dispute settlement and otherwise facilitate ECFA's implementation in an institutionalized manner.[8] SEF and ARATS also held periodic meetings to review
progress under their previously negotiated agreements.[9] In early 2012, there
was talk that each side would set up quasi-official representative offices in the
other's capital (the Taiwan External Trade Development Council was one candidate for the Taiwan side).[10] As a Shanghai scholar noted, those interactions
began to fill the "institution deficit" in cross-Strait relations that had impeded
both resolution of disputes and facilitation of cooperative interaction.[11]

Clearly, the agreements so far represented only the early stage of an
extended process. Some legacy issues remained. For example, Taiwan maintained existing tariffs on a number of Chinese products. It had been obli-
gated to reduce or eliminate the duties when it joined the World Trade
Organization in 2002 but was able to keep them legally by citing national
security and other grounds. Legacy issues aside, negotiations on the other
agreements promised by ECFA were going slowly. The pact on investment
protection was hung up over use of international arbitration (Taipei wanted
it and Beijing demurred) and over whether and how promptly PRC authorities that had detained Taiwan executives should inform their families.[12] An
agreement to prevent double taxation also was stalled. In addition, implementation of existing accords was sometimes problematic. For example,
China did not honor a provision in the agreement on protection of intellectual property rights that allowed distribution of Taiwan films in the Chinese
market without quota limitations.[13] One reason for the slowdown in the pace
of negotiations was certainly that the January 2012 Taiwan presidential elections were nearing, but another was that the supposedly "easy" economic
issues were getting harder.

The Rationale for Liberalization

There was a strong economic argument for the projected liberalization package. In a relatively near-term forecast, Taiwan's Chung Hua Institute of Economic Research predicted that ECFA would increase the island's economic

performance by 1.72 percentage points and add 260,000 new jobs to the labor force.[14] Daniel Rosen and Zhi Wang, in an econometric study prepared under the auspices of the Peterson International Institute for Economics, reached the following conclusions:

—By implementing ECFA along the lines of the FTA among China and the ASEAN countries, Taiwan would increase its 2020 GDP by about 4.4 percent, or US$20.6 billion, from the current trend line.

—Other regional agreements (for example, ASEAN Plus China, Japan, and Korea) would impose costs on Taiwan if it did not sign the ECFA, to the tune of almost –0.8 percent of GDP.

—The combination of ASEAN Plus China, Japan, and Korea and liberalization of China-Taiwan trade would produce a 3.5 percent increase in Taiwan's GDP by 2020.[15]

—GDP aside, there would be similar effects on domestic consumption (it would increase with ECFA, decline without).[16]

—The ECFA would make Taiwan an attractive gateway to the Chinese economy for multinational corporations (for example, as a site for their regional headquarters) and encourage Taiwan firms to invest more in Taiwan instead of China or third countries.[17]

—Their study's estimates of the positive impact of ECFA on the Taiwan economy understate the benefits because of "a variety of gains having to do with services trade and investment that models such as ours are likely to undercount."[18]

Tung Chen-yuan, who was a vice chairman of the Mainland Affairs Council under Chen Shui-bian and is now affiliated with National Chengchi University, surveyed Taiwan and foreign enterprises to learn how economic integration in East Asia would affect their decisions on whether to invest in Taiwan. He found that if Taiwan and China signed an economic integration agreement (which ECFA may lead to), 30 to 41 percent of the firms surveyed would increase investment in Taiwan. If Taiwan is included in the circle of regional economic integration, which ECFA may permit, 23 to 37 percent would increase investment. If it is excluded, 26 to 35 percent of the firms would reduce investment on the island.[19]

Near-Term Impact: Economics and Politics

The response in Taiwan to the ECFA was mixed. As might be expected, the government hailed its conclusion, with President Ma saying that it would significantly overcome Taiwan's economic isolation, enhance cross-Strait economic cooperation and reciprocity, and hasten economic integration in Asia.[20] Corporate CEOs on Taiwan also approved: 60 percent of those polled by *CommonWealth* believed that the ECFA would benefit their companies sooner or later. Eighty-nine percent of members of the American Chamber of Commerce in Taipei surveyed believed that the package would benefit Taiwan.[21] Some Chinese and Taiwan scholars praised ECFA because it would remove barriers, rationalize the distribution of resources, and facilitate two-way investment and cooperation in industrial supply chains.[22]

But others on Taiwan argued that liberalization would hurt the domestic economy. A group of scholars associated with the DPP detailed what they believed would be harshly negative impacts on Taiwan's trade, service, financial, and agricultural sectors and on employment. One scholar concluded that with liberalization, China's big economy would have a magnetic effect on Taiwan's smaller economy and that the island would become a peripheral unit of the Mainland's core economy—a kind of colony.[23] The *China Times*, a leading Taiwan newspaper that usually supports the Ma administration, echoed the anxiety about dependence. It called for a diversification of export markets, producing goods that meet American and European standards (to avoid exclusion), and increasing the added value of Taiwan's exports through innovation.[24] There were new worries about the "hollowing out" of Taiwan manufacturing as companies moved production to the Mainland and Chinese rivals became, with Taiwan's help, more technologically proficient and economically competitive.[25] Tsai Ing-wen, the chairperson of Taiwan's opposition Democratic Progressive Party, focused on the welfare effects: ECFA would open Taiwan to cheaper goods, there would be "less jobs for the people . . . a larger gap between rich and poor and more societal problems . . . causing the public to lose its confidence."[26] Tung Chen-yuan remarked that in 2007 the top 20 percent of Taiwan's households received 5.98 times as much income as the bottom 20 percent, whereas in 2010 the multiple was 6.34 (granted, there had been a global economic crisis in the intervening years).[27]

Economic Impact

The immediate impact of ECFA, through the early harvest, was to give nontariff treatment to 539 Taiwan products. In 2011, the first year of the program, the export of early-harvest goods increased by 9.9 percent over exports in 2010 and the companies concerned saved almost US$123 million in tariffs. Early harvest benefited only 267 Chinese products, and imports of those increased 21.3 percent over 2010, with a tariff saving of just under US$23 million.[28] ECFA therefore gave cross-Strait economic relations more of a straight trade component (as opposed to an investment component that drives trade) and benefited some Taiwan industries that had been excluded from investment-led growth.[29] Six months after early harvest began on New Year's Day 2011, Taiwan's machinery exports to China had already grown by 61.9 percent over exports one year before and exports of affected agricultural goods grew by more than three times. Government officials claimed that ECFA had made a significant contribution to Taiwan's growth, exports, and domestic investment.[30] Yet the benefits from early harvest may be less than projected because exporters must prove that 40 to 50 percent of their products' value was added on Taiwan to qualify for the lower tariffs. Initial reports suggest that the exporters had applied for certificates of origin for only a fraction of Taiwan's export products, thus limiting the advantage of tariff reduction, although applications picked up toward the end of the year.[31]

Individual agreements yielded specific results. Because of direct flights, there were more than 12 million "person-trips" in the almost three years between July 2008 and May 2011, and the flights took less than two hours instead of the six to seven hours that indirect flights had taken. Direct shipping saved sixteen to twenty-seven hours per voyage and more than US$300 million over the same period. Through the notification procedures established pursuant to the food-safety agreement, 284 cases of unsafe food were identified (although some cases were not addressed to Taiwan's satisfaction). Each side began accepting patent and trademark applications from the other.[32] And so on.

Generally, cross-Strait economic relations in Ma Ying-jeou's first term had a mixed impact on Taiwan. The only sector that showed more than limited "monetary gains" was tourism, with more than 3 million PRC Chinese visiting Taiwan between May 2008 and December 2011.[33] Yet, even there, the sector's full economic potential was not realized because of policy (Taiwan places significant restrictions on individual Chinese tourists, as opposed to groups) and the interests of the travel agencies that managed the tours (Taiwan travel agencies believe that they are being short-changed by their Mainland counterparts). The number of direct flights rose to almost 600 by the end of 2011, and those flights probably stimulated more Mainland investment by large Taiwan firms than smaller ones. But if there had been an expectation that some Taiwan firms would relocate operations back home because the ECFA eliminated tariff walls, that did not happen right away. The impact of lower duties was limited by the number of initial product lines affected, but exports of Taiwan machinery and agricultural goods got a boost. Still, Taiwan's exports to China did worse than Korea's, and its share in China's growing market continued to decline. Taiwan's preferential access to the Chinese market may attract investment from third markets like Japan, but not right away.[34]

Longer term, liberalization will benefit Taiwan only as the full ECFA package is implemented. Tung Chen-yuan has correctly argued that its true value would be a function of yet-to-be negotiated agreements on goods, services, and investment, because they will transform Taiwan's economic structure: "There will be both winners and losers, and income distribution in Taiwan may become even more unequal as a result."[35] Rosen and Wang would agree with Tung's conclusion about winners and losers and with the statement that "nearly everyone will be faced with competitive pressures and have to bear the cost of adjustments."[36] Their analysis seeks to identify precisely which sectors fall into which categories. The winners are leather and sporting goods, processed food products, textiles, and some agricultural commodities. The losers are electronic equipment, machinery and equipment, mineral products, and, in the unlikely event that trade in these products is liberalized, sugar and fruits and vegetables.[37]

Different business sectors will face different fates. The many Taiwan companies that have thrived by managing assembly operations in China on behalf of overseas multinationals and have thereby secured a valued intermediate position in global supply chains face the danger that they will be squeezed out of that position as, on one hand, ambitious companies in China seek to move up the technology ladder and displace them and, on the other, their overseas clients cut the cost of final products. Those companies that excel in advanced manufacturing on Taiwan (of semiconductors, for example) must constantly struggle to remain on the cutting edge of technology. The situation for small- and medium-size enterprises is complex because of their great variety. China presents a great opportunity for some, particularly those in the service sector, which on Taiwan have already mastered the art of meeting the demands of urban consumers.[38] Still others that have remained on Taiwan in order to service both local and external markets may face a choice as ECFA opens the domestic market to their Chinese competitors: fight and die on Taiwan or seek to survive by moving production to China and gaining preferential access to Southeast Asian economies.[39] Taiwan's SME sector has declined in any event because some companies have been squeezed out of their subordinate position in supply chains and must compete with larger companies for scarce capital from banks.[40]

But Rosen and Wang assert that specific gains and losses are less important than the "considerable structural adjustment" that liberalization would cause.

They write that "in addition to the gains for the winning sectors in Taiwan, the agreement would generate dynamic gains for the economy as it more rapidly reallocated resources including money and people away from sunset industries toward areas of promise for the future."[41] In short, they believe that Taiwan will be worse off if it seeks to wall itself off from greater competition in the face of the large and modernizing Chinese economy, fighting just to preserve every last existing job. Ensuring economic survival in the long term will require policies that help create new, high-quality jobs. Their principal message is that Taiwan's economic growth would suffer if it *does not* liberalize trade and services with China.

Political Impact

On Taiwan, economic stabilization in general and ECFA in particular have been politically controversial and divisive, casting doubt on the durability of the Ma administration's cross-Strait economic policies. To put it concretely, if the public does not support the Ma administration's cross-Strait economic policies, Ma will be in a weaker position to implement them or his party will lose power altogether.

The politics of cross-Strait liberalization can be assessed at two levels. The first is the level of public opinion, wherein Blue voters who support the ruling KMT also support Ma Ying-jeou's cross-Strait policies and the Green adherents of the DPP oppose those initiatives. A poll by the government's Research, Development, and Evaluation Commission in May 2011 found that 63.5 percent of respondents had an essentially positive view of Ma's policies while 29 percent said that they were dissatisfied.[42]

The popular support for Ma's policies contrasted with the public's generally negative view of his personal performance. In fact, Ma's approval rating appears to correlate less with cross-Strait policies per se than with two other factors: the state of the global economy and Taiwan's economy and the government's response to high-visibility issues. For example, his approval ratio dropped soon after he took office as the international economic crisis kicked in and demand for products produced or assembled in China for Taiwan companies declined in the United States and Europe. It gradually rebounded through June 2009, when agreements with China opening direct transportation links were concluded. Then it dropped sharply after a poor response to a serious typhoon in August 2009, only to recover incrementally thereafter, probably as Taiwan's economic growth revived.[43]

The second level is that of political sociology. Here, Kevin Tze Wai Wong of the Chinese University of Hong Kong has found that Taiwan's economic interdependence with China has already created winners and losers among the island's population, with significant political consequences. High-skilled managers, professionals, and office workers have participated in and benefited from cross-Strait economic relations, while the lower middle class, workers, and farmers, who do not participate, are excluded from integration and have lost out. Indeed, class has become the basis of political cleavages in ways that it has not before, and the Blue and Green camps have sought to exploit that cleavage to their own advantage. People in the first set of occupational groups tend to support the KMT and its coalition partners, while those in the second set tend to support the DPP and its allies. Those tendencies are demonstrated in island-wide elections.

Finally, Wong finds that the class cleavage on economic benefits coincides with that hardy perennial of Taiwan politics, the ideological split over Taiwan independence: anti-independence for the pro-KMT skilled and professional classes and pro-independence or anti-unification for the pro-DPP lower middle class, workers, and farmers. Thus the economic and ideological cleavages are cumulative and mutually reinforcing and become key elements of each party's identity. According to some scholars, cumulative cleavages reduce the effectiveness of a political system, unlike cross-cutting cleavages. Future economic liberalization will likely exacerbate existing political divisions and complicate the formulation of economic policy even further.[44]

So the stabilization of economic cross-Strait relations through a policy of liberalization is not without its problems. It will not necessarily bring stability for Taiwan companies and their employees or relief from dog-eat-dog competition. Some firms will gain marginal benefits, in the form of better market access. Others will have to strive to stay ahead of potential rivals as they always have; now, the rivals will be in China. Still others will not survive. Nor will stabilization necessarily bring stability to Taiwan politics. Those who lose from liberalization are likely to give political voice to their grievances, and the health of the Taiwan economy and public support for liberalization policies will be as much a function of trends in the global economy as it is of cross-Strait economic relations. These are dynamics that China can affect on the margin but not change. The only question is how much worse Taiwan's economic and political plight would have been without liberalization.

Implications for Final Resolution: Persuasion

Even if the path to economic stabilization that the two sides have chosen did not contain its share of obstacles, there is always the possibility that the process of stabilization will shift the balance in favor of one side with respect to resolving the fundamental political dispute between them. This is a concern for Taiwan in particular since it is the weaker power. Has Taiwan's sovereignty claim suffered from attrition? Will economic integration lead to political integration? Will China use its economic power to leverage political outcomes unfavorable to Taiwan?

Taiwan's DPP has regularly accused the Ma administration of undermining Taiwan's sovereignty in negotiating its various agreements with Beijing. Thus, To-Far Wang of National Taipei University writes that the Closer Economic Partnership Arrangement (CEPA) between China and Hong Kong is

> a special free trade "arrangement" between central and local governments, working under the principle of "one China." . . . The Ma Administration agreed on ECFA—quite similar to CEPA—and with it sacrificed Taiwan's sovereignty. Through the signing of ECFA . . . Taiwan has become Hong Kong.[45]

The Taiwan Brain Trust, a think tank aligned with the DPP, made a similar claim, but justified it on highly technical grounds.[46] Just as regularly, government officials counter that the DPP has no evidence for its allegations.

If the Ma administration allowed the attrition of Taiwan's sovereignty as it negotiated economic stabilization, as some have alleged, it would have occurred on matters like the premise of negotiations; which entities (official or unofficial) negotiate the understandings; which entities are charged with implementing an agreement's provisions; how the two sides and the agencies of the two governments are referenced in any agreement; and whether equality is maintained in both the negotiations and the language of the agreement.

First Premises

For negotiations on economic issues, the two sides agreed to use the 1992 consensus concerning the matter of one China. As discussed in chapter 2, their parallel statements had points of agreement and disagreement, but after Ma Ying-jeou's election, the two sides simply chose not to make an issue of the points of difference because they thought that getting cross-Strait relations back on track was more important. Only if pressed would Ma say that the "one China" that Taiwan upholds is the Republic of China. Only when the 1992 consensus became a political issue on Taiwan would Beijing specify that it "stresses adherence to the one-China principle."[47] A related matter is whether the 1992 consensus is stated in any agreements concluded. So far, it has not been. Generally, during Ma's first term, the two sides adopted the approach of "mutual nondenial" when it came to how the other side defined core principles. On the basis of this tacit agreement, they have been able to expand the areas of cooperation. As one Taiwan scholar put it, "If either side sabotages the tacit agreement, the other side will do the same, and the relationship will therefore sour. . . . Only fools would like to tear it apart."[48]

Who Negotiates?

Chiang Pin-kun, the chairman of SEF through September 2012, and Chen Yunlin, the head of ARATS, signed the agreements reached after the summer of 2008. Formally private bodies, SEF and ARATS have been entrusted by their respective governments to act on the government's behalf. Thus SEF is the exclusive authorized agent of the Taiwan government "to contact and negotiate directly with mainland China on matters concerning the exercise of public authority."[49] Using these "white glove" organizations has facilitated the expansion of cooperation at a time when neither side has been ready to address fundamental political issues.

The likely model here is the structure that the United States and Taiwan created in 1979 to ensure that their substantive relations continue even in the absence of diplomatic relations. The American Institute in Taiwan (AIT), which has an office in Taipei, and its Washington counterpart, the Taipei Economic and Cultural Representative Office (TECRO), perform just about all the functions of embassies vis-à-vis the other.[50] But the staffs of the two organizations are composed of officials from the various agencies of the home government, who are technically on leave from those organizations, and behind the AIT-TECRO façade of unofficiality, it is they who conduct bilateral affairs.

The same phenomenon has emerged with respect to Taiwan and China. Representatives of SEF and ARATS may open their joint meetings and then attend to preserve the fiction that these are not governmental interactions, but the individuals who are conducting the negotiations are officials from the relevant government agencies. When the two sides got to the consultations on ECFA, the interaction occurred at the vice ministerial level.[51] The Cross-Straits Economic Cooperation Committee, formed pursuant to ECFA, has as its conveners the vice chairman of SEF and the vice president of ARATS, but vice ministers from Taiwan's Ministry of Economic Affairs and China's Ministry of Commerce are the "top trade representatives."[52] The Taiwan members of the committee include the directors general of the Bureau of Foreign Trade and the Industrial Development and Investment Center, both in the Ministry of Economic Affairs; the director of the Department of Economic Affairs in the Mainland Affairs Council; the deputy director of the Ministry of Finance's

Customs Administration; and the deputy director of the Financial Supervisory Commission's Banking Bureau. Aside from some SEF staff, all the Taiwan members of the committee are government officials, as are their Chinese counterparts. Moreover, when officials of one government meet in their own capital with their counterparts, the meetings can take place in their office, and officials of the two sides talk regularly by phone with their counterparts.[53]

It is worth noting that Beijing took a more restrictive approach during the late Chen Shui-bian period. Pressure was building to allow "charter flights" by air carriers of the two sides for the convenience of Taiwan business executives working in China. The first step was to allow such flights on major holidays like the Lunar New Year, after which they might be liberalized. Because the Chen government would not accommodate Beijing in any way on the idea of one China, the PRC insisted that any negotiations on charter flights be convened by officers of the relevant commercial associations, such as the air transport associations. The Chen administration went along, but government officials were members of the nominally private delegations, and they negotiated the agreements. After the arrival of the Ma administration, the job of convener shifted to SEF and ARATS and participation by government officials increased to the point that they are the ones who conduct the negotiations, in an essentially open manner.

In short, it appears that the Ma administration has been able to conduct its economic negotiations with Beijing on essentially a government-to-government basis and that the "white gloves" of SEF and ARATS are becoming increasingly nominal. Moreover, the PRC has accommodated this trend. By sustaining cross-Strait interactions on an intergovernmental basis, Taiwan has preserved the idea that it is a sovereign entity.

Mutual Nondenial in Action: The Financial Cooperation Agreement

SEF and ARATS signed an agreement on cross-Strait financial cooperation on April 26, 2009. The purpose of the agreement was to facilitate supervision of financial institutions and management of monetary affairs as well as "to strengthen broad cooperation in the financial domain, and to jointly maintain financial stability."[54] Several features of the agreement are relevant to sovereignty concerns.

First, there was no reference in it to any political basis for the agreement, whether the one-China principle, the 1992 consensus, or the idea that Taiwan is a sovereign entity. The implication, of course, was that the 1992 consensus was the basis.

Second, the names "SEF" and "ARATS" and the term "the parties" were used to refer to the entities that negotiated the agreement. That is, there was no hint that Taiwan was somehow politically or legally subordinate to the PRC.

Third, the entities charged with carrying out the agreement were, to translate from the Chinese text of the agreement, the two sides "financial supervision and management institutions" (*jinrong jiandu guanli jigou* [金融監督管理機構]). It happens that the Chinese name of the organization in the Taiwan government that is responsible for these matters is *Jinrong jiandu guanli weiyuanhui* (金融監督管委員会). That is, the term for the functions covered by the agreement is exactly the same as the title of the government agency responsible for those functions; *weiyuanhui* (委员会) simply means "commission." China could have insisted on a euphemism for that term to obscure the governmental character of the agreement, but either it chose not to do so or Taiwan held out for transparency.

Fourth, the agreement specified that cooperative mechanisms would be created for cross-Strait interaction in the areas of banking, securities and futures, and insurance. Those three areas happen to be the scope of three commissions that are under the direct jurisdiction of the PRC's State Council. Again, while the agreement did not name those agencies explicitly, the implication was that the cooperation in these areas would be intergovernmental.

Fifth, in the area of monetary management (*huobi guanli*), the agreement indicated that "the parties" would provide organizations such as commercial banks with mechanisms for cash exchange, currency supply and flowback, and anti-counterfeiting technology.[55] These mechanisms were described as the "first steps in gradually establishing a currency settlement mechanism to strengthen cross-Strait cooperation in monetary management."

Sixth, the agreement authorized access of commercial financial institutions on one side of the Strait to the financial services sector of the other. But the scope of that access was to be discussed by "the Parties' supervisory institutions" and, once established, it was to be subject to supervision by the relevant institutions (a government function).

Finally, to facilitate continuing liaison on these matters, the agreement authorized each side to designate contacts. The designation was to be made by "the financial supervision and monetary management institutions of each side"—that is, by government agencies.

Thus, the agreement on financial supervision and monetary management contemplates that China and Taiwan will cooperate on matters that are usually in the purview of national governments. Government agencies will conduct the cooperation, on a direct basis, without intermediation by "white glove" organizations. When it comes to who does the implementation, other agreements do not make such a clear-cut reference to government agencies as this one does. More often, as in the legal cooperation and nuclear safety cooperation agreements, the reference is to *zhuguan bumen* (主管部门)—"competent" or "responsible" authorities. Moreover, the interaction that occurs between Beijing and the government of the Hong Kong Special Administrative Region, under the aegis of the one-country, two-systems formula, is between government agencies.[56] So the way in which Taiwan has negotiated and implemented these agreements does not mean necessarily that it has ruled out any possibility of a one-country, two-systems outcome in the long term. But neither does it mean that China has ensured such a result or precluded one that would be more favorable to Taiwan. In negotiations, Taipei preserved its claim of sovereignty, and the fact that officials of the Republic of China will be implementing the agreements along with their PRC counterparts fortifies that claim.

International Space

How ECFA and other agreements are negotiated does not affect Taiwan's claim of Westphalian sovereignty alone. It indirectly affects the ROC's effort to reassert its role in the international community after three decades of retreat. Taiwan's desire to expand its international space surfaced in places where it might not be immediately expected. For example, talks on the Cross-Strait Investment Protection Agreement, something that Taiwan companies with operations on the Mainland have sought for some time, were deadlocked for over a year because the two sides disagreed on where arbitration, if necessary, would take place. Taiwan insisted on international arbitration while Beijing wanted a bilateral mechanism.[57] (The agreement was finally signed in August 2012 and included a compromise on arbitration.)

More significant economically was the rash of agreements since the late 1990s among East Asian countries (except Taiwan) to deepen regional economic integration , a trend that created a new challenge for Taiwan. This new architecture included free trade areas within the ASEAN region and then among ASEAN, China, Korea, and Japan. Exclusion of Taiwan from regional trade collectives was not just a political slight; it had concrete consequences, by denying Taiwan companies the benefits of liberalization. A Taiwan firm that competed in the China market with a Southeast Asian company in a given product line would now be at a competitive disadvantage because it would have to pay higher tariffs. Indeed, it was the entry into force of the ASEAN-plus-China FTA that led Taiwan to seek the ECFA with China when it did. Korea's bilateral free trade agreement with the United States puts added competitive pressure on Taiwan because Taiwan competes with Korea in a number of product areas, such as plastics, textiles and apparel, chemicals, and machinery. Consequently, the government tried to assure the business community that the damage would not be too great but conceded that it could amount to as much as a 30 percent loss in the island's trade with the United States.[58]

The Ma administration understood that any unilateral and direct attempt on Taiwan's part to break into these new circles of trade liberalization would fail, because Beijing would oppose such an effort and other countries would defer to Beijing. That was certainly the outcome of the frontal attacks that the Lee and Chen administrations mounted regarding the United Nations and the World Health Organization. So Taipei has sought an indirect route into the circle: negotiating ECFA with Beijing in order to reduce its reasons for opposing Taiwan's entry into East Asian economic groups. This assumption received initial support after the signing of ECFA, when Singapore began (or resumed) work on trade liberalization with Taiwan. Other regional economies, such as India, the Philippines, and New Zealand, were also willing to engage Taiwan. In September 2011, Japan and Taiwan signed an investment agreement.[59]

The terms and conditions are important here: what formal name Taiwan would use; whether the agreement would be called a free trade agreement (Beijing prefers not). For its part, Taiwan wishes to avoid creating too clear an impression that it has somehow sought Beijing's permission to negotiate these arrangements, which would weaken Taiwan's claim of sovereignty. Being a part of a regional trade regime made up of nation-states improves its claim.

The Democratic Progressive Party has charged that any moves to elicit Beijing's tacit concurrence for Taiwan's trade liberalization initiatives are tantamount to reducing Taiwan's sovereignty.[60] It argues that Taiwan should engage the world first and then China, rather than the other way around. Yet that assumes that the DPP's preferred route is practicable and that Taipei can gain international space without in some manner consulting with the PRC. The history of the 1995–2008 period suggests otherwise: third countries are generally unwilling to risk Beijing's ire by dealing with Taipei if China might object. So Taiwan's choice is between expanding its international presence by securing at least an implicit Chinese green light or remaining isolated. The latter choice is especially self-constraining when it comes to economic interests.

Is Economic Integration a Political Slippery Slope?

Among those on Taiwan who warned that economic integration between Taiwan and China would lead to political integration was Lu Hsiu-lien, Chen Shui-bian's vice president, who said that ECFA's "historic meaning" was that it "has laid the foundation for China's attempt to use economic integration to reach its ultimate goal of political unification."[61] For some on Taiwan, it might have been an ominous sign that China's twelfth five-year economic plan, presented in 2011, included for the first time a section on Taiwan, even though the passage only affirmed what was already happening.[62]

Some Chinese scholars gave Lu and her fellow critics ample reason to fear the slippery slope when they argued that the signing of ECFA opened the door to talks on political issues. Beijing and Taipei, they said, had done the easy issues and could now move to hard ones. Zhao Liqing of the Communist Party's Central Party School argued that "after signing ECFA the two sides of the Strait, observing the objective laws of building trust and cross-Strait peaceful development, should make a choice to advance on the road of military [talks] first and political [talks] later."[63] Yu Keli, the director of the Institute of Taiwan Studies at the Chinese Academy of Social Sciences, argued that "after the signing of the ECFA, the two sides should no longer avoid political issues in the course of their consultations and dialogues. . . . Efforts to resolve difficult cross-Strait political issues . . . will be an important topic that both sides of the Strait must face."[64] Other scholars, like Zhang Nianchi of the Institute for East Asian Studies in Shanghai, were far more cautious: "It is impossible to fundamentally solve cross-Strait relations today by sitting down to talk about 'politics' since the proper groundwork has yet to be laid."[65]

THE ANALOGY OF WESTERN EUROPE. In this regard, the process of integration in Western Europe after World War II provides a contested point of reference for observers on each side of the Strait. People on the PRC side would likely find superficially attractive the orthodox neofunctionalist understanding of European integration. In this perspective, the dismantling of walls between national economies created the need and the incentive to build institutions and eventually an economic and political union. But China had responded badly to how the Chen Shui-bian administration interpreted the European experience. In late 2000, Chen proposed what came to be called his "integration theory" (*tonghelun*). That was during the first year of his presidency, when he pursued a relatively moderate stance toward China. He appealed to Beijing to "gradually build trust between the two sides, starting from the integration of cross-strait economic, trade, and cultural affairs and then jointly searching for a new framework of lasting peace and political integration."[66]

Chen was willing to talk in terms of political integration for two likely reasons. The first was that the process would occur only over a long period of time; the other was that the participants in European integration, which was the main historical precedent, were sovereign states and Chen claimed the same status for Taiwan. That became clearer in an article by David Huang Weifeng, a scholar at Taiwan's Academia Sinica who later worked in the Chen administration. He saw integration along the lines of the European experience as a long-term process and thus a win-win option for both sides. It was good for China because, although the final outcome would not be certain, unacceptable outcomes (Taiwan's independence) would become much less likely. Taiwan should be open to integration because it would bring economic benefits and constitute Chinese recognition that Taiwan possesses sovereignty: "Once the integration process kicks off, China will in fact have admitted that Taiwan has a certain form of sovereignty or autonomy."[67]

The European experience is actually problematic as a model for cross-Strait relations, for a variety of reasons. First, Beijing and Taipei are only in the first stage of what Christopher Dent terms the "five progressive stages of regional integration." That is the creation of a free trade area, for which the Economic Cooperation Framework Agreement signed in June 2010 is the starting point. The later stages are a customs union, common or internal markets, an economic and monetary union, and an economic and political union (Europe is in the fourth of these stages). So even economic integration has a long way to go.[68]

The second problem is that integration is not simply a matter between Taiwan and China; it is also occurring throughout East Asia. Taiwan was not a part of the free trade area among China and the countries of the Association of Southeast Asian Nations that took effect at the beginning of 2011 and can suffer economically from the trade diversion that it will engender. In addition, the political isolation that such arrangements create for Taiwan raises questions among the island's public about whether Taiwan's dignity is being accorded the proper respect.

Third, of course, is the growing crisis in the European project. Economic integration occurred among very different political economies, with the main cleavage occurring between northern and southern countries. When economies like Greece, Italy, and Ireland accepted the Euro, they gave up what traditionally were basic elements of sovereignty (foreign exchange policy and currency issuance). However, they did not make appropriate changes in monetary and fiscal policy and discipline, and no higher European authority had the power to impose economic policies on them. Probably most important, the principal debate in Europe has always been between the relative priority of intergovernmentalism on the one hand and supranational authority on the other. Will national governments enter into obligations as the result of negotiations among them, or will those obligations be the result of a decisionmaking process that occurs within the European Union? For cross-Strait relations, however, the key point of division is whether understandings are reached by two essentially equal governments or by two entities, one of which (Taiwan) is fundamentally subordinate to the other (China).

Even if the differences between Europe and East Asia were not enough, scholars have long called into question the neofunctionalist idea that the transition from economic integration to political integration is somehow automatic and self-directed. They question whether the slope is really as "slippery" as it seems. They observe that, even after six decades of effort, today's European Union still exhibits an essential tension between nation-states and the federal government constituted by those states and between the competing policy styles that are characteristic of the two levels.[69] As European states sought to deepen economic integration, the process faltered at a number of critical points when one or more of their number imposed obstacles for political reasons. As Andrew Moravcsik puts it:

> Neofunctionalists maintained (as I do . . .) that the pursuit of economic interest is the fundamental force underlying integration, but they offered only a vague understanding of precisely what those interests are, how conflicts among them are resolved, by what means they are translated into policy, and when they require political integration.

In fact, any transition is highly contingent and subject to negotiation and consensus building both within countries and between them.[70] Hence, economic integration does not create an automatic process that deprives the parties concerned of their freedom of choice. A former Taiwan official confirmed the political factors that will determine the degree to which economic integration leads to political integration. In an interview, he said:

> Economic integration is still ongoing. Political integration would be a quantum leap and only a remote possibility at this moment. We in Taiwan are still busily managing the process and consequences of economic integration. Political problems have been dealt with in the last two years only on [an] ad hoc basis and only when necessary. Sometime in the future, we may begin to manage the political process. But it is just "management" which will render continuing stability to the cross-strait relations. It's far from any "settlement." Because Taiwan is a democracy, any political decision will be taken collectively through a due process. Hence, without a rough consensus, even "management" would be difficult, let alone "settlement."

Yet the inevitability of collective political decisions does require that those decisions be well made. And the former official warned that the challenge facing Taiwan was not economic integration per se or a neofunctionalist dynamic but paralysis in the island's political system:

> What I am afraid of is that the political gridlock and bickering at home will not only hamper the "management" process in the short run, and so be potentially destabilizing, but in the long run damage our internal strength, politically and economically. This will put Taiwan in a very disadvantageous situation when the two sides of the Strait have to sit and negotiate "settlement."[71]

Conclusion

In both China and Taiwan, the government and business sector saw benefits to be gained through normalizing, liberalizing, and institutionalizing the two sides' economic relationship—benefits that exceeded the perceived costs. Implementing this project has certainly stabilized economic relations, but it has also had a positive political effect, fostering greater predictability and habits of cooperation. As Chiang Pin-kung, chairman of SEF, put it when talking about liberalization: "ECFA was not only an economic agreement but also a political symbol of peaceful cross-Strait development."[72] On careful examination, the risks that some on Taiwan highlighted—such as a political slippery slope and loss of sovereignty—are less serious than imagined. Not everyone in Taiwan benefited from the new economic relationship, to be sure, but enough people did to sustain political support for the venture.

Yet the course of economic stabilization has not been one of unalloyed progress. For Taiwan, liberalization only altered the content and time frame of a constant challenge: how to maintain the island's competitiveness in a world of globalization in which its neighbor is a major actor. The economic model that China pursued for three decades after 1979, which relied on foreign investment and foreign management, benefited Taiwan companies, but that model may be changing (see chapter 8). The two sides have grabbed the "easy" gains, the low-hanging fruit. They already are finding it hard to complete other elements of economic stabilization, such as the investment protection agreement. Agreements on trade in goods and services are likely to be difficult because they affect domestic economic interests on both the island and the Mainland. Whether there will be smooth and effective implementation of understandings on issues like the protection of intellectual property rights, which are critical to the future of Taiwan's leading companies but bump up against the fundamentals of the PRC political economy, remains an open question. Finally, as I discuss more fully in chapter 8, Taiwan has considerable "homework" to do to ensure that its companies have the tools that they need to meet the competitive challenge.

5

Political and Security Stabilization

During Ma Ying-jeou's first term, China and Taiwan made significant progress in normalizing and liberalizing their economic ties and, more broadly, in reducing the mutual fear that had previously clouded their relations. They did not complete the liberalization agenda by any means, but a lot was accomplished nonetheless. And during the 2012 elections, when Ma's policies and performance were the focus of debate, Taiwan voters endorsed his record.

In contrast, Beijing and Taipei were unable to do much to formally stabilize the political and security dimensions of their relationship. That should not be surprising, since the fundamental disagreement between the two is essentially a political dispute that has become militarized over the last two decades and the balance of risks and benefits involved is very different from that of their economic relationship. The two sides suggested as much when they implied that economic issues were relatively "easy" and political ones were "hard."

The lack of movement was not for lack of trying on the part of China, which in 2009 began to push toward beginning political discussions. Wang Yi, director of the Taiwan Affairs Office, dropped a hint in April of that year, when he spoke of the need to "give precedence" to economic issues, implying that political issues were not off the agenda.[1] Hu Jintao, in a meeting with Kuomintang chairman Wu Po-hsiung in early May 2009, remarked that "the two sides, however, should be prepared to create conditions for solving these [political and difficult] problems," even if it meant that discussions would be gradual.[2] Scholars got into the act during the summer. Yu Keli, director of the Institute of Taiwan Studies at the Chinese Academy of Social Sciences (CASS), warned that even though cross-Strait relations had developed to a certain extent, they would "encounter political bottlenecks and . . . have difficulties to continue their in-depth development." Only complete normalization could prevent stagnation or reversal. Guo Zhenyuan of the Foreign Ministry's think tank repeated the "bottleneck" metaphor four months later.[3]

There was a certain logic for moving into the political dimension. As People's University scholar Huang Jiashu would later observe, expanding business and people-to-people interactions "produced a host of legal issues that were not possible to solve through only tacit agreements and 'policy flexibility.' Only reliance on public authority and institutionalized mechanisms can assure orderly and stable development."[4] Chang Ya-chung of National Taiwan University said that economics and politics must be addressed together: "To avoid the political and only discuss the economic doesn't necessarily make it possible to lay a good foundation for resolving political disputes and may in fact exacerbate the confusion."[5]

But Beijing's 2009 initiative was a false start, manifested in November 2009 when a delegation of twenty-eight Mainland retired officials and scholars traveled to Taiwan for a conference with their Taiwan counterparts. The leader of the PRC delegation was Zheng Bijian, a prominent Communist Party intellectual. Although much of his keynote speech in Taipei reflected Hu Jintao's authoritative policy statement of December 2008, he also suggested that while the momentum of cross-Strait reconciliation was increasing, Taiwan was slow to make the necessary policy readjustments. He raised hackles in the Democratic Progressive Party by asserting that "the downfall and ruin of 'Taiwan independence' is inevitable."[6] Yang Jiemian, the head of a government think tank in Shanghai, sparked ire among more conservative Taiwan participants by highlighting the importance of the one-China principle. Shuai Hua-min, a retired Republic of China general, suggested that Beijing would not advance its interests unless it "liberated its thoughts" on the principle.

Bau Tzong-ho, vice president of National Taiwan University, advised that what Taiwan needed most in any political talks was Beijing's recognition of the existence of the Republic of China.[7] Not surprisingly, Mainland participants "were struck by the total lack of positive resonance from among the Taiwan participants, even from KMT supporters, who they had anticipated would be more enthusiastic."[8] Soon, Chinese officials were declaring that "at present, the Mainland does not have a timetable for political talks."[9] Before too long, China got the message that initiatives like the Zheng Bijian delegation were politically counterproductive. In the second half of 2009, Ma Ying-jeou was under fire for a weak performance on issues other than cross-Strait policy, and PRC pressure to move from economics to politics was undermining him even more. Indeed, DPP media outlets exploited this advantage:

The Chinese officials who spoke in Taiwan [at the forum] made it very clear that they are in Taiwan to dictate and to threaten—not to listen or learn. . . . For the Taiwanese independence movement, this is a good thing, and more CCP officials should be allowed to speak in Taiwan. If they're willing to crucify themselves in public by putting their intolerance and ignorance on display, then so be it.[10]

So Beijing backed off, picking up on Taipei's idea that educational and cultural exchanges should be the next new area for discussions.[11]

There was also a false start in the security realm, where the two sides had already floated the idea of some sort of peace accord. During his 2008 presidential election campaign, Ma Ying-jeou called for negotiation of a peace accord to last from thirty to fifty years and include confidence-building measures (CBMs).[12] He spoke of a "possible" peace accord in his inaugural address.[13] And Hu Jintao, in his authoritative policy statement at the end of 2008, reiterated a PRC appeal: "On the basis of the one-China principle, formally end the state of hostility across the Strait through consultation [and] reach a peace agreement." Hu also suggested military dialogue and "exploratory discussions on the issue of establishing a mechanism of mutual trust for military security."[14] Furthermore, the two defense establishments endorsed CBMs in principle in their respective defense white papers.[15] The Kuomintang, in a policy paper issued in October 2009, emphasized the danger of delaying military CBMs: "To limit [negotiations] to only . . . economic, cultural and social exchange between the two sides is not enough to secure long-term, peaceful and stable cross-Strait relations, in that military threats, confrontations and competition . . . increase the risk of armed conflicts." It suggested ending the state of hostility, concluding a peace accord, and agreeing to mutual renunciation of the use of force.[16]

Elements within the PRC system began to argue during the summer and fall of 2009 that the time had come for the two sides to negotiate a peace accord. Emblematic of this viewpoint was Yu Keli, who argued strenuously in a series of articles that a peace accord was urgently necessary. In an essay written in August, Yu argued that only by ending the state of hostility and signing a peace accord could the two sides break through the political bottleneck in cross-Strait relations, avoid reversals, and facilitate general normalization of relations and peaceful development.[17] It was the situation of mutual hostility that fostered the "shadow and suspicion resulting from mutual mistrust or even hatred remaining in the hearts of the compatriots on both sides of the Strait." He assembled evidence to suggest that there was widespread support for a peace accord on the island—even Lee Teng-hui and Chen Shui-bian had proposed the idea. He argued that the two sides were a "community of fate" based on common ancestry and so should abandon "the antagonistic way of thinking and ideological confrontation. . . . Is it so difficult for the two sides to overcome misunderstanding, remove barriers, abandon enmity, and put an end to the state of hostility?"[18]

As with proposals for political talks, proposals for a peace accord got no traction. One reason, again, was politics on Taiwan. For example, in the fall of 2011, in presenting his vision for Taiwan's future during his presidential campaign, Ma stated that sometime in the next decade Taiwan might consider a peace accord with China under certain conditions. He was roundly criticized and his support in the polls declined. But there are also conceptual obstacles to both a peace accord and political talks.

Why does it matter that the two sides have not made progress in these areas? On the one hand, it obviously affects the degree of stabilization that is achieved. If Beijing and Taipei can reach mutually acceptable understandings in matters other than economics, they will have a firmer foundation for preserving peace and advancing cooperation. On the other hand, it has implications for the incremental process through which Beijing and Taipei have sought to stabilize their relationship. Given the mutual mistrust that has developed since the mid-1990s, gradualism makes perfect sense. It often is easier for two adversaries to allay their suspicions about each other through a series of modest reciprocal initiatives. If each side responds positively to the steps of the other, confidence and the stakes in the relationship grow. If, on the other hand, the other side does not respond positively but rather pockets the concessions and demands more, the losses are not so great. The alternative approach is a "grand bargain," whereby two adversaries seek to resolve all differences all at once. But underlying mistrust makes such an approach risky, and the costs of failure are large.

The problem with a step-by-step approach is that each side still wants to be confident that the outcome will be something that it desires or at least something that is not harmful. In the cross-Strait relationship, Beijing wants some assurance that this approach will amount to more than walking in circles and that the result will be unification. Taiwan wishes to ensure that the step-by-step approach will not end in Taiwan walking off a cliff. Although Taiwan is divided internally over the endpoint that it seeks, there is a broader understanding of what should be avoided: subordination. Xu Shiquan, a prominent PRC specialist on Taiwan, has made the insightful observation that scholars from China and Taiwan differ in their views of the nature of the process that began in May 2008. For the Chinese, it had the clear purpose of achieving an objective (unification); for their Taiwan counterparts, "the process would decide the objective."[19] An agreement establishing a political framework, for example, could provide Beijing with a greater degree of long-term certainty.

The two sides approach the process-versus-outcome problem differently. China has a well-defined goal (unification), and it has a political system in which the setting of goals is done within the Communist Party leadership. It fears that Taiwan will either subvert that goal by moving toward independence or simply engage in avoidance and delay tactics. Beijing is willing to pursue an incremental approach because it believes that the existing power asymmetry will continue to shift in its favor and that over time the incentives that engagement provides will erode the Taiwan public's aversion to a settlement on China's terms. China would have greater confidence in the current strategy of engagement and gradualism if it could induce Taiwan to signal somehow that it shares Beijing's ultimate goal. So for China, some sort of political understanding and peace accord would make it easier to tolerate a gradual process.

Taiwan's situation is different. It sees incrementalism as a useful means to delay a decision or to gain a clearer sense of Beijing's intentions. Of course, Taiwan's views are divided on political and security matters. Some fear that an understanding in these areas will make unfavorable outcomes (unification) more likely and preferred ones (such as independence) less so. For the skeptics, such understandings make cross-Strait relations not more but less stable because it creates a bias toward a certain way of resolving the fundamental dispute. Others think that it is precisely because of China's growing relative power that political and security agreements should be reached.

The following discussion examines how the two sides addressed both political and security issues during Ma Ying-jeou's first term and elucidates the conceptual and political obstacles to each. Strictly speaking, security is one type of political issue. But it is a very special one because it includes military power and the conditions under which it might be used. For that reason and for analytical clarity, the two are separated here.

Was the Political Really Ignored?

At the outset, it is worth noting that the two sides did not strictly follow the mantra of economics first, politics later. Of the sixteen formal agreements concluded in Ma's first term, three are clearly non-economic in character: Joint Crime-Fighting and Mutual Judicial Assistance (2009), Medical and Health Cooperation (2010), and Nuclear Safety (2011). Three are really about government regulation, not economics and trade: Financial Cooperation; Quarantine and Inspection of Agricultural Products; and Inspection and Certification of Industrial Standards (all in 2009). Cooperation in these areas may facilitate interaction among business entities, but the activity is governmental.

The agreement on crime fighting and judicial assistance clearly concerns a core responsibility of the state. It establishes institutionalized, operational cooperation between Taiwan's Ministry of Justice and Ministry of the Interior on one hand and, on the other, the PRC's Ministry of Public Security, Supreme People's Procuratorate, Supreme People's Court, and Ministry of Justice. The agreement focuses law enforcement efforts on high-profile criminal activities—such as telecommunications fraud, economic crimes, narcotics smuggling, and human trafficking—through the exchange of information and intelligence, collaboration and concerted action on cases, and repatriation of criminals. The modes of judicial assistance include document delivery, case investigation and collection of evidence, restitution of proceeds of crime, recognition of judgments, facilitation of humanitarian visits, and repatriation.[20]

The agreement resulted in a series of exchanges by senior officials. A PRC vice minister of public security visited Taiwan in mid-September 2010 and met with Taiwan officials in the Ministry of Interior, Coast Guard Authority, judicial bodies, and the Central Police University. The director general of Taiwan's National Policy Agency made a trip to the Mainland in late October and early November of the same year and met with his central and local government counterparts, particularly on the matter of telecom fraud. The island's procurator general led a delegation of prosecutors to meet with his counterparts at the Supreme People's Procuratorate and also at the Supreme People's Court, the Ministry of Public Security, and the Ministry of Justice (he had also visited in 2009 when he was vice minister of justice).[21]

From the signing of the agreement in April 2009 until March 2011, the two sides exchanged information on 729 cases and provided mutual assistance on cases concerning telecom fraud, kidnapping, drug trafficking, and murder. And not all cooperation was strictly bilateral. In June 2011, police agencies in Taiwan, China, Indonesia, Cambodia, Malaysia, and Thailand arrested almost 600 individuals in their respective countries who were engaged in a telecom and Internet swindling operation. Over 400 of those arrested were Taiwan citizens; almost 200 were from China. Each group was repatriated.[22]

Disaster relief is another field in which the two sides have cooperated that has nothing to do with economic activities. After Typhoon Morakot caused significant damage on Taiwan in August 2009, Beijing provided houses, tents, and medical supplies to its "compatriots" on the island and simultaneously eased the transfer of relief funds from Mainland organizations and individuals. The Taiwan government and nongovernmental humanitarian organizations have provided disaster assistance to China since 1988—for example, after the May 2008 Sichuan earthquake. The Tzu Chi Foundation, Taiwan's premier charitable organization, set up offices on the Mainland in 2010. Of course, each side undertakes these good works in part to score political points with the other, but it is cooperation all the same.[23]

Perhaps the political issue that has the greatest significance in the stabilization of cross-Strait relations and beyond is that of Taiwan's participation in the international community, the extent of which is one measure of Taiwan's sovereign status. The more international organizations in which it is active, for example, the more Taipei can confirm to itself that it is a sovereign entity. Beijing understands that and therefore has worked since the founding of the PRC to drive the Republic of China from the international community, in part to weaken Taipei's resistance to unification. The PRC has been largely successful in its campaign. Most countries in the world have formal diplomatic relations with the PRC, leaving only twenty-plus countries for Taiwan. Taiwan is a member of only a few international governmental organizations, most notably the Asian Development Bank, the Asia-Pacific Economic Cooperation forum, and the World Trade Organization. It was able to avoid exclusion from those organizations only through the efforts of the United States and by accepting nomenclature that did not challenge China's view that Taiwan was not a sovereign state.[24]

Taiwan's international space is important in another way. A widespread majority on the island believe that Taiwan has a role to play in the international community and that Beijing's effort to exclude it is improper. Both the DPP and the KMT have sought to gain a political advantage on the issue. The DPP was on the offensive during the 1990s, when it got the Lee Teng-hui administration to seek first a return to the United Nations and then observer status in the World Health Organization (WHO). The Chen Shui-bian administration intensified those efforts but soon overreached. Its tactics created the impression that it was recklessly provoking Beijing, which saw the campaign as a way of promoting an independent Taiwan. Challenging China in that way may have been good politics in Taiwan, but it ignored the fact that Beijing had sufficient influence in international organizations of which it was already a member to block any Taipei initiative. So in the 2008 election campaign, Ma Ying-jeou argued that a more effective way of expanding international space was to reassure Beijing about its ultimate intentions and play on its stated aspiration to "win the hearts and minds" of the Taiwan public.

Ma's policy of engaging with China has yielded some benefits. Since he took office, no country has switched diplomatic relations from Taipei to Beijing (the so-called diplomatic truce). Some wished to (Paraguay, for example), but Beijing declined. Since 2009 Taiwan has participated as an observer in the World Health Assembly (WHA), the annual meeting of the WHO. Once the two sides signed the Economic Cooperation Framework Agreement (ECFA), China apparently signaled that it had no objection to a similar agreement between Taiwan and Singapore to liberalize their trade.[25] In late February and early March 2012 (after Ma's reelection), a delegation from Taiwan that included government officials attended the annual session of the UN Commission on the Status of Women at UN headquarters in New York.[26]

Yet those achievements were relatively modest. While the diplomatic truce prevented losses for Taiwan, it blocked it from winning new diplomatic partners. Beijing reserved the right to review Taiwan's attendance at the WHA on an annual basis. It has been unresponsive to Taipei's proposals that Taiwan also participate in the work of organizations like the International Civil Aviation Organization and the UN Framework Convention on Climate Change, saying that Taiwan's participation must not create "two Chinas" or "one China and one Taiwan." It was unclear whether the Ma administration would be able to conclude trade liberalization agreements with countries other than Singapore. And China has exerted low-level pressure on the nomenclature used for Taiwan in international nongovernmental organizations. Bonnie Glaser comes to the "irrefutable" conclusion that "Taipei continues to face very difficult challenges in its efforts to enhance its role in participation in international organizations and Beijing continues to prevent Taiwan from gaining much ground."[27]

Two reasons were likely behind the limited expansion of Taiwan's international space. First, the PRC was concerned that the DPP might come back to power and use Taiwan's greater access to the international system to advance a Taiwan independence agenda, something that Beijing vigorously opposed during the Lee Teng-hui and Chen Shui-bian years. Second, Beijing also suspected the motives of the Ma government, worrying that it could use greater global participation to legitimize the government of the Republic of China. Beijing, of course, worked for decades to delegitimize the ROC, and under its one-China principle, a two-Chinas outcome is almost as unacceptable as Taiwan independence.[28]

Finally, it is worth noting that even though the two governments may not negotiate on political issues, the Kuomintang and the Chinese Communist Party have their own platform for engagement. Indeed, when Hu Jintao and

Lien Chan, who was then the KMT chairman, met in April 2005 and together set the broad framework for what was to happen in the event that a KMT candidate won the presidency, they did so in their capacity as party leaders. To institutionalize the interaction, their two parties established an economic and cultural forum in 2005, which from its title is clearly not confined to economic matters.

Taipei has not been completely happy with the implementation of bilateral agreements that are more governmental in character. That Beijing failed to hold the Chinese producers of melamine-tainted milk accountable or to permit the import of Taiwan-produced films depleted confidence in the agreements on food safety and intellectual property.[29] In the spring of 2011, the Taiwan public reacted badly when the Philippine government arrested Taiwan citizens accused of telecom fraud and then repatriated them to China. The Ma administration convinced Chinese judicial authorities to send the accused criminals to Taiwan, but having to go through Beijing did not sit well with some on the island.

So far then, the two sides have established a mixed record on the political issues that they have addressed. Intergovernmental cooperation preserves Taiwan's sovereignty. Still, the work on crime and judicial matters has been generally but not totally successful. There are gaps in the implementation of agreements in the area of government regulation. On the expansion of Taiwan's international space, the issue for which the Taiwan public has the highest expectations, Beijing has been only modestly responsive. The question is whether a more ambitious effort to conclude understandings in the political realm would further stabilize cross-Strait relations or make matters worse.

Culture: A Prelude for Political Matters?

Not only did Beijing and Taipei engage to some degree on political matters, they also flirted with cooperation in the cultural sphere. Enhanced activity in this area, broadly defined to include issues of political identity and people-to-people contact, could prepare the ground for addressing the "hard" aspects of their political relationship.

The PRC certainly seems inclined to use culture as a prelude for the political, with its emphasis on the "Chineseness" of the two sides of the Strait. In his major address on Taiwan policy on December 31, 2008, Hu Jintao said the following:

> Chinese culture . . . is a common precious asset of the compatriots on both sides and an important cord that underlies the national emotional

bond between the compatriots on the two sides. . . . The compatriots on both sides should jointly inherit and promote the fine tradition of Chinese culture, conduct various forms of cultural exchange, and enable Chinese culture to be carried forward from one generation to the next and enhanced, so as to boost national awareness, build up a common will, and generate spiritual strength for the joint endeavor toward the great rejuvenation of the Chinese nation [of which unification is by definition a major component].[30]

Beijing's focus on culture stems not from sentimentalism but from anxiety about the past trend of political attitudes on Taiwan. After the island's democratization began in the late 1980s, politics on the island centered on questions of identity, and China watched as the Taiwan public adopted an increasingly Taiwanese identity at the expense of a Chinese identity.[31] Both Lee Teng-hui and Chen Shui-bian sought to shift the Chinese-Taiwanese balance in public life—for example, in education, where the curriculum in history, geography, and literature had ignored Taiwan altogether in favor of China. The result, as measured by polls, was a shift in identity away from China and toward Taiwan. A December 2009 survey conducted by *CommonWealth* magazine revealed that 62 percent of respondents considered themselves Taiwanese, 22 percent said that they were both Taiwanese and Chinese, and only 8 percent said that they were Chinese. Younger people were more likely to pick a purely Taiwanese identity. Other polls had a lower figure but still a majority for respondents identifying as solely Taiwanese and a higher percentage for those identifying as both Taiwanese and Chinese.[32] Beijing found this trend worrisome, and it has feared that a stronger Taiwan identity would lead inexorably to the quest for a Taiwan republic, which, if successful, would constitute a fundamental defeat for the CCP.

In light of the PRC's fears, it was a salutary development that Hu Jintao, in his December 2008 speech, stated that the "Taiwan awareness of the compatriots in Taiwan who love their home and love their land is not the same as 'Taiwan independence' awareness," and acknowledged that a separate "Taiwan culture" had "enriched the substance of Chinese culture."[33] Ma Ying-jeou was willing to meet Hu part way on the issue of culture. He has affirmed that the residents of Taiwan are ethnically and culturally Chinese and, like people on the Mainland, are "descendants of the legendary emperors Yan and Huang." They possessed, he said, the traditional Confucian "core values" of benevolence, righteousness, diligence, honesty, generosity, and industriousness, and it was these core values and "way of life" that mattered in resolving cross-Strait disputes, not issues like sovereignty. "Guided by the wisdom of our common ethnic Chinese culture, we can surely work out a very satisfactory solution." But Ma added a couple of twists. For him, "the ROC will be the standard-bearer at the leading edge of Chinese culture. . . . Having preserved the rich roots of Chinese culture intact over the past six decades or so, Taiwan now dazzles the world with an aesthetic sense and artistic verve that are firmly grounded in a deep vein of traditional culture." Moreover, he noted, democracy was the heart of Taiwan's modern way of life and a point of difference with the PRC.[34]

Moving beyond general statements, Hu Jintao spoke in December 2008 of Beijing's "readiness to negotiate an agreement on cross-Strait cultural and educational exchange." He was, perhaps, responding to Ma's call in his inaugural address to "normalize" cultural relations along with economic ones. In July 2009, the fifth session of the KMT-CCP Economic and Cultural Forum, which met in the central China city of Changsha, focused on the issue of culture. The Taiwan side had a large delegation that included officials from the cultural arena, legislators, students, and individuals from the spheres of education, culture, and religion.[35] The forum produced a five-point "joint proposition" that called for cooperation in these areas: "tightening up" cultural exchange work and carrying forward Chinese culture; deepening cooperation between the cultural industries of the two sides and enhancing their global competitiveness; promoting cross-Strait educational exchange and cooperation; improving information exchange; and fostering and studying "the possibility of signing an accord on cross-Strait cultural and educational exchange, and build[ing] a mechanism for cross-Strait cultural and educational cooperation." The statement suggested that institutions, experts, and scholars would lead the effort, but conceptually the idea was to create a formal framework like the one that became ECFA.[36]

After that start, the process later stalled. After the PRC's minister of culture visited Taiwan in September 2009 (using a nongovernmental title), there was talk suggesting that a cultural agreement was in the offing that would foster exchanges on a reciprocal basis by removing restrictions and addressing copyright and patent violations.[37] But Taiwan apparently got cold feet. At a January 2011 conference in China on traditional culture and cross-Strait relations, Wang Yi reiterated the call for a "systematic mechanism" for exchanges, and Mainland participants urged the signing of an agreement. But Lai Shin-yuan, chair of Taiwan's Mainland Affairs Council and Wang's counterpart, replied in Taipei that there was no need for a separate agreement because existing pacts addressed the key issues (like protection of intellectual property rights) and "no major problems have resulted from these exchanges to date, [so] it is unnecessary to sign a cultural agreement."[38]

There also were efforts to formalize interaction in the field of education. Here, Taiwan had an incentive to do so, because the island had more spaces in universities than it had local students to fill them. The Ma administration had proposed in 2009 that Taiwan authorize admission of Mainland students to fill the gap and also expose younger Chinese to life on Taiwan. But legislation was required, and the opposition DPP blocked action by the Legislative Yuan for almost a year. To end the impasse, the administration made concessions on the maximum number of students, what Chinese students would pay (full tuition), and whether they could get jobs in Taiwan after graduation (no). The legislation was finally passed in August 2010, and a Taiwan vice minister of education revealed that an "education cooperation framework agreement" had been drafted and sent to the Mainland Affairs Council (MAC) in order to institutionalize the handling of cross-Strait student affairs (for example, how to ensure that visiting students who became ill would be guaranteed health care). But the MAC, which is responsible for formulating policy toward China, did nothing to put the issue into the queue of matters for cross-Strait discussion. There was some expectation that an agreement would be discussed during 2011, but no discussion occurred.[39]

Certainly, some aspects of culture did evoke what the two sides have in common. That was manifest in the case of a landscape painting, "Dwelling in the Fuchun Mountains," that was painted in the late Yuan dynasty but split into two different parts in 1650. The two parts of the painting remained separate for over three centuries, and the larger part was taken to Taiwan at the time of the KMT's defeat on the Mainland. It was not until 2011 that the two parts were rejoined and put on display at the National Palace Museum in Taipei, attracting large crowds. Officials in China, of course, saw the painting as a metaphor for political reconciliation. For Taiwan, however, the situation is not so simple. Its National Palace Museum has so far been unwilling to send items in its collection to the Mainland, including its part of "Dwelling in the Fuchun Mountains," until Mainland authorities negotiate a legally binding agreement to guarantee that those items, which came originally from the National Palace Museum in Beijing, will not be seized. The two sides have conducted negotiations on such an agreement but with no success as of the fall of 2012.[40]

The opening of Taiwan to Mainland tourists during Ma Ying-jeou's first term also has had mixed results. Although these visits may help foster cross-Strait reconciliation over time, the initial impact was to expose the gaps between the two societies. Mainland visitors are impressed by the quality of service industries, the degree to which Taiwan people have internalized norms of restrained public behavior—in contrast to their PRC cousins—and the vibrancy and accountability of the island's democratic system (which is one reason that the Ma administration gave tourism a high priority). A Mainland journalist reported that "Taiwan and the PRC have been apart for more than sixty years, and have thus formed two entirely different societies that greatly differ in many aspects, from daily living habits to their value systems." The journalist noted the intense competition that occurs in Chinese public places—for subway seats, service at banks and restaurants, and so on. For him, Taiwan was a "totally different [and positive] experience." Taiwan people, on the other hand, are turned off when the tourists display relatively boorish behavior traits as they move around the island.[41] Han Han, a well-known Chinese writer, visited Taiwan in the spring of 2012 and drew a larger implication from the contrast between the societies. He wrote:

> I saw many special things and met kind-hearted people everywhere dur-
> ing my three-day trip to the island. What most interested me were the
> numerous small protests [street demonstrations] taking place almost
> every day.... In Taiwan, I felt lost when people I didn't know treated me
> with kindness and sincerity, and my first reaction was to suspect duplic-
> ity.... Indeed, I need to thank Hong Kong and Taiwan for protecting
> Chinese culture. They have preserved the virtues of the Chinese people,
> preventing many deep-rooted qualities from being destroyed.[42]

The starkest difference between the two societies is that Taiwan picks its leaders through elections and China does not, and Mainland observers took great interest in the 2012 elections, for their own sake and as a point of comparison with the PRC authoritarian system.[43]

So cultural and people-to-people exchanges may have seemed like a useful proxy for a new approach to political issues, a step that was somewhere between easy and hard. Yet taking that step was constrained by the reality that Taiwan and China are two different societies, the factor of competing political identities on Taiwan ("Just how Chinese are we?"), and the temptation to gain political advantage. If all of that has been true for culture, it has been even more so for purely political issues.

Defining "Political"

If Beijing and Taipei undertook to address truly political issues, what form would the discussion take? The answer has not been completely clear because China has not specified what it seeks. The Chinese proposals of 2009 spoke variously of trust building and more formal dialogue, talks, and negotiations. The implication of terms like "talks" and "negotiations" is that the outcome would be some sort of agreement. Would it be, perhaps, a framework agreement like that for economics? At least one PRC scholar spoke of a process that would culminate "eventually" in an "accord."[44] The thread that runs through official statements and scholarly writings from the PRC is a cross-Strait agreement on a more precise definition of Taiwan's relationship to China. For those on Taiwan, the priority is Beijing's acceptance of the Republic of China. Hence, a significant gap remains.

Governments' Views on a Political Undertaking

When it comes to China's approach to a political undertaking, the starting point is Hu Jintao's authoritative speech on December 31, 2008, which addressed matters from a variety of perspectives:

—*The source of the dispute*: "Although the mainland and Taiwan have not yet been reunified since 1949, it is not a state of division of the Chinese territory and sovereignty. Rather, it is a state of political antagonism that is a legacy, and a lingering one, of the Chinese civil war that took place in the mid to late 1940s."

—*The essential starting point*: "To scrupulously abide by the one-China principle and enhance political mutual trust." Hu defines the one-China principle as follows: "There is only one China in the world; China's sovereignty and territorial integrity tolerate no division; . . . the mainland and Taiwan belong to one China."

—*The effect of a basic political understanding*: "When the two sides of the Strait develop a common understanding and united position on safeguarding the one-China framework, which is an issue of principle, it will form a cornerstone on which to build political mutual trust and anything can be discussed. . . . Continuing to oppose the 'Taiwan independence' separatist activities is an essential condition for advancing . . . peaceful development."

—*The focus of near-term discussions*: "The two sides should make joint efforts, create conditions, and gradually solve the legacy issues in cross-Strait relations and any new issues that arise in the course of development through consultation on equal footing. . . . In the interest of conducting consultation and negotiation across the Strait and making arrangements for their interactions, the two sides can hold pragmatic exploratory discussions on their political relationship in the special context where the country has not yet been reunified."

—*The near-term objective*: "On the basis of the one-China principle . . . build a framework (*kuangjia* [框架]) for the peaceful development of cross-Strait relations."

—*On Taiwan's international space*: "Regarding the issue of Taiwan's participating in the activities of international organizations, fair and reasonable arrangements can be made through pragmatic consultation between the two sides, provided that this does not give rise to 'two Chinas' or 'one China and one Taiwan.'"

Finally, in addition to other cross-Strait channels of interaction, Hu reaffirmed the practice of "exchange and dialogue" between the Chinese Communist Party and the Kuomintang.[45]

Several aspects of Hu's formulation are worth noting. First of all, it is based on long-standing precedents in PRC policy. The emphasis on the one-China principle and the proposal for an agreement to end the state of hostilities go back to Jiang Zemin's authoritative statement of January 1995. The three-part definition of the one-China principle was enunciated by former vice premier Qian Qichen in January 2001. The absence of a common position on "safeguarding one China" is consistent with Beijing's understanding of the 1992 consensus—that is, "in routine cross-Strait consultations, the political meaning of 'one China' will not be discussed." By implication, any negotiations on nonroutine, political issues would require a discussion of the political meaning of one China. And the use of a party channel of communication, which Beijing has advocated for decades, was revived in 2005.[46]

Yet Hu's announcement also reflected his own elaboration of policy. It was during his meeting with former KMT chairman Lien Chan in April 2005 that the idea of a "framework for the peaceful development of cross-Strait relations" was first proclaimed. The term "framework" implies a greater degree of convergence and of formalization and institutionalization. One Chinese scholar, Li Peng of Xiamen University, sought to bring precision to the term:

> To apply the concept here, the framework for the peaceful development of cross-Strait relations means an architecture constructed by the two sides across the Strait which is based on prescribed political prerequisites, follows certain rules or regulations, provides logical coordination of the relations between elements affecting the peaceful development of cross-Strait relations, and ensures a stable, sustaining, and orderly development of cross-Strait relations.[47]

Note also that the Chinese term that Hu used in his speech was the same that Beijing used for the title of the Economic Cooperation Framework Agreement. Taiwan used a different word (*jiagou* [架構]), but the meaning is essentially the same.[48] The implication is that a framework can be expressed—and perhaps should be expressed—through a formal agreement.

In contrast, Ma Ying-jeou was restrained when it came to political relations. He did speak of the interim objectives of peace and mutual prosperity (or development). But he also stressed that the status quo would be maintained; there would be no discussion of the PRC's ultimate goal of unification; the ROC constitution would remain the framework for Taipei's policy; and to him, "China" meant the ROC. He understood that Beijing could not recognize the ROC, as it does other countries, but he saw emerging a situation of "mutual nondenial." In speaking to a group of international lawyers, Ma opined that it was necessary to look for "new theories to define cross-Strait relations."[49] But he never echoed Hu's call for building a framework for peaceful development. Ma's priorities in the political sphere were ensuring that the principles of parity, dignity, and reciprocity formed the basis for cross-Strait relations and expanding Taiwan's role in the international arena.

The Scholar Track

As noted above, when Beijing recognized in the latter part of 2009 that political talks with Taiwan were premature, it retreated to having those issues discussed by scholars of the two sides. As Wang Yi, of the PRC Taiwan Affairs Office, told a journalist in April 2010: "To resolve political differences, we may as well start with discussions of scholars and experts from the two sides and, then, gradually form a consensus."[50] But the interaction that has occurred may have simply clarified differences rather than facilitated consensus.

There were certainly a number of scholarly encounters, at a series of conferences held in China, Taiwan, or Hong Kong (technically a part of China). Two months before the November 2009 meeting of senior scholars in Taipei described above, the PRC's Academy of Social Sciences (Yu Keli's institution) and the Chinese Integration Association (a Taiwan organization headed by Chang Ya-chung) met in Beijing.[51] In April 2010, Chinese and Taiwan scholars met near Mount Fuji in Japan at the Motosu temple of the Fo Guan Shan Buddhist organization. In June 2010, China's National Society of Taiwan Studies held a symposium on the peace and deepening of the cross-Strait relationship.[52] Around the same time, organizations in Hong Kong and Macau convened a joint seminar in Hong Kong that three individuals associated with the DPP attended.[53] In October 2010, the Taiwan Research Institute of Xiamen University (in Fujian province, opposite from Taiwan) convened a symposium at which some scholars pushed for the beginning of political dialogue.[54] Four organizations held a "think tank forum" in Taipei a few days later.[55] And in January 2011 the Ninth Seminar on Cross-Strait Relations was held in Guilin.[56] Just as important as these face-to-face encounters were writings in both China and Taiwan on the various issues that political talks might address.

WRITINGS: CHINA. Mainland scholars were quite prolific in putting forth ideas on cross-Strait policy, particularly after Hu Jintao made his authoritative statement in December 2008. Many of their ideas have appeared in *Zhongguo Pinglun* (*China Review*), a Hong Kong journal that favors unification. They agreed strongly on fundamentals like opposing Taiwan independence but displayed a range of views on other political matters.

On one side of the argument were scholars who had some sense of urgency. One example was the already cited Yu Keli, director of the Institute of Taiwan Studies at the Chinese Academy of Social Sciences. It was he who warned that political issues were a "bottleneck" in the development of cross-Strait relations.[57] He labeled the establishment of a framework as a "pressing task" and specified that it should have a "certain mechanism that serves as a guarantee" against retrogression.[58] He proposed that the two sides should agree on the three elements of the one-China principle cited above.[59] And he suggested that Taiwan had to exorcise "the ghost of 'Taiwan independence'"—in effect, discipline its democracy—if Beijing was ever going to trust Taipei's intentions.[60]

On the other side of the argument were scholars who opposed rushing negotiations before conditions were right, particularly on Taiwan. A premature rush would damage cross-Strait relations with very little gain. Zhang Nianchi, director of the Shanghai Institute of East Asian Studies, stressed that "we must . . . be conscious of the instability and vulnerability of the basis of cross-Strait relations." The evolution of those ties will be a "new, lengthy historical stage," one in which "blindness and impatience are of no help to the matter." Instead, China "must not lose confidence, doubt the correctness of the 'peaceful development' policy, or employ a confrontational approach in handling possible conflicts."[61] Wang Jianmin, a scholar at Yu Keli's institute, warned of the "increasingly prominent and sharp contradiction between the mainland's urgency for holding political dialogue and negotiation and the Taiwan authorities' vigorous effort to ambush political dialogue and negotiation. On this, we must fully recognize the complexity, sensitivity, tortuous course, and the difficulty of the development of cross-Strait relations."[62] Huang Jiashu of People's University identified "structural conflicts" that will impede political talks: the definition of the Republic of China, international space, Taiwan's security concerns, and the political gap between the two sides:

> We are actually at . . . a starting point at which cross-Strait relations are seeking reconciliation after a long period of hostility and both sides are cooperating on a cracked foundation. . . . The hostility accumulated . . . over the past sixty years cannot be eliminated overnight. . . . Priority should be given to things that are beneficial for both sides."[63]

Chu Shulong of Tsinghua University believed that the best the two sides could do under current circumstances was to reach a bilateral agreement or framework merely to maintain the political status quo, thus formalizing their unilateral commitments.[64]

Other scholars acknowledged the obstacles that any sort of political agreement would encounter, but they still believed that it would have value. One example is Chen Qimao, president of a Shanghai think tank. On the one hand, he affirmed the progress made in the economic relationship since Ma took office. On the other, he identified negative factors on Taiwan that might reverse that progress: the persistence of independence sentiment; the majority belief that the ROC is a sovereign state; the potential return to power of the DPP; and the fact that legally speaking, a state of war still exists. Because of this conflicted situation, Chen argued, "The present task is to make every effort to establish a framework of peace and development across the Straits in the coming years, so as to create a stable cross-Strait situation . . . and to make it irreversible"; the present, he said, presents an opportunity that must be seized. One specific objective should be a peace agreement; the other should be a framework "with relevant necessary mechanisms" to cope with political disputes that will exist even after any peace agreement is signed.[65]

PRC scholars offered more specific ideas about the substance and process of a cross-Strait political framework. One issue was the basis for talks. Chen Qimao insisted that movement into political negotiations, including talks on a peace accord, required further clarification of the content of the consensus on one China. The 1992 consensus was enough for economic matters, but at a minimum, Taiwan must "reaffirm that both sides of the Straits stand for the one-China principle."[66] Zhang Huangmin, a legal expert, argued for a similar "shared interpretation of one China," with two regional governments within a single country.[67] As already noted, Yu Keli favored Taiwan acceptance of the elements of the one-China principle as China defines it (the Mainland and Taiwan belong to one China; sovereignty and territory are indivisible, and so forth). Liu Guoshen of Xiamen University was probably most creative regarding how to think about this relationship, with his "planet theory." He compared China to a planet in a solar system (the international system). Like the other "planets," that entity possesses territory, people, and sovereignty, and it has both an internal function (governance) and an external one (protecting its sovereignty). Unlike the others, the China "planet" has two faces, each of which has an international presence and competes with the other to represent the whole planet. One face is the PRC and the other is Taiwan, which calls itself the ROC.[68]

Official thinking was similar. In a December 2010 speech, Sun Yafu, deputy director of the PRC's Taiwan Affairs Office, said: "The crucial point is that we should reach a more explicit and definite common understanding that the Mainland and Taiwan are parts of the same China."[69]

Zhang Huangmin, the legal expert, offered an unusually full treatment of the nature of any political negotiations between the two sides. The standard PRC position is that consultations should be "on equal footing" and that "anything can be discussed." Zhang specified that negotiations would be between two regional governments regarding one country's domestic affairs. Neither should disrespect the other. Beijing would be silent regarding Taiwan's "governing power over its region" and vice versa. Yet Zhang was honest enough to admit that whatever the form of political negotiations, the "objective reality" is that they are unequal. The PRC's strength and international standing are greater than Taiwan's. The two sides' "governing power" is unequal. This "reality" will inevitably affect any talks:

> It can be predicted that once future cross-Strait political negotiations begin, wrangling for position between the two principals will be a 'pit' they will not be able to circumnavigate. In terms of managing the relationship between large and small, a sage of the past has already left with us the wise principle of "the large should treat the small with kindness, and the small should treat the large with wisdom."[70]

In short, Chinese scholarly writing focused mainly on how fast to move to political talks and the basis of those talks. Some scholars see the need to move quickly; others counsel patience. Some are more flexible on the one-China principle than others. Those who advocate caution are most sensitive to the reluctance on the Taiwan side to make political commitments.

WRITINGS: TAIWAN. On the Taiwan side, scholars sought to elucidate the political differences between the two sides but have shied away from endorsing political talks. For example, Chang Hsien-chao of National Sun Yat-sen University, after reviewing issues like sovereignty in the context of international politics, international law, and the PRC and ROC constitutions, concluded that "at present, the mutual gap in understanding and values is too great, making it hard to facilitate a true opening." Political talks would require Taiwan to abandon options other than unification, which would render it a subordinate of the sovereign, the PRC. In the current stage, "no Taiwan leader, political party, or the people as a whole would lightly accept such an outcome." To embark on negotiations without adequate political understanding and preparation would only open Pandora's box; Chang advocates the continuation of gradualism.[71]

The most prominent exception to this Taiwan allergy to political talks was Chang Ya-chung, a professor of political science at National Taiwan University, who was as prolific as his Mainland counterparts. The head of the Chinese Integration Association and an opponent of U.S. arms sales to Taiwan, Chang was part of a small group of scholars and former officials that produced a "white paper" on cross-Strait relations in 2011; he also served as the drafter of the document. The most important element of the white paper was the formulation of a draft "basic agreement on peaceful cross-Strait development," which Chang regarded as an interim measure rather than a way to resolve the fundamental dispute. (For the text, see appendix A.) As a "basic" agreement, it could not cover all issues at once. He believed that given the growing economic imbalance between the two sides, a political understanding was the best way to stabilize cross-Strait relations and protect Taiwan's fundamental interests.[72]

Chang developed this draft over time. The first version was written in late 2008 and appeared as part of a longer article in a European journal in 2010. The same year, Chang revised his draft to take account of various comments, and it was this version that appeared in the white paper. In explicating both drafts, Chang makes a number of points.[73]

First, a key issue for Chang is what he calls positioning, or legal status. As a point of departure, Chang introduces the concept of the "Whole China" or "Entire China," by which he means the Chinese people and not the PRC or the ROC. The two sides of the Taiwan Strait belong to the Whole China, but it has been divided or separated in terms of governance since 1949.

Second, although the draft agreement says nothing about how to resolve the fundamental dispute (unification or otherwise), its bias for the medium term is against further separation. Because Chang understands that people of the same ethnic nationality can form different countries, he proposes that the two governments commit to not separate from the Whole China and pledge to jointly maintain Chinese territorial integrity and sovereignty. This is "a mutual promise between the two sides."[74] This promise is important for Beijing because it fears that a prolonged status quo will become permanent. Also, Chang has a more legalistic argument for reassuring China: because it might regard constitutional revisions in democratic Taiwan as the act of another country, Taiwan is designated as "a specific political order within the 'Whole China.'"[75]

Third, Chang addresses the relative status of the two parts of the "Whole China." The draft states: "The two parties agree simultaneously to respect the other as a constitutional order subject, and promote a normal relationship on an equal basis." Here, Chang wishes to avoid the historical baggage and debates associated with the term "one China" and the zero-sum conflict between the PRC and ROC. Within the context of the "Whole China," he stresses that the relations between the two sides "are equal in legal terms."[76] Specifically, both Taipei and Beijing are "constitutional order subjects" (*xianfa zhixu zhuti*; 宪法秩序主体). "The Taipei constitutional body and the Beijing constitutional body each [governs] its people in [its] own territory. Neither belongs to the other or is subordinate to the other."[77] Accordingly, the draft agreement stipulates that it should be approved on each side pursuant to the respective constitutional procedures of each.

On the basis of these principles, Chang specifies the modes of interaction that would occur under the basic agreement. In the military sphere, the two sides should pledge not to use or threaten force because they have agreed that they belong to the Whole China and have made a commitment not to separate from it. Obviously, such a pledge would require an unprecedented concession by Beijing. In the realm of functional issues, the two sides should form "communities": "issue-based cross-Strait institutions . . . to regulate common policies." Modeled substantively but not legally on the process of integration in Western Europe, these institutions would emerge to supplement the two governments, would pursue their functional tasks, and would foster "an overlapping identity" within the Whole China.[78] In the international arena, the two sides would mutually cooperate in international organizations "to maintain the common interests of the Chinese people." The optimal method for this cooperation would be for Taiwan to have observer status in these organizations, but there might be a way for the functional communities to be represented as well.[79] For routine interaction, the two sides should set up representative offices in each other's capital.

Chang's proposal is exceptional in two ways. First of all, it is rather courageous because it appears to lean further in China's direction than most on Taiwan would probably be prepared to move and further than the media would accept. Second, regardless of whether he successfully reconciles the two sides' conflicting positions, he is at least willing to present a detailed proposal for public comment. That has elicited a mixed but somewhat grudging response from individuals in China. Zhang Mingqing, vice chairman of the PRC's Association for Relations across the Taiwan Strait, labeled it "an important approach to turning a new page of the peaceful development of cross-Strait relations." Zhang Huangmin calls Chang's ideas clear and forward-looking, with theoretical integrity.[80]

In contrast, people on Taiwan basically ignored Chang's proposal. One person told me that it was not discussed by either scholars or practitioners. Another felt that it was premature and unnecessary: ECFA could provide an institutionalized and legal basis for the relationship, and if it were successful, other functional agreements might be possible. There was "no urgent need" to conclude a political agreement, and serious conceptual differences between a "Whole China" and the one-China principle remained.[81] A Taiwan scholar close to DPP circles says that he cannot accept the "Whole China" as a concept of sovereignty to include Taiwan. Because the PRC has already been "the only legal and legitimate government of that sovereignty in the international community for many years," agreeing to the concept is tantamount to being annexed by the PRC: "We will lose our autonomy." That scholar noted that the DPP itself had used integration theory (Chang Ya-chung's point of departure) to shape a conciliatory approach to China but that it was based more explicitly on the premise that Taiwan was already a fully sovereign entity with membership in the international community; that was one reason that China rejected the overture.[82]

Still, the draft agreement has more substance than most discussions of cross-Strait political relations, which generally do not go beyond floating competing verbal formulas, like the 1992 consensus. Such formulations can certainly reflect contending schools of thought; they may even stimulate creative thinking. But often they are limited to the wordplay itself, as if the only obstacle to cross-Strait reconciliation is a failure to find the right combination of Chinese characters. Instead, what is required for a stable and enduring relationship is a shared understanding of the substance behind the words, and Chang makes a start at providing it.

One manifestation of Chang's depth is his emphasis on the ROC as a "constitutional order subject" ("subject" here is a term in international law that contrasts with "object," that which is acted on). He understands, correctly, that the PRC "treats Taipei as an 'unequal [or lesser] jurisdiction' and denies the reality that the Republic of China has existed." Furthermore, he has no illusions about Beijing's preferred method of resolving the fundamental dispute: "If Taiwan accepts the 'one country, two systems' arrangements, the two systems will not be equal. This is undoubtedly an arrangement [by which] our side [abandons] the ROC Constitution and gives up its legitimacy."[83] Without saying so explicitly, Chang understands that Taiwan's Westphalian sovereignty must be vigorously defended. Moreover, because the two sides of the Strait are equal entities with their respective constitutional orders, he sees the need for another constitution for the "Whole China" to which the two sides each belong (an idea reduced to the slogan, "one country, three constitutions").[84]

On the other hand, Chang became more implicit as his proposal evolved. His late 2008 version included the following article: "'Both sides agree to respect its counterpart as the highest power in its own area, and that neither side may represent the other in international relations, or act in the name of the other.' Both sides respect the authority of the other party in internal constitutional order and external affairs." In the 2008 version, Chang used the terms "highest power" and "constitutional order" as substitutes for "sovereignty," and he avoided the term "state" when it came to external activities.[85] By the time of the 2011 white paper, he had clearly decided that greater ambiguity was necessary and dropped the whole article—which, of course, included an indirect assertion of Westphalian and international sovereignty— in favor of the first clause in the new Article 2 ("The two parties agree simultaneously to respect the other as a constitutional order subject").

If there is a bias in Chang's thinking, it is toward strengthening the idea of the "Whole China" and being open to a certain kind of unification as the solution for the fundamental dispute. Yet he is under no illusions about what is at stake for the ROC in how the "Whole China" is defined. Chang deserves credit for actually submitting a text for discussion. His approach does not undermine Taipei's position in the medium and long term because it understands the minefield that the sovereignty issue has created. What is most striking about his effort, however, is how little traction it has in Taiwan, a demonstration of the broader public's deep reluctance to engage on cross-Strait political issues.

The Gap Remains

There is an obvious value in having scholars from China and Taiwan address these issues. Intellectuals should not shirk their responsibility to offer creative suggestions on how to resolve difficult policy problems, and there have been cases in which track-two diplomacy by private individuals has served to reduce interstate tensions. But in the China-Taiwan case, it is clear that interaction has not yet resulted in consensus, as Wang Yi of the PRC's Taiwan Affairs Office had hoped. Rather, the gap remains for both procedural and substantive reasons.

On the procedural side, one issue is who gets included in cross-Strait dialogues and who does not. The "dialogue entrepreneurs" on the Taiwan side are individuals with whom the Mainland is relatively comfortable; Chang Yachung is an obvious case in point. It appears that Taiwan delegations are composed of mainstream scholars and those who favor unification. Scholars who are associated with the DPP or who favor independence are seriously underrepresented.[86] That no doubt ensures a better atmosphere for discussions, but it also excludes points of view that have resonance on the island. Another issue is the sheer number of meetings. Does more talk necessarily produce clear and convergent thinking? Finally, there is the degree to which the scholars who participate are conversant with their government's policies (and, in the case of Taiwan, the views of the opposition party). If they are not, then scholars of the other side may read more into what they say than is justified.

Then there is the question of what happens next. Even if scholars from Taiwan and China can expand the common ground between them, will it necessarily be acceptable to their government and public? The proposals that have received the most attention in face-to-face dialogues have exposed significant differences, and it is not clear that they have traction in the societies from which they originated. At the October 2010 conference in Xiamen, participants discussed Chang Ya-chung's proposal and one by Liu Guoshen of Xiamen University. Each proposal was relatively creative, and consequently some Mainland scholars predicted that Chang's ideas would never make it into the Taiwan mainstream and Taiwan scholars had a similar opinion on Liu's. The main consensus of the meeting was fairly general: political negotiations were inevitable at some point and the two sides should "seek common ground and set aside differences."[87] Two months before, Zhang Huangmin, in commenting on Chang's proposal, warned that it was premature to address "the complex problem[s] of constitutional government . . . and future shared governance." Instead, the two sides should focus their "wisdom and good faith . . . on resolving the issue of 'a shared interpretation of one China.'"[88]

Concerning substance, cross-Strait scholarly encounters exposed the gap on conceptual issues rather than closed it. That was obvious at the April 2010 meeting of Chinese and Taiwan scholars in Japan, on which there is a useful, published report.[89] Among other issues, there was extensive discussion of Chang Ya-chung's draft. Mainland scholars asserted that the one-China principle was Beijing's bottom line and that China's sovereignty could be shared but not divided. Taiwan scholars acknowledged that there were points of overlap between the two sides but that given the fact that each side had its respective constitutional order plus Taiwan's internal democratization, equality of the two sides was Taiwan's bottom line. Xu Shiquan, a PRC Taiwan specialist, suggested that there was consensus among participants that "peaceful development" was a process and so could not be rushed; he also observed, as noted at the beginning of this chapter, that Chinese scholars believe that the purpose of the current process is to achieve unification, while for those from Taiwan "the process would decide the objective." Finally, there was broad agreement with a Taiwan suggestion that, because the concept of one China was so controversial, expressing it in a "relatively concealed (*yinxing*) manner" could avoid a lot a trouble.

In their writings and discussions, there is a tendency for scholars in China and Taiwan to focus on verbal formulas and metaphors. They have used their principal currency—words—to try to reconcile their differences over complex issues. For example, Huang Jiashu has offered these alternatives to Taiwan's current rendering of the 1992 consensus (one China, different interpretations): one China, no interpretations; one China, limited interpretations; one China, shared interpretation; one China, same interpretation; and one China, new interpretation.[90] Other scholars search for the perfect metaphor, and Zhang Nianchi reviews some of the offerings:

> There is a theory which compared the "Republic of China" to a cup and compared the people of Taiwan to the water in the cup. How can the water in the cup exist if cross-Strait relations do not want the cup? There is another theory, which compared the "Republic of China" and the People's Republic of China to the surfaces of a planet, which is China [see discussion of Liu Guoshen, above]. There is another theory, which compared the "Republic of China" and the People's Republic of China to the two sides of a body. Speaking in terms of moral principles, perpendicular relations are relations between father and son, and horizontal relations are relations between brothers. They are people of the same family.[91]

Some solutions are more historical. One, "a country in a country," draws on periods when China was divided into different kingdoms; under it, Beijing would accept the ROC as a part of China but Taipei would accept the PRC as the government of China after unification.[92]

Metaphors and historical antecedents may capture some aspects of the dispute and so create a mutually acceptable basis for discussion and provide some indication of ultimate direction. In these cases, the ambiguity that accompanies the analogy can facilitate the search for common ground, whereas clarity only creates obstacles and mistrust. On the other hand, analogies only skirt important substantive issues.[93] Even worse, there is the danger that each side interprets an ambiguous formulation in very different ways, which creates problems later when the misunderstanding becomes apparent. Even if scholars use verbal formulas in a clear and constructive way and understand that there is substance behind the slogan that must be addressed, discussions in the media and public understanding of the issues remain at the level of slogans alone.

In the case of cross-Strait relations, a key distinction is at play but not always recognized: that between the territory associated with a sovereign unit and whether and how governing authorities of parts of that territory exercise sovereignty.[94] The 1648 Treaty of Westphalia established the principle that each sovereign unit has its own defined territory and that no territory is "owned" by two sovereigns.[95] On the different dimensions of the state itself, chapter 3 cites four. Who rules within? Does the state control its territorial borders? Does it have the absolute right to rule within its territorial jurisdiction (nonsubordination)? And is it a full member of the international system? As it happens, the two sides of the Strait are on different sides of this distinction: the PRC emphasizes the first (the territory associated with a sovereign unit) and Taiwan the second (whether and how parts of the territory exercise sovereignty).

The PRC and the ROC claim the same territory: both the Mainland and Taiwan. The ROC constitution was written in 1946, when the ROC claimed both the Mainland and Taiwan. Amendments to the constitution in the early 1990s designated Taiwan and its associated islands as the "free area" of the ROC (by implication, the non-free areas also were within the ROC's territory). On the other hand, Taiwan's leading opposition party, the DPP, takes a different view: it asserts that according to international law, Taiwan was not returned to China after World War II because no peace treaty transferred sovereignty (or ownership) from Japan. Therefore, the DPP argues, Taiwan deserves its own state. (Note that all the metaphorical formulations cited by Zhang Nianchi above assume that Taiwan belongs to the state called China.)

Yet when Mainland scholars stress the importance of the two sides agreeing that Taiwan is a part of China, they are only addressing part of the problem from Taiwan's point of view.[96] To state, as they do, that "the Mainland and Taiwan belong to one China," ignores in what way Taiwan and its governing authorities might become part of a unified Chinese state.[97] Is it as a subnational, autonomous, but subordinate unit, essentially like Hong Kong? Or is it as a sovereign entity that is in some sense equal to the PRC? Analogies thus ignore the central obstacles to stabilizing the cross-Strait dispute, to say nothing of resolving it. The difference here is essentially about the status of the Republic of China, which is a very old issue. Beijing has consistently held that the ROC ceased to exist on October 1, 1949, the day that Mao Zedong declared the founding of the People's Republic of China at Tiananmen Square. Taipei has just as consistently maintained that it does exist, and the DPP maintains that "Republic of China" is the current, formal name of Taiwan. One Taiwan participant at the Motosu meeting told me that for him and his colleagues whether Beijing accepts the existence of the Republic of China was "the bottom line."[98]

One verbal formula expressed by some Chinese scholars that might seem to hold promise is that China's sovereignty can be shared. The idea has been around since the 1990s but has resurfaced in scholarly discussions and writings (at the Motosu conference in April 2010). Xia Liping writes: "Sovereignty cannot be divided, but can be shared." But what precisely does it mean, for example, to say that sovereignty can be shared? Addressing this question requires a close look at how a scholar like Xia understands it. I quote his essay at length:

> Sovereignty is a kind of supreme, political authority displayed/exercised over a certain territory, people, or individual. As the highest authority for "independent initiative and self-determination," it is internally the source of legislative, judicatory, and administrative powers and externally the power and will to preserve independence and initiative. Internally, the legal form for sovereignty is normally stipulated in the constitution or the basic law; externally it is mutually recognized internationally.... The term "One China" indicates that there can only be one sovereignty for China.
>
> Under the framework of shared sovereignty, the Chinese mainland and Taiwan belong to the same one China. The Chinese central government has the supreme, exclusive political authority in the Chinese mainland region, and maintains the force and will of independence and initiative toward the rest of the world. Taiwan authorities administer in fact the Taiwan-Penghu-Jinmen-Matsu region. The Chinese mainland and Taiwan can share China's sovereignty based on consultation and cooperation, especially in dealing with the issue of Taiwan's international space.[99]

On the territory-state issue, Xia restates Chinese official policy: that the geographic territory of Taiwan is included in the Chinese state.[100] But he never makes clear exactly how the two territories might "share" sovereignty. On the different dimensions of sovereignty, Xia does at least distinguish between its internal and external aspects. But in both respects he treats the PRC and the ROC quite unequally. Internally, the "government" in Beijing is the supreme, exclusive authority over the Mainland, but the Taiwan "authorities" only "administer" the territory currently under their jurisdiction. That is, the PRC government is the Westphalian sovereign for its territory and Taiwan is something less than that for its territory. Externally, Xia says that the Beijing government "maintains the force and will of independence and initiative toward the rest of the world" but is willing to consult with Taipei on an external role.[101] Again, the ROC is not equal to the PRC. It was perhaps for this reason that Taiwan scholars at the April 2010 Motosu conference stressed that equality between the two sides was Taiwan's bottom line. Even a Taiwan scholar like

Chang Ya-chung, who tries to accommodate the PRC as much as possible, understands that the equality of the two sides is the bottom line.

This difference over equality exists with respect to Taiwan's international sovereignty. Taiwan wishes to reverse its marginalization from the international community, which began in the late 1960s and accelerated after the United States terminated diplomatic relations in 1979. But it also concerns Westphalian sovereignty—whether its authorities have the absolute right to rule within its territory. As I read it, the PRC view on whether Taiwan or the ROC has the right to rule for purposes of Westphalian sovereignty is "no." Beijing's preferred outcome for resolving the fundamental cross-Strait dispute is a national union in which it is the exclusive sovereign and in which entities like Taiwan have autonomy but are still subordinate (à la Hong Kong and Macau). The Taiwan view on whether it is a sovereign entity has been most assuredly "yes," even though there are different views on the details. The history of cross-Strait disagreement over the last two decades has been over Taiwan's international and Westphalian sovereignty. The conceptual gap is not only central to any ultimate solution but also highly relevant to any effort to stabilize the China-Taiwan political relationship.[102]

So the conceptual gap remains basically as wide as it ever has. "Shared sovereignty" is as yet an idea that confuses as much as it reveals. It may in fact be possible to flesh out the idea so that it goes beyond the formulation that Taiwan and the Mainland both belong to one China and addresses the international and Westphalian dimensions of sovereignty. Thus far, however, whether and how sovereignty can be shared in these areas remains opaque. If scholars have disagreed at this fairly conceptual level of policy, it does not offer much hope that an understanding can be facilitated between the two governments on political matters. Failure to achieve such an accord may impede the stabilization of cross-Strait relations. But an understanding that skates over these fundamental issues will produce a superficial stabilization and complicate any effort to resolve the fundamental dispute.

Domestic Sovereignty

Besides the difficulties that the two sides face in finding a mutually acceptable conceptual approach to Taiwan's legal status and its relationship to China and the international community now and in the future, another aspect of sovereignty is lurking beneath the surface of scholarly investigation: the role of Beijing in Taiwan's domestic political system. The original concept of sovereignty concerns the entity that rules within any political unit: the sovereign, whether a monarch, an elite, or the people at large, and so on. To what extent might the government in China dictate who may assume power on Taiwan after unification and what issues may be placed on Taiwan's political agenda? Would it expect to control personnel and policy the way that it does on the Mainland? The discussion among scholars also has demonstrated that the difference between the two political systems—democratic Taiwan and authoritarian China—has consequences as well. On this, Beijing and Taipei have conflicting expectations.

It is not just within the thirty-one provinces and autonomous regions of the PRC that central government control is exercised; it also is exercised less directly in the special administrative regions (SAR) of Hong Kong and Macau. An SAR of the PRC is what Taiwan would become if it accepted the one-country, two-systems arrangement, and the concrete experience of the Hong Kong SAR is not reassuring. Beijing crafted the territory's political system in a way that allows it to block unwanted outcomes: the opposition Democratic Party can neither win control of the legislative council nor secure the election of one of its leaders as chief executive. In addition, Beijing acts in political ways to strengthen the forces within the SAR that uphold its rule and undermines those from whom it fears a challenge. Thus, it seeks to marginalize Hong Kong's analog to Taiwan's Democratic Progressive Party.[103] China's effort to impose limits can extend to what should be fairly routine matters. A visit to Hong Kong by PRC vice premier Li Keqiang in the summer of 2011 was marred by restrictions on demonstrations, which are normally allowed in Hong Kong, that many in the territory thought were improper and at odds with the existing rules for political expression.[104]

There is no way of knowing, of course, whether the PRC might revise the one-country, two-systems formula to take account of the fact that Taiwan is already a democratic system (Hong Kong and Macau never were). But there is evidence that it would prefer even now to limit who rules on the island and what they do. Beijing has demonized the DPP at times and sought to use economic influence to strengthen the Kuomintang—for example, by giving preference to Taiwan agricultural products as a way of weaning farmers away from the DPP.[105] Recall also Yu Keli's statement about how Taiwan would have to change its political system to reassure Beijing:

> Now, only if the Taiwan authorities resolutely and bravely lead Taiwan society to carry out radical reform, abandon the separatism of "Taiwan consciousness" . . . and remold the identity of Chinese culture, the Chinese nation, the Chinese and the motherland can the ghost of "Taiwan independence" awareness lingering over Taiwan be fundamentally

driven away . . . and the problems related to cross-Strait political differences and the consensus be naturally solved.[106]

Chen Qimao, the Shanghai scholar, called on the KMT to "state its political
outline in a clear-cut manner so as to guide the people, lead the people, . . . and
make great efforts to eliminate the pernicious influence of the 'desinification'
campaign launched by Chen Shui-bian." If the KMT does not refute the accu-
sation that it is selling out Taiwan, Chen asks, "doesn't that mean the KMT is
throwing away its political flag and relieving itself of its political weapons?"[107]
In short, Chen wants the KMT to behave a bit more like the Leninist party that
it once was.

Security Stabilization: A Peace Accord

In and of itself, the virtuous circle that began in 2008, replacing the vicious circle of previous years, made both sides more secure. Beijing could take heart
from Ma Ying-jeou's repeated pledge of "no independence." Taiwan could
take heart from China's continued emphasis on *peaceful* development. Tensions in the Taiwan Strait and the danger of conflict declined significantly, and
much of the Taiwan public felt less sense of danger from the People's Liberation Army. In an August 2010 poll conducted by the *United Daily News* that
asked respondents to rate the possibility of peace and war on a 1-to-10 scale,
the aggregate score was 3.2 (relatively low chance of war).[108] Another survey,
done three months later, found that around 41 percent of the Taiwan public
thought that the PRC government was "unfriendly" to the Taiwan people and
46 percent felt that it was unfriendly to the ROC government. Around 41
percent thought Beijing was "friendly" to the Taiwan people, but only 33 percent believed that it was friendly to the government.[109] This less conflicted situation also benefited the United States.

Yet a reduction in tensions does not necessarily eliminate the cross-Strait
security dilemma, in which each side has viewed the actions of the other with
some alarm and responded with "self-help" actions to enhance its own security, which has only increased the anxiety of the other and created a negative
spiral. A key variable here is the intensity of the security dilemma—how much
each suspects the intentions of the other and how it acts in response. If intensity is high, Charles Glaser predicts, intense competition and war are more
likely. When it is mild, it "creates opportunities for restraint and peace
[because] a state will be more secure when its adversary is more secure."[110] The
question, therefore, is how much China and Taiwan can further reduce the
intensity of their security dilemma and encourage mutual restraint.

Official Proposals

On January 1, 1979, the day that the United States and the PRC extended diplomatic recognition to each other, the Standing Committee of China's legislature issued a statement to "Taiwan compatriots" that called for talks to end the existing "state of military confrontation" between the two sides.[111] Taiwan refused any direct negotiations and generally took the position that Beijing had to unilaterally renounce the use of force. Then, in February 1991, the Lee Teng-hui administration issued the National Unification Guidelines, which proposed that the two sides eliminate their mutual state of hostility and solve all disputes through peaceful means. Beijing responded positively to that idea. For example, in his authoritative statement on Taiwan policy in January 1995, PRC president Jiang Zemin elaborated his position and reiterated the offer to open talks in China's most extensive, formal statement of Taiwan policy up until that point: "I suggest that, as the first step, negotiations should be held and an agreement reached on officially ending the state of hostility between the two sides in accordance with the principle that there is only one China."[112] Jiang also explained that Beijing could not renounce the use of force because doing so would make a negotiated solution impossible, but he did say that "Chinese should not fight fellow Chinese." He also reiterated a PRC pledge dating from 1981 that Taiwan could retain its armed forces after unification and that Beijing would not station troops on the island.

After the Taiwan Strait crisis of 1995–96, Lee Teng-hui reaffirmed the need to address how to terminate the state of hostility and offered to make a "journey of peace" to the Mainland to meet there with Beijing's leaders.[113] Moreover, Lee did not restate explicitly his previous precondition that the PRC renounce the use of force. Although the two sides had agreed in principle on a common negotiating objective, they could not go any further, partly because of the PRC requirement regarding the "one China principle" and partly because of deepening mutual mistrust about broader intentions. But the idea of an agreement to conclude the state of hostilities did not die. Hu Jintao mentioned it in a statement of policy in March 2005, along with "establishment of military mutual trust," a euphemism for military confidence-building measures. The Anti-Secession Law that China's legislature enacted the same month mentioned it as an issue for negotiations, assuming good relations.[114] And in April 2005, Hu and KMT party chairman Lien Chan agreed that the two sides should "promote a formal ending to the cross-strait state of hostilities, reach a peace accord, and build a framework for the peaceful and steady development of cross-strait ties, including the establishment of a military mutual trust mechanism, to avoid cross-strait military conflict."[115]

Envisioning a Peace Accord

Among Western scholars, Phillip Saunders and Scott Kastner have provided the most comprehensive analysis of a possible peace agreement.[116] They argue that the core elements are straightforward: "Taiwan would pledge not to seek de jure independence so long as China did not use (or threaten to use) force" (and vice versa).[117] And they identify a set of choices on which the two sides would have to find common ground as they approach and enter into negotiations:

—Who are the parties to the agreement? Options range from trusted representatives, at the most informal level, through party leaders and SEF and ARATS officers to the leaders of China and Taiwan acting in their official capacity. On this issue, the pro-unification *United Daily News* [*Lien Ho Pao*] editorialized that "Beijing is aware that it cannot sign a peace agreement while simultaneously denying that the ROC government was one of the warring parties, and therefore one of the signatories to the agreement.[118]

—What is the form of the agreement? It could range from an essentially tacit understanding about the ways in which each side would exercise restraint toward the other to a formal agreement that had binding legal force.

—Should there be more than one agreement? Some proposals distinguish between a proposal to terminate the state of hostilities and a peace accord. Hu Jintao's December 2008 statement suggested that termination would be a key element of a peace accord. An agreement to engage in CBMs could be a separate step. And if there are to be separate steps, there is the question of how the steps are sequenced.

—What would be the premise of negotiations? Would it be the 1992 consensus, which Taipei would likely prefer, or the one-China principle as Beijing defines it, which Hu Jintao's December 2008 statement indicated was its desire?

—What is the scope? Would the agreement merely state the basic no independence–no use of force bargain noted above, or would it undergird that general commitment with specific mechanisms like CBMs, arms control provisions, verification measures, and institutional structures?

—What would be the duration of the accord? Would it be permanent? Would it last several decades? Until resolution of the fundamental dispute?

—How would the U.S. security relationship with Taiwan be treated? Would Beijing insist that because the two sides would now be in a state of peace, there would be no need for the American security commitment and arms sales to Taiwan?[119]

Among Chinese and Taiwan scholars, Sun Zhe, a Columbia University–educated political scientist at Tsinghua University in Beijing, has addressed these questions in the most detail. On the parties to a peace accord, he argues that existing platforms, such as the SEF-ARATS channel, are not appropriate and advocates instead the creation of a new body, the "Cross-Strait Special Issues Commission," that would bring together officials at lower and higher levels, legislative officials, and nongovernmental experts. On the form of the agreement, he argues that in order to have lasting binding force, it must be a legal treaty and not a declaration, joint declaration, communiqué, or oral understanding. In addition, it must be totally public, with no secret provisions. It must be approved through the "constitutional process" of each side: that is, endorsement by China's National People's Congress and Taiwan's Legislative Yuan. Sun prefers that the agreement focus on stabilizing cross-Strait peace and stability, rejecting the more ambitious goal of some Mainland scholars that it be an explicit stepping-stone to unification. On the question of time frame, he advocates a flexible approach: initially defining the duration (say, twenty years) and then reviewing it periodically to determine whether an extension is necessary. The reason is that the two sides have conflicting goals over the purpose of a peace agreement: China regards it as an interim agreement on the way to unification; Taiwan prefers it to reinforce an unchanging status quo. On the question of premise, Sun says that the two sides must address the one-China principle in order to "guarantee a political foundation" for the peace accord. He realizes the difficulty involved but suggests that they "use their areas of common understanding as a basis and then creatively come up with an interpretation that they can at least temporarily accept while making reservations [where they cannot]."[120]

Sun Zhe does not address the scope of the agreement. Nor does he mention the treatment of the U.S. security role in his article on a peace accord, although he has written elsewhere that there can be a breakthrough in relations only if Ma Ying-jeou agrees to no longer request American arms.[121] He is not clear on how his special issues commission can produce a legally binding treaty. Most significant, he and other Mainland scholars do not endorse the reciprocal commitments that Saunders and Kastner propose: no independence by Taiwan; no use of force by China. The likely reason is that Beijing believes, on the basis of its experience as it interprets it, that Taipei might manipulate a "no independence" pledge to serve separatist aims. That being the case, China is better served by maintaining ambiguity with respect to "no force" than by making a categorical commitment to it.

Sun does raise other pertinent issues that Saunders and Kastner neglect. By what mechanism should the agreement be revised if that became necessary? How should its implementation be monitored and deviations rectified? On the question of sovereignty, he suggests that the two sides draw on international law to forge a mutually acceptable consensus.

No Taiwan scholar has looked into a peace accord as systematically as Sun Zhe, but Chang Hsien-chao, of National Sun Yat-sen University, has done his own inventory of the issues that one would entail. Among them are Taiwan's security cooperation with the United States; legal and constitutional obstacles to an agreement; the parity of the two sides in the negotiations (or lack of it, given China's greater power); and the need to ensure political support for any agreement, particularly on Taiwan. But key for Chang are the underlying political issues: sovereignty, including Taiwan's role in the international system; the status of the two parties to the agreement; the objective of the agreement (China wants a prelude to unification); and so on.[122] Commentary on a peace accord by other Chinese and Taiwan scholars confirms the continuing mistrust that each side feels about the true motivations of the other and therefore the difficulties facing any kind of negotiated stabilization of security relations.

On the PRC side, Wang Weixing, a PLA scholar, argues that building political trust is the key both for cross-Strait relations in general and for reducing military mistrust.[123] Liu Guofen, a scholar at the Chinese Academy of Social Sciences, warns against setting preconditions (but what about Beijing's one-China principle?). He focuses in particular on the activities of Taiwan independence forces, because of which "it is difficult for Taiwan to reciprocate goodwill to the Mainland."[124] As reported earlier in the chapter, Yu Keli, also at CASS, asserted that Taiwan can allay Mainland mistrust only by eliminating "Taiwan independence sentiment." On CBMs, Sun Zhe wrote that they would require a credible declaration from Taiwan concerning arms sales and other security cooperation with other countries.[125] Luo Yuan, a semi-retired senior military officer, specifically says that if Taiwan insists on a redeployment of PLA missiles away from the island, then Taipei's commitment to forgo arms purchases would be necessary.[126]

On Taiwan, views on security issues vary with political standpoint. But again, political mistrust is a common theme. Chen Ming-tong, a professor at National Taiwan University and an official during the Chen Shui-bian administration, regards a cross-Strait peace accord as a poison pill. To sign one, he argues, is to establish "unification" as the only option for the future and to use the accord as a transitional framework toward that end.[127] On the Blue side is Andrew Nien-tzu Yang, a respected Taiwan defense scholar who joined the Ma administration as deputy minister of defense. In an essay written before he joined the government, Yang argued that building cross-Strait military confidence requires two things. One is that neither side fears that the other will threaten its existence, its territory, or sovereignty through invasion, annexation, or other means. The other is that both foster mutual political confidence through actions so that there is mutual respect, equality, benefits, and peaceful coexistence.[128] Specifically, mutual military trust is impossible unless each side refrains from undermining the other's definition of its sovereignty, which, for Taiwan, is a fundamental issue. Mainstream scholar Bau Tzong-ho, vice president of National Taiwan University, concurs. What Taiwan needs most from a peace accord is Beijing's recognition of the existence of the Republic of China.[129] Lin Bih-jaw, a vice president at National Chengchi University and a prominent scholar, welcomes the new trend of peace building but says that it must be based on "strong self-defense and mutual trust."[130] He also emphasizes the political context for security stabilization: "political trust is far more important than military CBM[s]." What are needed, he suggests, are "civilian CBMs" to foster political trust by fostering better mutual understanding between the two societies, plus a "new domestic consensus" on Taiwan concerning Mainland policy. Drawing on the European experience, Lin argues that these will come only through a period of "mutual learning."[131]

Confidence-Building Measures

Within any discussion of cross-Strait security issues, confidence-building measures have received special attention—from observers in China, Taiwan, and the United States. CBMs are specific means by which two actors set benchmarks for acceptable behavior and facilitate mutual signaling. The use of CBMs was most prominent in Europe during the cold war and can be especially useful when the armed forces of the two actors operate in close proximity to each other, thereby creating the possibility of accidents that might escalate out of control. CBMs may be construed broadly or narrowly. Broadly, they include any measure, either political or military, taken to reduce uncertainty. One government's unilateral declaration of peaceful intent toward its adversary is an example. Obviously, these declarations will have the desired impact only if they have credibility, which is where narrower and more specific measures that make *military* intentions more predictable and transparent come in. When effective, they reduce the chances of accident and miscalculation.[132] Military CBMs, which are probably best established in a phased manner because of the general environment of mutual mistrust, can take a variety of forms and have different purposes:

—declarations (for example, pledging not to attack or use force)
—communication (for example, establishing a military hotline)

—transparency (for example, providing calendars of military maneuvers or activities)

—self-restraint in operations (for example, establishing a code of conduct for military contacts/activities)

—verification (for example, on-site inspection).[133]

The Taiwan Strait in the 2010s is not cold war Europe, but CBMs might still be used in the cross-Strait context.[134] They could certainly be one important element of a peace accord, to reinforce broader undertakings. But they could also be done in the absence of a general agreement and so could be a concrete way to improve the security situation in the Taiwan Strait. To the extent that there is a danger that the normal operation of PRC and Taiwan forces might lead to accidental clashes, CBMs can reduce that risk.[135] They are also ideally suited to an incremental negotiating process.

The Kuomintang favored the "establishment of a military mutual trust mechanism to avoid cross-strait military conflict" in the years before Ma Ying-jeou took office. Indeed, Taipei reportedly undertook planning for CBMs during both the Chen Shui-bian and early Ma Ying-jeou administrations.[136] Consistent with a phased approach, Taiwan's Ministry of National Defense suggested in October 2009 that the two sides begin with a telephone hotline, proceed to a code of conduct regarding "unexpected contact" between their naval vessels and aircraft, and then work on restrictions on deployments, maneuvers, and even the number of troops.[137]

China has resisted use of the term "confidence-building measures" when it comes to Taiwan because it believes that the term applies only to relations between states and it denies that Taiwan is a state. Yet the two sides have done what amounts to CBMs on a limited basis. Chinese and Taiwan leaders have each made unilateral, political statements designed to reassure the other about their long-term intentions. Beijing has emphasized that its policy is one of "peaceful development" and "peaceful unification." Ma Ying-jeou has promised "no independence" to allay China's worst fears. Reportedly, the two sides have in place an informal understanding concerning their routine military operations in the Taiwan Strait, so that naval vessels and aircraft maintain some distance from each other. "Both sides have established unilateral rules of engagement that are clearly understood by the other side."[138] The two sides' coast guards have done modest search-and-rescue exercises together to help ensure that their ships would not get in each other's way in case of a true emergency.[139] Retired officers from the PLA and the ROC's armed forces have met one another at conferences and on the golf course.[140]

The cross-Strait CBM that has received the most attention is the proposal that China withdraw the short- and medium-range missiles that are within range of Taiwan. The chief advocate of this measure is Ma Ying-jeou, who has made it a precondition for talks on security issues. Not long after his inauguration, he told a Japanese newspaper: "In order for China and Taiwan to truly reconcile, it is necessary to hold cross-Strait peace talks. I request that threats be cleared up, first by removing missiles and by other means."[141] More than a year later, he said: "If we are to negotiate a peace agreement with the mainland, certainly we expect them to do something about those missiles, either to remove them or dismantle them."[142] Removal would be more a gesture of goodwill than a change in the underlying threat that the PLA poses to Taiwan, since these are mobile missiles. Deployed once, they can be deployed again should circumstances change.[143]

Assessment: Will Negotiated Understandings Actually Enhance Mutual Security?

Instruments like a peace accord and confidence-building measures are not ends in themselves, only means to an end. Their objective is to enhance mutual security for the parties concerned, and it is on that basis that they ultimately should be evaluated. Saunders and Kastner, for example, believe that the benefits of a peace accord would outweigh any costs and foster security.[144] But close analysis suggests that under the circumstances that are likely to prevail, a cross-Strait peace accord is unlikely to have that effect. It would be politically controversial in Taiwan and might, depending on how it is crafted, undermine Taiwan's claim of sovereignty. More serious, it is doubtful that an agreement would in fact produce mutual security and allay the fears that each has had about the other's intentions.

Saunders and Kastner themselves identify some of the problems associated with concluding a peace accord:

—Preconditions like the one-China principle make talks less likely.

—The bargaining process contains traps. Each side may be tempted to make excessive demands to ensure getting more than it needs. Or the two sides could discover, only after negotiations begin, that there is less common ground than they thought.

—If the provisions are vague and obligations limited, neither side can be confident that its fears about the other's intentions have been allayed. Each has less to lose by backing out.

—New leadership on either side might abandon the cooperative policy of its predecessor, a scenario that is more likely on Taiwan because of its regular elections.[145]

Nonetheless, Saunders and Kastner remain optimistic that the obstacles can be managed because they believe that the benefits of an agreement for each side will outweigh the obstacles.[146]

The basic understanding that Saunders and Kastner and most other outside analysts propose for a peace accord—that Taiwan pledges not to seek de jure independence so long as China does not use or threaten to use force—is not as straightforward as it seems. One issue is how "de jure independence" is defined. If it means only a formal declaration of independence through some authoritative process, then it is a cut-and-dried issue. It either happens or it doesn't. But what Beijing feared from Lee Teng-hui and Chen Shui-bian was a series of incremental and covert steps whose cumulative effect would be the functional equivalent of a declaration of independence. In any agreement designed to place limits on Taiwan's future actions, Beijing would certainly seek the broadest possible definition of what constituted independence, while Taipei would seek a narrow one.

And there is a more fundamental problem: there appears to be little evidence that China would accept that basic understanding. Most Chinese scholars suggest that the purpose of a peace accord is to eliminate the "hostility" that Taiwan purportedly displays toward China, most notably through the idea of Taiwan independence.[147] One Chinese scholar rejects any effort by Taiwan to set the PRC's renunciation of the use of force as a precondition.[148] At a minimum, they think that China should have an "ambiguous" stance on the use of force, because a renunciation vis-à-vis Taiwan would "compromise its position on a sovereignty issue" (that is, Taiwan is a part of China's sovereign territory so the central government has the right to use force if it deems it necessary).[149]

The second issue is what is meant by the use or threat of force. On the surface, this also seems clear cut. The PLA either attacks Taiwan (or threatens to attack), or it doesn't. But there are other coercive actions, such as aggressive exercises, that also can have a coercive and intimidating effect. On this matter, Taipei would seek a broad definition and Beijing a narrow one.

A related issue is the degree to which any agreement that one Taiwan administration concludes with China is binding on the next administration. Specifically, Beijing would want to ensure that a future DPP government would not renege on an understanding made with a KMT administration. Its anxiety operates on two levels. The first is that it regards Taiwan as a subnational "authority" rather than a state, which rules out putting the agreement in the form of a treaty, which is the most legally binding mechanism. Perhaps there might be a lesser mechanism that is both legally binding and satisfies the

PRC's view that Taiwan is not a state. But the other level is more consequential: China would likely assume that any DPP government would find a sneaky way to renege on the accord.

Finally, there is the question of verification and enforcement: who gets to decide whether Taipei has kept its commitment concerning Taiwan independence? No doubt, Beijing would seek the right to make the final judgment. That it would want that added guarantee is understandable, but it begs the question of whether it would exercise its right in a fair way. China's response to Lee Teng-hui and Chen Shui-bian is instructive here: in at least some cases, China arguably misinterpreted their initiatives and exaggerated their negative impact on its interests.

Confidence-Building Measures: Problems and Obstacles

PRC officials and commentators have thrown cold water on Taiwan's proposal that Beijing unilaterally withdraw missiles targeting Taiwan; instead, China would likely seek a reciprocal change in Taiwan's military posture in return for doing so. Examples include withdrawal from an offshore island, a reduction in the security relationship with the United States, or credible evidence that "Taiwan independence" no longer poses a danger to China.[150] Peng Guangqian, a retired general, has even suggested that the missiles are good for Taiwan: "In fact, the mainland's missiles are for protecting Taiwan. The more missiles the mainland has, the safer Taiwan will become" (after unification, presumably).[151]

More generally, China believes that military CBMs should result from greater trust rather than create it—and that the other party should take unilateral steps to reduce mistrust. Finally, China does not see much value in being transparent about its capabilities and intention. It opts to keep Taiwan "off balance, rather than enhancing [its] sense of security."[152] Indeed, Bonnie Glaser has identified several CBMs that, given past PRC practice, Taiwan should *not* expect Beijing to adopt, even though they include measures that Taipei has long sought to increase its sense of security: any unilateral measures, such as a drawdown of ballistic missiles or renunciation of the use of force; recognition of the center line of the Taiwan Strait as a de facto border; creation of a buffer zone in the Strait that would be free of military operations; and so on.[153] Finally, when China has agreed to CBMs with other countries, implementation has not always met expectations. Commenting on the U.S.-PRC military maritime consultative agreement, an American observer said that "the Chinese are not particularly interested in a rules-based, operator-to-operator approach to safety on the high seas. They have other (probably strategic) objectives in play."[154] Tsai Ming-yen of Taiwan's National Chung

Hsing University identifies two significant points of difference between the two sides on CBMs. In terms of expectations, China wants to create political trust whereas Taiwan wants to avoid sudden incidents and so foster a more peaceful environment. Concerning the path, Taiwan wants to reduce China's military threat before moving to CBMs themselves, while China wishes to settle the underlying political issues first.[155]

The Capabilities Imbalance

The main problem with the sorts of peace accords that have been discussed is that they are fundamentally imbalanced. They focus on the intentions of each side—for example, the basic no independence–no force bargain. In addition, there is some expectation China would seek to restrict Taiwan's acquisition of advanced equipment ("If we have peace, why do you need to prepare for war?"). Yet there has been no discussion about China's capabilities.

Those capabilities are not trivial. The U.S. Department of Defense (DOD), in a report on Chinese military power that it released in May 2012, concluded that Taiwan remained the People's Liberation Army's "most critical potential mission"; that the PLA continued to build its capabilities with respect to Taiwan; and that the military balance ("personnel, force structure, weapons, and doctrine") continued to shift in China's favor.[156]

As it prepares for possible coercive measures against Taiwan, China also has to worry, in its own mind at least, about the likelihood that the United States will intervene against it. To ensure that an attack on Taiwan succeeds in achieving its objectives, China is acquiring the ability to "deter, disrupt, or deny third-party (including U.S.) intervention."[157] The 2011 report specifically states that China has embarked on

> a sustained effort to develop the capability to attack, at long ranges, military forces that might deploy or operate within the western Pacific. ... China is pursuing a variety of air, sea, undersea, space, counterspace, information warfare systems, and operational concepts to achieve this capability, moving toward an array of overlapping, multilayered offensive capabilities extending from China's coast into the western Pacific.[158]

For example, China is developing an anti-ship ballistic missile that would put at risk the principal platform for the defense of Taiwan: aircraft carrier battle groups.[159] The U.S. Department of Defense characterizes these as "anti-access and area denial" capabilities; the PLA uses the term "counterintervention." The idea is the same.[160]

Acquiring new and better equipment is not the only way that a military improves its capabilities; training, readiness, and deployment also are important.

The majority of the PLA's more sophisticated equipment is "deployed to the military regions opposite Taiwan" and military exercises relevant to a Taiwan conflict continued through the Ma administration.[161] Regarding ways that China might employ military force, the DOD report says that the PLA lacks the means for a Normandy-style amphibious invasion but possesses other options that it could execute with more success:[162]

—*Limited force or coercion*: a campaign of disruptive, punitive, or lethal military actions, including computer network or limited violent attacks against Taiwan's political, military, and economic infrastructure, and special operations forces attacks against infrastructure or leadership targets.[163]

—*Air and missile campaign*: missile attacks and precision strikes against air defense systems, including air bases, radar sites, missiles, space assets, and communications facilities.

—*Maritime quarantine or blockade*: executing a traditional maritime quarantine or blockade would be beyond the capabilities of the PLA navy for the remainder of this decade, but China could do the next best thing by announcing exercise or missile closure areas in approaches near ports, in effect closing them to traffic.[164]

With respect to Beijing's intentions—whether it might actually use force to achieve its political objectives—the PRC stresses continually that its policy is one of peaceful development in the medium term and peaceful unification in the long term. It appears that China is unlikely to use its growing capabilities *if* it believes that it can achieve its political goals through persuasion and other political means and *if* those goals are not negated by the actions of others. The 2012 DOD report concludes that "Beijing appears prepared to defer the use of force, as long as it believes that long-term reunification remains possible and the costs of conflict outweigh the benefits."[165]

However, the PRC government has never renounced the use of force against Taiwan, and believes that it is right not to. The 2011 DOD report confirms: "Beijing argues that the credible threat to use force is essential to maintain the conditions for political progress, and to prevent Taiwan from making moves toward de jure independence."[166] In PRC eyes, those forces have not gone away. As China's defense white paper released in March 2011 put it, "the 'Taiwan independence' separatist force and its activities are still the biggest obstacle and threat to the peaceful development of cross-Strait relations."[167]

Yet Beijing does not worry just about a future DPP government that would pursue de jure independence, as unlikely as that may seem objectively. Its "anti-secession" law of 2005, in which Beijing codified the circumstances under which "non-peaceful means and other necessary measures" would be authorized, specified other worrisome contingencies. In

addition to the contingency in which "the 'Taiwan independence' secessionist forces should act under any name or by any means to cause the fact of Taiwan's secession from China," it added two more: "that major incidents
entailing Taiwan's secession from China should occur, or that possibilities for
a peaceful reunification should be completely exhausted."[168] Note that these
criteria are deliberately ambiguous and that China reserves for itself the discretion to decide whether they have been met. The Pentagon concurred, concluding that China was acquiring capabilities for two purposes concerning
Taiwan itself: to deter moves toward Taiwan independence and to develop
"the prerequisite military capabilities to eventually settle the dispute on Beijing's terms."[169]

The combination of China's growing capabilities and its less-than-clear
intentions creates vulnerability for Taiwan. Even if the probability that Beijing
might decide to use its military arsenal to compel Taiwan to submit is low, as
it is now, and even if Taiwan seeks to reassure Beijing that its own intentions
are benign and so encourage China's strategic patience, as the Ma administration has done, some degree of insecurity persists. Taiwan's formal assessments of the shifting military balance reflect that insecurity. Ma Ying-jeou has
said that "despite easing cross-Strait ties, Beijing remains the biggest threat to
us militarily. We must not drop our guard and be lulled into a false sense of
security."[170] The island's Ministry of National Defense concluded in the 2011
version of its defense white paper:

> Although the possibility of conflict has decreased after cross-Strait rela-
> tions relaxed, and dealing with the "Taiwan issue" might be delayed, the
> PRC's objective to unify Taiwan has not changed. As the military
> strength of the two sides of the Taiwan Strait becomes even more imbal-
> anced, we are bound [to] face growingly severe military threats.[171]

In turn, this imbalance calls into question the very assumption that a peace
accord might actually promote mutual security. The sort of understanding
that Beijing would seek and accept would likely not limit the damage that
China could do to Taiwan if it chose to attack. At the same time, Beijing might
well seek to limit the assistance that Taiwan receives from the United States,
which is the ultimate source of its security.

Implications of a Peace Accord for Taiwan's Sovereignty

A cross-Strait security accord is by definition an interim measure, a way of stabilizing relations before the two sides undertake any effort to resolve their
fundamental dispute. Neither side, particularly Taiwan, would be willing to
make commitments in an interim accord that might prejudice its interests for

the long term. Yet Beijing's apparent insistence that the one-China principle be the political premise of a peace accord would appear to do exactly that for Taiwan. That is, Beijing's definition of that principle arguably negates Taiwan's claim that it is a sovereign entity. At least, Taipei interprets it that way.

Of concern here are three issues. The first is how Taiwan's legal status is addressed in any resolution of the fundamental dispute. No government in Taipei would be willing to negotiate stabilization arrangements in ways that would foreclose options for resolution. The second is Taiwan's role in the international community and, in this case, its freedom to have security relations with third countries, including the purchase of advanced weaponry and the protection of a security guarantee. In the absence of a clear, binding, and enforceable renunciation of force by Beijing, those security relations remain very important. The third concerns political arrangements within Taiwan. As noted above, Mainland scholar Yu Keli has indicated that China will not feel secure—and therefore will not be willing to take steps to make Taiwan feel more secure—unless Taiwan leaders take steps to ensure that independence is eliminated as a political force on the island. That is tantamount to defining who may and who may not rule there.

In a discussion of CBMs that also applies to a peace accord, Steven Goldstein pinpoints the corrosive effect of Beijing's precondition: Beijing would seek to use security talks and CBMs to blunt independence sentiment, promote unification, and attenuate Taiwan's security relationship with the United States: "In short, the central paradox . . . is that Beijing's apparent present stance on negotiating CBMs puts the most intractable issues in cross-Strait relations at the *beginning* of a trust-building exercise rather [than] at the end, where they belong." It imposes too high a political cost on Taiwan and is thus a "deal-killer" and "détente-consuming."[172]

Saunders and Kastner express some confidence that Beijing might be willing to back down from that stance and use the 1992 consensus as the premise, as it has for economic agreements. If so, then some type of accord is possible. But there is really no basis for such confidence. For almost two decades, China's top leaders—first Jiang Zemin and then Hu Jintao—have been explicit that the one-China principle should be the basis, leaving less flexibility to move to another approach. Beijing's acceptance of the 1992 consensus would be a major concession, but it would appear to be essential to ensure that Taipei sat down at the peace-talks table without fear that its fundamental claim of sovereignty had been undermined.

That does not mean that more modest cross-Strait understandings are useless in producing limited security stabilization. Formalizing the conflict avoidance mechanisms that already exist and creating new ones would be useful, as long as Beijing does not set political preconditions and Taiwan's leaders can make the case to the public that those steps *do* make Taiwan secure in concrete ways.[173] If the no independence–no use of force trade-off is flawed for various reasons, perhaps the two sides can develop a conditionality that is more acceptable. For example, if Beijing could come forward with a precise definition of a Taiwan action that would justify the use of force, then a pledge not to use force might have more reassurance value. Its fear, of course, would be that a new Taipei government would find some loophole and move toward independence.

It should be no surprise, therefore, that during his first term Ma Ying-jeou became increasingly skeptical regarding the utility of a peace accord and CBMs. He did suggest them during the 2008 election campaign and spoke of a "possible" peace accord in his inaugural address. By the third anniversary of that speech, he had a different emphasis. He spoke of determination to "protect the security of Taiwan" and noted that he had called on the United States to provide more advanced fighters and submarines to help "maintain a balance of power in the Taiwan Strait and make Taiwan more willing and confident about pursuing further dealings with mainland China."[174] In talks before military audiences, he was even more explicit about the threat that the PLA posed and the need to "avoid war without fearing it, and prepare for war without seeking it." Although Taiwan would not engage in an arms race with China, he said, it should "be able to engage in asymmetric warfare and . . . utilize innovative tactics."[175] Su Chi, who was Ma Ying-jeou's first secretary general in the National Security Council, indicated in May 2010, two years after Ma's inauguration, that CBMs were premature.[176] Immediately after his reelection, Ma took a new tack. Even in the absence of a peace accord, "we have other means to achieve its purpose that will institutionalize the cross-Strait status quo of peaceful development." He even suggested that the agreements already signed could be seen as a "broadly defined" peace accord.[177]

The Taiwan Politics of a Security Agreement

If the substance of a negotiated understanding was not difficult enough, politics make one even more problematic. Not surprisingly, defense is a sensitive political issue on Taiwan. In any society, political leaders do not voluntarily foster the impression that they do not care about the security of the country; to do so only puts them on the political defensive. But the politics of security have been complicated on Taiwan.

The island's political history is one factor. Chapter 2 discussed the impact to this day of the manner in which the KMT regime imposed its rule on Taiwan after World War II. The Nationalist military was a part of this narrative of resentment and suspicion. It was made up of KMT army units from the Mainland, which carried out a violent, badly disciplined suppression after the February 1947 uprising. The military was part of the system of hard authoritarianism that was imposed thereafter. By and large, it was Mainlander officers who lorded over Taiwanese conscripts. To this day, the officer corps of the ROC's armed forces has a larger share of Mainlanders than does any other institution. On top of that, there is the anxiety about "traitors in our midst," an anxiety that was manifest in the titles of two July 2011 editorials in the pro-DPP *Liberty Times*: "Ma [Ying-jeou] Acting as China's Trojan Horse" and "A Vote for Ma is a Vote for China."[178] A peace accord thus raises not only questions of policy (does it contribute to the security of Taiwan?) but also, for some Taiwanese, questions about the loyalty of those who would be charged with its implementation.

The concern about "traitors" was on full display in June 2011 when the Taiwan media reported that a retired general from Taiwan who participated in an exchange of officers of the two sides had said, "Let's not make divisions between the Nationalist army and the Communist army; we are all in the Chinese army." That created a momentary firestorm on Taiwan whose flames the media were happy to fan. A senior DPP figure asked: "How can our high-ranking military officials receive taxpayers' money on the one hand and have banquets with the PLA on the other?" A pro-DPP paper asserted that "mainlanders have never regarded themselves as Taiwanese and still think they are Chinese." In light of the reaction, Ma Ying-jeou said that the retired general's remarks should be "sternly condemned" if they were true. Xia Yingzhou, the general who was supposed to have made the remark, declared that the media report was without foundation. He did admit that retired generals from the two sides had discussed deployments and operations, even though they were not authorized to do so by their governments—an admission that would only confirm the fears of those skeptical of such interactions.[179]

Politics was again at the fore in October 2011, in the middle of the presidential campaign, when the issue of a peace accord resurfaced. In one of several presentations on his vision for the next decade, Ma Ying-jeou said that "we are currently considering that . . . both sides should discuss in a gradual step-by-step process the concluding of a peace agreement in a meticulous and prudent manner." Yet he also said that such a pact should not be concluded unless it had a high degree of popular support; met the actual needs of the country; and was supervised by the legislature. Taiwan should not do a peace accord merely for the sake of doing so, and it should make "comprehensive preparations in advance."[180] Some media outlets ignored the conditions and regarded the agreement as a done deal. The DPP, sensing a political opportunity, sought to exploit a vulnerability. A party spokesman charged that Ma had submitted to a PRC demand and established a "timetable for unification," and a think tank scholar associated with the DPP warned about "de jure annexation." Tsai Ing-wen, the DPP presidential candidate, termed the proposal "irresponsible," "impetuous," and "reckless."[181] One set of newspaper polls suggested that Ma had lost his lead over Tsai in the four weeks that followed the announcement. He struggled to recover, offering a series of assurances to the public, culminating in "ten guarantees" made up of "one framework, two preconditions, three principles, and four assurances." The sovereignty and security preconditions had become so onerous that they realistically ruled out any sort of agreement. Furthermore, he promised that there would be a referendum to probe public sentiment before beginning negotiations—a promise that likely produced an allergic reaction in Beijing, given its opposition to Chen Shui-bian's referenda.[182]

Conclusion

As China and Taiwan consider stabilizing their relationship through formal agreements on political and security issues, they have more questions than confidence. Thus far, they lack a conceptual foundation for creating a more peaceful environment. And the fervid response to Ma's remarks on a peace accord demonstrated once more that, on Taiwan at least, there is no political foundation either.

Cross-Strait engagement on political issues was not totally absent in Ma Ying-jeou's first term. Crime control, culture, and education were addressed, at least to some extent. But as the two governments discovered, they could not go beyond those limited encounters to reconcile their core political differences, as Beijing had hoped. The issues that had bedeviled cross-Strait relations for more than two decades—most important, the status of the Republic of China—still festered. Neither side was willing to make concessions on those matters—which are, after all, at the heart of the fundamental cross-Strait dispute—for the sake of stabilization, because each believed that to do so would weaken its position when it came to negotiating a final resolution. Moreover, as the 2009 visit of the Zheng Bijian delegation to Taiwan illustrated in microcosm, the Taiwan public is not ready to move forward on political issues.

Similarly, a peace agreement, which seems attractive in principle, is hard to construct when it comes to specifics. One problem is the PRC's inclination to use a security agreement to make progress on political issues like the one-

China principle, which affects Taiwan's claim of sovereignty. Just as important is Beijing's desire to exclude treatment of China's military power as relevant to Taiwan, although an agreement that did not restrain China's military capabilities in some way would leave Taiwan with an irremediable and irreversible vulnerability. For Beijing, any pact that left open even the possibility of future separation would only reinforce the anxiety that it has lived with over the past two decades. A peace accord that was not accompanied by an amendment of the PRC anti-secession law would be less reassuring to Taiwan than one that did. An agreement that limited or ended U.S. arms sales would cheer Beijing but only deepen Taiwan's sense of insecurity. The chance that China would choose to compel Taiwan's submission may be very low, if only because of the costs that Beijing would pay in terms of its reputation on Taiwan and worldwide. Yet the probability is not zero, and the stakes are very high for Taiwan: the loss of everything that it has been. If a peace accord does not leave each side feeling more secure and if neither gains much confidence in the other's formal commitments, of what value is it?

At the current stage of mutual persuasion on political and security matters, the two sides remain far apart. It is hard to see how the ideas now on the table can facilitate political convergence and mutual security through formal accords and so stabilize cross-Strait relations in these areas. For the moment, it appears that each prefers maintaining the relative certainty of the status quo to accepting the risks implied in formal agreements. The danger for Taiwan is that Beijing may grow impatient with mutual persuasion in a status quo that is not completely stabilized and choose to exploit its growing power advantage.

Appendix A:
"Basic Agreement for Cross-Strait Peace and Development (Draft)"

(translation by author)

The two sides undertaking this agreement:

Recognize the fact that since 1949 the entire China has existed in a state of separated jurisdictions but that both are still parts of the Chinese nation.

Recognize that, in view of the shared responsibility of the people[183] on the two sides to promote the restoration/revival of the entire Chinese nation and national peace and prosperity, the two sides belong to the entire China and that one [side]'s equal treatment of the other is the basis for promoting peace. The two sides [also] understand that establishing a cross-Strait integration mechanism is a path for peaceful development,

Based on the common interests of the people on the two sides and the aspiration to terminate the state of hostilities and create conditions for cross-strait cooperation [the two sides] reach the following agreement:

Article 1
The two parties [literally "the two shores"] commit themselves not to split the entire China and commit themselves to safeguarding its sovereignty and territorial integrity.

Article 2
The two parties agree simultaneously to respect the other as a constitutional order subject and to promote a normal relationship on an equal basis.

Article 3
The two parties agree not to use force or threaten to use force against the other and agree to resolve bilateral disputes by peaceful means only.

Article 4
The two parties agree to establish communities on mutually agreed on subject matters in order to promote [their] cooperation.

Article 5
The two parties agree to cooperate in international organizations. The presence of both parties in international organizations does not mean the splitting of China, and each party has the responsibility to safeguard the entire interests of the Chinese people.

Article 6
The two parties agree to exchange representative offices. The establishment of these offices and the status and forms of their representation internationally will be negotiated separately.

The Agreement should be ratified through each party's constitutional process, and it will take effect from the day of exchange of documents.

Signatures:

Representative, Beijing China government

Representative, Taipei China government

"Liangan Tonghe yu Hoping Fazhan: Yitiao Huli Shuangying di Wenjian Daolu" ("Cross-Strait Integration, Peace, and Development: On a Stable Path Leading to Win-Win Mutual Benefits")

Drafter: Chang Ya-chung
Chief Convener: Sun Chen
Co-Conveners: Raymond Tai, Hwang Kwang-kuo

6

The 2012 Transitions
and Scenarios for the Future

The Taiwan elections of January 2012 demonstrated the impact of politics on China policy. Any election is a contest in at least three different arenas: the first concerns the character and reputation of the contenders; the second, the relative ability of the competing parties to mobilize their loyal voters; the third, how voters, particularly swing voters, rank various issues. Taiwan's elections were no exception.

In the first arena, Ma Ying-jeou and Tsai Ing-wen, the two major candidates, were remarkably alike. Each came from an elite family, though Tsai's forebears had arrived on Taiwan long before Ma's parents, who arrived in 1948. They both received a superior education and focused on law. Each served in government. Ma was in the central government in the early 1990s and was Taipei mayor from 1998 to 2006. Tsai was an adviser to Lee Teng-hui and held senior positions for most of the Chen Shui-bian administration. Those surveyed in a fall 2011 poll had mixed but fairly positive assessments of their leadership abilities.[1] *Time* magazine offered this overall assessment:

> Neither Ma nor Tsai can resolve the island's existential problem.... Still, they do Taiwan proud. Both are informed, confident, articulate ... well educated ... well traveled, passionate about making a difference and genuinely concerned about the future of their land—traits any electorate would want in its leaders. Too bad one of them has to lose. But whatever happens, as the freest place in the Chinese world, Taiwan wins.[2]

James Soong Chu-yu was the spoiler candidate in 2012. A Mainlander, he had risen through the ranks of the KMT and was the first elected governor of the now-dormant Taiwan provincial government.[3] He was both a capable and ambitious politician, and he ran as an independent when Lee Teng-hui refused to make him the party's candidate in the 2000 presidential race. After dividing the Blue vote, Soong created his own People First Party, which occupied an ideological position to the right of the KMT. His campaign was more about politics than policy.

When it comes to the second arena, mobilizing core voters, for historical reasons the DPP has had the advantage. During the authoritarian period, when the KMT was the only major legal party, it relied on patronage and vote buying by local political machines (factions) to get out the vote. Lacking such organizational advantages, the KMT's Taiwanese opponents had to compete by stirring up popular resentment of the KMT, to the extent that the regime allowed. The skills thus acquired served the DPP well once it established itself in 1986 and as the political system became more democratic. In the island's increasingly complex media environment, the KMT's organizational mobilization and the corruption associated with it (vote buying) could not always overcome the mass enthusiasm that the DPP was so good at generating. So increasingly the KMT has sought to rely less on organization and more on mass mobilization, and the political machines have become less important in the large urban municipalities, where around 60 percent of voters live.[4] Understandably, the KMT's shift has caused resentment among the heads of the local machines, whose power stemmed from brokering turnout, and the closeness of the 2012 election led the party organization at least temporarily to reconnect with them to secure their help in getting out the vote.[5]

A key target group for KMT mobilization was in China most of the time, not on Taiwan. It consists of business executives with operations in China, who tend to favor the KMT but who, because Taiwan does not allow absentee voting, have to return home to vote. Whether they would vote for Ma in the numbers that they did in 2008 was in question, because rising labor costs and other factors had hurt their economic opportunities.[6] There also were charges that scheduling the presidential election in January one week before Lunar New Year reduced turnout because some people could not return home twice in two weeks. In the event, approximately 200,000 people returned home for election day.[7] In all, 74 percent of Taiwan's eligible voters went to the polls, which was not out of line with turnout in previous elections.[8]

The contest in the third arena—to define which issues are most salient, particularly for swing voters—was the most important. Ma Ying-jeou's engagement of China was the primary issue. Ma argued that his policies of economic normalization, liberalization, and institutionalization had benefited Taiwan in general and that the island's long-term political interests had not been sacrificed in the process. At least one public opinion poll suggested that voters agreed. Asked in November 2011, two months before the election, about their view on the pace of "cross-Strait exchanges," only 25.7 percent thought that it was too fast, 48.1 said that it was just right, and 12.0 percent thought that it was too slow.[9] The implication of these results is that only core DPP supporters (about 25 percent of the electorate) believed that Mainland engagement was happening too quickly.

Tsai Ing-wen, on the other hand, claimed that Ma's policies had worked to the advantage of large corporations and the wealthy rather than the middle class and that they had undermined Taiwan's interests. Ma emphasized growth while Tsai stressed justice and fairness. Tsai charged that Ma had undermined the island's sovereignty; Ma rejected the charge.[10] Those with strong party loyalty endorsed this difference in emphasis. Blue supporters thought that the government's emphasis should be on economic development and cross-Strait relations. Green supporters thought that reducing the gap between rich and poor should get the highest priority.[11]

Ma also asserted that the flow of benefits that his policies purportedly had produced would stop if Tsai Ing-wen became president. Tsai countered that Beijing would accommodate a new DPP administration. A central issue was the 1992 consensus, which the KMT was prepared to accept even before Ma began his 2008 campaign and which had been the basis for all the cross-Strait agreements concluded during his first term. The DPP, on the other hand, had consistently rejected the consensus. In August 2011, Tsai herself denied that the formula ever existed and drew this inference: "Since it doesn't exist, neither does the problem of whether or not I should admit or accept it."[12] At several points during the campaign, the KMT charged that this stance would bring disaster. Ma responded to Tsai by saying that abandoning the 1992 consensus would cause uncertainty in cross-Strait relations: "Both sides would feel the negative impact. Taiwan, in particular, would be hit hard."[13]

Former KMT officials asserted that the 1992 consensus did in fact exist. For example, Chen Chang-wen, who was secretary general of the Straits Exchange Foundation in the early 1990s, said that an understanding was reached in 1992 and that it had facilitated the positive developments since May 2008.[14] Beijing also weighed in. The spokesman of the State Council's Taiwan Affairs Office asserted that "if [Tsai's] policy [of denying the 1992 consensus] is put in place, it will make it impossible for the two sides of the Taiwan Strait to continue the talks and cause instability in cross-Strait relations."[15] That assertion was consistent with China's oft-repeated statement that "the peaceful development of cross-Strait relations is based on opposition to Taiwan Independence and adherence to the 1992 Consensus."[16]

In this thrust and parry, Tsai made two tactical moves. First, she warned that China was working in various ways to bias the outcome of the election in its favor. For example, she said that "in recent elections, the Chinese government has exerted influence on Taiwan's elections to compel their desired outcome. They have attempted to threaten the Taiwanese people. . . . Lately, they have emphasized the use of economic leverage. . . . The long-term impact of these tactics is yet to be seen, but from our part we must be vigilant in defending our hard-won freedom to choose and decide our future."[17]

James Soong, the candidate of the small People First Party (PFP), charged that Beijing was opposed to his campaign because of its fear that he would drain votes from Ma Ying-jeou in a close election.[18] And indeed, China did seek to affect the outcome. PRC officials suggested with varying degrees of clarity and precision that the results of the election would affect "the stable development of cross-Strait relations," a warning that a pro-DPP newspaper called on Ma to refute.[19] Mainland scholars were not shy about discussing the benefit of arrangements like the Economic Cooperation Framework Agreement for southern Taiwan (the DPP's geographic base), and the Green media were quick to see China's special purchases of Taiwan's agricultural products as part of China's united front strategy. In a reference to one transaction, the *Liberty Times* editorialized that "what China really wants to buy is the Taiwanese banana farmers' hearts, not their bananas" and that Ma Ying-jeou was Beijing's "Trojan horse."[20] The same paper charged that a vote for Ma was a vote for China.[21]

Tsai's second move was to seek to shift the argument away from the 1992 consensus by calling for a "Taiwan consensus" to serve as the basis of negotiations with Beijing. She presented her proposal at a speech to the American Enterprise Institute during her September 2011 visit to Washington, D.C.: "I have raised the concept of a Taiwan consensus, which highlights the democratic process of decisionmaking and emphasizes the fact that policy is only sustainable when it is a realistic response to the consensus and needs of the people. Any political precondition that is not democratically agreed upon is fragile at most." In subsequent comments, Tsai indicated that this process would be inclusive in terms of participants, iterative (starting at the lowest common denominator), and open-ended in terms of ultimate content. But she also said that the consensus "must be passed by law," a requirement that might foster anxieties in Beijing depending on whether the legislation suggested that Taiwan was not a part of China.[22] Tsai's proposal stimulated a debate on Taiwan: DPP proponents supported her, and the KMT criticized her.

Why did Tsai ignore suggestions to shift China policy and apparently create a vulnerability for herself on issues like the 1992 consensus?[23] Why did she reject that formulation rather than foster ambiguity about what she would do if elected, since vagueness might have been modestly reassuring to the Taiwan public and to China? First, there is, of course, the possibility that she truly believed that the 1992 consensus significantly undermined Taiwan's sovereignty, in addition to whatever consequences economic engagement entailed. If that was the case, she did little to explain specifically why and how Taiwan had suffered from the use of the formula. Second, she argued, in essence, that Beijing was bluffing. That is, if she were elected, China would have such a stake in the current status quo that it would have to accommodate her. If so, she and her party would secure the real gains of Ma's administration but avoid what she regarded as the unacceptable costs of his policies *and* unwanted political concessions.

Another likely but not inconsistent explanation is that she did not wish to alienate the DPP base even as she sought the support of swing voters in the middle. She had already received criticism from the Deep Green wing of the party. Some faulted her for not mobilizing the enthusiasm of the base in the way that Chen Shui-bian did so well—she had gone out of her way to demonstrate that at least stylistically, she was not like Chen.[24] Her decision to moderate her criticism of the Economic Cooperation Framework Agreement was termed "throwing in the towel."[25] When, in October 2011, she said that an open-minded DPP was willing to accept the proposition that "Taiwan is the ROC and the ROC is Taiwan" (not a new position for the DPP), Koo Kwan-min, a DPP elder, charged that she had "dangerously legalized and rationalized" the ROC.[26] So electoral imperatives helped shape her policy proposals.

Ma Ying-jeou created his own political vulnerability with his October 2011 statement that Taiwan might consider a cross-Strait peace accord over the next decade (see discussion in chapter 5). Whether he was simply stating a fact or worried that the DPP was gaining traction by playing up domestic issues is unclear. But even though he set fairly onerous conditions for such negotiations, the opposition exploited the opportunity that he had provided. Tsai Ing-wen charged that he had "put the nation's future at risk" and "pushed the future of Taiwanese into a political danger zone." The DPP central standing committee passed a resolution asserting that Ma had sacrificed sovereignty, changed the cross-Strait status quo, jeopardized Taiwan's democratic values, and damaged the island's "strategic depth" for negotiations. The controversy persisted for longer than normal, and Ma's support in the polls dropped.[27]

2012 Election Results

In the end, Ma appears to have won the overall argument over which policy issues were most salient, as voters opted for the continuity that they knew over uncertain change.[28] He received 51.6 percent of the vote, while Tsai got 45.6 percent. James Soong got the rest, and because he came from a KMT background, his supporters were likely to be more ideologically aligned with Ma than Tsai. A modest majority apparently accepted Ma's view that the island by and large had benefited from his cross-Strait policy, that those benefits would continue only if he remained president, and that his policies would not jeopardize the island.[29] Taiwan's swing voters were less prepared to vote for him in 2012 than they were in 2008, but not by too much. Ma won in both northern and central Taiwan (the south is DPP territory) and got majorities from all age cohorts, including the young people on whom Tsai had counted.[30] Yet although Tsai Ing-wen failed to make a credible case that she could simultaneously sustain the benefits of economic relations with China and protect the island's political interests as her party defined them, she did bring the DPP back from the defeat of 2008 and make the 2012 contest competitive.

In the Legislative Yuan election, the KMT dropped from seventy-two seats to sixty-four, and the DPP rose from thirty-two seats to forty. Both James Soong's People First Party and Lee Teng-hui's Taiwan Solidarity Union (TSU) got three seats each, and nonparty candidates received three seats. In the party vote, the KMT received 47.6 percent, the DPP 37.0 percent, the PFP 5.9 percent, and the TSU 9.6 percent (the total does not equal 100 percent because of rounding). Adding results for the Blue parties (KMT and PFP) and for the Green ones (DPP and TSU) suggests that the balance of sentiment among voters was 53.5 percent Blue and 47.5 percent Green. The TSU's unexpectedly strong showing in the party vote indicates that Deep Green sentiment remains.[31]

In the end, the key variable, which determined the outcome of both the presidential and legislative elections, was party identification. Here, the Blue parties enjoyed a margin of around 55 to 45 percent and so a structural advantage. Those who favored the KMT or the PFP agreed with Ma's approach on China policy; those who identified with the DPP or the TSU did not. The KMT ensured that it translated that advantage into victory by getting its voters to the polls on election day. The most revealing measure of the power of party identification as the key predictor came in areas of southern Taiwan, which traditionally vote for the DPP but to which China had directed economic benefits. In the 2012 election, the support rate for the DPP declined only a modest amount.[32] At least those voters were able to keep their economic interests and their political preferences separate.

The Politics of Taiwan Policy in China, 2012 and Beyond

It happens that 2012 is also the year that China begins a political transition as the membership of leading party, government, and military bodies turns over. Most important are the Chinese Communist Party's Politburo and its Standing Committee, the State Council (cabinet), and the Central Military Commission (CMC), which are the ultimate policymaking bodies in China.[33] The transition occurs every five years when the National Party Congress and the National People's Congress (China's legislature) meet. The National Party Congress (the eighteenth, historically) met in November 2012; the National People's Congress (the twelfth) will occur in spring 2013. The turnover can be quite substantial, mainly because of strictly enforced age limits for officials. Thus in 2012, at least fourteen and possibly sixteen members of the twenty-five-person Politburo will retire. Seven of the nine members of the Standing Committee will retire.[34] Seven or eight of the ten members of the State Council's Executive Committee will retire or be promoted out.[35] And seven of the ten members of the Central Military Commission will retire.[36] Competition for the vacated chairs can influence policy.

The even-numbered congresses are critical for Taiwan, because it is there that a new "paramount leader" emerges, with the expectation that he will serve for two five-year terms. Thus, Hu Jintao became general secretary of the party at the Sixteenth National Party Congress in the fall of 2002 and president of the PRC at the Tenth National People's Congress in the spring of 2003. He had to wait a couple of years to become chairman of the party's Central Military Commission, for reasons that are not completely understood. It is expected that Xi Jinping, the son of a CCP leader who was prominent both before and after 1949, will succeed to Hu's party and state positions in the fall of 2012 and spring of 2013 respectively. (Hu did not remain as CMC chairman, and Xi replaced him.[37]) The paramount leader has the dominant voice on policy concerning Taiwan.

The competition for the thirty-five or forty party, government, and military positions at the top of the PRC system takes place not in public campaigns like Taiwan's but mainly behind closed doors.[38] Still, the rivalry is intense. Also unlike in Taiwan, the competitors are more successful in climbing the ladder of power if they refrain from proposing new policies, even if they have new ideas. Reinforcing this incentive, the CCP has carried out a process of formal evaluation whereby "rising stars" must state their views on the gamut of policy issues, and on Taiwan they have not strayed from the conventional.[39] If such an evaluation was used for the 2012–13 succession, there is no information on what Xi Jingping might have told party evaluators about his views on Taiwan policy, so it is hard to predict what changes he might make once he takes power. It happens, however, that Xi served as party head in Fujian and Zhejiang provinces on China's southeast coast and in that capacity had substantial contact with Taiwan corporate executives with business operations there. He reportedly "immersed himself in the details of China's relationship with Taiwan" as he sought investment from the island.[40] A biography of Xi, published in Hong Kong, describes an instance in which he worked through the night to resolve problems in a Taiwan-invested joint venture during the time that he was in the leadership of Fuzhou, the capital of Fujian province, which is directly across the strait from Taiwan. But that was consistent with his general effort to attract investment from outside, particularly from "overseas Chinese."[41] He also may have been instrumental in formulating the "developmental plan for the western Taiwan Straits economic zone" and, in particular, the plan for the Pingtan Island comprehensive economic zone. Those proposals to draw Taiwan businessmen more deeply into the economic development of southeast China became public after Xi Jinping moved to Beijing, but an "all politics is local" psychology may have led him to wish to bring benefits to his former turf.[42] Still, those experiences may suggest that he would not radically change Hu Jintao's approach. More generally, the emerging system of leadership change in China encourages gradual transitions and denies any new "paramount leaders" excessive stature. And Xi and his cohort will face a number of domestic challenges that will give them little incentive to rock the boat on Taiwan.[43]

As Xi replaces Hu at the top of the party, government, and PLA hierarchies, his initial approach to Taiwan policy will likely be cautious, initially because the officials who have managed cross-Strait relations on a day-to-day basis will likely be replaced, creating a hiatus in implementation as new personnel learn their briefs.[44] Over the longer term, Xi will have to gradually establish his authority, master the intricacies of the Taiwan Strait issue himself, and then forge consensus among different bureaucratic interests. Ma Ying-jeou's victory may foster expectations among some in China that the momentum of cross-Strait relations can accelerate.

In looking beyond the leadership transition itself, it is interesting to speculate how Xi might adjust Taiwan policy as he becomes the new paramount leader, assuming that he seeks changes. One source of clues is to recall from chapter 2 how Hu Jintao executed his policy innovations regarding Taiwan after becoming general secretary of the CCP in 2002 and president of China in 2003.[45] First of all, even though he quickly became head of the leadership team responsible for guiding Taiwan affairs (the Taiwan Work Leading Small Group), he had to move slowly to reshape the content of policy, because the policy approach of Jiang Zemin, his predecessor, was well entrenched and Jiang himself remained as chairman of the Central Military Commission. Once Jiang finally stepped down in fall 2004, Hu gradually deployed a series of policy statements that shifted Beijing's emphasis away from promoting unification and toward blocking Taiwan independence; they also clarified the costs to Taiwan of continuing with the DPP's policies and the benefits of engaging with Beijing. Those statements then became the basis for under-standings reached with the leaders of the KMT and the PFP who visited Bei-jing in spring 2005 (which later became the starting point for the Ma administration's policy initiatives). Hu's new political message to Taiwan was "Put these parties in power and benefits will flow." As Hu put it, China was "placing its hopes in the Taiwan people."[46]

The point here is that if an incoming Chinese leader like Xi Jinping wishes to alter Beijing's Taiwan policy, he will have to do so gradually and methodi-cally. It took Hu Jintao two and a half years from the time that he became CCP general secretary to complete the foundation of his revised approach. With Jiang Zemin looking over his shoulder and Chen Shui-bian sowing division with China, incrementalism was the only way to build consensus for innova-tion among China's various power centers.[47] So too, Xi will have to defer to a healthy Hu and, perhaps, to a not-so-healthy Jiang. Moreover, relevant agen-cies, including the PLA, have a stake in the current policy. Reinforcing the inevitability of gradualism is that Hu Jintao was able to do the so-called "easy" economic issues, while Xi's agenda will be more difficult, particularly in the political and security arenas.

The deliberate pace required for policy innovation in the PRC may actu-ally facilitate the stabilization of cross-Strait relations. As discussed, the Tai-wan public is not yet ready for rapid movement on the political and security dimensions of relations with China. Although the KMT retains control of the legislature, its margin over the DPP and the TSU declined. The time that Ma Ying-jeou needs to prepare public opinion in conceptual terms on these issues—if he chooses to do so—is time that Xi Jinping can spend building consensus within the PRC system for whatever initiatives he might wish to undertake. Zhang Nianchi, one of China's leading Taiwan specialists, argues that political attitudes on the island will change only gradually and that Hu Jintao's patient policy should be continued. Because the trend begun in 2008 is positive, China should not panic about polls or elections that are not favor-able for China. Instead, it should have confidence that, "[although] the iceberg between the two sides of the Taiwan Strait cannot be melted overnight ... the iceberg is melting."[48]

Mid-Term Scenarios

It happens that Ma Ying-jeou's second term will overlap significantly with Xi Jinping's "first term," the five years that he is likely to serve as China's paramount leader. What then are the prospects for cross-Strait relations in the medium term? Will stabilization through mutual persuasion continue? If so, at what speed? Or will either China or Taiwan lose patience with the process that Ma Ying-jeou and Hu Jintao set in train in 2008? What happens next? After examining various scenarios for the period 2012 to 2016, I conclude that the momentum of cooperation on stabilization that began when Ma took office in 2008 will decelerate and most likely stall. Beijing and Taipei have grabbed the low-hanging fruit, and if they are to get what is on higher branches, a "ladder" will be necessary. (To complicate matters, China hopes that the apple of unification awaits at the very top of the tree, while Taiwan fears that the apple will be rotten). The more likely task for the two sides is to manage unmet expectations and conceptual differences. Yet with a certain amount of skill, they may transform the loss of momentum, with all its attendant difficulties, into a process of consolidation that lays the foundation for future progress. Yet I cannot rule out, at least analytically, that the paradigm of power asymmetry will replace the paradigm of mutual persuasion.

A scenario that is unlikely (but not hypothetically impossible) is that the stabilization of cross-Strait relations unexpectedly morphs into rapid movement toward resolution of the fundamental dispute, leading to some type of unification. Although the current leaders of both China and Taiwan hold that any resolution of their fundamental differences will be a long-term process, one cannot rule out the possibility that their predictions are wrong. Several routes to rapid resolution come to mind. First, Beijing might decide to concede to Taiwan on the sovereignty issue and alter its one-country, two-systems formula in a significant way. Second, the Taiwan public might judge, based on favorable economic interactions and persistent dilemmas in other policy areas, that China's formula for unification is not all that bad and that China's power advantage will only increase anyway. Third, China might make token revisions to the one-country, two-systems formula that Taiwan misperceives as truly significant and then naively accepts, leading to unification. None of those routes to resolution are especially likely in the medium term. Even if they were opened, the DPP would no doubt oppose taking them, roiling Taiwan politics for some time to come.

Three other scenarios seem far more likely. One is that the gradual stabilization that began in 2008 continues indefinitely and broadens in scope. The two sides conclude more agreements on economic relations and find greater common ground on political and security issues, each gaining greater confidence that the other will not challenge its fundamental interests. In particular, the two sides reach a peace accord whereby China limits the growth of its military capabilities that are most threatening to Taiwan and accepts formal confidence-building measures to regulate routine military activities. The result is a stable and institutionalized relationship in which the chances of reverting to past tensions are low. As time passes, the older, the more ideological generations of Taiwanese politicians retire from the scene and attitudes toward the Mainland become more pragmatic. Beijing bases new proposals on a clear sense of what the Taiwan public is willing to accept. In the medium term the key obstacles to resolving the fundamental dispute remain, although the possibility of accelerating toward unification is low. Taiwan remains unwilling to accept the one-country, two-systems formula, and Beijing is not ready to change it, but the two sides understand that stabilization of relations is important for its own sake and that it is a process that should not be rushed.

Nonetheless, the thrust of the analysis in chapters 4 and 5 suggests that achieving economic stabilization will become more difficult and that achieving political and security stabilization will be quite hard. However much Beijing may like to see stabilization broaden into the political realm, a second and more likely scenario is that the current process will stall, frustrating the creation of a fully institutionalized and cooperative order. Although there is no return to the level of tension that existed prior to Ma Ying-jeou's 2008 election and economic interdependence continues and perhaps deepens, the two sides are unable to conclude any significant agreements, such as those of Ma's first term. They not only fail to conclude the understandings mandated by the Economic Cooperation Framework Agreement, such as agreements on trade in goods and services (probably because domestic interests in both China and Taiwan oppose market openings that hurt their interests), but also fail to reach understandings on political and security issues. In particular, negotiations on a peace accord founder because one side or the other feels compelled to introduce issues like sovereignty. (Hu Jintao has already telegraphed that the one-China principle, not the 1992 consensus, should be the basis of talks on a peace accord.) Although confidence-building measures are useful in regulating the activities of the two militaries (and reducing somewhat Taiwan's sense of insecurity), creating them becomes impossible because each side views the purpose of CBMs differently. Public support in Taiwan for reconciliation declines, and the Taipei government therefore adopts a more "Taiwan-first" stance to stay in power. The benefits appear to accrue to one side or the other, not to both. The politics of cross-Strait relations become more complex. Each government faces the challenge of managing expectations.

A stall would have been the most likely scenario had Tsai Ing-wen won the January 2012 election, but it may also be the most likely one in the second Ma administration, given the difficult issues involved. The early signals did suggest that Beijing does not have excessive expectations for Ma's second term, but a uniform view was not expressed in the months after Ma's reelection. The most authoritative statement came from Premier Wen Jiabao, who signaled that economic issues would remain the focus. In his most detailed exposition, he said:

> I would first consider accelerating the follow-up negotiations of ECFA. In strengthening cross-Strait economic and trade exchanges, we will pay particular attention to accommodating the interests of Taiwan's small and medium-sized enterprises, the industries with local characteristics, and the grassroots people, particularly those in central and southern Taiwan. We will promote further development in cross-Strait financial cooperation, including pushing forward cooperation in bank clearing systems, encouraging banks on both sides to acquire stakes in each other so that banks will be able to play their due roles in boosting economic and trade cooperation. We will pay particularly high attention to the development of Taiwan-invested enterprises on the mainland. We will create favorable conditions to help them achieve transformation and upgrading, and expand their domestic markets.[49]

In a late January essay, Wang Yi, director of China's Taiwan Affairs Office of the State Council, also placed primary emphasis on easy and economic issues and "pragmatically promoting the sequential, progressive, forward development."[50]

Yet Mainland officials did not ignore the political dimension of the cross-Strait relationship. Wen Jiabao wondered "why the nourishment of our common cultural bond that has stretched over several thousand years cannot possibly resolve the political grudges that have lasted just several decades," and he called for an expansion of cultural and educational exchanges. Wang Yi suggested that the two sides "create conditions in areas such as politics and the military." In particular, he said that a top priority for promoting the peaceful development of cross-Strait relations was to "deepen the common understanding that both sides of the Taiwan Strait belong to one and the same China."[51] (Note, in light of the discussion in chapter 5, Wang's emphasis on the territory that encompasses China but avoidance of the status of the ROC government.) Chen Yunlin, Beijing's lead cross-Strait negotiator, advocated introducing more coherence and complexity into the institutional relations between his organization and its Taiwan counterpart.[52] He also said that once the two sides determined that the time was right for a peace accord, "we should make efforts to push for it."[53]

PRC scholars went further than the officials did. One, Li Jiaquan, argued for political contacts to complement economic negotiations.[54] Luo Yuan, a semi-retired general, criticized Ma's rejection of unification as a near-term issue and his caution about military exchanges. "For mainland China, it is the time for 'pushing for peaceful unification vigorously.'"[55] Guo Zhenyuan, who works at the Foreign Ministry's think tank, argued that forward movement was possible because the election had demonstrated that Taiwan's political mainstream was ahead of Ma and had not shown the restraint that he did.[56] Shanghai scholar Yan Anlin wrote that Ma's second inaugural address was "excessively conservative and propos[ed] inadequate development" and that enhancing public support for advances on political and security issues was an "urgent task."[57] Xu Shiquan, a senior scholar, was more patient. "China," he said, "will continue to focus on economic matters rather than political ones. There are many economic issues that the Mainland needs to address with Taiwan." Any worries about a rapid rush to unification were "totally unfounded. . . . The mainland's Taiwan policy at least for the mid-term is to 'build up the framework of peaceful development across the Strait.'"[58]

In my view, neither continued, gradual stabilization nor a stall is likely to divert China from its current Taiwan policy or lead it to abandon mutual persuasion. Continued, gradual stabilization is perfectly consistent with Hu Jintao's policy of peaceful development and the strategic patience that comes with it. A more permanent stall would no doubt be a disappointment to Beijing, since any optimism about achieving the goal of unification in the foreseeable future would vanish. It might confirm the views of those Chinese who favored some measure of pressure or coercion. Yet advocates of "strategic patience" could argue that a stall had slowed the realization of China's goals, not made it impossible. They could argue, as Wang Yi did in an April 2012 article, that Beijing's policies exert "an increasingly extensive influence on the social conditions and opinions of Taiwan people" and undermined "the radical 'Taiwan independence' roadmap."[59] The chance of the worst case—that Taiwan would seek de jure independence—would still be low. The door to unification would not have closed, it would just not be opening as fast as had been hoped; moreover, there is a risk in pushing the process faster than the Taiwan public is prepared to accommodate.

A third scenario, an alternative to both continued stabilization and a permanent stall, is that the two sides use the stall period to consolidate the stabilization that has occurred, defend the gains that they have already made, minimize the negative consequences of a slowdown, and take time to create the conceptual and political foundation for further steps.[60] Preventing a stall from becoming permanent and engendering mutual accusations of bad faith will not be easy, and it will require both skill and maturity. Political dynamics in each society will constrain the choices of the two governments. Yet Beijing should be able to adapt to the need for consolidation, because it recognizes the need for the two sides to lay a better foundation together and for a willingness to do so. Indeed, in a major speech on cross-Strait policy in March 2012, Wang Yi said that "a new phase of consolidation and deepening" had begun. It was necessary to consolidate mutual political trust and past achievements in economics and trade, exchanges, and public opinion.[61]

What would the consolidation of past gains require the two sides to do? Two projects come to mind: implement their past understandings well and seize new but modest gains where they are possible. In executing those projects, Beijing and Taipei also need to gear the substance of what they do to the process by which they interact.

Implementation

Agreements of the sort that Taiwan and China concluded are of little value if the benefits that they promise are not delivered. Good implementation will be needed to ensure that benefits flow and to sustain mutual confidence even as progress slows. Yet implementation is not automatic. A survey by Taiwan's National Federation of Industries found that Mainland customs authorities did not enforce the duty-free treatment that ECFA provided for specified Taiwan goods, failed to revise tariff schedules in accordance with ECFA, created non-tariff barriers when tariffs were removed, and demanded unnecessary or irrelevant documentation. "China still reportedly maintains . . . barriers despite Taipei and Beijing having significantly improved their economic relations after implementing the landmark bilateral economic cooperative framework agreement (ECFA) signed in 2010."[62] In its annual white paper, the federation specifically called for rapid implementation of the June 2010 agreement on protection of intellectual property rights: "As Taiwan manufacturing moves in the direction of advanced science and technology and innovation, enterprises will only invest in innovation and research and development if their intellectual property rights are protected."[63] Obviously, if either side fails to implement well the agreements reached in Ma's first term, when the focus was on "easy" issues, the other will be more cautious about reaching new understandings, particularly when the issues are "hard."

Seize Possibilities

The "easy" issues have not necessarily been exhausted. As Chu Yun-han, a prominent Taiwan political scientist, said at a post-election Washington symposium, "While many low-hanging fruits were picked [during Ma's first term], there are many more left to be picked." They include some economic opportunities, increased tourism, and expanded cultural and educational exchanges.[64] A panel of scholars assembled by the Taipei Forum Foundation, a think tank established by Su Chi in 2011, recommended that Ma use his second term to complete ECFA, pursue economic liberalization with other major trading partners, creatively encourage Taiwan business people in China to return investment to the island, work out a monetary settlement mechanism with Beijing, and promote cultural and educational exchanges. It also urged using the second term to foster a broader consensus on Taiwan concerning China policy, including creation of a "council for cross-Strait peaceful development" under the office of the president. Finally, the group said that Taiwan should "remain conscious of the risks in dealing with cross-Strait relations."[65] Wang Yi laid out a rather full agenda in January 2012: completing the ECFA agenda (for example, trade in goods and services and investment protection), expanding cooperation in the financial sector, and supporting cross-Strait industrial cooperation.[66] Taiwan's Ministry of Economic Affairs targeted eight areas in which there was potential for deeper business cooperation: herbal medicine, telecommunications, automobiles, business services, renewable energy, LED lighting, metallic materials, biotechnology, and medical equipment.[67] In the field of education, Taiwan universities were allowed to admit 2,000 Mainland students from six provinces. Relaxing those limits would fill empty spaces in Taiwan institutions and also provide greater opportunities for Chinese graduate students.[68]

That economic issues are getting harder—in part because they impinge on the interests of domestic actors on each side—is no reason not to keep trying. Completing the ECFA agenda will be mutually beneficial, forcing economic structural adjustment on Taiwan and confirming PRC confidence in Taipei's goodwill. Accordingly, in August 2012 Beijing and Taipei took new steps in stabilizing the economic relationship by signing agreements on customs cooperation and investment protection and a memorandum of understanding (MOU) regarding currency clearing. The first of the agreements, which seeks to remove obstacles to the movement of legitimate goods in both directions and to reduce smuggling, was modeled on existing agreements that the two sides had with other trading partners. The second—investment protection—had been long in gestation, hung up on questions of third-party arbitration and the security of Taiwan business people on the Mainland. In the end, the agreement was a compromise of the wishes of each side. Regarding arbitration, the agreement set forth five different mechanisms by which disputes could be resolved. Third-party arbitration, which Beijing had resisted because it might be interpreted as conferring sovereignty on Taiwan, was one of them, but only if it was specified in the original agreement. Thus, the PRC party would have an implicit veto—it could simply refuse to sign a contract with that option in it. Regarding personal security, Beijing pledged that if any Taiwan business person was arrested, the person's family would be notified within twenty-four hours. Some in Taiwan were concerned that this commitment was conveyed in a side memorandum of understanding and not in the agreement itself, which led Beijing's Taiwan Affairs Office to clarify that the MOU was binding in its effect. Both scholars and business executives in Taiwan concluded—correctly—that the value of the agreement would depend on its implementation. A comment by an executive of Hon Hai, the parent company of Foxconn, the world's most prominent electronics contract manufacturer, reflected the initial skepticism: "China does not uphold rule of law and its local governments, public security offices, and judicial authorities may not necessarily obey its central government."[69]

Completing the ECFA agenda is certainly not the only thing that Taiwan must do to ensure its future competitiveness (chapter 8 discusses other steps in detail). Effective implementation will be a bigger challenge for China's central government, since economic actors and local governments will resist the requirements of agreements on intellectual property rights and investment protection. If concluding and implementing these agreements proves to be too "hard," it will demonstrate concretely the limits of cross-Strait cooperation.

Finally, there is potential for incremental progress in the political and security areas. China could earn a lot of goodwill on Taiwan by expanding the international space that Taiwan may occupy. There are international governmental organizations of a functional sort in which Taiwan has a role to play— for example, those related to civil aviation, meteorology, and climate change. Giving Taiwan entré into the circle of countries that have adopted multilateral economic liberalization in the Asia-Pacific region would strengthen the island's competitiveness. For Beijing to permit Taiwan more international space would strengthen the KMT's argument that Mainland policy is broadly beneficial. After all, Beijing can take comfort from the fact that Ma was able to win reelection in 2012 despite the DPP's assertion during the campaign that economic engagement of the Mainland cost more than it benefited the population as a whole. In contrast, restricting Taiwan's global participation will only alienate the Taiwan public and raise doubts about the PRC's intentions. Yet there were vague indications in February 2012 that Beijing might do exactly that, which provoked predictably negative reactions on Taiwan.[70] Finally, concerning the routine operations of the two armed forces in the Taiwan Strait, the two sides could formalize those conflict avoidance understandings that already exist informally and perhaps create new ones. Here, Beijing would have to abandon its desire to use confidence-building measures for broader political purposes and restrict the freedom of action of the PLA navy and air force. The Ma administration would have to convince the public that such mechanisms benefit Taiwan's security and do not entail any deleterious political cost.

Coordinating Substance and Process

Whether the two sides are dealing with the remainder of the economic agenda or opening talks on political and security issues, they will have to consider how to coordinate both substance and process. Too often it is assumed that the "correct" substantive solution to a problem will automatically be adopted. Yet a flawed process can undermine adoption of mutually acceptable substantive provisions, while a sophisticated approach to problem solving can facilitate action on different issues of substance. The following are among the elements of a productive process:

—Each side should accept the value of concluding agreements incrementally for building mutual trust but should not act in ways that cause the other side to fear that the ultimate outcome is impossible. Thus, Taipei must not foster Chinese doubts about the possibility of unification, while Beijing should not confirm Taiwan fears about losing sovereignty.

—The two sides should maintain authoritative, high-level channels so that the top leader of each can reassure the other of his good intentions, particularly on initiatives done for domestic political purposes that appear to undercut cross-Strait relations.

—The top leader on each side should have the power and the will to ensure that the agendas of individual agencies are consistent with broad policy.

—For negotiations on sensitive issues like a peace accord, the two sides should be as sure as they can in advance that the outcome will be mutually acceptable. Because they may have only one chance to reach agreement, they should not begin the enterprise if failure is possible.

More broadly, China might "lighten up" on those aspects of its Taiwan policy that arguably will be perceived as indicating a shift on its part to the paradigm of power asymmetry. They include the part of the PLA's military buildup related to Taiwan, obvious steps to "buy" the goodwill of Taiwan voters, and efforts to block Taiwan's entré to Asia-Pacific economic integration arrangements, international space, and so on. The Taiwan public is pretty smart, and it can see such initiatives for what they are. They may undermine Taiwan confidence about the future of cross-Strait relations, and they undermine Beijing's stated goal of winning hearts and minds.

Negative Scenarios

In addition to the scenarios above, there are others that are not so benign. If the former scenarios imply satisfaction with the paradigm of mutual persuasion and continued commitment to it, the latter assume a shift, by one party or another, to a less cooperative mode.

The least likely of the negative scenarios is one in which China would use force or threaten to use force to compel the second Ma administration to negotiate on its terms. The hypothetical reasons that it might do so are national ambition, the belief that Taiwan will never accept unification, the maturing of its coercive capability, low regard for the will and capability of Taiwan to defend itself, and the belief that the U.S. commitment to defend the island is a bluff. Yet those motivations pale in significance when compared with reasons for restraint: the relative success of the peaceful development policy and the absence of any evidence that the window for unification is closing permanently. Beijing will likely continue to have confidence that time is on its side and that the KMT government's reluctance to deal on political and security issues will gradually diminish.

Also improbable is a scenario, at least in the medium term, in which Taipei is the one that loses patience and returns to a policy of provoking the PRC, as Lee Teng-hui and Chen Shui-bian did. Ma Ying-jeou has been more willing than they were to take risks to stabilize cross-Strait relations, and he got reelected in the process. He has struck a different balance than they did between firmness and reassurance in his dealings with Beijing, more in favor of the latter. Yet having secured the easy gains, it is not inconceivable that Ma might become frustrated with Beijing's demands in the future, because he felt that they were substantively wrong and politically problematic (or both). He might choose to emphasize firmness more and reassurance less, and so increase PRC doubts about his intentions. As of the fall of 2012, however, such a scenario and any resumption of a negative spiral seemed unlikely. What happens after his term ends in 2016 and Taiwan has a new president is an open question. But there is no reason to infer that if Tsai Ing-wen, the DPP's candidate for president in 2012, had become president, she would have provoked Beijing simply because she was the leader of the DPP—nor is there any reason to infer that any future DPP president would.

A third scenario, more likely that these two, is that Beijing would lose patience with Taiwan over the pace and direction of cross-Strait relations, abandon mutual persuasion, and shift to exploiting its power advantage over Beijing. The use or threat of use of force would not be part of the ensuing strategy, but the PLA's growing capabilities would be one facet of a multifaceted strategy of pressure and intimidation. The next chapter explores what such a strategy would and would not entail.

7

The Dynamics of Power Asymmetry

The idea that China might somehow use its power to get other relatively weaker actors to do what they previously were unwilling to do is eminently plausible. It is based on an underlying premise of political philosophy: influence is a function of power. It also informs the growing literature on the impact of a stronger China on the international system.[1] So, it is reasonable to hypothesize that should Beijing grow frustrated with endless cross-Strait negotiations, it might seek to secure through pressure what it cannot get from Taipei through persuasion.

Curiously, how the contemporary Chinese state manipulates or might manipulate power asymmetry to achieve its goals is an understudied question. When it comes to external relations, perhaps the explanation is that the PRC was relatively weak for much of its history and its weakness dictated that it play the power game in a defensive mode, which it often did very well. As the power asymmetry between China and other actors shifts in its favor, China's policies may shift to a different, more offensive mode.[2]

A starting point is the insight of Robert Sutter of George Washington University concerning leverage as a dimension of Chinese statecraft. "Leverage" is a metaphor borrowed from mechanics, whereby the force exerted on a lever is magnified by the lever's interaction with a fulcrum. Both the initial force and the fulcrum are necessary for leverage. Sutter writes:

> Chinese leaders throughout the history of the . . . PRC have understood leverage as a key variable in world affairs affecting China's interests. They have seen great-power adversaries such as the United States and the Soviet Union endeavoring to place China in a vulnerable and compliant

position by means of establishing greater leverage and suspected strategic dominance over Beijing. . . . Chinese leaders have focused for decades on building such leverage and eventual dominance over Taiwan, with the objective of reunification on terms agreeable to the PRC. Private conversations with Chinese officials . . . underlined the widespread belief that China's economic, military, and international importance to Taiwan ultimately will reach a point where Taipei will have little choice other than pursuing a path toward a settlement agreeable to China.[3]

Note Sutter's point that the PRC regime has always understood how to use political fulcrums to enhance the effect of its power, both from a position of weakness and, he anticipates, from a position of strength as it gains greater power to apply to the lever.

There is no question that Beijing tries to exert political leverage whenever it can, as most governments do. When faced with pressure from the United States that had economic consequences for China (for example, when President Clinton issued an executive order in 1993 that linked China's most-favored-nation trade status to its human rights policies), Beijing has mobilized American companies dependent on the China market to lobby Washington to back down.[4] Two German scholars demonstrated a drop in China's exports to countries whose senior leaders meet with the Dalai Lama, particularly in the last decade as China's global economic clout has increased. The inference is that Beijing uses trade as a lever to encourage restraint from those countries on the issue of Tibet.[5] After the Philippines got into a spat with China concerning access to a shoal in the South China Sea in the spring of 2012, Philippine bananas exported to China were suddenly subject to rigorous safety inspections.[6]

Exerting Leverage: What We Think We Know

The idea of leverage is a starting point for understanding how China might seek to achieve its fundamental Taiwan objectives in a mode different from mutual persuasion. That is the subject of this chapter, which is perforce exploratory in character. It looks at specific ways—economic, military, and domestic political—in which Beijing might seek to pressure Taiwan to make concessions that do not accord with the island's interests. It then broadens the discussion to consider how people in both China and Taiwan might think about the opportunities and perils of power asymmetry.

For one side to abandon persuasion as the mode of interaction and to exploit power asymmetry implies that persuasion no longer yields the benefits expected; it therefore sets aside the norms that come with persuasion. It would, for example,

—no longer emphasize the minimum that it needs but what it wants
—no longer worry about fully understanding the other's substantive position
—no longer search for substantive common ground
—no longer have to coordinate politics and negotiations so carefully.

Referring back to the formulas that Vincent Siew and Hu Jintao exchanged, a China that was abandoning mutual persuasion would no longer set aside differences and seek common ground. Instead, it would emphasize differences and ignore common ground. It would refuse to recognize realities important to Taiwan. It would no longer seek to build Taipei's trust. And it would seek solutions whereby it won and Taiwan did not.

Economic Leverage

The fear here is that both Taiwan companies and the economy as a whole will become so dependent on China as a production platform and market that the island will become vulnerable to Chinese pressure to resolve the fundamental political dispute. The American Chamber of Commerce in Taipei, which has historically favored the expansion of cross-Strait relations, actually issued a warning in its 2011 white paper: "Longer range, over-reliance on any one market is always risky, even without the political complications present in the cross-Strait relationship."[7] Taiwan's senior intelligence official has said publicly that the procurement missions that China sends to Taiwan "might be part of China's strategy to promote unification."[8]

There is no question that the Mainland economy is becoming more important to Taiwan. Table 7-1 shows the post-1993 trends in exports, imports, two-way trade, China's share of Taiwan's trade, and Taiwan's trade linkage with China. ("Trade linkage" represents the average of Taiwan's exports to China as a percentage of Taiwan's total exports and Taiwan's imports from China as a percentage of Taiwan's total imports. Some economists use this indicator to measure economic interdependence.)[9] Setting aside periods of global recession, the overall trend is one of growth in all categories. Of China's total imports in 2009, 8 percent came from Taiwan, and of those Taiwan imports, 80 percent went to wholly foreign-owned or joint venture firms. Those firms were mostly Taiwan firms, and the imports went predominantly into assembly of goods for export to other markets. Rosen and Wang worked their way through a thicket of incommensurate statistics to arrive at the conclusion that China was the destination of 80 percent of Taiwan's outward foreign direct investment (FDI) in 2008 and that Taiwan was the biggest external investor in China, constituting 15 to 17 percent of China's inward FDI.[10]

Table 7-1. *Taiwan's Foreign Trade and Trade with China, 1994–2011*
U. S. dollars, millions

| Year | Foreign trade | | | Trade with China | | | China's share of Taiwan's trade (percent) | Trade linkage (percent) |
	Total	Exports	Imports	Total	Exports	Imports		
1994	179,998	94,300	85,698	17,881	16,023	1,859	9.93	9.58
1995	217,354	113,342	104,012	22,525	19,434	3,091	10.36	10.06
1996	220,503	117,581	102,922	23,787	20,727	3,060	10.79	10.30
1997	239,125	124,170	114,955	26,371	22,455	3,915	11.03	10.75
1998	217,825	112,595	105,230	23,955	19,841	4,114	11.00	10.77
1999	234,929	123,733	111,196	25,841	21,313	4,529	11.00	10.65
2000	292,682	151,950	140,732	31,239	25,010	6,229	10.67	10.44
2001	234,284	126,314	107,970	31,510	25,607	5,903	13.45	12.87
2002	248,562	135,317	113,245	39,497	31,529	7,969	15.89	15.17
2003	278,611	150,601	128,010	49,311	38,293	11,018	17.70	17.02
2004	351,128	182,370	168,758	65,723	48,930	16,792	18.72	18.39
2005	381,046	198,432	182,614	76,365	56,272	20,094	20.04	19.68
2006	426,715	224,017	202,698	88,116	63,332	24,783	20.65	20.25
2007	465,929	246,677	219,252	102,261	74,246	28,015	21.95	21.44
2008	496,077	255,629	240,448	105,369	73,978	31,391	21.24	21.00
2009	378,046	203,675	174,371	86,514	62,091	24,424	22.88	22.25
2010	525,837	274,601	251,236	120,784	84,832	35,952	22.97	22.60
2011	589,695	308,257	281,438	134,711	91,105	43,605	22.84	22.52

Sources: *Taiwan Statistical Data Book 2011*, Council for Economic Planning and Development, Executive Yuan, R.O.C. (Taiwan), July 2011; "Major Indicators of Taiwan Economy," *Taiwan Economic Forum*, vol. 10 (April 2012), pp. 102–03.

Thus the Chinese and Taiwan economies have grown increasingly more important to the other. Ironically, the trade linkage between the two grew at a faster rate during the administration of Chen Shui-bian than in the KMT administrations before and after, but the ultimate outcome is the same. Also, Taiwan's market share in China declined from 12.9 percent in 2002 to 7.4 percent in the first half of 2011.[11] That is, Taiwan is becoming more dependent on China economically while China is becoming less dependent on Taiwan.

These trends raise the question of whether China might threaten some form of economic sanctions—to either withdraw economic benefits or impose punishments—in order to get the island's political leaders to negotiate on its terms. Has Taiwan become China's economic hostage?[12] After all, the interdependence is asymmetrical. If China has less to lose from a rupture than Taiwan does, it has greater leverage.[13] Nonetheless, the answer that I deduce from the scholarly literature is "not yet."

In a Taiwan-specific study in 2007, the RAND Corporation examined how different kinds of Chinese sanctions might play out. A ban on imports from Taiwan would be very difficult to enforce, whether the object of enforcement is corruptible Chinese local officials or companies from third countries. A ban on Taiwan investments would also be difficult to enforce, in part because some Taiwan funds come into China through third parties. Moreover, the most valuable assets of Taiwan companies that invest in China remain in Taiwan, including their "intellectual, executive, and managerial talent; their design, research, and development facilities; their best intellectual property; and many of their marketing facilities."[14] Given time and government support, these companies could reconstitute production in other places. A ban on Chinese exports to Taiwan would likely not be effective because Taiwan's dependence is relatively low, except for dependence on some commodities, such as coal. Finally, China could harass Taiwan business people on the Mainland, but it is far from clear that doing so would have the desired political impact.[15] Moreover, some of the ways in which China might sanction Taiwan would hurt China itself. Many of the imports and much of the investment that China receives from Taiwan relate to Chinese factories that assemble and produce goods for export. Any ban would therefore create large-scale unemployment and potential instability. Moreover, in all of these cases, China's international reputation would suffer enormously, in part because its business ties with Taiwan are part of a much larger network of global economic activity.[16] Other scholars have reached similar general conclusions.[17] Concerning Taiwan specifically, Tung Chen-yuan has concluded that "China has no economic leverage over Taiwan in terms of imposing economic sanctions and that Taiwan's vulnerability to such a scenario is almost nonexistent."[18]

Finally, the RAND study concludes that when it comes to economic sanctions, "political factors—in particular domestic politics within the initiating and target countries—usually have a greater impact on the initiator's ability to convert economic influence into political leverage. . . . Thus, China's growing capacity to inflict economic pain upon Taiwan has not automatically provided Beijing with . . . powerful political leverage."[19] How Taiwan leaders might respond to hypothetical Chinese sanctions would be a function of the domestic political pressure that the government would face. Sanctions could certainly produce a panic that might lead to the capitulation that China sought; Chinese missile tests in March 1996 created a run on the Taiwan stock and foreign exchange markets. But economic coercion could just as well create anger and resistance on the part of the public. Even if Taiwan capitulated, it would likely leave China with a hostile population to deal with.

Nor is politics irrelevant on the Chinese side. In conducting a detailed analysis of the presence of Taiwan business operations on the Mainland, Shelley Rigger of Davidson College and a collaborator were struck by how much the Chinese jurisdictions in which they were located had to lose from any PRC effort to exert political leverage. "Without Taiwanese investors," they write, "many of China's wealthiest provinces and cities would lose the crown jewels of their local economies, and China's exports, especially IT exports, would decline sharply."[20] The various Chinese entities that began investing in Taiwan in 2009 also have a stake in stable cross-Strait political relations. Taiwan's investment commission approved 120 direct Chinese projects with a pledged value of $140 billion by February 2011, and funds come in through subsidiaries in other economies.[21] "In other words, cross-strait economic interactions have given actors within China a strong interest in avoiding events that would disrupt those interactions." Whether those actors have sufficient influence in Beijing to dissuade decisionmakers who might consider coercion and the will to exercise that influence is another question.[22]

Other factors complicate any effort to manipulate economic relations for political purposes. The Chinese central government has far from complete control of the activities of Chinese entities that interface in some way with the Taiwan economy. Therefore, it cannot precisely calibrate the effect that any sort of economic coercion might have on the political calculations of the island's decisionmakers and its public. Similarly, Taiwan's entrepreneurs, not its government, have the primary responsibility to assess the risks of their companies' dependence on the Chinese economy.[23] The government and the public likely have different definitions of Taiwan's interests.

More generally, it does not appear that economic sanctions are especially successful as a tool of statecraft. Gary Hufbauer and Jeffrey Schott, of the

Peterson Institute for International Economics, looked at a large number of cases in which economic sanctions were used to discover the circumstances in which they have and have not worked. They find that in most instances of successful economic sanctions, the economy of the "sender" country is more than ten times that of the "target country." It is true that China's gross domestic product is now estimated to be almost thirteen times greater than Taiwan's ($11.29 trillion versus $885.3 billion for 2011),[24] but it is not clear that the size differential *per se* would be the reason for the success of sanctions and so would be the determining factor in the case of China and Taiwan. Moreover, when the GDP differential is less than ten times, the chances of success or failure are about equal.

According to Hufbauer and Schott, trade linkage is a more significant causal factor: "In [sanctions] cases we have scored as successes, the sender country accounts, on average, for almost one-third of the target country's total trade." When the sending country tries to compel "major policy changes" by the target country, the average trade linkage (see definition above) was 34 percent for successes and 24 percent for failures.[25] For Taiwan to agree to political negotiations more or less on Beijing's terms would certainly qualify as a major policy change, but a one-in-three success rate is not that high. And as the data above reveal, Taiwan's trade linkage with China was only 22.6 percent in 2010. Taiwan, it seems, is less vulnerable to Chinese sanctions than has generally been thought.[26]

This review of the sanctions literature suggests that any effort by China to leverage Taiwan's economic dependence to achieve unification on its terms would be fraught with risks. The business relationship of the two sides is complicated, and Taiwan's political response to such a move, which cannot be predicted, would likely determine the outcome. China would have to cope with a number of negative consequences of unknowable severity and duration. Any decision to act would be judged by the costs of not acting. Beijing would be more likely to act if it perceived that the window for achieving its Taiwan goals was closing. In the meantime, it has nothing to lose by restraint. As long as Taiwan does not act in ways that make it impossible for Beijing to reach its political goals someday, the rewards of patience outweigh the risk of waiting. Finally, there is the historical fact that China itself was the victim of economic sanctions during the cold war, by both the West and, after 1960, by the Soviet Union. At least in interstate relations, it prefers to avoid their use.

Yet the sanctions literature takes one only so far. A variable such as trade linkage is fairly general. For one economy to have a significant business dependence on another does not mean that it has become an economic appendage and therefore politically defenseless. That Nazi Germany was able to exert influence in Central and Eastern European countries was not because of their general trade dependence on Germany as much as it was the deliberate and entrapping way that Germany conducted business and trade, with the effect that its trading partners could not reduce their resulting dependence or compensate for it.[27]

Military Leverage

PRC leaders have long believed that military power is a necessary condition for achieving its political objective of unification. As Qian Qichen, then a vice premier, stated in a May 2000 speech:

> Comrade Deng Xiaoping used to say that we should use "two hands" in settling the Taiwan issue and not rule out any of the two ways: Doing as much as we can with our right hand to settle the issue peacefully because the right arm is stronger. However, in case this does not work, we will also use the left hand, namely military force.[28]

For the last two decades, Beijing has placed even more emphasis on the military "hand." Since the 1990s, it has sought to improve its capability to deter any effort by Taiwan's political leaders to make permanent and formal the current state of division (either incrementally or suddenly, covertly or overtly) and to complicate or block any U.S. intervention to help Taiwan defend itself.[29] In particular, it has improved its ability to damage Taiwan from long distances, to degrade its cyber-infrastructure, and to degrade U.S. command and communications capabilities.[30] As a result, the People's Liberation Army is much stronger than it was in the late 1990s, while Taiwan has seen only moderate improvement in its military capabilities. The PLA's budget is growing steadily, while Taiwan's military budget, although basically stable, has actually fallen during the Ma administration.

Of course, the aggregate defense budget of any country is only a rough measure of changing capabilities, but it does suggest a trend. The PRC's official budget, which likely understates the true level, increased from US$35.3 billion in 2006 to $76.4 billion in 2010 (at market exchange rates). Taiwan's reported budget was $7.73 billion in 2006, rose to $10.5 billion in 2008, fell back to around $9.3 billion in 2010, and rose again, to $10.2 billion, in 2011.[31] Expenditures for equipment are more revealing, and here again, the trend is one of steady PLA progress. By one expert estimate, the level of PLA's overall spending on new equipment has increased approximately six times, even when inflation was taken into account.[32] The U.S. Department of Defense has estimated the degree to which the PLA modernized its equipment in various areas from 2000 to 2009. It reports that while less than 5 percent of surface ships and aircraft were modern in 2000, the share was around 25 percent by 2009. The submarine fleet progressed from being less than 10 percent modern to being 50 percent modern over the course of that decade. And air defense equipment, which was less than 5 percent modern in 2000, was more than 40 percent modern in 2009.[33] Meanwhile, Taiwan's expenditure for "military investments," which includes procurement, has been under 30 percent of the military budget in recent years, and it is likely to decline relative to personnel costs as the island's armed forces make the transition from a conscript to a volunteer army.[34]

Furthermore, there is a difference in the military capabilities that each side is acquiring. The PLA's focus is clearly on offensive assets, even though their stated strategic purpose is deterrence. They are designed to inflict damage on Taiwan. Taiwan's capabilities, which are declining in relative terms, are mostly defensive, intended to deter China from attacking. To enhance deterrence, Taiwan does have a program to develop cruise missiles that can hit targets on the Mainland, such as airfields, missile bases, and naval bases. Still, in general, attack is becoming easier for China and Taiwan remains in a primarily defensive mode.[35] The island's Ministry of National Defense, in its first quadrennial defense review released in 2009, warned that despite declining tensions since Ma took office, "the ROC still faces palpable military threats ... [and] vigilance for readiness preparation cannot be relaxed. ... [The PRC's] capabilities in launching a war against Taiwan have increased dramatically."[36]

The mere fact that the PLA is acquiring more robust capabilities does not, of course, mean that China's leaders will use them. As long as Beijing believes that it will achieve its goals sometime in the future, it has little reason to incur the costs that coercion might entail: the alienation of much of the island's populace, destruction of part of its physical infrastructure, war with the United States, and international reprobation.[37] But from the point of view of any defender, a potential attacker that has the capabilities that it needs to engage in coercion or that is on the way to acquiring them is more dangerous than one that does not.

More likely from a logical point of view is that China might *threaten* to use its military power in the expectation that the mere act of intimidation would lead to Taipei's capitulation. The concept that scholars of international relations use in considering how one actor bends a weaker one to its will without war is "coercive diplomacy": "the use of threats and assurances in combination to influence the behavior of real or potential adversaries."[38] Such a strategy is not easy to implement. The successful coercing state must finely balance its threats and assurances to achieve its goals and at the same time avoid both going to war and backing down. Tactically, it must signal its intentions properly. It must carefully assess the intentions of the target state's allies, if it has them.[39] Yet China's buildup has a couple of features that suggest that coercive diplomacy is not out of the question.

First, the PLA buildup continues even though the Ma administration has made deliberate efforts to reassure Beijing that it need not worry about the main motivation for the PLA buildup—deterring Taiwan independence.[40] Among the possible explanations for China's continued procurement, a couple are relatively benign. One has to do with civil-military relations: the PLA may have convinced a weak civilian leadership that it was premature to decrease its acquisitions in light of changes in the political situation.[41] Another is the rigidity of procurement schedules: that is, the PLA is probably still receiving equipment that it decided to purchase long ago, when China perceived a greater political threat from Taiwan.[42] This factor may be at work to some degree. In the last two reports on Chinese military power, the estimate for the number of Chinese short-range ballistic missiles has remained constant at 1,000 to 1,200, and the number of cruise missiles has been between 200 and 500.[43] Of course, the accuracy of the estimate is only a function of the underlying methodology, but it does suggest that a prior procurement schedule has been completed. Nonetheless, even if the number of missiles may have reached a plateau, Chinese capabilities are still improving in other areas. And even with missiles, the PLA has "upgraded the lethality of its existing force by introducing variants with improved ranges, accuracies, and payloads." That is, if the number of missiles has not grown, their destructive power has.[44]

But two other explanations for continued acquisitions, which stem from continuing Mainland mistrust, are more worrisome. First, Beijing may fear that Ma's policy of reassurance is insincere—that he may just pocket Taiwan's economic gains and do nothing to reciprocate politically—and there is no doubt a concern that the DPP may come back to power and resume a challenge to China's interests. As the Chinese defense white paper released in March 2011 put it, "the 'Taiwan independence' separatist force and its activities are still the biggest obstacle and threat to the peaceful development of cross-Strait relations."[45] The 2010 DOD "Annual Report to Congress" confirms this Chinese logic for continuing to build a deterrent: "Beijing argues that the credible threat to use force is essential to maintain the conditions for political progress, and to prevent Taiwan from making moves toward de jure independence."[46]

Whatever the case, China's coercive capabilities have clearly taken on more and more of a dual-use character. That is, not only can the PLA increasingly deter what Beijing fears (independence), over time it will be able to compel what it seeks (unification on PRC terms). The Pentagon therefore concluded in its 2011 "Annual Report to Congress" that China was acquiring capabilities for two purposes concerning Taiwan itself: one was to deter moves toward Taiwan independence; the other was "to develop the prerequisite military capabilities to eventually settle the dispute on Beijing's terms."[47]

This growing asymmetry in military power is relevant in any PRC effort to exert pressure on Taiwan to resolve the fundamental cross-Strait dispute on its terms. An actual attack may be quite unlikely, at least under current political circumstances, but coercive diplomacy is less so. Recall that China's antisecession law authorizes "nonpeaceful means" if "possibilities for a peaceful reunification should be completely exhausted."[48] In an intimidation scenario, what Taiwan leaders believe about the damage that the PLA could wreak on the island will influence how they respond to Beijing's demands.

By some estimates, the PLA can already do quite a bit of damage. Among the nonpeaceful options for dealing with Taiwan is an air and missile attack, and a 2011 analysis by the RAND Corporation concluded that Taiwan is already seriously vulnerable to such an attack.[49] It would begin with attacks on the information infrastructure (important for command and control); move to ballistic and cruise missile attacks on Taiwan radar installations, air force bases, surface-to-air missile batteries, and command and control units; and then proceed to attacks by manned aircraft and cruise missiles to eliminate the remaining assets. China's missiles, the study predicted, would overwhelm Taiwan's air and missile defenses, make it difficult for planes of the Taiwan air force to take off and land, and impair communications between commanders and field personnel. Should the United States intervene in support of Taiwan, its bases in Japan would be the object of a similar campaign. Layered defensive capabilities—both aircraft and surface-to-air missiles—would support the effort to gain air superiority over the Taiwan Strait and the island itself and to counter attacks by Taiwan and American air forces against targets on the Mainland.

A related RAND study, published in 2009, comes to the dire conclusion that merely "between 90 and 240 sufficiently accurate, submunition-equipped SRBMs [short-range ballistic missiles]—less than a quarter of the number of such missiles that Beijing currently has deployed—would give China a better-than-fair shot at shutting down Taiwan's fighter force in a matter of minutes. If Taiwan's surface-to-air defenses can also be suppressed, a window would open through which the PLA Air Force . . . could fly hundreds of sorties delivering precision-guided munitions . . . on [hardened aircraft shelters] and other targets too small or hardened to be at risk from SRBMs. Blows like this could essentially knock Taiwan's air force out of the war in the opening hours of the conflict."[50]

PRC Leverage in Taiwan Domestic Politics

Another fear on Taiwan has been that Beijing might create a political coalition among Taiwan people to support and promote unification on China's terms. Groups that benefit from the economic dependence on China would be likely candidates for inclusion in such a coalition. As Albert Hirschman commented in his study of economic coercion, "If conditions are such that the possible loss from a stoppage of trade would fall with special weight upon certain groups within the country, these groups are likely to form a sort of 'commercial fifth column' [and] will exert a powerful influence in favor of a 'friendly' attitude toward the state to the imports of which they owe their existence."[51] In Leninist terms, this is a "united front from below."

Indeed, there is credible evidence that political constituencies in Taiwan have already had an effect on broader cross-Strait relations. Scott Kastner's detailed study of the Lee Teng-hui and Chen Shui-bian periods found that even during that time of political conflict between the Taiwan and PRC governments, Taipei's economic policies were favorable for cross-Strait relations when companies with a stake in China were more powerful within Taiwan politics. When their domestic political influence waned, Taipei's policies were less favorable. Moreover, the Chinese government had an interest in protecting the interests of Taiwan companies that did not overtly support the Lee or Chen governments, because of their domestic influence. Kastner also found that economic interdependence probably moderated the political dispute, although the evidence there was less obvious.[52]

Taiwan companies with a stake in positive Mainland relations may have had a moderating impact on Taipei's policy toward China, as Kastner suggests, but the issue here is rather different. That is, in the event that Beijing decided to exert its leverage to bring about a change in the Taiwan government's fundamental cross-Strait policy, would those companies' economic interests cause the leaders of the companies to take China's side and magnify pressure on their own government to concede to Beijing?

The most likely members of a supposed "fifth column" in cross-Strait relations are Taiwan business executives (*taishang*) who have a presence in China. The anxiety that they would advocate "China-friendly" policies to protect their own narrow economic interests comes from two sources. One is the knowledge on Taiwan that building a "united front" is a time-tested tactic of

Leninist parties, including the Chinese Communist Party. So it was likely not surprising that associations of Taiwan business people doing business in China began forming in the PRC in 1990. As one might expect of a united front approach, these associations have links to the Taiwan Affairs Office of the State Council, China's key policymaking body for cross-Strait relations, and its subordinate offices in local party and government units; moreover, the secretariats of the associations are drawn from those Chinese organizations. Second, people on Taiwan are aware of Chinese formulations about using business people to steer politics (*yishang weizheng*) and manipulating economics to promote unification (*yijing cutong*). Moreover, there is the fear of "traitors in our midst" (see chapters 2 and 5).[53]

The human interaction that has accompanied cross-Strait trade and investment can be grist for this mill. Around 1 million Taiwan people are now living in Shanghai and its suburb Kunshan, in Dongguan in Guangdong province, and in other Chinese urban areas. According to Taiwan government estimates, there have been several hundred thousand cross-Strait marriages; some have endured and others have resulted in conflicts within families.[54] Taiwan schools have been established in Dongguan and Kunshan to cater to the children of the Taiwan people in those areas. More significant is the flow of sophisticated talent among Silicon Valley in California, Hsinchu in Taiwan (where a science-based industrial park is located), and Kunshan, much of it made up of ethnic Chinese. U.S.-educated Taiwan engineers have fostered the movement of technology, capital, and expertise between the United States and Taiwan and the development of productive business partnerships. As Taiwan companies moved more production to China, they put their second-generation Taiwan executives in charge of mainland operations and recruited talented Chinese engineers. Young Taiwan IT entrepreneurs have built relationships with China's young entrepreneurs and the children of high-ranking officials, and they sometimes have attended Chinese business schools. In turn, Silicon Valley is a magnet for talented engineers from both China and Taiwan.[55] These contacts, some argue, have created a community of interests that can be exploited by the Chinese government to alter the balance of opinion within the Taiwan political system.[56]

Yet Beijing's united front approach and affiliated organizational network do not necessarily mean that Taiwan companies and executives have the influence to change Taipei's fundamental policy approach to China, even if they want to. Shu Keng and Gunter Schubert conclude that their influence is rather weak. First, their business interests vary considerably and forging a common position on an intrinsically political issue such as how Taiwan should resolve the fundamental dispute with China would be extremely difficult. More likely is a consensus on changing or repealing Taiwan government policies that are bad for business, a consensus that probably existed regarding the Chen Shui-bian administration. Even if *taishang* could agree on the desirability of unification, they lack the institutional channels through which to advocate their preferences in Taiwan. (And anecdotally, it is said that *taishang* believe that they would lose much of their preferential treatment from Beijing if unification happened.) The main ways that *taishang* influence the political process is through their votes (if they are willing to return to the island to cast their ballots) and through campaign contributions. With respect to votes, they constitute only a small share of the electorate, but they may have a large impact in a close election. Corporations reportedly give about twice as much in campaign contributions to the Kuomintang as they give to the DPP, yet Keng and Shubert still conclude that "even if China tried to exert pressure or influence on Taiwan by making use of the *taishang*, such a strategy would not work."[57]

Based on extensive research among Taiwan executives in China, Gunter Schubert has constructed a useful ideal type of the *taishang*:

—They possess a "situational identity," shifting between "Chinese" and "Taiwanese" identities as circumstances dictate.

—They see a substantial gap between Mainland and Taiwan society and believe that they and their colleagues are creating "a parallel *taishang* society within Chinese society."

—They are interested in Taiwan's domestic politics, follow developments on the island regularly, and return to Taiwan to vote in important elections, even though it may not affect the result.

—They support KMT but did not make public their critical attitude toward the Chen Shui-bian administration or other sensitive political matters. Even during the drama of the Chen period, they were more worried about the impact of economic factors on their business than political ones.

—They regard ties with local government officials to be much more important than trends in national cross-Strait politics, and they otherwise maintain a low political profile. Nor do they believe that *taishang* can influence Mainland policy.

—They do not believe that *taishang* should play a role in the conduct of cross-Strait relations and deny being Beijing's "hostage" or a "lobbyist" of the Chinese government.

—They are not opposed to cross-Strait integration along various dimensions, and they believe that economic integration is not only the key to survival for their business and for Taiwan as a whole but also an avenue to resolving the China-Taiwan conflict. To them, the battle between independence and unification is becoming passé.

—They prize political stability more than political integration. Preserving the status quo is a good option.[58]

If Beijing were to exploit its power asymmetry over Taiwan, having a fifth column would likely help its cause but it would not be the decisive factor. Currently, however, the point is moot since Taiwan business people active in China do not yet appear to have formed that fifth column.

Does Taiwan Have Leverage?

This analysis does raise the question of whether Taiwan has any tools of counter-leverage to use against China. A couple of years ago, Alan Romberg and I engaged in a mini-debate with Robert Sutter regarding his analysis of Beijing's increasing influence over Taiwan. While Romberg and I did not dispute the possibility that Beijing might seek to use leverage to achieve its ultimate goal of unification, we argued that Taiwan's democratic system was (or should be) a principal line of defense. "What is not open to question is that Taiwan voters have the clear option of punishing Ma and the KMT if his promise [that an engagement policy would benefit Taiwan] is not realized. What China *should* fear is that its failure to cooperate with Ma on these issues will bring the DPP back to power and with it the potential for a replay of 2002–2008. It is the possibility of that outcome that is the most powerful instrument to encourage PRC moderation."[59]

Interestingly, Taiwan officials appear to be thinking along the same lines. The main example is Lai Hsin-yuan, the chair of the Mainland Affairs Council. In a speech in August 2010 at the American Enterprise Institute, she identified three "bargaining chips" that Taiwan had in negotiations with China. The first was the role that Taiwan plays in the Mainland economy. The second was its role in the global economy, particularly its "well-established position and networks in markets worldwide." Third, there was the requirement of a democratic system that "government policy must be rooted in the will of the people." Taiwan, she said, should employ a tactic of Chinese martial arts: "borrowing the opponent's force and using it as one's own."[60] To do that, of course, it must preserve and expand its advantages.

Initial Assessment

It is premature to conclude prima facie that China is likely to choose to use its growing capabilities to attain its ultimate objective of unification through pressure and intimidation. China's military posture appears still to be a function of what it fears—independence—and of the need to maintain the capacity to deter that outcome.[61] Beijing can cling to the Marxist confidence that as economic interdependence grows, political views on Taiwan will become more China friendly. It can continue its Leninist, united front tactics of trying to cultivate forces within the Taiwan political system that are more sympathetic to its goals and marginalize those that are not. It can assume that time is on its side and that with time Taiwan will understand even more clearly that it has no choice but to submit to China. And it can continue to recognize the risks of pursuing a more aggressive strategy.

On the other hand, the discussion so far has assumed that if Beijing were to chose to abandon mutual persuasion and exploit its power asymmetry with respect to Taiwan, it would employ only one kind of leverage: economic sanctions, coercive diplomacy, or manipulating a fifth column. Yet it is far more likely that it would exert leverage along several different dimensions at the same time. Indeed, Lin Chong-pin, a Taiwan security scholar, argues that China has pursued a "grand strategy that utilizes 'extra-military instruments' to gradually diminish the preponderant influence of the United States."[62] As Lin writes elsewhere, "With regard to the China-Taiwan situation, it is certain that if the economy of mainland China continues to develop, its Taiwan policy will be correspondingly stable and peaceful. In the long run, economic cooperation with Taiwan will be more beneficial than attacking Taiwan and mainland China will have no need to use arms against Taiwan."[63] The possibility that China might apply such an approach to Taiwan requires a deeper exploration of how that might occur, one in which traditional Chinese approaches to power may be relevant.

Winning without Fighting

The basic idea is that success in political combat is not necessarily most easily achieved through a frontal assault along one dimension of power. Rather, an indirect and multifaceted effort may be more successful. That is, von Clausewitz is not as effective as Sun Zi, who famously asserted that "not fighting and subduing the enemy" is best. Of course, Sun Zi is not traditional China's only strategist, and his and others' thinking about how to exercise military power is more complex than is usually inferred. Alastair Iain Johnston of Harvard University has argued convincingly that traditional Chinese strategic thought, including Sun Zi's, in no way ignores making preparations for war and the use of violence. Whether states use violent or nonviolent means depends on the circumstances and the costs and benefits of each.[64]

Whatever the historical facts, contemporary Chinese give Sun Zi's military thought pride of place, and they emphasize its nonviolent side. So the conventional wisdom about Sun Zi is therefore a useful point of departure in exploring how Beijing might seek to achieve its goals. The central element of that wisdom is the need for a state to identify *all* its adversary's weak points and exploit them with *all* the dimensions of its power while minimizing its own weaknesses. The last thing that a state should do is try to attack points of strength. In exploiting vulnerabilities, the adversary's unity, morale, hopes, fears, goodwill, plans, and alliances are all fair game. A more direct attack should be undertaken only if it is both necessary and cost-effective. Conserving one's own power, broadly defined, and preserving freedom of action are high priorities.[65] In a more philosophical vein, the outcome of political struggle depends on the disposition of various causal factors and the potential created by their disposition. An apt analogy is the configuration of a water course, which dictates the flow of the stream.[66] A flood control and irrigation system guarantees a positive outcome, but an unregulated torrent brings destruction.

Applying this approach to cross-Strait relations, China would take advantage of Taiwan's diplomatic isolation, its doubts about U.S. support, its desire for peace, its need to sustain its economic prosperity through globalization, and the difficulties that it faces in coping with China's more robust military capabilities. Such a Chinese strategy does not rule out the occasional need for "aggressive" action, such as when it appeared that Chen Shui-bian was moving toward independence, but even then Beijing targeted Chen's weak link, which was the U.S. belief that he was making trouble. Generally, such an approach would dictate patience while a favorable disposition of China's assets is prepared gradually, creating the potential for greater policy success. (Patience is on display in China's approach to territorial disputes in the East and South China seas. It delays resolution of the disputes while it builds up its power vis-à-vis other claimants, eschewing both compromise and intense conflict.[67])

In the world of board games, the best analogy to this approach is the Chinese game of *weiqi* (literally, "surround game"; *go* in Japanese). It captures metaphorically the ideas of proper disposition of forces and strategic patience. Each player seeks to establish incrementally a position of strength in each part of the board ("territory"), limiting and eventually eliminating the presence of the other player, and defending itself against the other player's effort to achieve a balance of power in each sector. *Weiqi* captures some of the dynamics of military conflict, and the game has been used to illustrate warfare in modern China.[68] But it is also a useful metaphor for political struggles in which the probability of violence is low.[69] The player that deploys assets well and wins tactical engagements in the different arenas of conflict by exploiting the poor positioning of the other player gradually establishes a commanding position. Applying that metaphor to Taiwan, Beijing has already established a dominant position over Taipei in the international arena. It is enhancing its relative power vis-à-vis Taiwan in both the economic and military dimensions of national power. It seeks to limit and eliminate U.S. support—particularly security support—and cultivate political support on the island. Taiwan, meanwhile, seeks to preserve American backing and assert itself in other arenas.

China's hope, of course, is that Taiwan will ultimately conclude that its situation is hopeless and then capitulate. In that contingency, China's military and economic policy would shape the calculus of Taiwan's decisionmakers but actual economic sanctions or threats of force would never be necessary. Su Chi, the first secretary general of Taiwan's National Security Council under Ma Ying-jeou, worries about Taiwan's growing vulnerabilities as the military balance shifts in favor of China and against Taiwan and the United States. "Between the two sides across the Taiwan Strait, Taiwan is small, therefore it will not be easy to look for a bargain [favorable to Taiwan] in the push-and-pull situation." Unfortunately, he observes, Taiwan people are not aware of the growing asymmetry; in his view, they naively think that everything will be all right.[70] Chinese foreign minister Yang Jiechi offered his perspective on the phenomenon of power asymmetry when reacting in July 2010 to Southeast Asian criticism of China's increasing assertiveness in the South China Sea: "China is a big country and other countries are small countries, and that's just a fact." The implication is that the small countries should defer to the wishes of the larger, an implication that likely animates Chinese views of Taiwan.[71] In characterizing PRC behavior in Southeast Asia, Denny Roy, of the East-West Center in Hawaii, bluntly used the word "bullying."[72]

Chas Freeman is a retired U.S. diplomat and Pentagon official who has extensive contacts within the PLA. Based on that interaction, he offers this assessment of Beijing's approach:

> The Chinese see weapons [along with economic, diplomatic, and other forms of power] as tools with which to change men's minds, not as instruments whose value is to be measured in how much physical damage they inflict.... Beijing is using the allure of mainland markets skillfully to vest a widening range of Taiwanese economic and social groups with interests in cross-Strait interdependence.... When Beijing judges that the moment is ripe, it will know how to use inducements as well as implied threats to help Taiwanese rationalize agreement to a long-term cross-Strait

accommodation that meets the requirements of Chinese nationalism. . . . China's endgame with Taiwan envisages its eventual preemptive capitulation to the inexorable in response to an offer Taiwan cannot refuse.[73]

With respect to economic sanctions specifically, Freeman notes that Beijing opposes them in principle but would not mind producing "a bit of anxiety-driven reflection about the pain a crisis could inflict on the large chunks of Taiwanese society that are now dependent on cross-Strait trade and investment."[74]

Beijing's strategy for the reversion of Hong Kong, which occurred in 1997, displayed elements of Sun Zi–*weiqi* thinking and is relevant for Taiwan if only because it was the first successful case of applying the one-country, two-systems formula.[75] Of course, Hong Kong is different from Taiwan in that Great Britain, which "owned" Hong Kong before 1997, never claimed that the territory possessed sovereignty. Moreover, Britain accepted that Hong Kong was indefensible. Yet it initially sought to preserve the essence of the colonial status quo by proposing a nominal transfer of sovereignty back to China and retaining British administration. Deng Xiaoping, however, demanded an end to British sovereignty and administration and insisted that "Hong Kong people would rule Hong Kong." Mutual persuasion had produced a stalemate, so China sought to tilt the balance of power in its direction. It cultivated the Hong Kong business elite economically by allowing them to move production from the colony into South China, where labor costs were much less. It fostered political support by promoting patriotism and anti-British feeling (and demonizing those who sided with the British). Deng used the clock to his advantage by manipulating the end of the lease on most of Hong King's territory in 1997 to press the British, who worried about falling confidence in Hong Kong, to make concessions. And he was willing to sow anxiety in the territory to serve his ends. China was prepared to contend with London when necessary, particularly when Britain sought late in the process (the early 1990s) to create a more democratic system than Beijing was willing to tolerate. At that point, the business community's dependence on the Chinese economy and its fear of Hong Kong becoming a costly welfare state ensured that it backed Beijing rather than Britain.

What Would Sun Zi Do?

If, purely hypothetically, Beijing were to develop a playbook based on Sun Zi–*weiqi* logic, what would it look like? How would it use its various assets to contest Taiwan's initiatives, exploit its vulnerabilities, and cumulatively guide the island's leaders and people to the conclusion that they have no choice but to accept China's terms? My guess is that the following fifteen items would probably make the list:

—Increase Taiwan's economic dependence on the PRC economy and so raise the costs of any political challenge.

—Play up the idea that people on both Taiwan and the Mainland share a Chinese identity.

—Encourage social and cultural exchange to create the impression that the PRC's political intentions are not hostile.

—Cultivate social and economic constituencies that have a stake in the continuation and improvement of cross-Strait relations.

—Demonize those on Taiwan who seek de jure independence as unpatriotic and dangerous.

—Foster the view that unification is inevitable.

—Promote the idea that China is the victim of continuing division and needs to be reassured about Taiwan's long-term goals.

—Point out the success of Hong Kong in preserving the territory's way of life without significant cost.

—At election time on Taiwan, point out the costs of choosing leaders hostile to China.

—Show no flexibility on China's fundamental approach to resolving the fundamental dispute, while suggesting that there is flexibility on details.

—Oppose any significant expansion of Taiwan's participation in the international community but grant token concessions.

—Create military capabilities to deter any move toward independence while offering constant reassurance that Beijing will use peaceful means to attain unification.

—Oppose overt moves toward Taiwan independence through political and diplomatic means if necessary and by displays and use of force if necessary.

—Constrain arms sales and other forms of U.S. support for Taiwan's security and get American help in blocking Taiwan independence.

—Encourage American officials and thinkers in the belief that U.S. relations with China are much more important than those with Taiwan and that the two are increasingly mutually exclusive.

China has in fact done all of these things, to one degree or another and at one time or another. It now controls some parts of the cross-Strait *weiqi* board—for example, by having limited Taiwan's international space and made a Republic of Taiwan highly unlikely as a future option. It is maneuvering to control other "territory": who holds power in Taiwan and the policies that they pursue. This strategy is similar to the strategy that Beijing has deployed against Hong Kong and to the one that it uses to control groups in China that might pose a challenge to its rule, such as workers and intellectuals.[76] It is consistent with a united front approach to politics, and it is useful to various parts of the PRC state. The PLA has used the threat of Taiwan independence to secure more modern military capabilities. The Ministry of Foreign Affairs can demonstrate its patriotism by limiting Taiwan's international space. Provinces and localities have used Taiwan investment to foster economic development. And so on.

There is, of course, no official Chinese document publicly available that confirms that Beijing is in fact carrying out a Sun Zi–*weiqi* strategy in parallel with its program to negotiate agreements with Taipei on economic, political, cultural, and security ties. Yet the correlation between what such a strategy would look like in the abstract and what Beijing is actually doing is at least suggestive. And we can assume that China's leaders believe that as China's power grows, its chances of "winning without fighting" will improve.

But this line of speculation also raises a question. Under what circumstances might China be tempted to abandon a stance of strategic patience and the paradigm of mutual persuasion to exploit the advantages that it has created and actively press Taiwan to recognize the need to resolve the fundamental dispute? Several come to mind:

—It concludes that Taiwan will always avoid such negotiations, even under continued KMT rule.

—It decides that the unification window is closing or that a serious Taiwan independence window is opening;

—It overestimates the benefits of pressure and underestimates both the resistance that such an approach would provoke on Taiwan and other costs.

—It believes that the political forces on Taiwan in favor of final resolution are much stronger than those actively against it and that people in the middle no longer see any value in resisting.

Making these assessments is tricky, and there is a danger that Beijing will miscalculate regarding both the need to increase pressure and the benefits that it will yield. That the PRC system has been prone to misperceptions concerning Taiwan and other actors in the past suggests that it might be in the future.[77] If China were to overestimate the prospects for success but then face unexpected resistance from Taiwan, it would have to consider carrying out the threats implied in a pressure policy.

What repertoire of actions would indicate that China's hope in the paradigm of mutual persuasion is declining and that China will place greater stress on exploiting power asymmetry? A few come to mind. China could:

—call for a timetable for negotiations on unification

—begin a propaganda campaign that complains about delay by Taiwan (for example, by reviving the argument on the linkage between progress in the economic and political arenas)

—withhold benefits that the Taiwan government seeks and threaten to retract some already given

—manipulate the dependence of Taiwan firms on the Chinese economy

—create "reminders" that China is more powerful—for example, through overt exercises near Taiwan

—encourage Taiwan figures friendly to unification to criticize government recalcitrance.

Will such a strategy work? The prewar history of Czechoslovakia, to take just one example, is not encouraging. To be sure, China is not Nazi Germany, and Taiwan is not Czechoslovakia. The leaders of the PRC and Taiwan are very different from their German and Czech counterparts during that era. Land frontiers are harder for the weaker party to defend than maritime ones. But there are similarities. It was German policy to increase the economic dependence on Germany of smaller European powers.[78] Germany had an authoritarian system whose leader knew exactly what he wanted and was skilled in making a series of incremental yet cumulative demands that put Eduard Benes, the president of Czechoslovakia from 1935 to 1938, constantly on the defensive. Czechoslovakia had a fairly well developed but still polarized democracy, which found it hard to make resolute decisions in the face of a more powerful adversary. And, as much as Prague wished to rely on support from London and Paris, it never had total confidence in its allies and, in the end, they abandoned the Czechs for the sake of "peace in our time." One observer asks: "Might there not have been something wrong, something undemocratic, in this best of all possible democracies, some missing ingredient, some structural flaw that made it vulnerable to antidemocratic forces, something that might perhaps have been fixed, had they mustered the will to do so?"[79]

Of course, Beijing would have to gauge whether, even if it were to adopt a pressure strategy and win, the victory would be worth the candle. PRC decisionmakers might worry that however powerful it gets, whatever the degree of Taiwan dependence that it can create, and no matter how many Taiwan "hearts and minds" it wins, there will still be a significant and irreducible core in the population that is profoundly suspicious of PRC intentions. Even if this part of the public has had to abandon the dream of Taiwan independence, it will continue to resist unification.

Are there things that Taiwan can do to improve its position in this contest of wills and so reduce the probability that the PRC will even consider a pressure strategy? That is the subject of chapter 8.

8

What Taiwan Might Do to Help Itself

It is clearly in Taiwan's interest to keep cross-Strait relations in the paradigm of mutual persuasion and out of the paradigm of power asymmetry. One way of doing so is to consolidate the gains of Ma's first term and seize opportunities where they exist; that will help foster the PRC's confidence that someday it will achieve its fundamental objective ("Keep hope alive," to quote Jesse Jackson). But more seems to be needed in order to strengthen its position in the realms of economics, security, politics, and the U.S. relationship. Such efforts would be beneficial for their own sake, but they would also strengthen the island's self-confidence, which is probably the greatest point of potential vulnerability as the island contemplates the "shadow of the future" cast by a more powerful China.[1]

To be sure, the social and political context for a program of self-strengthening is not especially favorable. A predominantly middle-class society, Taiwan has serious points of weakness, many of which are products of its very success in social and economic development. The island's population will peak relatively soon, so an increasing share of old people will depend on a declining share of working-age people to support them—from a ratio of 7 working–age people to 1 older person in 2010 to a ratio of 3.2 to 1 in 2026.[2] Income inequality is trending upward. In 1998, the highest quintile's average disposable household income was 5.51 times that of the lowest; in 2008, it was 6.05 times. The unemployment rate was higher in the first decade of the 2000s (around 4–5 percent) than it was in the 1990s (1–3 percent).[3] The central government budget has been basically flat over the last few years, and although Taiwan's public debt as a percentage of GDP is relatively low in comparison with that of many countries (only about 35 percent in 2011), government debt per capita continues to grow (US$7,453 in early 2012).[4] Compounding these problems, the Ma administration reduced taxes on corporations to facilitate their competitiveness, but it has yet to offset the revenue loss and promote fairness by closing tax loopholes. One observer commented:

> The loophole-ridden system has resulted in reductions in spending on national public works projects and education, contributing to a vicious cycle of national weakening, sluggish economic growth, and a widening wealth gap. The tax system has become the chief culprit in the wholesale theft of Taiwan's future.[5]

Whether the political system will summon the will to increase taxes to meet the inevitable demands for increased social welfare spending is an open question. Compensating for China's growing military power will create a separate set of budgetary demands.[6]

I confess to some degree of reluctance in offering "advice" to Taiwan on how it might cope with its predicament. On the one hand, I do feel strongly that the leaders and the people of the island can better meet the challenge of China if they remedy or mitigate what I regard as points of weakness. On the other hand, I am a citizen of the United States, not of Taiwan, and there are limits to the liberties that any outsider should take in making suggestions. The choices are really for the leaders and people of Taiwan to make. Moreover, there is value in drawing their own conclusions instead of relying on what foreigners tell them to do. So a tentative approach is in order.

Preparing for Political and Security Talks

Even though the near-term prognosis for political and security talks may be low, it would still be worth Taiwan's while, as a precautionary measure, to prepare for them. Obviously, Taiwan would be much more willing to enter political talks if Beijing were willing to accept the 1992 consensus as their basis, but Hu Jintao has signaled that the premise will be the one-China principle as Beijing defines it, something that Taipei so far has refused to accept.[7] So the impasse persists, in part because of a fundamental disagreement over the Republic of China. If mutually acceptable progress is to occur on these issues and if China is to stay in the mode of mutual persuasion, then the two sides will have to work harder to close the conceptual gap between them. Yet if Taiwan refines its approach to negotiations on political and security matters, it will be better prepared for any talks that occur, keeping the negotiating ball in Beijing's court and discouraging it from giving up on mutual persuasion.

If Taiwan is to defend its sovereignty, as Ma asserts, it probably needs a clearer sense of what it is defending. Taiwan leaders since the early 1990s have specified sovereignty as a key obstacle to the improvement of relations (a view with which I concur). Yet a lack of clarity on why that is the case can complicate Taiwan's conduct of cross-Strait relations.[8]

Analytically, there may be aspects of sovereignty that are so important to Taiwan's survival that they must defended at all costs, as Ma promised to do. In contrast, there may be other aspects that are less important to its future and so can be safely conceded. There also may be dimensions that are in the middle. But it is important to know the difference, both for negotiations on resolving the fundamental dispute with Beijing, should those ever occur, and for talks and agreements in the stabilization stage. Conceding something important in the near term will undermine Taipei's negotiating position in the long term. At any stage, defending the trivial and compromising on what is important makes bad sense. The idea that sovereignty has different dimensions (Westphalian, international, and so forth) makes the task of negotiating even more complex.[9]

Within Taiwan, the dimension of sovereignty that has received the most attention is the island's limited international role. It was on this front that Lee Teng-hui first sought to challenge China's Taiwan policy, in part to co-opt challenges from the DPP but also because "going out" globally was popular with most of the island's public. The debate has not been whether to expand international space but how to do so. If the concept of sovereignty means anything to the average citizen, it is in the international domain.

With respect to other aspects of sovereignty, the situation is mixed. Only Chang Ya-chung has looked at Westphalian sovereignty in any detail, as discussed in chapter 5. He clearly understands the concept and why it is important to Taiwan, but he became less explicit about its content as time went on. Also, he is handicapped within Taiwan by the perception that he is pro-China. There has been little attention to the question of domestic sovereignty (who rules at home), but the thinking of PRC scholars like Yu Keli, who said that Taiwan had to exorcise the "the ghost of 'Taiwan independence'" and discipline its democracy, is antithetical to the island's civic identity.[10]

Sovereignty issues can surface in very specific ways, such as whether it is appropriate for Taiwan's people to accept appointment to public bodies in the PRC. It was revealed in March 2012 that some individuals who spent most of their time on the Mainland (for example, business executives) had done so. The most controversial of the organizations were local branches of the Chinese People's Political Consultative Conference (CPPCC), a semi-official structure created to incorporate and so control people who are outside the

Communist Party but who generally support its objectives. Technically, such appointments not only violate existing Taiwan law but also suggest that the individuals involved are citizens of the PRC, thus devaluing the integrity of ROC citizenship. When the revelations put the government on the defensive, Beijing called on Taipei to "adopt a positive and constructive attitude" on the issue.[11]

What is more, sovereignty issues are politically contentious as well as conceptually complex. The question of what aspects of sovereignty are trivial and which are vital has roiled Taiwan politics since the 1990s. Those on the Green side of the spectrum generally believe that asserting sovereignty is Taiwan's only defense, and they claim that the concessions that the Ma administration has made to China on various dimensions weakens Taiwan's fundamental position. For example, they object to giving Beijing what they regard as a veto over Taiwan's participation in the international community, and they say that economic liberalization has undermined sovereignty. The Ma administration, of course, rejects those claims and believes that whatever concessions it has made stem from a pragmatic calculation of what is necessary to achieve larger goals. The more that various dimensions of sovereignty become the subject of public discussion, the more contentious the political debate is liable to be, with the potential for increased hostility toward China.

Therefore, for both substantive and political reasons, Taiwan has "homework" to do in clarifying its understanding of sovereignty. Concerning international space, the task is to define the priority among various goals and to devise a good strategy for achieving the most important ones. How much to open Taiwan's economy to the PRC should be studied as part of the broader assessment of how to ensure overall economic competitiveness, and in that regard, expanded entré into the process of Asia-Pacific economic liberalization is becoming more important. If any aspect of Taiwan's international space deserves priority, this is it. On domestic and Westphalian sovereignty, the challenge is to foster an informed public debate on what each involves and what aspects are worth defending.

But clarifying sovereignty issues in a divided political system is not easy. The inherent difficulty was on display during the 2012 campaign, when the KMT and DPP debated the idea of a "Taiwan consensus" (see chapter 2). In theory, such an idea makes sense. Broad agreement concerning China would both consolidate the island's negotiating position and endow it with political support. In fact, forging such a consensus is neither a new idea nor solely a Green idea. Taiwan leaders and observers have long recognized that policy division gives China a negotiating advantage, and some have used the absence of consensus to delay negotiations. Chen Shui-bian tried to cultivate a cross-party agreement early in his presidency. Su Chi used the term "Taiwan consensus" in December 2010, arguing that the lack of an accord was "dragging Taiwan down."[12] On the Green side, Tung Chen-yuan went further, defining in advance what he thought constituted the Taiwan consensus: that Taiwan was a sovereign and independent state with the name of Republic of China; that Taiwan people "at this stage" wished to maintain the status quo; that they did not wish to move toward unification or change the national title (Beijing would interpret the latter as code for Taiwan independence); and that the future should be decided by the 23 million people of Taiwan. Tung also endorsed in essence the Lee Teng-hui idea that cross-Strait relations were "special."[13] Of course, Tung's view does not reflect the views of all Taiwan people or even a majority; hence, a consensus-building process will be necessary.

In that regard, a significant factor will be the future stance of the DPP concerning China. During the 2012 presidential campaign, Tsai Ing-wen, the DPP's candidate, rejected the 1992 consensus as a basis for cross-Strait relations but still claimed that she could preserve Taiwan's post-2008 benefits. She gave little indication of how she would square that circle (see chapter 6). She likely positioned herself in this way because she did not wish to alienate her party's base voters or dilute their enthusiasm. She thereby created an opening for the KMT to appeal to swing voters who valued the status quo and did not wish to risk losing it.

In the wake of the election, the DPP conducted an assessment of why Tsai lost the election. It cited factors other than Tsai's approach to China: voters' doubts about the DPP's capacity to be the ruling party; the way in which both the KMT and China engaged in scare tactics about a DPP victory; the KMT's access to resources that were available to it as the ruling party; the difficulty that some DPP voters had in returning to their home town to vote one week before they would return again for Lunar New Year (Taiwan has no system for absentee voting); lower-than-expected voter turnout; and the tendency of supporters of the independent candidate to vote for Ma in order to block a Tsai victory. The interaction of those factors, the DPP argued, deflated support for Tsai in the final two weeks of the campaign.[14] But some in the DPP stressed Tsai's approach to China policy. One DPP legislator asserted that it was the major reason for her defeat, allowing the KMT to paint the DPP as "anti-business" and "anti-cross-Strait exchanges"; unless the party corrected that image, he warned, it would lose again. Similarly, former DPP vice president Lu Hsiu-lien said that Tsai had not given voters an in-depth explanation for opposing the 1992 consensus.[15]

So both formulating a broad-based political consensus and defining what is important and what is not about the idea that Taiwan is a sovereign entity provoke a number of questions. How, as a matter of process, should a consensus be constructed, given the hostility that exists between the Green and Blue camps, including mutual suspicion of the other's objectives? Should the political parties negotiate understandings, for example? What would be the role of the Legislative Yuan, the island's principal representative institution? How should public opinion polls be used? On the Taiwan consensus, what breadth of consensus should be sought? Would it be acceptable, for example, if 25 percent of those polled opposed the consensus and did so intensely— which is likely if the consensus reflected the views of the Blue camp and Light Green voters but not Deep Green ones?

Su Chi has called for a three-stage process in which, first, the DPP reconciles its internal conflict between those who support Taiwan independence and those who see the need for pragmatism in formulating China policy. On the basis of that understanding, the DPP and the KMT would then work on a cross-party agreement. Then and only then would Taiwan "negotiate with China on more complicated problems such as the 'one China' issue and Taiwan's sovereignty."[16] Perhaps an incremental process would work best, beginning with scholars who reflect the views of the more centrist parts of the two major political camps and working from there to include other scholars, the political parties themselves, and so on. In March 2012, a policy team established by the Taipei Forum Foundation suggested that the government set up a committee on the peaceful development of cross-Strait relations, to include representatives of political parties and social elites. It would be "the official platform for forging domestic consensus" on policy toward China.[17]

Economics: Why Liberalization Is Not Enough

During Ma Ying-jeou's first term, Taiwan and China took a number of steps to normalize, liberalize, and institutionalize their economic relationship (see chapter 4). Better access to the Mainland economy brought benefits for many economic actors on Taiwan, though not all. Yet steps like direct transportation links and the Economic Cooperation Framework Agreement (ECFA) address only one part of the island's fundamental economic challenge: how to maintain its competitiveness in an open, globalized economy subject to rapid technological change. Liberalization itself will likely stimulate a structural readjustment of the Taiwan economy, accelerating the decline of some sectors and encouraging the growth of others. Yet it will merely reduce the downside risk of continuing prior, more protectionist policies. Many Taiwan companies have done well by managing global supply chains for products like computer laptops and tablets and using their operations in China for assembly, and others have excelled at advanced manufacturing in Taiwan, but they all must constantly innovate to stay ahead. Still others have focused on providing goods and services for the growing China market, yet they have recently lost market share to outside competitors.[18] All businesses face pressures to cut costs. Many worry how, specifically, to survive the competition with up-and-coming Chinese companies.[19] In short, how do Taiwan businesses continually reengineer themselves in the creative destruction that is globalization so that they can deliver profits to their shareholders and jobs for Taiwan residents? What should the government do or not do to ensure an environment in which prosperity can be maintained?

That Taiwan's economic liberalization with China alone is a necessary but not sufficient condition of future competitiveness is true in another way. If Taiwan opens its markets to China alone and not to other trading partners, it will exclude itself from the circle of economic integration in East Asia and the Pacific. Over time, even the best Taiwan companies will be marginalized. Continued liberalization with the Mainland through ECFA therefore must be paired with economic liberalization with other trading partners. The worst outcome for Taiwan would be to have a liberalized economic relationship with the PRC but with no one else, creating the risk that Taiwan becomes an appendage of the Chinese economy. Yet in the face of PRC opposition, Taiwan's other trading partners have been reluctant to cut their own liberalization deals with Taiwan. The Ma administration understood the competing imperatives and waited until the approval of ECFA to pursue agreements with third countries, but during Ma's first term the targets were relatively small economies like those of Singapore and New Zealand.

The Problem of China's Changing Economic Strategy

One important reason for Taiwan to pursue diversification is that the China that created opportunities for Taiwan firms under the post-1979 policies of reform and opening may be changing. The PRC Chinese leadership has signaled a fundamental shift in their model of economic growth. If the regime executes that transition, it will undermine the preferential position that Taiwan firms and other outside firms have enjoyed since the early 1980s, using China as a low-cost platform for the production and assembly of finished goods for which they provide materials and components. Already, such firms have had to adjust to a variety of constraints imposed by the Chinese government: increases in industrial wages; the end of preferential tax treatment for foreign-invested companies; the appreciation of the Chinese currency from 2005 to 2008 and then from the summer of 2010 through the writing of this book; tighter policies on land use and export processing; and more stringent environmental standards.[20] Some Taiwan firms, particularly small and medium-size ones, have found China to be an increasingly inhospitable business environment. As one report noted: "The highway from Shenzhen airport to Dongguan in Guangdong province used to be lined with Taiwanese firms. . . . Now most of these factories are deserted."[21] These trends did not slow the rate of Taiwan investment in the Mainland, however. The total amount for investment projects approved by the Taiwan government actually doubled from 2009 (admittedly a bad economic year) to 2010. An October 2011 report revealed that Taiwan's one hundred top companies regarded China as their leading investment target, and the top ten garnered 25 percent of their revenues in China. But business locations were shifting from the east coast of China to the interior, and in some cases locations were changed to expand existing enterprises rather than start new ones.[22]

Those changes in PRC policy appear to be part of a broader movement away from depending on foreign firms for capital, technology, and management expertise, as evidenced by the roll-out in the late 2000s of an industrial policy that sought to foster "indigenous innovation" based on science and technological development. The goal was to transform China into a technology player by 2020 and into an international leader by 2050 and to reduce reliance on foreign technology in areas like electronics and communications. The regime planned to use various tools: making it even more difficult for foreign companies to secure protection of their intellectual property rights in the Chinese legal system; using product testing and approval regimes to delay the entry of imports that compete with new Chinese products; facilitating a monopoly position for state-owned industries ("national champions") and discriminating against foreign firms through anti-competition policies; using government procurement policies to favor domestic products and place foreign ones at a disadvantage; and employing standards to create market barriers.[23]

The PRC leadership may not be able to carry off this transition, because some domestic economic entities have a vested interest in the policy of export-led growth.[24] But to the extent that it happens, the shift will mean that Taiwan firms will likely face challenges from Chinese firms, either by being displaced from their more privileged positions in global supply chains or, for those that sell to the Chinese domestic market, by losing market share. Taiwan observers are alert to the dangers posed by China's new policy direction, as is clear from a series of articles in *CommonWealth* (*Tien Hsia*), the island's leading business journal. These observations exemplify the concern:

—On preserving a beneficial place in global supply chains: "What Taiwan needs to look out for is, in the years following the paradigm shift [in the electronics industry], China will become capable of doing what Taiwan does, and when that happens, Silicon Valley and China could squeeze Taiwan out."[25]

—On Taiwan companies' collaboration with China's "national champions": "In many industrial sectors, Taiwan cannot take advantage of the opportunities in front of it [to collaborate with new strategic industries]. It can only pick up some of the crumbs left behind by large Chinese enterprises."[26]

—On the issue of product standards: "China's ambitions . . . are grand and exceed cooperation with Taiwan. Indeed, it ultimately seeks to eclipse Taiwan. . . . The question remains whether the day China sets the international standard will be the day Taiwan loses its comparative advantage."[27]

—Another sign of the times is that Chinese firms are hiring talented Taiwan engineers, luring them with much higher salaries than they have made with Taiwan firms.[28]

Finally, there is the deterioration in the rule of law in local jurisdictions in China. This has been a general problem with Chinese governance, but it has affected in particular non-PRC business people who get into a dispute with either PRC business people or authorities, who then use the Chinese police, prosecutors, and courts to get their way.[29]

Promoting an Innovation-Based Economy

Even though a policy of liberalization will hurt some sectors on Taiwan, it is probably a necessary condition for structural adjustment and new competitiveness. But it is not a sufficient one. Without other policy steps, it seems the result will be marginalization within the global economy, slow growth, and loss of self-confidence.

One course of action that Taiwan should consider with some degree of caution is to pursue itself an industrial policy, whereby it deploys various measures (credits, taxes, subsidies) to encourage sectors that it believes are ripe for rapid growth rather than let the market work its will. Taiwan did so in its period of most rapid development, but a scholarly assessment finds that those policies did not contribute much to economic growth. The more significant variable was macroeconomic policy.[30] Similarly, protectionism is probably not a good option. That would preserve jobs for some people for awhile, but it imposes costs on consumers and aggravates the misallocation of resources over the long run. Finally, although Taiwan has some comparative advantage in services, to place all its eggs in that basket to the exclusion of advanced manufacturing and the high-wage jobs that it creates would likely cause an unwanted imbalance.[31]

The alternative to industrial policy and protectionism, therefore, is for Taiwan to emphasize innovation in order to cut costs at one or more technological levels. Harvard Business School economist Michael Porter believes that Taiwan already has a highly innovative economy, with strong intellectual property protection, creative entrepreneurs, a flexible business culture, a large pool of researchers, strong institutions for science and technology education and research, some deep technology clusters in closely related industries, a strong logistics capability, and a stream of outbound FDI. Based on that foundation, Taiwan should ensure future success by becoming the research, technology, and complex manufacturing base for multinational corporations in Asia. Porter suggests that Taiwan should

—become the most attractive site for R&D centers

—create a welcoming, transparent, and highly efficient investment climate

—make Taiwan the easiest place in Asia to do business

—serve as the secure technology gateway to China

—provide world-class logistics and business services

—develop Taiwan as a knowledge and education center

—become a hub for information.[32]

Denis Fred Simon of Arizona State University concludes that Taiwan has no choice but to upgrade its role as a global and regional R&D center, especially in the field of industrial design. To do that, it must enhance ways to attract more foreign direct investment with higher-value-added products. It must become further embedded in the knowledge networks that are defining the shape of global innovation. In particular, it must develop and deploy the critical talent needed to support innovation and become fully engaged in the networks of global education with links to the best universities. It must balance its search for opportunities in China with strong economic ties to the United States, Japan, and Europe.[33]

The Ma administration appears to agree with those proposals. As negotiations on ECFA neared their conclusion, officials emphasized that the agreement was only one means to the end of stimulating the economy. In May 2010, Ma Ying-jeou stated that "we need to resort to innovation to enhance Taiwan's competitiveness. Taiwan's industrial structure needs to be changed. . . . Taiwan . . . can only survive with the ability to make innovations. . . .We must strengthen our own research and development and improve our self-manufacturing capability."[34] In his New Year's address for

2011, he stated that "experience teaches us that the greatest amount of value added comes from innovation, research, and development."[35] By implication, Taiwan should not only rely on the improvement of service industries, which would be the obvious post-industrial option, but also emphasize advanced manufacturing.[36]

In May 2010, Taiwan's legislature passed a comprehensive administration-sponsored bill on industrial innovation covering issues such as tax incentives, financial support, encouraging investment, information sharing, human resource development, and science and industrial parks. Tax incentives targeted research and development, employee training, running operational headquarters, and international logistics and distribution.[37] There is also some understanding that a good education system is a precondition for innovation. To quote Ma Ying-jeou: "Education is the cornerstone of national power, and children are our hope for the future."[38]

Emphasizing innovation is relevant even for some of Taiwan's star IT firms. Despite all the success of the firms in securing a key position in global supply chains, some observers believe that the small profit margins under which they operate allow too little investment in R&D and branding. "The Taiwanese industry is particularly weak where the most valuable intellectual property is created these days: in software, services and systems."[39] Writing in 2005, Douglas Fuller argued that the same firms will remain competitive only with public and private investment in research and design. To that end, the government should shift tax incentives and subsidies away from underperforming sectors; rationalize the industrial structure so that strong firms can take over weaker competitors; encourage creation of high-level research and development centers on the island; and consider developing Taiwan brands (as opposed to producing goods that are marketed under the brands of American and other companies).[40]

Promoting innovation is proposed not just for high-technology firms but also for small and medium-size enterprises (SMEs) to reduce the vulnerability that liberalization poses for them. Soon after the signing of ECFA, the Ministry of Economic Affairs announced a series of measures to help increase the SME sector's competitiveness. The ministry pledged to foster cooperation between universities and industry; encourage technology transfer to promote innovation; assist SMEs to expand sales in domestic and foreign markets; increase business opportunities for service industries; and integrate industrial supply chains. An example of the last measure is ensuring that Taiwan auto parts manufacturers take advantage of the reduction in PRC tariffs to supply automobile manufacturers.[41]

Moreover, the Ma administration has understood that there is a certain contradiction within an economic strategy that combines innovation and trade liberalization with China (among others). Specifically, the intellectual property that innovation creates must be protected to uphold that part of the strategy. But liberalization with the Mainland creates the danger that Chinese entities will abuse Taiwan intellectual property rights (IPR). As Terry Gou, a leading Taiwan entrepreneur, put it, "because China is protectionist at the local level, Taiwanese companies there have absolutely no [IPR] protection."[42] Hence, in parallel with ECFA, the Taiwan government pursued an agreement with Beijing on IPR protection, and that agreement was signed on the same day as ECFA. In it, the two sides agreed

> to strengthen exchanges and cooperation on the cross-Strait protection of patents, trademarks, rights pertaining to new plant varieties . . . and other intellectual property rights, resolve relevant issues through consultation, and enhance the innovation, application, management and protection of intellectual property rights on both sides of the Strait.

In particular, they agreed to create a coordination mechanism for law enforcement that would crack down on piracy and counterfeiting; enhance market monitoring, investigation, and punishment; and prevent various abuses of IPR.[43] But the frustrating, two-decade effort of the United States to limit Chinese abuses of American companies' intellectual property and to secure protection of those rights at the local level should be a cautionary tale for Taiwan.[44] Similarly, it was at the Ma administration's initiative that the ECFA package included the promise of agreements on investment protection (long a goal of Taiwan) and on settlement of disputes. The two sides reached agreement on investment protection in August 2012 (see chapter 6), but officials and business executives understood that its success depended on proper implementation of its provisions within the Chinese legal system.

That Taiwan should face difficulties in securing protection for its Mainland investors and their intellectual property rights should not be a surprise. These issues are at the heart of China's political economy. The Communist Party sets broad policy and retains a monopoly over personnel appointments down to the county level but then grants county officials wide latitude to carry out the regime's objectives, particularly with regard to economic growth. That flexibility can benefit outside investors, but it has also led to local protectionism, abuse of intellectual property rights, corruption, and a legal system that does the bidding of local party bosses.[45] Removing past artificial limits to cross-Strait economic interaction (such as indirect flights) and removing trade barriers at the border are relatively easy. Securing and enforcing rights that are inconsistent with the prevailing political economy will be hard.

More broadly, it is one thing for the Taiwan government to set a strategy and formulate objectives; it is another to execute them within a difficult context. There is some indication that the government is falling back on the industrial policy playbook from a previous era (which, as noted, probably didn't help much). It has now identified sectors that deserve special focus, such as "six rising industries" (biotechnology, sightseeing tours, green energy, health care, intensive agriculture, and cultural and creative industries) and "four intelligent industries" (cloud computing, intelligent electric cars, intelligent green construction, and turning inventions into competitive products).[46] To the extent that government does have a role to play in facilitating growth, the quality of the civil service becomes important, yet its capacity is in question. As one observer noted: "Many civil servants feel that they have a mission . . . yet over the years government has become increasingly entangled in red tape, and ultimately they become resigned to reality."[47] There is also sometimes a tendency in Taiwan to measure success in innovation according to global rankings, number of patents, and performance in international competitions. These are not trivial, but neither are they reliable indicators. A new patent may reflect only a modest change in an existing design. Rankings and competitions are only as good as their assessment methodologies.

A central question is whether Taiwan's economic institutions are agile enough to support an economic strategy of innovation. The most obvious reform in that direction is a plan to consolidate government agencies. But the American Chamber of Commerce in Taipei correctly argues that redrawing organizational charts and retraining government employees to make them more service oriented is not enough. Moreover,

> AmCham members are constantly struck by the sharp disconnect between the vigorous efforts of senior officials seeking to promote Taiwan's further economic internationalization and the seemingly random and idiosyncratic efforts by parts of the bureaucracy to erect barriers that make it more difficult to do business in Taiwan. Apparently a concerted top-down campaign by the President and Premier would be required . . . to drive policy consistency and predictability.[48]

AmCham's 2012 report argued that "the government leadership will need to consolidate support among the civil servants who carry on the day-to-day work of policy execution and to ensure a sufficient legislative majority when votes are needed. . . . President Ma will need to be not just the commander-in-chief but also the communicator-in-chief.[49]

If Taiwan is to base its growth on innovation and the cultivation of talent, it will have to address the problems of the education system. Generally, the expansion of tertiary education—a 22 percent increase in the number of students between 2000 and 2010—has raised concerns about the quality of university graduates.[50] Specifically, reforms that began in the late 1990s created incentives for schools to focus on the minority of students—the most academically qualified—while ignoring the needs of the majority. In part because of pressures from politicians, the number of universities and Ph.D.s available for teaching jobs expanded far beyond the number of students to be taught. The neglect of technical and vocational training has made it more difficult to sustain a manufacturing base, and interest in science among young people is declining, in part because of the way that science is taught.[51] Not surprisingly, the global rankings of major Taiwan universities are slipping.[52] Again, the Ma administration appears to recognize the need for reform, but implementation is the key.

Security Issues

As the imbalance between China's military power and that of Taiwan grows, so will the island's objective vulnerability and, perhaps, subjective fears that Beijing might choose to exploit its overall advantage. Of course, the fact that China is increasingly able to carry out serious military action does not mean that it will do so. It has reason to believe that it can achieve its political goals by peaceful means. Still, Ma Ying-jeou has warned against complacency: "We should not entrust our national security to the goodwill extended by the Mainland; otherwise, if a crisis erupted in cross-Strait relations, we might be incapable of defending ourselves."[53]

To be sure, if China's leaders ordered the PLA to attack the island, it could inflict a lot of damage. As Thomas Mahnken, a former Pentagon official, and several colleagues conclude, "In time of war, it is increasingly likely that Chinese missiles would be able to shut down operations on Taiwan airfields, preventing Taiwan from controlling the Taiwan Strait. These missiles could also shut down U.S. airfields in Japan, preventing the United States from supporting Taiwan."[54] If American analysts can so contemplate ways that Beijing might use force to compel Taipei, PLA war planners can do so as well. And Taiwan's formal assessments do not ignore the danger that the island faces. Ma Ying-jeou has said, "Despite easing cross-Strait ties, Beijing remains the biggest threat to us militarily. We must not drop our guard and be lulled into a false sense of security."[55] For now, China appears to understand that the costs of a PLA campaign against both Taiwan and the United States would be severe. Pin-pointing those costs has been part of Taiwan's strategy. As Ma put it in a December 2011 speech: "We don't rely only on weapons; we also rely on ideas to maintain peace. Now, either side, if they want to change the status quo uni-laterally, they will incur a prohibitively high cost. So nobody wants to do that. Both sides want to maintain the status quo, so peace could be maintained."[56]

As the previous chapter suggested, if China embarked on a political cam-paign to pressure Taiwan by exploiting a range of power asymmetries, it is more likely that it would rely on the mere *existence* of its robust military forces, as opposed to their use, to lead Taiwan to capitulate. As the 2012 Pen-tagon report states, Beijing almost certainly views the *prospect* of using force as an important point of leverage in cross-Strait relations.[57] American offi-cials therefore have stressed the need for Taiwan to be "confident that it has the capacity to resist intimidation and coercion as it continues to engage with the mainland."[58]

Even if the odds that China will lose patience and resort to pressure are modest, no Taiwan government can ignore them. Strengthening the island's military capabilities is one way of lowering the odds. Taiwan's leaders certainly convey a strong rhetorical commitment to ensuring the island's security mili-tarily. In May 2011, Ma Ying-jeou said, "Taiwan has the resolve to defend itself. . . . We are confident that we will succeed in building a small but strong mili-tary force."[59] The quadrennial defense review issued by Taiwan's Ministry of National Defense in March 2009 stated that "during ROC's pragmatic cross-strait interaction with the PRC, the Armed Forces must still maintain strong defense capabilities, so that Taiwan can enjoy protected national security and establish a more lasting peace over the Taiwan Strait."[60] These official views are reflected in public opinion: even in the relative calm of the Ma Ying-jeou period, between 40 to 50 percent of those surveyed have stated that they believe that China is hostile to both the Taiwan people and their government.[61]

Taiwan could, of course, choose to muddle through by continuing its cur-rent three-prong approach: use rhetorical reassurance and greater cross-Strait ties to increase Beijing's stake in peace; seek advanced weaponry from the United States in line with its current defense strategy; and maintain defense spending at recent levels, below 3 percent a year. But muddling through would not promote security, because China would likely invest more in military power than Taiwan does. The island's vulnerability to intimidation and pres-sure (if not to outright attack) would likely increase.

Taiwan's alternative to muddling through is to strengthen itself militarily in order to reduce the intimidation value of the threat that a PRC shift to a Sun

Zi–*weiqii* strategy would imply. To use Ma Ying-jeou's formulation, Taiwan would rely a little more on weapons without ignoring ideas. While Taiwan has pursued a mixed hedging strategy to cope with vulnerability and uncertainty by combining reassurance of China with some degree of deterrence, security self-strengthening would place somewhat more emphasis on deterrence.[62] Taiwan can do so by strengthening its indigenous capabilities (internal balancing), deepening its quasi-alliance with the United States (external balancing), or both.

But if Taiwan's security self-strengthening is to be effective it must be credible, by raising to some degree the risks that Beijing believes that it would run by acting on the threat implied in a strategy of pressure and intimidation. What is important here is for Taiwan to adopt steps that truly change Beijing's calculus rather than serve other purposes. And there's the rub. It appears that Taiwan's current defense strategy is less and less appropriate for the threat environment that Taiwan faces. If that is the case, the steps that Taiwan takes pursuant to that strategy may actually not improve the credibility of deterrence.[63]

Even though the military part of a Sun Zi–*weiqii* pressure strategy is more implied than real, it is still there. That simplifies the analysis of what Taiwan needs to do to strengthen deterrence in its own eyes and Beijing's. Its assessment of its threat environment, defense strategy, and procurement options is the same whether it is preparing for an attack or for an implied threat. Beijing will understand that a threat, implied or otherwise, includes the possibility of the use of force, and so its willingness to make the threat will be a function of its calculation of whether the use of force will be successful.

Defense Strategy and Force Structure

Taiwan's defense strategy is embedded in its security strategy. Officially, that strategy has five objectives: war prevention, homeland defense, contingency response, conflict avoidance, and regional stability.[64] The key strategic concept, which is central to the first two goals, is "resolute defense and credible deterrence." For resolute defense, according to the *2011 National Defense Report* (NDR), Taiwan "needs to be able to survive the enemy's first strike, averting decapitation, maneuvering forces to counter strikes, and sustaining combat power so as to achieve the objectives of 'strategic protection and tactical resolution.'"[65] Credible deterrence requires ready capabilities that, combining firepower, joint operations, and training, will force "the enemy to rationally calculate the costs and risks of invasions."[66] Regarding war scenarios, the NDR implicitly proposes a staged defense of the island:

—The task of the first stage is to oppose a blockade designed to exploit the reality that Taiwan depends on trade for economic and political survival. The battlefield would be the sea and skies surrounding the island. Taiwan's armed forces would "integrate joint operations capabilities to counter the enemy's blockading forces, open safe aerial and sea transportation routes, maintain communications to the outside world, and ensure continuity of government functions."[67]

—In the second stage, the task would be interdiction to stop an invasion force from getting close to Taiwan. Here, the *Quadrennial Defense Review* (QDR) advocates going on the offensive, at least tactically, in support of strategic defense. Taiwan would attack "the enemy's important military targets [probably naval, missile, and air-defense bases] and amphibious forces as they assemble and move." The objective would be to "stop and destroy the enemy when its war-fighting capabilities are relatively weak while transiting across the Taiwan Strait."[68]

—The emphasis of the third stage, if necessary, is defense of the Taiwan homeland: resisting an amphibious invasion. The objective would be to "execute multilayered interdictions to destroy enemy forces before the lodgments of landed amphibious and airborne troops are secured."[69]

That is the official strategy. The real strategy is based on the simple assumption that Taiwan would survive a sustained Chinese coercive campaign only if the United States intervenes. So far, the possibility that the United States will come to the defense of Taiwan has strengthened deterrence. China has not attacked because it has assumed that the United States will fight for Taiwan and is able to inflict substantial damage on the Mainland. If, on the other hand, Beijing were ever to conclude that Washington lacks either the will or the ability to defend Taiwan (or both), its temptation to exploit its power advantage would grow (assuming, of course, that it concluded that it had reason to do so). If Taipei decides that Washington lacks that will or ability, its vulnerability to pressure increases.

Taiwan cannot state overtly that reliance on U.S. intervention is an element of its security strategy, because the United States itself has not been willing to extend an explicit commitment. For Washington to openly pledge to defend Taiwan when Beijing believes that Taiwan it is a part of China and that their relations are an internal affair is not a good way to foster U.S.-China relations. American ambiguity on the subject has allowed Chinese leaders to maintain support within the regime for a policy of accommodation toward Washington. An explicit U.S. pledge to defend Taiwan also runs the risk of encouraging reckless behavior on Taipei's part. Yet implicitly the United States has warned China not to use force, particularly if there is no provocation from the island's leaders. The fact that PLA is acquiring capabilities that would complicate the access of U.S. armed forces to the maritime areas east and west of the Chinese coast—and, in the event of a Taiwan conflict, block those forces from coming to the island's defense—suggests that it assumes that the United States will indeed intervene.[70]

It is only implicitly, then, that Taiwan can base its security strategy in part on U.S. intervention. But it really has had no choice, and that creates an imperative and a challenge. The imperative is for Taipei to foster a good political relationship with Washington and to strengthen U.S. confidence that Taiwan will not act in ways that are inconsistent with the American interest in peace and stability in the Taiwan Strait. U.S. confidence was undermined during the Lee Teng-hui and Chen Shui-bian administrations but strengthened under Ma Ying-jeou.

Taiwan's challenge is to create the impression in Beijing's mind that it has the confidence to stand up to the implied military threat embodied in a Chinese pressure campaign because it has the ability to survive a PLA attack on its own for as long as the United States takes to decide whether to intervene and, assuming that the United States does, to mobilize its forces to enter the fight. That period is usually assumed to be around a few weeks. Taiwan's need for strategic endurance in turn provokes the question of what defense strategy and what force structure would best facilitate it. If China believes that Taiwan could survive until "the cavalry" arrived, then it would be less likely to resort to pressure in the first place. If, on the other hand, it concludes that Taiwan's defense strategy is flawed and its confidence is misplaced, it would be less deterred.

As suggested above, Taiwan's defense strategy is one of forward defense, what might be called "extending space to buy time"—that is, mounting a defense in and over the Taiwan Strait, as far from the island as possible, and so prolonging the time available to the United States to intervene. A critical element is achieving air superiority in order to make a PLA blockade or amphibious campaign too risky to contemplate. This approach has relied on the relative quality of Taiwan's weapons platforms and the strategic depth that the ninety-mile-wide Taiwan Strait affords. Securing advanced weapons platforms from the United States for the navy, the air force, and the army was intended to preserve the qualitative edge conferred by Taiwan's weapons against more numerous PLA forces.

Yet this strategy may no longer be viable, because the balance of capabilities has shifted in China's favor and Taiwan is losing its qualitative margin of safety. Thus Bernard Cole, the dean of American defense specialists concerning Taiwan, wrote in 2006: "China may be superior to Taiwan in 2005 and will clearly be superior by 2008 across the military spectrum. . . . In the event of armed conflict, Taiwan by itself does not appear capable of prolonged defense against the PLA."[71] William Murray worries that the growing accuracy of China's missile force will give it the ability not just to wreak general damage on Taiwan targets but to destroy or degrade the island's assets for conducting naval and air warfare.[72] In the face of PLA missiles, combat aircraft, and ground-based air defenses, the Taiwan air force would be hard pressed to win a fight for air superiority.[73] If Chinese decisionmakers share this skeptical assessment of Taiwan's ability to execute its defense strategy, then they will not be deterred from coercion or pressure, should they decide to employ them.

One reason that Taiwan's force structure no longer fits its defense strategy is that its leaders have failed to mount a vigorous response to the island's growing vulnerability. Writing during the Chen Shui-bian period, Cole speaks of a "lack of popular will to build a stronger deterrent force to confront the mainland" that places the Ministry of National Defense "in a politically difficult position when it comes to asking for its needed share of national revenue."[74] Defense budgets therefore have ranged between 2 and 3 percent of GDP since the early 2000s, which, Murray says, "hardly seem[s] commensurate with the increased threat."[75] Cole cites a "strategic syllogism" that he attributes to Taiwan's leaders in order to explain this inconsistency: "China is not serious about employing military force against Taiwan; if China does employ military force against Taiwan, the United States will intervene immediately and effectively; therefore, Taiwan does not need to strengthen and modernize its military forces."[76] Compounding a shortage of budgetary resources, which is correctible in the short term given the requisite political will, Taiwan's demographic trajectory will reduce the number of young people available for military service—a problem that can be solved only over a long period and by choices outside government control.[77]

There has been some effort to prepare for new modes of PRC coercion. Writing in 2007, Andrew Yang, a deputy minister of national defense in the Ma administration, summarized measures taken to counter China's improving capabilities: protection of critical command, control, and communication facilities; modernization of air defense; better shelter for advanced aircraft; improved ability to conduct anti-submarine warfare; and streamlining ground forces and equipping them with more modern attack capabilities.[78] Yet these measures only slow the negative shift in the balance of capabilities. Some analysts believe that war planners have displayed more realism by modifying the definition of victory, from total defeat of the enemy's forces to "preventing enemy landing forces from establishing a secure foothold on the island."[79] Yet that is not inconsistent with extending space to buy time and making significant investments in the navy and air force.

To be sure, there are ways that Taiwan and the United States could strengthen deterrence under the current strategy. Perhaps the most important are intelligence, reconnaissance, and surveillance. The PLA could not mount a coercive campaign based on air and missile strikes without ample preparation—exercises, mobilization, and deployments—and at least some of those steps could be detected with adequate intelligence assets. (A PLA attack from a "standing start" would likely be too risky to undertake.) In addition, Beijing would probably precede such a campaign with a propaganda offensive to create a justification for coercion or to intimidate Taiwan into submitting. As the PLA readied its attack, the United States would have time to deploy its own forces more quickly and make more explicit its warning that it would defend Taiwan.

In theory, Taiwan has other defensive options. First, it can significantly improve its missile defenses by acquiring more Patriot batteries, a sufficient number of reload missiles, and a second long-range, phased-array radar to detect incoming PLA missiles in a timely manner. But that would be very expensive, and the legislature has sometimes declined to provide sufficient funding for a robust program. Second, it can emphasize passive defenses such as hardened shelters and command and control facilities, camouflage, decoys, and rapid runway repair—but the repair of inoperable runways still takes time. Third, it could disperse its air assets to a smaller and less accessible installation, but that requires logistical preparation and practice. If done properly, these three steps would require Beijing to begin an attack at a higher level of lethality.

Finally, Taiwan can develop long-range strike capabilities of its own in order to put the PLA's airfields and missile bases at risk. Indeed, it has sought to acquire land-attack and anti-ship cruise missiles to exploit the vulnerability of China's missile bases, ports, and so forth. Early in his presidency, Ma Ying-jeou reportedly authorized the Ministry of National Defense to procure 300 surface-to-surface Hsiung Feng 2E (HF-2E) missiles, which have a range of 600 kilometers, or around 373 miles.[80] One American defense analyst reportedly stated: "Given China's increasingly formidable air defenses, using fixed-wing air assets, such as F-5s or F-16s, to strike mainland targets has become increasingly costly. Therefore, investments in systems, such as the HF-2E, could be viewed as necessary to maintain a limited retaliation capability."[81] The acquisition of HF-2E missiles does raise questions. Would such missiles be effective without robust intelligence assets to identify targets and do battle damage assessments? Could Taiwan get enough cruise missiles to seriously degrade PLA offensive capabilities and convince China's decisionmakers of that possibility? Moreover, for Taiwan to acquire a significant independent deterrent would raise concerns in Washington about preserving escalation control in a crisis. For Taiwan to raise such doubts on the part of its quasi-ally is at odds with a key element of its security strategy. But setting those concerns aside, purely in terms of enhancing deterrence, it is hard to argue with Taiwan's view that having its own long-range precision-strike capability would reduce Beijing's confidence in the success of its own strategy.[82]

Time for a Change in Strategy?

The growing gap in Taiwan between a defense strategy of extending space for time and a deteriorating threat environment puts in ever sharper relief a fundamental question: if the PLA's more robust capabilities are indeed making Taiwan's current strategy unviable, is it time to change the strategy?

A growing number of American defense scholars are coming to the conclusion that the only defense strategy that makes sense for Taiwan is one that better exploits its key strategic feature: the fact that it is an island. The task then is to make the island as impervious as possible to invasion, isolation, and political despair, what William Murray calls a "porcupine" strategy. Michael Lustumbo argues that Taiwan should base its defense on exploiting the PLA's greatest weaknesses: that is, the vulnerability of an invasion force to attack while it is transiting the Taiwan Strait and coming ashore on Taiwan.[83] Obviously, Taiwan would be better off if it could both render the island impervious to conquest *and* conduct a forward defense in and over the Taiwan Strait. But given scarce defense resources, the first priority should be the defense of the island itself. To focus those resources solely or mostly on platforms for forward defense is to leave the island relatively defenseless.

A porcupine strategy for Taiwan would better ensure two strategic imperatives. The first is to give the United States the maximum amount of time to intervene and do so in an effective way. Mounting a defense of Taiwan is growing ever more complicated as China assembles the capabilities to place at risk key U.S. assets: power projection platforms like aircraft carriers; advanced command, control, and communications systems; and so on.[84] That is not to say that a defense is impossible. China has vulnerabilities of its own, which U.S. forces can exploit with their own long-range, precision-strike, and other capabilities. But Taiwan's ability to endure is all the more important because the PLA is better able to complicate U.S. intervention.

The second strategic imperative is to sustain the will to fight of the Taiwan leadership and public. If Taiwan has a security "center of gravity," this is probably it. In truth, there is no way to know how Taiwan would respond to a PLA coercion campaign. A survey commissioned in October 2010 by the Ministry of National Defense found that 76.5 percent of those polled were willing to take up arms voluntarily if Taiwan was "under military threat," the highest percentage in recent years. Whether such attitudes would prevail in an actual conflict is unknowable, and even if they did it would probably be too late to turn determination into military capability. That should be done now if it is to be effective.[85]

All that can be said at this point is that if China conveys an implied military threat to Taiwan and if the political elite and the people doubt that defense is possible, then they will be tempted to sue for peace in order to protect what they can. If, on the other hand, there is confidence that a "resolute defense" is difficult but still feasible, it remains an alternative to capitulation and so a disincentive for Beijing to mount a pressure campaign in the first place. For Taiwan to place most of its defense chips on the increasingly problematic strategy of forward defense and then face the reality that in a real fight the capabilities associated with that strategy would either be quickly destroyed or made irrelevant would make it harder to sustain the will to fight.

What steps should Taiwan take to make the island more impregnable? Peter Lavoy of the U.S. Department of Defense argues that Taiwan requires a "more holistic approach" to its military vulnerability and limited budget resources. "Lasting security cannot be achieved simply by purchasing limited numbers of advanced weapons systems. Taiwan must also devote greater attention to asymmetric concepts and technologies to maximize Taiwan's enduring strengths and advantages." He suggests acquisition of maneuverable weapon systems; more hardening of defenses; greater use of decoys, deception, and concealment to complicate PLA targeting; and exploiting the island's geography to protect key resources and raise the cost of coercion.[86]

Lustombo identifies two criteria concerning any new capabilities Taiwan might consider: lethality and survivability. "Will the investment enable a capability to target vulnerable PLA forces, and can they survive formidable precision-strike capabilities?"[87] Murray and Lustombo identify types of equipment that would help Taiwan resist an amphibious invasion:

—coastal defense cruise missiles, cued by a variety of accurate sensors, to target amphibious shipping, particularly ships carrying tanks

—attack helicopters, such as the American Apache AH-64D

—mobile multiple-launch rocket systems

—anti-armor weapons

—more extensive ground-based air defenses, particularly mobile ones

—surf-zone sea mines.[88]

Because China might opt for a maritime blockade in order to cut trade-dependent Taiwan's lifeline to the international economy and so break its political will, Murray suggests stockpiling critical items (energy, food, medical supplies) and planning ahead for how to ration them. That would extend the time available for the United States to intervene and break the blockade.[89] Murray also suggests a number of measures that could make a long-range precision-strike campaign by the PLA less effective both militarily and politically:

—hardening key civil and military facilities (leadership facilities, command posts, communications systems) in order to preserve the chain of command

—making redundant key infrastructure (distribution systems for food and water, medical services, wartime command and control facilities, radar, civil defense, and, in particular, the electrical grid)

—using decoys to frustrate PLA targeting

—making the key targets of PLA missiles mobile

—improving training to ensure that personnel know how to fight should they have to.[90]

All of these measures have the distinct advantages of being relatively inexpensive and, cumulatively, raising the cost of coercion by China. Taiwan is already taking some of them. But any effort to shift from forward defense to defense of the island and from platforms like advanced fighter aircraft and submarines to items associated with coastal defense confront an institutional problem: the opposition of Taiwan's air force and navy. As Murray predicts:

> Air force leaders would be understandably loath to admit that their fighters cannot defend Taiwan's skies; their navy counterparts might similarly resist suggestions that their fleet is acutely vulnerable in port. Both services' political champions would certainly challenge the implications of this . . . analysis. So too would the arms manufacturers who stand to benefit from the sale of aircraft, ships, and supporting systems to Taiwan.[91]

Publicly, Taiwan's Defense Ministry said that it welcomed "new concepts" but still asserted that the navy and air force were "extremely important" in its strategy of "keep[ing] war as far away from Taiwan as possible."[92]

I observed above that I feel some reluctance to tell Taiwan what to do. Military self-strengthening is the area in which I feel the most reluctance, if only because I am not a defense expert. Moreover, it is Taiwan's government leadership, including its military leaders, who must judge in a very objective and hard-headed way whether these American specialists are correct in their conclusion that the PLA's improving capabilities have made forward defense less feasible and have complicated the task of U.S. intervention. It is they who must assess whether Taiwan's current defense strategy is still viable and whether the procurement preferences that stem from it are still appropriate. If it is their considered conclusion that past priorities are no longer a good use of scarce defense dollars, then the priority should be on formulating a defense strategy and procurement priorities that are realistic in light of the island's current security situation, striking the right balance between engagement and deterrence. A "whole of government" approach to security and defense strategy seems necessary in light of the institutional issues cited above. Whatever approach is adopted, moreover, has to make sense in strategic, budgetary, and political terms and must fit well with Taiwan's relationship with the United States. These may be the most important choices that Taiwan's leaders have to make, and because the stakes are high, it is all the more important that the choices be made well.

Taiwan's Democratic System

Chapter 2 describes the way in which Taiwan's democratization has had a profound effect on its cross-Strait policy. Taiwan's long-term future depends on how skillfully it engages Beijing in the near and medium term, in either the paradigm of mutual persuasion or the paradigm of power asymmetry. It follows that the island's political system must do a good job of assessing dangers and opportunities, defining interests and trade-offs, and choosing courses of action that reflect the public's will. Therefore Taiwan should strengthen its democratic system as it strengthens the areas already discussed—and ensure that all projects are done well. In chapter 7, I suggest that Taiwan's democratic system could provide it with a source of counter-leverage, but that is more likely in a system whose choices reflect sound policy and in which a broad public consensus provides a source of negotiating strength. A dysfunctional system is a source of weakness. There is a general sense that Taiwan's political system does not always work very well, thus distorting the popular will. This is another area for Taiwan's self-strengthening.

The Problem

It is tempting to attribute the dysfunction of Taiwan's democratic system to the idiosyncrasies of its leaders (for example, Lee Teng-hui and Chen Shui-bian) or to the divided government that existed from 2000 to 2008. If those explanations were correct, one could infer that the return of unified government in 2008 and the rise of leaders with moderate views and temperament would have solved the problem. But the united government that was in place after 2008 did not foster a political paradise, and there has been something of a consensus that much of the political difficulty is structural in origin.

That is, leaders, politicians, parties, and publics are operating, often in spite of themselves, in a democratic order that is only partially constructed and not yet consolidated. The behavior that results may make sense for the individual actors in the system, but it is dysfunctional for the public at large and will likely continue until the democratic order is more responsive and effective. The problems associated with its various institutions (semi-presidentialism, the legislature, the party system, the electoral system, and the mass media) work together in an interlocking way to reduce accountability, foster a zero-sum political psychology, promote policy deadlock, ensure suboptimal policy performance, and defer consensus on the rules of the game.[93] As Su Chi, an official during the Ma administration put it, "Taiwan's leaders are 'squirrels in a cage.' They run and run, only to find themselves in the same place."[94] Some Taiwan scholars blame the island's divided political system for the economy's failure to modernize and keep pace with the rest of Asia's "little dragons" (South Korea, Hong Kong, and Singapore), with which Taiwan is often grouped.[95]

A key measure of the effectiveness of the Taiwan political system is how the public evaluates its performance. Larry Diamond's paper for a June 2011 conference in Taipei provides relevant polling evidence for the last decade or so. Generally speaking, the Taiwan public has vacillated in its satisfaction regarding "the way democracy works." The share of those surveyed who were satisfied stood at 67.2 percent in 1996; fell to 53.4 percent in 2001; rose a bit to 55.9 percent in 2006; and jumped to 68.6 percent in 2010.[96] The picture was also mixed when it came to specific features of Taiwan's system, summarized in table 8-1.

On most measures, there was little or no change. The only exception was growing confidence about the control of corruption, but that may be simply because the more numerous Blue citizens approved of corruption prosecutions against former officials of the Green Chen administration. More disturbing was the low share of those surveyed who believed that the system is responsive and that the legal system can hold law-breaking officials to account and the decline in confidence in the ability of the Legislative Yuan (LY) to hold the executive to account.

The LY should have a key role in ensuring responsiveness and accountability, but Hawang Shiow-duan of Soochow University has identified a number of institutional features that limit that role. Legislators are allowed to

Table 8-1. *Specific Measures of Taiwan's System Performance*

Measure	2006	2010
Freedom	74.9	76.4
Competitiveness	56.4	58.6
Vertical accountability	46.4	48.2
Horizontal accountability	51.1	47.5
Rule of law	40.8	42.5
Control of corruption	45.8	56.1
Responsiveness ("to what people want")	35.8	38.5

Source: Larry Diamond, "How Good a Democracy Has the Republic of China Become? Taiwan's Democracy in Comparative Perspective," paper presented at the INPR conference "A Spectacular Century: The Republic of China Centennial Democracy Forums," Taipei, June 24–25, 2011. Data drawn from the Asian Barometer surveys. Vertical accountability refers to the people's power to change their government; horizontal accountability refers to the ability of the legislature to check the executive.

switch committee assignments on a regular basis and so have no incentive to specialize and become expert in particular policy areas. The majority party does not have a monopoly over the power to convene committee meetings. The procedure committee can sometimes block floor consideration of bills, even though the majority party might disagree.[97] Then there is the consultation committee for interparty negotiations on bills before they go to the floor for a final vote, somewhat analogous to the conference committee in the U.S. Congress. It can change the content of a bill in ways that are not transparent and that permit no floor amendments. The committee allocates significant power to the speaker, who chairs it, and gives one seat to a party or nonparty group that has at least three members in the LY. The majority party may find that it can pass bills on a second reading but that the consultation committee will block final passage unless it makes significant concessions. The committee, says Su Chi, "distorts the results of democratic elections and is the darkest corner of our democratic system."[98] Finally, there are no effective mechanisms for deterring and punishing legislators for corruption and conflicts of interest.[99]

Semi-presidentialism, a mix between a presidential and a parliamentary system similar to that of Weimar Germany and the French Fifth Republic, introduces another layer of complexity. Originally, the ROC constitution gave the premier (formally called the president of the Executive Yuan) the authority to lead the executive branch and thus significant power relative to that of the president of the republic. That was unimportant from the late 1940s to the early 1990s, when the constitution was suspended. Under Lee Teng-hui, the constitution became operative and a series of amendments strengthened the powers of the island's president, who was now directly elected. He would appoint the premier and a host of other officials to be responsible for national security policy. The premier was still accountable to the legislature, but the LY now approved the initial appointment and could remove him/her through a vote of no confidence. At that point, the president could dissolve the LY. But because elections are costly for LY members, the vote of no confidence is a lever that legislators have been reluctant to pull.

Such a system works moderately well when the same party controls the presidency and the LY, subject to the problems just cited. But it works badly when one party controls the presidency and the other the legislature. That was the case during Chen Shui-bian's tenure, when the KMT maintained control of the LY. In that case, one Taiwan scholar concludes, "constitutionalism will be unstable and the duration of governments [that is, premierships] will be short."[100]

The degree of political polarization may also affect leaders' capacity to govern. Generally, if the Deep Green and Deep Blue forces dominate the political spectrum, with each justifying its existence by attacking the policies of the other, polarization increases and good governance is impeded. A centrist consensus of the "Light" tendencies is more likely to foster policy progress. Lee Teng-hui fashioned such a centrist coalition of moderate elements of the DPP and his ruling KMT and so was able to complete the process of democratization. Chen Shui-bian toyed with a centrist approach during the 2000 campaign and for a while thereafter. But frustrated by KMT resistance, he shifted to an electoral strategy of mobilizing the DPP's Deep Green base, ensuring that he achieved few of his policy goals. Political polarization may be useful as a domestic political strategy, but it can be counterproductive at a time when Taiwan faces, as the pro-Green *Taipei Times* put it, "a threat to its survival." Surprising for the *Taipei Times*, this particular editorial proposed a more centrist approach:

> Rather than launch attacks on what is regarded as the "proximate enemy [Ma Ying-jeou and the KMT]," the pan-green camp would be far more effective if it sought to establish constructive relationships with officials in the pan-blue camp who have the same democratic values and pride in Taiwan as they do, in an effort to focus on the one external force that can truly dissolve the nation: China.[101]

Finally, in an era of media-based politics, whether the print and broadcast media contribute to good governance rather than undermine it is a function of their professional standards. But Gary Rawnsley of the University of Leeds provides a mixed assessment of the political role of Taiwan's media. He makes several points. First of all, Taiwan media are fully autonomous, free from state interference; they are able to foster political accountability and transparency, and they provide a platform for a range of conflicting views. They have served as both "agents of change" and "agents of restraint."[102] Second, various media outlets have responded to the pressure of market forces by competing to be the most sensational and confrontational, with little regard for the privacy of individuals.[103] Third, the partisan character of many media organizations raises questions about who owns them and how ownership is used inappropriately to influence politics. Thus the 2011 report of Freedom House on the freedom of Taiwan's press noted that "press freedom advocates raised concerns that media owners and some journalists were whitewashing news about China to protect their financial interests."[104] Fourth, the Blue-Green polarization of the media, fueled by "crisis discourse" and simplistic, us-versus-them analysis, only exacerbates the polarization of the political system. Rawnsley concludes: "Where does freedom of speech end and moral responsibility begin? Too many people in Taiwan, particularly journalists and politicians, suppose freedom of speech absolves them from any responsibility for caution, sensitivity, and sometimes accuracy."[105]

The return of the KMT to government-wide power in 2008 ameliorated some of the negative features of the political system. Conflict between the legislature and the executive was not as severe as during the Chen Shui-bian years, although the LY was not a passive instrument of the Ma administration. The results of the 2012 election reflected pretty well the balance of sentiment between the 50-plus percent of the population that is comfortable with current policies and the less than 50 percent that is either skeptical or opposed. Still, the fundamental dysfunction appears to remain. To repeat, the problems here are mainly structural. The dysfunction will continue and politicians will respond to the cues that the system creates, unless and until systemic solutions are devised for what are systemic problems.

Solutions?

It is one thing to diagnose the problem of Taiwan's democracy; it is another to prescribe remedies, particularly from America, whose political system has its own share of dysfunction. Moreover, while it is fine to recommend what are, in theory, good changes, they may never be adopted in practice because of inherent difficulties and political vested interests. If they are adopted, they may have unintended and negative consequences.

One example of such an imperfect remedy was the proposal to activate the provision of the ROC constitution that authorized the people's right of referendum. Along with initiative and recall, this measure was promoted in Western countries in the early twentieth century as a tool of direct democracy to counter the way that small but powerful minorities (for example, corporations) were able to monopolize or corrupt institutions that provided indirect or representative democracy and so distort or block the popular will. It was from the American progressive movement that Sun Yat-sen borrowed the instruments of direct democracy, which he then introduced into the original political program of the Kuomintang, and those instruments were later incorporated into the ROC constitution. In the late 1980s, Taiwanese activists in the United States saw the utility of a referendum in promoting their political goals, and they sold the idea to the DPP once they were permitted to return to Taiwan in the early 1990s.[106] The party found the referendum power especially attractive because it believed that KMT dominance of the government (particularly the legislative branch) would negate what it believed to be the wishes of the Taiwanese majority. As a result, its charter, adopted in 1991, stated that "the establishment of a sovereign, independent and self-governing Republic of Taiwan and promulgation of a new constitution should be carried out by all residents of Taiwan through a national referendum."[107] The LY finally passed legislation to operationalize the constitutional right of referendum on policy issues in the fall of 2003, as Chen Shui-bian was running for reelection and the KMT was trying to replace him. In those fraught and exceptional political circumstances, the DPP and KMT competed to promote the most "democratic" mechanism.[108] The upshot was a measure that generally required a high number of signatures on any petition calling for a referendum but that gave the president authority to call for one unilaterally in cases involving national security. Chen Shui-bian was able to exploit this loophole and schedule a referendum on election day in both 2004 and 2008. Yet his purpose was not to measure the popular will on issues where it was uncertain but to mobilize the DPP's base to go out and vote.[109] Neither of the Chen-sponsored referendums passed because the KMT called on its supporters to boycott them and not enough people voted to make them valid.

It is perhaps regrettable that this democratic mechanism became so politicized. Granted, direct democracy can distort the popular will just as indirect democracy can (witness how special interests in California seek to manipulate the initiative and referendum power in support of their narrow interests). Taiwan's LY has a mixed record in representing public views. Yet there remains a value in employing selective and carefully crafted referendums to address fundamental policy issues on which there is genuine disagreement. That the Taipei government has the option of calling one can fortify its negotiating mandate and so increase its leverage with Beijing. Moreover, any policy change that requires a constitutional amendment would be subject to a popular referendum if it first passed the legislature.

A commonsense point of departure for reforming Taiwan's political system would be to identify measures that are, on the one hand, relatively simple and specific and, on the other, something that Blue and Green forces can unite on. The institution in which reform may be most feasible is the Legislative Yuan. At least some of its weakness is specific, and legislators would benefit as a group from modest changes. First of all, Lin Cho-shui, an independent-minded leader of the DPP, has recommended reform of the central government so that powers and responsibilities are more clearly defined. Toward that end, he suggested an overhaul of the Legislative Yuan to create "a normal parliament structure and rules of discussion."[110] Increasing staff resources for members certainly falls into that category. Second, ending the rotation of committee assignments and reducing the number of panels on which members can serve might be another. It would certainly have the benefit of creating substantive expertise, which would strengthen the LY's ability to monitor seriously the performance of the executive branch. LY members might fear losing the ability to cultivate useful political constituencies (and garner campaign contributions), which they can do by having a variety of committee assignments, but if they concluded that they could satisfy that priority by acquiring expertise and seniority on a few committees, they might well go along. Third, tightening rules on conflicts of interest would improve the low regard in which the legislature is held. Getting members to agree would probably be difficult, for obvious reasons—it is the institution that has the poor reputation, not each of them as an individual. It may take a scandal to fix this.

Yet the feature of the LY that is probably most problematic for good governance is the consultation committee, on which each party has a seat and retains the right to affect decisions concerning the content of legislation and whether it gets enacted at all. In the wake of the 2012 LY elections, the KMT, the DPP, the conservative People First Party (PFP), Lee Teng-hui's Taiwan Solidarity Union (TSU), and a nonparty caucus each has a vote on the committee, even though the KMT has twenty-four more seats than the DPP and 57 percent of the total membership. The PFP and TSU have only three LY seats each, but they too have a vote in the committee. The speaker, who serves as the chair, has one vote and can act independently even though he is a vice chairman of the KMT. This balance of power certainly protects minority rights, but it also undermines majority rule and effective policymaking. At a minimum, the committee's membership should reflect that of the LY as a whole.

If a Blue administration wished to correct some of these problems, what could it offer the Greens to secure its agreement? One possible step would be for the administration to agree to tighten regulation of vote buying and then carry out its commitment. Vote buying—an organization-intensive and "retail" mode of voter mobilization—has benefited the KMT more than the DPP. But vote buying is a hallmark of politics in predominantly rural societies (it was common in Japan as well), and Taiwan is becoming a predominantly urban society where "wholesale" mobilization is more the norm. So to remain competitive, the KMT has to move in this direction anyway. Tsai Ing-wen hinted at such a bargain in a September 2011 speech: "The legislative process and campaign financing regulations can be further improved to ensure greater transparency and accountability as well as fairness in the political system."[111]

Another way to leverage reform of the Legislative Yuan would be to give it more authority to approve cross-Strait agreements. Currently, the LY has a rather limited role in this regard. True, the relevant officials consult with legislators before and during talks on each agreement and must provide reports and briefings to the appropriate committees of the LY.[112] But the Ma administration went by the letter of Article 5 of the Taiwan law governing cross-Strait relations, which specifies that any agreement should be submitted to the LY only "where the content of the agreement requires any amendment to laws or any new legislation." If no such action is necessary, the agreement is submitted to the legislature only "for record" and through a confidential procedure when necessary.[113] If an agreement involves issues of cross-Strait commerce or transportation but does not entail changes in existing law, the LY has the option of passing a resolution of disapproval within thirty days. In fact, the ECFA was the only agreement that required deliberation by the legislature, and in that case the Ma administration argued that it was an international agreement that did not affect the fundamental rights of citizens. Consequently, it was subject to an up-or-down vote and not subject to amendment.[114]

Ironically, during his first term, Ma Ying-jeou did not overtly use the advantage that Taiwan domestic politics might have conferred on him in negotiating agreements with China. Political scientists like Robert Putnam would be likely to suggest that his administration had the option of changing the law to provide the legislature with a more extensive role in order to increase the administration's bargaining power with Beijing. Clearly, priority was given to reducing legislative scrutiny, no doubt to minimize the possibility that parochial interests might excessively disrupt the administration's diplomacy.[115]

Just as ironically, the results of the 2012 election create even more incentives for Taiwan to take full advantage of the dynamics of what Putnam calls a "two-level game." Indeed, some on Taiwan have expressed anxiety that "the winner of [the 2012] presidential election will face more hurdles in talks with mainland China due to a diminished political mandate."[116] That Ma has relatively less political clout gives him an incentive to seek agreements with China that provide such clear benefits for Taiwan that they are more likely to obtain formal LY approval. To formalize this diminution of its autonomy, the administration could propose amendments to the law on cross-Strait relations whereby the LY would approve all cross-Strait agreements. Such a role makes sense since any future pacts will be more controversial than those of the first term.

There are legitimate reasons for Taiwan's negotiators to emphasize to their PRC counterparts the limits that public opinion places on their flexibility. One is that those limits are real. If the administration concludes a draft agreement that does not command public support, opponents have ways of scuttling it. Witness the LY's passage of legislation in late 2009 concerning market access for imports of foreign beef that essentially rejected an agreement that the Ma administration had negotiated with the United States. A second reason is that, should Beijing and Taipei ever get around to attempting a resolution of their fundamental dispute, they should work on the plausible assumption that the resulting agreement will require an amendment to the ROC constitution. The procedure is extremely demanding, requiring approval of a proposed amendment by both three-fourths of the members of the LY and 50 percent of *eligible* voters in a referendum. Because only around three-fourths of eligible voters generally cast ballots, passage of a referendum would require approval by 60-plus percent of those who actually vote. So both Beijing and Taipei should craft agreements that have broad public support.

Some positive steps have been taken concerning the media. The decision of the two political parties to end ownership of and other links to media organizations encouraged their separation from politics; whether the spirit of those changes has been honored is another question. Regulation of television and radio was transferred from the Government Information Office to the National Communications Commission, although disputes over membership limited its work for a while. Rawnsley argues that a reliance on the market mechanism to determine the number of media outlets or the quality of their "product" will neither protect the public against manipulation and interference nor ensure quality journalism. Instead, when it comes to programming, it produces a "race to the bottom"; therefore a greater yet still measured role for the state is necessary. Policy steps to reduce the number of newspapers, radio stations, and satellite television stations (high for an island of 23 million people) and so the competitive pressures among them might be a step in the right direction.[117] Ensuring greater transparency regarding the ownership, operations, and commercial side of media organizations and giving non-governmental organizations and media activists more of a say in deciding government policy on media content and on licensing of media organizations might also have positive impacts.[118] Yet finding the right level and scope of regulation will require time, experience, and measured reflection.[119]

The prospects for changing Taiwan's semi-presidential system are probably slim, since it is embedded in the ROC constitution. And, as indicated, passing a constitutional amendment is not easy, since it effectively requires super-majorities in both the legislature and a referendum and so a broad social consensus. Probably the best that can be done is to maximize coordination of policy both within the office of the president and the Executive Yuan and between them.

How might political polarization be addressed? If political actors take a zero-sum, "you live–I die" approach to politics, as they tend to do when "Deep" segments of each party dominate the political spectrum, compromising on policy becomes very difficult. But structural factors also influence the degree of polarization. The first has to do with the consequences of parties' electoral strategy. If, in a presidential election, the voters reject a candidate who pursues a strategy of playing to the base, the experience of defeat may have a moderating effect on future candidates from that party. In the 2012 election, the Deep Green wing of the DPP apparently restricted Tsai Ing-wen from adopting a more moderate China policy, which was one reason that she lost. The lesson seems to be that the DPP should take a different approach. Second is the method for drawing legislative districts. If the priority of those who draw district lines is to create homogeneous constituencies, it will likely encourage candidates to play to their party's base—as the United States has discovered with respect to elections to the House of Representatives. Less homogeneous districts give incentives to candidates to appeal to middle voters and thereby represent a broader range of views. Here, the record so far seems good. The process for drawing districts for the 2008 legislative elections was relatively fair and scientific, but it should be preserved.[120]

Another cause of polarization is an electoral system in which voters cast one ballot for a candidate for the legislature in their geographic election district and another for their preferred political party. The total vote that each party secures in the second vote determines how many candidates on its "party list" will become legislators.[121] Moderate candidates are more likely to be nominated for geographic seats where swing voters have an impact (assuming heterogeneous districts) while more "radical" candidates are placed on the list and do not have to face the voters. Removing the party list provision would reduce the polarization that it encourages but simultaneously would foster the principal defect of a pure single-member district, first-past-the-post system: overrepresentation in the legislature of the winning party.[122] Admittedly, any effort to get a different balance within the electoral system between representativeness and polarization is likely to fail because any change would require a constitutional amendment.

The reform of institutions along these lines, where possible, would likely enhance Taiwan's ability to fashion a more coherent policy toward the PRC. It would increase the probability that decisions on economic and security policy and on the ROC's self-definition would better reflect the mainstream national interest and the public's wishes. Obviously, making such decisions will not be easy, given the trade-offs that Taiwan faces in ensuring economic competitiveness, social welfare, and security. But a political system in which parochial minorities can block or distort policy choices to the detriment of the broader public interest does not serve Taiwan well. Among the casualties are sound policies for both the stabilization phase and any effort to resolve the fundamental dispute and, most important of all, the public's confidence in the system itself.

That is easy for me, an outsider, to say. But it is clearly hard to do. It will be necessary to construct a process to facilitate reform to remove the obstacles that actors in the current system impose in order to protect their parochial interests. Two elements of such a process come to mind. First, change is more likely if a draft reform agenda exists. Taiwan is blessed with many intelligent political scientists, lawyers, and former legislators. Perhaps a commission of such people might come together to develop, on a consensus basis, an agenda for political reform. It should be a centrist body, made up of individuals of Light Green and Light Blue perspectives. Second, to consider such a reform agenda, there will have to be an understanding between the moderate leaders of the Blue and Green camps that change is necessary. Leaders will have to let their subordinates—including those in the Legislative Yuan, where minorities can block legislation—know what is expected of them. Leaders will have to cope with one common problem of any reform process, which is that in the middle of the effort, no one is happy with the results, so they will have to sustain public support for the effort. In effect, I suggest that the same sort of cross-party process that Su Chi has suggested for China policy, in which specialists who span at least the center of the political spectrum seek to formulate policy consensus, should also be applied to the task of political reform.

Taiwan's Relationship with the United States

Finally, if Taiwan is going to strengthen itself and so reduce the likelihood of a PRC shift to pressure, positive ties with the United States will help.[123] U.S.-Taiwan relations did improve during the first Ma administration, particularly in the conduct of bilateral relations, and the United States took several steps to indicate its approval of Ma's cross-Strait policy. The Bush administration notified Congress of one major arms sales package after Ma came to power, and the Obama administration subsequently approved two. The Obama administration resumed visits to Taiwan by high-level economic officials. And in late 2011, Washington announced its intention to include Taiwan in the visa-waiver program, which will save time and money for the millions of Taiwan people who travel to the United States each year.

Yet there are a couple of other areas in which it is in Taiwan's national interest to deepen relations with the United States (including strengthening itself vis-à-vis Beijing), even if it is politically complicated to do so. The first area is economic. Above, I argue that if Taiwan is to ensure future competitiveness, it must liberalize its economic relations with all major trading partners, not just with China. Unless it does so, it risks being excluded from the circle of economic integration occurring within Asia and across the Pacific and ignored by companies in the countries that *are* included as they make trade and investment decisions. It will be more likely to become an economic appendage of China and less likely to remain what Shelley Rigger has called a "global powerhouse."[124]

The United States is key to Taiwan's multidirectional liberalization. It is still the world's largest economy and Taiwan's third-largest trading partner, after China and Japan. With a high level of per capita income, its consumers buy high-value products, including many of those that are manufactured or assembled in China for Taiwan firms. Washington controls access to high-standard multilateral arrangements like the Trans-Pacific Partnership (TPP), which would foster continued structural adjustment of the island's economy. Yet Taiwan has constrained itself by maintaining and even tightening barriers to American goods and services. The most serious case was market access for American beef. Due to political pressures concerning food safety, Taiwan ended up reneging on a formal agreement with the United States as well as an informal understanding on this issue. Consequently, American trade officials have come to doubt the credibility of any commitments that their Taipei counterparts make and have refused to discuss broader liberalization issues of interest to Taiwan until their confidence is restored.[125]

It was in Taiwan's interest to remove those problems unilaterally, so that liberalization discussions under the bilateral trade and investment framework agreement could resume. The Ma administration understood this logic, and it expended considerable political capital in order to get the LY to reopen the Taiwan market to American beef, which it did in July 2012.[126] Aiming for inclusion in TPP is a worthwhile *long-term* goal for Taiwan, but Taipei can have no illusions about the high bar that TPP sets, and the nagging feeling in the U.S. government is that Taiwan is incapable or unwilling to clear even low bars. Domestic political forces in Taiwan (farmers, doctors, and so forth) will oppose reform and unilateral steps, but this may be a case in which the interests of all should take precedence over the interests of a few.

Taiwan will, no doubt, worry that Beijing will exert pressure on any of its major trading partners who consider undertaking liberalization negotiations with Taiwan. Beijing might take the position, for example, that such agreements violate the one-China principle. Actually, China lacks a legal basis to oppose such pacts, for the rules of the World Trade Organization permit "special customs territories"—which was the status that Taiwan used to enter the WTO—to conclude free trade agreements with their trading partners. It might have a stronger argument if Taiwan were seeking such agreements in ways that suggested that it was a country equivalent to China, through, for example, use of a particular nomenclature. But that is not an issue. Taiwan is prepared to use terminology for itself and for an agreement that does not create "two-China" issues. Beijing's pressure would be more political in nature—for example, leveraging its own relations with any Taiwan trading partners, particularly smaller countries, to get them to back off. That is another reason that the United States—which is least likely to submit to Beijing's view of what is acceptable and what is not—should also be Taiwan's most attractive candidate for liberalization. The United States, Japan, and the European economies are less likely to accommodate China—*if* they believe that it is in their economic interest to liberalize with Taiwan.

Moreover, Taiwan can make a case to Beijing when it comes to trade liberalization deals with its major trading partners by conveying a simple message: this is an important way of expanding the island's international space that does not just boost Taiwan's dignity but is also critical to the island's prosperity. If Beijing undermines Taiwan's global strategy to secure its competitiveness, it will have no hope of achieving its long-term political goals. Thus, Taipei may turn what seems like a point of weakness to its advantage.

In addition to trade liberalization, security is an area in which Taipei can continue to improve relations with the United States. The Ma administration has taken some important steps by reducing what Washington feared during the 1995–2008 period: that Taiwan and China would slip into a conflict through accident or miscalculation. Those steps gave first the Bush and then the Obama administration the confidence to go forward with major arms sales. Yet the gap between China's offensive power and Taiwan's defensive capabilities continues to grow. And there is a gap between Washington and Taipei in how they look at their security relationship—that is, between the military utility of U.S. arms sales and the broader political commitment that they reflect. Taiwan emphasizes the political importance of arms sales and the psychological confidence that they produce. The U.S. government does not dismiss the commitment value of arms sales but believes that the weapons should be militarily useful as well.

Taiwan's emphasis on the political aspect of arms sales reduces its incentive to better align its procurement decisions with a sensible defense strategy. As Peter Lavoy noted, "lasting security cannot be achieved simply by purchasing limited numbers of advanced weapons systems."[127] In order to reduce Taiwan's insecurity vis-à-vis the PLA, Taiwan should, as suggested above, objectively reassess its threat environment, defense strategy, force structure, and procurements and do so in coordination with the United States. The hope is that it would pursue American systems that not only reflect the U.S. commitment to Taiwan's security but also are militarily useful and so reduce China's temptation to undertake a campaign of coercive pressure.

Conclusion

A serious effort by Taiwan to strengthen its sense of sovereignty, economic competitiveness, security, political system, and U.S. relationship will not guarantee a completely satisfactory outcome with China. What is certain is that refusal to engage in self-strengthening or failure to do it well will give Beijing significant advantages in how it deals with Taiwan, whether through mutual persuasion or exploiting power asymmetry, and in how its fundamental dispute with the island's government is ultimately resolved. Taiwan's most important asset is confidence that it has been and will be able to act to promote the island's prosperity and security and that it has a political system that is effective enough to make decisions that are in the best interests of Taiwan's people. But Taiwan can create that confidence only through what are primarily its own efforts. To ignore what is at stake, to make bad choices through a dysfunctional political system, or to give up because the challenge is too hard are all bad options.

9

What China Might Do

Staying within the paradigm of mutual persuasion is certainly good for Taiwan, because it means that whatever choices it makes about the medium- and long-term future will be voluntary. It is also good for the United States, because it will avoid having to decide what to do in complex circumstances in which Taipei faces Chinese pressure, a scenario that is technically peaceful because there is no violence but in which coercion is still present.

I would also argue that it is also in China's interest to continue mutual persuasion and its effort to convince Taiwan's leaders and its public that an increasingly close relationship with the Mainland—even a resolution of the fundamental dispute—is good for the island. The main reason for doing so is quite practical: the dynamics of Taiwan politics. Although a majority of the public appears to favor the Ma administration's policy approach, it is not a large majority, and what that majority has endorsed so far are steps where the benefits to Taiwan outweigh the costs. The public is more cautious on political and security issues, because it fears that on those issues the cost-benefit ratio will be reversed. Skepticism turns to outright opposition when it comes to China's proposal for unification. That is perfectly understandable, because most Taiwan people are more comfortable with the status quo than with an alternative that is vague at best and perhaps unknowable. Not only would they be unable to judge fully the implications of a unification agreement; at least some Taiwan people would view unification through the lens of history and memories of KMT authoritarianism and see a dark future. Their fears of yet another round of constraints imposed by a new group of Chinese outsiders may be unfounded, but the reality of their fears is what counts. Some PRC analysts interpreted Ma's 2012 victory—erroneously—to mean that he was actually lagging behind Taiwan public opinion and that he had no reason not to catch up.[1] For Chinese officials to think that they understand Taiwan politics better than Ma does would be a mistake.

The depth of this certainty-uncertainty dilemma will depend on the terms of any agreement that the two sides reach to resolve the fundamental cross-Strait dispute. Specifically, how the sovereignty issue is addressed in such a deal will dictate the mechanism by which it is approved in Taiwan. A solution that requires legislative approval will be hard enough to achieve, because members of the Legislative Yuan (LY) do not wish to open themselves to the charge that they are "selling out Taiwan." As discussed in chapter 8, amending the ROC constitution requires supermajorities both in the legislature and in a public referendum. So without a broad consensus of the major parties and of the public at large, it would be difficult to ensure that an agreement would endure and not provoke chronic partisan bickering, instability, and polarization.

Beijing should therefore work under the assumption that any effort to coerce unification—even a nonviolent effort—would be blocked, if not in the LY then through a referendum. It should also assume that any offers that it made in a persuasion mode would have to be immensely attractive to secure approval. And, of course, the implications of unification for Taiwan's sense of security—will the PLA be on Taiwan?—would also affect support for any accord.

Also, China should continue persuasion, with the attendant willingness to accommodate somewhat the views of the other party, for the sake of its international image. Other countries, particularly nations in East Asia, will be watching how Beijing pursues its Taiwan objectives for clues about how it will behave toward them. A willingness to resort to pressure and leverage and the exploitation of power asymmetries will only increase anxieties that the same tactics will be used against them and so shape perceptions about the trajectory of China's revival as a great power. Such an inference on the part of China's neighbors may not be valid, but it is their views that count.

Finally, Beijing might modulate its use of tactics that Taiwan might perceive as indicators of preparations to shift from mutual persuasion to a campaign of political pressure (chapter 7 identifies some of them). To continue these tactics only makes persuasion more difficult because of the mistrust that they engender. Instead, China should

—permit Taipei to negotiate economic liberalization accords with its other trading partners to reduce Taiwan's exclusive economic dependence on the PRC

—be more flexible on Taiwan's participation in international organizations

—play down efforts to foster a Chinese identity on the island

—continue social and culture exchange but avoid any pointed political message

—rethink the idea that it can "buy" the political loyalty of Taiwan people through economic incentives

—cease demonizing those on Taiwan who seek de jure independence

—play up the view that "peaceful development" is a long-term process and play down the inevitability of unification

—at election time on Taiwan, do not point out the costs of choosing leaders hostile to China

—suspend the acquisition of military capabilities relevant to Taiwan and tolerate U.S. arms sales.

The remainder of the chapter discusses some more general things that Beijing can do to stay within the paradigm of mutual persuasion.

Clarify Mistrust and Its Sources

In March 2012, Wang Yi, director of the PRC Taiwan Affairs Office, stressed the following in a major speech: "The further cross-Strait relations go, the more necessary it becomes for both parties to cherish mutual trust and also to enhance and expand mutual trust. Only if we do this, will we then be able to effectively manage and control disagreements. Also, we can do a better job to gather common things together and resolve disagreements."[2] His emphasis on trust is both entirely proper and another way to address the matter of mutual persuasion. Yet it is useful to clarify the different sources from which mistrust can flow, something that any effort to reduce mistrust must take into account.

The first source of mistrust is simple misunderstanding: that two parties look at the same set of facts concerning each other's actions and draw very different conclusions about what those behaviors say about underlying intentions. Ma Ying-jeou may seek to expand Taiwan's international space to improve the economy's competitiveness (through trade liberalization agreements with other East Asian economies) or to improve the KMT's political position at home (by showing that its strategy of engaging Beijing on international organizations is more successful than provoking Beijing). Yet some in China may conclude that those initiatives reflect a desire for "peaceful separation" by solidifying Taiwan as a "second China." Beijing may believe that it is necessary to continue its military buildup in order to maximize its ability to deter Taiwan independence and to limit the ability of the United States to come to Taiwan's defense in the event of a conflict. But Taipei may see its growing capabilities as increasing China's capacity for coercion through intimidation or worse.

Such misunderstanding may occur in a variety of ways. It may happen when one side is ignorant in some way about the reality at hand and views the actions of the other too harshly or too lightly. It can occur when two parties reach an agreement through compromise but have different interpretations of what the words of the compromise mean. It is often the result of flawed analysis by the intelligence agencies of the two parties, with the result that policymakers make bad decisions based on misperceptions. In the case of China and Taiwan, neither side is immune from flawed analysis. Misunderstanding may also stem from a pathology known as attribution error: the tendency to judge one's own actions in the best possible light and those of the adversary in the worst. (Thus, Taiwan: "How could China possibly imagine that our search for international space is something other than a desire for dignity?" China: "Can't Taiwan people understand that we have reasons to improve our military capabilities that have nothing to do with them?")

The second source of mistrust is problems in implementation of agreements. Of course, problems may occur first of all because one party to an understanding has no intention to fulfill its stated obligations; in that case, mistrust is justified. But they may occur also because policymakers come to an agreement in good faith but then one side or both cannot secure the domestic political support to carry out its commitments. In 1979, China questioned the intentions of the Carter administration when Congress passed the Taiwan Relations Act, which Beijing interpreted as reversing the U.S. government's commitments under the normalization communiqué. Sometimes, political leaders make commitments to another country that they have every intention of fulfilling but then cannot because the agencies of their own government act contrary to the commitments.[3] The United States has secured many PRC pledges over the years on the protection of intellectual property rights, but the central government has been unable to secure satisfactory implementation at lower levels. The end result in both cases is that the party to which the commitments were made draws larger conclusions about the intentions of the other.

Third, mistrust can arise for the simple reason that two parties have conflicting goals. The actions of each reflect those differences and confirm the other's suspicions about long-term intentions. In this case, mutual mistrust has a factual basis.

Two conclusions can be derived from the different sources of mistrust. First, domestic forces, such as intelligence agencies, scholars, bloggers, government agencies with their own agendas, and so on, can shape how one party views the other. If mistrust is to be reduced, leaders on each side will have to rectify the internal institutional reasons for suspicion. This is true in particular for implementation failings. Second, any effort to mitigate mistrust between two parties must be tailored to the underlying source. Creating dialogue mechanisms may be useful to clarify true misunderstandings and provide reassurance, but they are probably useless in a situation of conflicting goals. In that case, creative management is usually the best that can be achieved. Conversely, steps taken to cope with a situation of conflicting goals would not be appropriate for a simple misunderstanding.

Be Smart about Questions of Taiwan Identity

In earlier chapters I observe that when it comes to nationalism, different Taiwan people identify with their island in different ways. The national loyalty of Deep Green people (about a quarter of the population) is based on geography and their definition of ethnicity and culture. They assert that Taiwan is in no way part of China. Other Taiwan people might be prepared to accept the idea that Taiwan is geographically and culturally a part of the Chinese nation (broadly defined), but they still have a strong attachment to the island as their home. Theirs is probably more a civic nationalism that identifies with the Republic of China and its democratic system.[4] Beijing, however, has focused only on the separatist nationalism of the 25 percent and has sought to reduce it. But it has yet to address the civic nationalism of the remaining 75 percent. It will have to do so if it wishes to advance its goals.

Not only does national identity have different dimensions, it also takes a long time to form and then to change. Taiwanese political nationalism did not suddenly materialize during the presidencies of Lee Teng-hui and Chen Shuibian. As noted, it took shape in the forty years after the KMT first arrived on the island in 1945, in a response to the KMT's repression. Although the Mainlanders who accompanied Chiang Kai-shek and the Kuomintang were attached to the ROC from the beginning, Taiwan's civic nationalism has been fired more in the crucible of the democratic system that emerged after 1986, reaffirming the loyalties of Mainlanders and capturing those of native Taiwanese alike. It should be no surprise therefore that the public's attachment to Taiwan and the ROC remains strong and has grown, even as benefits have flowed from cross-Strait economic relations. As previously noted, a television network poll from early 2011 found that 50 percent of those surveyed said that they were Taiwanese alone, 3 percent said that they were Chinese, and 43 percent said that they were "both Taiwanese and Chinese."[5] Shelley Rigger is probably correct in noting that the political nationalism of the Deep Greens is declining, but she is also right in noting that most people see Taiwan as their homeland and that the transition to more pragmatic attitudes toward China is generational in its pace.[6]

Beijing has emphasized culture as an important dimension of the "peaceful development" of cross-Strait relations. It has done so partly to strengthen the Chinese sense of identity on Taiwan and to diminish the strength of the Taiwanese identity. Doing so may well serve its goal of opposing Taiwan independence, but that covers only part of the identity problem; it does not speak to the civic nationalism that identifies with the ROC and all that it means. (Among some Taiwanese, any PRC effort to strip them of their "Taiwaneseness" constitutes even more evidence that it cannot be trusted to treat them well.)

But if Beijing decides to take seriously Taiwan's civic nationalism—its attachment to the ROC—it will face a dilemma. On the one hand, altering the civic nationalism aspect of Taiwan identity will likely be more difficult and take longer than mitigating the political nationalism of advocates of Taiwan independence—if it can be altered at all. That would raise doubts in China about whether unification will ever take place. On the other hand, accommodating Taiwan civic nationalism and the ROC, which is an option, would likely require a significant change in Beijing's one-country, two-systems formula for unification.

After Ma Ying-jeou's reelection, some Chinese scholars worried about the persistence of Taiwanese identity and its implications for achievement of Beijing's goals. Wang Jianmin, a scholar at the Taiwan Studies Institute of the Chinese Academy of Sciences, argued after the 2012 election that the policies of the KMT and the DPP were converging and differed only in name, not in substance. Consequently, he warned, "the formation and development of 'Taiwan subjective consciousness' [i.e., Taiwan identity] does not benefit the development of cross-Strait relations, and what is more will not benefit the peaceful unification of the country."[7] Leaving aside Wang's premise concerning a DPP–KMT convergence (which I dispute), his conclusion is sound *only if* Beijing assumes two things. The first is that Taiwan identity is tantamount to a desire for de jure independence, which it is not. The second is that China itself cannot be sufficiently creative to achieve unification on terms that accommodate the attachment that Taiwan people feel toward their homeland and to the Republic of China. Any calculation that strengthening the Chinese identity of the island's people is the way to suppress Taiwan identity and promote unification is probably flawed.

Taiwan's competing national identities are important not just because of how they relate to the substantive interaction between the two sides. They also affect the decisions that the Taipei government makes on all policy issues, but particularly those concerning China. The negative public and media response to Ma's October 2011 announcement about a peace accord (see chapter 5) is a clear, recent example of the limits that identity imposes. And although Taiwan's leaders have the responsibility to educate and lead public opinion, there are limits to their ability to do so. They cannot turn night into day. No leaders can take policy initiatives without first convincing the public that they have the island's best interests at heart. And Taiwan leaders who happen to be Mainlanders, like Ma Ying-jeou, have the additional burden of answering the allegation that they will sell out Taiwan simply because they are Mainlanders. If Chinese leaders do not understand the constraints under which their counterparts on the island operate, they are liable to undermine their own goals.

Talk More to the DPP

Beyond the general issue of Taiwan identity, there is the specific question of whether and how Beijing interacts with the Democratic Progressive Party, the main political force on the island that has goals that are antithetical to China's and that voices opposition to Ma Ying-jeou's policies. Thus far, the PRC's default approach has been to decline to talk with any representatives of the DPP in their DPP capacity. That is because in 1991 the party had formally stated the goals of establishing an independent country to be called "the Republic of Taiwan' and of promulgating a new constitution—goals to which the PRC is fundamentally opposed. Beijing therefore was generally unwilling to have any dealings with the Chen Shui-bian administration from 2000 to 2008. The only exception has been to meet sometimes with DPP figures who are willing to act in another, non-party capacity (as professors at such-and-such a university, for example).

Beijing has kept the DPP at a distance for a couple of reasons. On the one hand, it has generally believed that the party's goals are more than traditional rhetoric and that it really does wish to establish a Republic of Taiwan. Given that belief, China sees the DPP's goals as being in direct conflict with China's; it therefore has just cause to mistrust the DPP and so oppose it at every turn. To engage with it, perhaps through some type of dialogue, would only reward a hostile adversary and undermine Chinese interests. On the other hand, Beijing's stance toward the DPP is designed to have a political impact within Taiwan—to minimize the party's support and to increase the chances that the KMT will remain in power. So during the 2012 election campaign, PRC officials regularly stated that the way to achieve good cross-

Strait relations was to oppose Taiwan independence and adhere to the 1992 consensus, two things that it could be pretty sure that the DPP would not do. That was part of its broader united front strategy, one element of which is to marginalize one's "enemy."[8]

Yet, drawing on the different sources of mistrust above, China cannot be absolutely certain that it has reason to believe that its goals are in mutual conflict with those of the DPP. One good way to test that proposition is to engage in serious discussions with interlocutors from the DPP. Such conversations might in fact reveal that what it thought were conflicting goals was a simple misunderstanding, and that the talk of Taiwan independence is traditional rhetoric that has no consequence for the policies of a DPP government if and when it came to power. Even if it becomes clear that China and the DPP really do have conflicting goals, management of differences is an alternative to unqualified opposition and rejection of contact. But management does require communication. China itself was willing to have diplomatic contact with the United States during the cold war, even though the two countries really did have conflicting goals.

There have been hints that Beijing and the DPP may have some room for flexibility. On the Chinese side, there was a suggestion from private discussions during the summer of 2011 that the 1992 consensus was not the only way to convey a commitment to one China. If the DPP was opposed to that formula, perhaps another could be devised. That was certainly an interesting signal.[9] On the DPP side, Frank Hsieh Chang-ting, a prominent DPP leader, has periodically floated the formula of a "constitutional one China" as a basis for engagement between Beijing and the DPP. He argues that for better or worse, the ROC constitution is a one-China document and that the chances of amending that aspect of it are slim to none. So, he says, "the ROC Constitution should be used to seek the greatest interests of the Taiwan people, conduct exchanges with mainland China, and maintain stability in Taiwan."[10] At least one respected PRC scholar has responded positively to Hsieh's approach.[11]

It is true that the PRC quickly and publicly rejected the news that it was open to alternatives to the 1992 consensus, probably because it was inconsistent with its electoral strategy of isolating the DPP. The DPP has a problem with the 1992 consensus not because it includes any specific wording but because it expresses a commitment to one China and, by implication, to the view that the territory of Taiwan is a part of that China. It is also true that Frank Hsieh is not in the mainstream of DPP thinking on policy toward China and that Chinese scholars are generally skeptical of the import of any signs of new thinking from the party.[12] Yet if ideas like Hsieh's are to gain traction within the DPP and become the basis for more effective management of conflicting goals, then it probably is necessary to have an official signal from Beijing that it regards them as a basis for interaction.

As much as China would like to assume that the DPP will never again win the presidency in Taiwan, it cannot afford to do so. It is the nature of democratic systems that the party out of power does not remain so indefinitely. And China's efforts to avoid that eventuality by reducing DPP's domestic support through economic inducements to its loyal voters—to farmers in the southern part of the island, for example—has apparently not worked (see chapter 6). Beijing should regard engagement of the DPP not as a favor to its adversary but as a way of protecting its own interest in the effective management of a difficult relationship if and when the party returns to power.

Construct an Acceptable Conceptual Foundation

China must not only help lay a *political* foundation in Taiwan for further stabilization of cross-Strait relations, it must also work on a *conceptual* foundation for the discussion of political and security issues that is acceptable to Taiwan's leaders and most of its public. Otherwise, it appears, progress will stop in the economic area and the prospects for the longer-term future will be uncertain at best. Indeed, Shanghai scholar Zhang Nianchi warns that absent a proper foundation, pushing forward on cross-Strait relations would be dangerous.[13]

The easiest way for Beijing to broaden stabilization beyond the economic arena is to adopt the same negotiating basis for the political and security arenas that the two sides have used so far. That is the 1992 consensus, whereby the Ma administration has associated Taiwan with one China but asserted its own interpretation: that "China" is the Republic of China. Beijing has tolerated that disagreement-within-agreement for economic and cultural relations but has indicated that a more explicit definition of what one China is will be required to achieve any sort of political framework or peace accord.[14] There is a logic to that position: negotiating a political framework and a peace accord requires a specificity concerning the political and legal relationship of the parties to the agreement that is not as necessary when it comes to economic relations. For two decades, however, the two sides have held mutually contradictory positions, particularly over the issue of the ROC. Moreover, it must be acknowledged that for Beijing to use the 1992 consensus for political and security issues amounts to deferring an inevitable decision about the conceptual basis for resolving the fundamental dispute. Doing so does not foreclose options but may in fact make the preferred option more difficult to achieve.[15]

To mitigate the stalemate, Beijing has sought to expand common ground with Taiwan concerning the content of the idea of one-China. In particular, its officials and scholars placed more emphasis on the need for the two sides to "deepen the common understanding that both sides of the Taiwan Strait belong to one and the same China."[16] That formulation both reflected the long-standing PRC view that the island is a part of China and recognized that some people on Taiwan reject that view. It conveys an understanding that some on the island are motivated by a nationalism that is ethno-cultural in nature. But confining the discussion to which territories belong to the state called China ignores the question of the political and legal character of the authorities that govern Taiwan and the fact that other people on the island identify more with its democratic political system. In effect, Beijing's approach ignores the issues of the ROC.

Beijing's dilemma showed up in its dissatisfaction about Ma's devotion to the ROC during his first term. Thus, Sun Zhe, a well-informed scholar at Tsinghua University in Beijing, reported that despite the decline of "Taiwan independence forces" after Ma Ying-jeou won his first election, Beijing has "deep suspicions" that he intends to maintain Taiwan's separation in perpetuity even if he does not seek a state called the Republic of Taiwan.[17] He is seen as not being active in promoting unification and as doing nothing to "direct public opinion" that way.[18] Yet unless Beijing demonstrates more flexibility on this political issue, a permanent stall in cross-Strait relations is likely. Taipei also will be looking to the PRC to restrain its acquisition of combat capabilities.

What are the chances that Beijing, in order to advance its political agenda, would accommodate Taipei on the issue of the existence of the ROC? To do so in a meaningful way would jump-start cross-Strait relations. It would signal what it would be—a major change in the Chinese position and a willingness to take Taiwan's fundamental concerns into account. Such a decision would probably require abandoning the PRC's long-standing position that the ROC does not exist, restraining its campaign to isolate Taiwan in the international community, and changing the essence of the one-country, two-systems formula for unification because under that formula the second system is not a sovereign entity. It is a choice that might have implications for the use of the one-country, two-systems formula for Hong Kong and Macau and perhaps for the larger Communist Party political order.[19] It also would foster confidence that a settlement of the fundamental conflict that the island's people could live with might actually be possible.

At least some scholars in China understand the need to address the issue. Zhang Huangmin writes: "The core issue in whether or not the mainland will

acknowledge the 'Republic of China' as a principal of constitutional government order is that it must view the 'Republic of China' as a qualified dialogue
principal [or entity]."[20] Chen Qimao writes that Taiwan's view that the ROC is
"a sovereign state . . . is a very difficult and sensitive problem . . . which, if not
dealt with appropriately, could trigger tensions between the two sides at any
time."[21] Chu Shulong also regards the matter of whether the two governments
can "recognize each [the PRC and the ROC] as legal governments within the
'one China'" as a long-standing and difficult problem.[22] Zhang Nianchi calls it
a "forbidden zone" that the PRC "must face" because people on Taiwan regard
a failure by Beijing to recognize the ROC as a form of decapitation.[23]

How exactly the PRC would address its ROC problem is not so clear; if it
were, there would have been a solution long ago. It likely entails acknowledg-
ing that the governing authorities in Taipei are a sovereign entity for international, cross-Strait, and Taiwan domestic purposes. The hypothetical
conceptual space for a political union among sovereign entities includes
arrangements like confederation and federation. This sort of dual-sovereignty
set-up has been more common in North America and Western Europe than
it has in East Asia,[24] but perhaps smart people in Taiwan and China can formulate an innovative and mutually acceptable approach to the problem. At a
minimum, however, the Chinese will have to do more "homework" to determine what is conceptually and politically possible.

Past experience suggests that Beijing will have a difficult time coming to
terms with the ROC. Long-standing orthodoxy, the memories of the Lee Teng-
hui and Chen Shui-bian periods (which led to greater emphasis on the "one-
China principle" as the heart of Chinese policy), and the institutional
commitment of the Ministry of Foreign Affairs to the international marginalization of Taipei's goals are all obstacles against it. Even if Beijing were to adopt
the 1992 consensus as the starting point for cross-Strait discussions on political and security issues, it would still be a significant step, based on the judgment
that avoiding a stall is more important than upholding orthodoxy. That judgment and decision would probably have to come from the top leadership.

There is another thing that Beijing can do to increase Taiwan's confidence
on political issues. That would be to continue to move toward full, representative democracy in Hong Kong. One key step is to move to universal suffrage,
whereby the entire electorate would vote on who should be their chief executive and for the members of the Legislative Council. For the legislature, that
requires elimination of the distorting effects of functional constituencies,
which give some social groups—at least some of them friendly to the PRC
government—a much greater degree of representation than the voters of

geographic districts. For the chief executive, full democracy also requires a liberalization of the current nomination process—which is controlled by a small circle of social and economic elites—so that candidates that Beijing does not like can actually get on the ballot and have a chance of winning public approval. Finally, Beijing would have to be willing to accept opposition politicians' gaining control of the executive or legislature, or both. Such accommodations would be important signals that China is prepared to work with whomever the Taiwan public chooses for the island's leadership.

Reduce Taiwan's Security Fears

Beijing should consider adjusting its approach to the military dimension of cross-Strait relations. That would not be easy because it would require an unusual shift in strategic culture and in the assumption that the best way for China to protect and promote its interests is to accumulate power and apply it through pressure and leverage. There is also the Chinese tendency to exaggerate the challenge that an adversary poses to PRC interests. The idea that Beijing could increase its security by moderating its threat assessment and exercising restraint in the acquisition and use of power is quite novel.

The first step that China can take is to acknowledge that it has successfully achieved its immediate goal of deterring Taiwan independence. It has accumulated sufficient military and other power to punish any Taiwan leader who undertook a serious initiative to separate the island from China permanently; the costs for Taipei are simply too high. Moreover, its fears of Taiwan identity, as discussed, are exaggerated.

Indeed, a key part of China's deterrent, one that is probably as effective as its coercive might, is the democratic system on Taiwan and the constraint that it imposes on any adventurism by a future Taiwan leader. The same system that enhanced China's fear of Taiwan independence in the late twentieth century is becoming a hidden defender of China's interests in the twenty-first. Increasingly, the Taiwan public has become so sensitized to the dangers of Taiwan independence for cross-Strait cooperation that it is becoming impossible for an avowed advocate of independence to win a presidential election. Even if a "covert" proponent of separatism were to win, there are checks within the system (for example, the structural advantage that the KMT possesses in the legislature) against a radical initiative. If between 20 and 25 percent of those surveyed tell pollsters that they supports independence sooner or later, that means, in effect, that more than 70 percent are likely to oppose that objective.[25] Moreover, younger generations of Taiwanese appear more pragmatic about China than their elders: "Taiwan identity often coexists with neutral or positive views of China. For the [youngest] generation in particular, there is no contradiction between loving Taiwan and seeking one's fortune on the Mainland."[26]

Some in China understand the positive trends in Taiwan opinion. Shanghai scholar Zhang Nianchi expresses confidence in the evolution of the Taiwan political system:

> Some believe that certain parties out of power in Taiwan and those who vote for them still support "Taiwan Independence" and that there is a risk of "Taiwan Independence" making a comeback, so that the current period represents a risk rather than an opportunity. But in my opinion, we should believe that the compatriots in Taiwan will act wisely, as they vetoed the path of "Taiwan Independence" in 2008. . . . Even in the heyday of the reign of the DPP, I pointed out in an article that "Taiwan Independence" is just a "cold" which will be cured by Taiwan compatriots. It has been evident that Taiwan's "democratization" has determined its constant restructuring and that even the DPP is now changing its understanding on "three direct links," "communication," "cooperation," "dialogue," "ECFA," etc. It is impossible for the DPP to take office if it continues going against public opinion. The Taiwanese are also aware that "localization" must not be based on "de-Sinification" and that loving Taiwan is not supposed and is impossible to be grounds for a "split." In this regard, we should be more self-confident.[27]

Of course, the other component of China's deterrent, which it does not necessarily acknowledge but has not been shy to mobilize, is the United States. Before the 2004 and 2008 Taiwan presidential elections, for example, Washington acted in subtle yet clear ways to oppose actions by President Chen Shui-bian that created fears in Beijing of a breakout.

In effect, China should lower its threat assessment. Arguably, the forces on Taiwan that fostered its fears have weakened. The threat that Taiwan poses to China's political aspirations has declined and is unlikely to equal again the threat that China perceived during the Lee Teng-hui and Chen Shui-bian administrations. China's deterrent against that threat has worked and removed Taiwan independence from the island's political agenda. If Taiwan's willingness and ability to "attack" China's political interests has declined, the security dilemma between the two can become less intense, but only if Beijing is willing to adjust its own approach.

China also should consider better aligning its defense strategy with its security strategy. Its security strategy, the essence of peaceful development, has sought both to deter independence and to create circumstances that will lead to the end of Taiwan's separation. But ending separation is fundamentally a political transaction that must be approved within Taiwan's political system. If fears persist on Taiwan concerning China's goals and motivations, then that transaction is not likely to occur. The PRC's defense strategy and the growing force structure that has supported it fit well with the first and immediate part of the security strategy, and, as discussed, it has succeeded. But it seems that Beijing will be more successful in making progress on the second part if it restrains its military buildup in order to enhance Taiwan's sense of security. Only if Taiwan's security strategy succeeds will China's also succeed.

What could China do that would truly reduce Taiwan's insecurity—and so increase its own? The first and most important step is to place limits on the offensive capabilities most relevant to Taiwan, which enhance deterrence but also have enhanced the credibility of a pressure or coercion approach. Thinking in the abstract, without any regard to what Chinese strategists might instinctively reject, the following steps come to mind:

—Suspend procurement of systems that would be at the heart of any compellence initiative, including short- and medium-range ballistic and cruise missiles, mobile and fixed air defenses deployed on the Taiwan Strait, and amphibious landing craft.

—Withdraw and place in storage mobile versions of those systems.

—Disable the infrastructure for the ballistic and cruise missiles.

—Suspend exercises associated with a coercion initiative.

—Where feasible, create mechanisms for verification of the storage of weapons and the disablement of missile infrastructure, preferably by a third party (not the United States).

Some in China are certain to argue that the PLA's modernization has objectives besides deterring Taiwan independence. That is true, but Beijing should be willing and able to exercise the greatest restraint with respect to the systems that create the greatest vulnerability for Taiwan. Chinese will no doubt assert that the danger of Taiwan independence still exists so a deterrent must exist as well. The fear is real, but, as argued, it rests on an anachronistic understanding of the threat. Moreover, if there indeed was a return to the dynamics that existed before Ma Ying-jeou's election, China should be able to reconstitute its deterrent force rapidly enough to make a difference. And, as also noted, during the period that Beijing saw the greatest danger, it relied more on the United States than it did on its own military power to contain Lee Teng-hui and Chen Shui-bian.

Second, China might better modulate the deployment and readiness of its Taiwan-relevant capabilities so that they track changes in the political relationship and do so in ways that are readily observable. If the cross-Strait policies of Taiwan's government are favorable to China's interests and reduce its fears, at least for the medium term, Beijing should adjust where it puts its forces and how frequently it exercises them and do so in ways that Taiwan can observe.

Finally, just as China should reduce the vulnerability that its offensive capabilities create for Taiwan, it should be willing to tolerate Taipei's procurements that enhance Taiwan's defensive posture. Beijing has opposed such acquisitions on the grounds that their purpose was to "use arms to resist peace" and to "use arms to resist reunification."[28] Yet the premise of that opposition was that Taiwan was seriously seeking independence. If that PRC premise were to change, as I argue it should, then China should be willing to accept a Taiwan force structure that is designed to resist unification by force. China could improve its own security if Taiwan were to feel less vulnerable.

Stop Blaming the United States

China has a tendency to attribute its failure to achieve its political goals concerning Taiwan to policies and actions of the United States. Blaming America began way back in 1950, when Washington resumed security assistance to the ROC government (something that probably would not have happened if communist North Korea had not invaded South Korea). It continues to the present day. Continuing U.S. arms sales to Taiwan remain the focus of China's assertion, based on the long-standing assumption that the advanced weaponry transferred so enhances Taipei's confidence that it is unwilling to negotiate. The American view has been that if Taiwan has a deep sense of vulnerability it will not be willing to talk and that it will be willing to negotiate with Beijing only if it has the moderate degree of confidence that U.S. security cooperation provides.

The PRC faults the United States on the political front as well. Wang Jianmin of the Academy of Social Sciences argued in April 2012 that Washington, as part of its strategy for containing China, had pressured Taipei to refuse to negotiate on political issues, conclude a peace accord, or agree to military confidence-building measures. Indeed, for Wang, the United States was the principal reason for the lack of progress in those areas.[29] He draws that conclusion in spite of authoritative statements by the U.S. government that it approves of the cross-Strait progress that has occurred and that it specifically "looks forward to efforts by both sides to increase dialogues and interactions in economic, political, and *other* fields."[30]

In fact, U.S. security or political support for Taiwan is not the reason that China has failed to achieve its political goals regarding Taiwan. The obstacle to unification on China's terms is that it has not hitherto offered an approach to resolving the fundamental dispute that the island's government and public deem worthy of consideration. Beijing has focused on the minority that favors Taiwan independence and ignored the broad majority that opposes the one-country, two-systems formula. Arms from the United States may fortify that opposition, but they do not create it. Hence, the United States need not atone for an alleged offense against the Chinese nation by ending the U.S.-Taiwan security relationship. It is not the panacea that some propose.

Political Reform

Finally, would China more easily achieve its political goals concerning Taiwan if it became a democratic system? Polling in Taiwan up into the first decade of the 2000s suggests that people on the island take the Mainland's political system into account when they consider what they want for the future and what they are prepared to risk.[31] Their logic, probably, is that a China that is authoritarian is more likely to renege later on the conciliatory commitments that it makes now than a China that is not.

That does not mean that a democratic China would necessarily be more reliable than one that is not. There is a long-standing view that democracies are less likely to go to war with each other than nondemocratic countries are to fight with other authoritarian nations and democracies. Yet more recent research has concluded that the idea of "democratic peace" is truer of mature, institutionalized democracies than it is of ones that have only recently made the transition to democratic governance. Edward Mansfield and Jack Levy found strong support for the hypothesis that countries in the midst of "incomplete democratization" are more likely to initiate war and become involved in war. Politically, democratizing nations exhibit a strong, exclusive type of nationalism, and institutions within such nations that can channel and mitigate pressures for aggressive foreign policies are weak. Instead, elites play to nationalistic publics to sustain their power. It is only in democracies with consolidated democratic institutions that the inclination to war declines.[32] Elements of the Chinese public are already strongly nationalistic, and they exert pressure on foreign policy decisionmakers to take robust action in response to real or imagined external insults. If an authoritarian China is already having trouble channeling and mitigating anti-foreign nationalism, imagine the difficulties that a newly democratized Chinese political system would have. I hope that China will someday become a full democracy, but I worry that during any such transition it will become more dangerous externally than it already is.

That unhappy conclusion does not mean that there is nothing that China can do now about its internal system that would increase Taiwan's confidence in a deepening reconciliation. Ma Ying-jeou has spoken of the need for increased political participation, improvement of human rights and the rule of law, and the emergence of civil society: "This will reduce the feeling of 'otherness' between people on the two sides of the Taiwan Strait."[33]

Probably the most important measure is to institute the rule of law. China did create a legal system of sorts during the reform period that began in 1979. But however good it is on paper, its implementation is erratic at best. The laws and procedures of the Chinese legal system do not bind local authorities if and when they see a reason to violate them. The case of Chen Guangchen, the blind human rights lawyer who was convicted unjustly and then held under house arrest after serving his full sentence—a situation known to the central government—demonstrates the impunity under which local authorities operate. So it is no accident, as seen in previous chapters, that Taiwan people who lived and worked on the Mainland had sufficient concern about their personal security that Taipei, in seeking a cross-Strait investment treaty, insisted specifically that when local Chinese government authorities detain any Taiwan citizen, they notify the person's family in a matter of hours. And it is no surprise that this particular clause was the last one to be resolved, perhaps because PRC negotiators knew that they might be hard pressed to see it enforced.

10

Policy Implications for the United States

The United States has been an integral element of the Taiwan Strait equation from the time that North Korea invaded South Korea in 1950. For the next two decades, American military power and a mutual defense treaty with Taiwan deterred any PRC attempt at a takeover. Through economic assistance and policy guidance, Washington facilitated Taiwan's rapid economic growth and emergence as a middle-class society. U.S. diplomacy protected the position of the Republic of China in the international system. And Beijing drew the obvious conclusion: that the United States had obstructed its goal of unifying China after a century of disorder and division.

That configuration changed after 1969, when first the Nixon and then the Carter administration decided that China would be a useful counterweight against a rising Soviet Union. To secure this strategic asset, Nixon and Carter chose to concede somewhat to PRC demands and reduce America's commitment to Taiwan. That reduction, which was carried out in 1979 and affected diplomatic relations and security ties, had more to do with form than substance. The United States continued robust yet unofficial relations with Taipei, including close security cooperation.[1] As a matter of policy rather than a treaty obligation, it continued the U.S. defense commitment to the island, including selected arms sales.[2]

Washington's working assumption, both before and after 1979, was that neither China nor Taiwan was likely to change the status quo in the Taiwan Strait. To be sure, either or both tested that premise from time to time.[3] Chiang Kai-shek and Chiang Ching-kuo hatched illusory schemes to "retake the Mainland," but Washington restricted their freedom of action. Mao

Zedong twice attacked the offshore islands that Taiwan controlled to test American and ROC resolve, but he met a firm response and backed down. After the United States terminated diplomatic relations with Taipei in 1979 in favor of Beijing, there were new questions about the durability of the status quo. Some Americans believed that the island's absorption into the PRC was only a matter of time, but the policies of the Reagan administration negated those expectations. With the opening of cross-Strait business relations in the 1980s, the prospect of political reconciliation appeared vaguely on the horizon but vanished like a mirage in less than a decade.

At least until the early 1990s, two factors fortified Washington's status-quo assumption. First, Taipei's rhetorical goal—the unification of China—did not conflict fundamentally with Beijing's, although the two governments disagreed on just about everything else. Second, neither China under Mao and Deng Xiaoping nor Taiwan under the Chiangs had enough military strength on its own to end the division of China through force.

Of course, Chinese observers believe that the cross-Strait status quo is not just the policy assumption of the United States but also its goal. In the Chinese narrative, American intervention in the protracted Chinese civil war is the key obstacle to ending national division. "By inserting itself and meddling in the Taiwan issue, the United States inflicts severe harm on China's core interests, and there is no other instance in contemporary international relations where one large nation so severely inserts itself and meddles in the internal affairs of another large nation."[4] America's purported "scheming designs" began in the 1950s and took a new form after the end of the cold war. In Beijing's view, Washington supported both Lee Teng-hui and Chen Shui-bian in separatist adventures. Most offensive to China are U.S. arms sales to Taiwan. In December 20008, Hu Jintao reiterated the long-standing PRC position: "Settling the Taiwan question and realizing the complete reunification of the country is an internal affair of China and is not subject to interference by any foreign forces."[5] For decades, the goal of Chinese policy—at least rhetorically—has been to reduce and end the U.S.-Taiwan relationship.

In fact, the sole emphasis of all American administrations since the 1950s has been on the process by which the dispute between China and Taiwan might be resolved. It is an "abiding interest" of the United States that Beijing and Taipei resolve their differences peacefully, without violence or coercion,[6] and Washington has long held that the content of any agreement is a matter for Beijing and Taipei to work out for themselves. Washington also has assumed that Taipei would be smart enough to know and protect its own interests if negotiations ever began.

The U.S. status-quo assumption was tested between the mid-1990s and 2008, when it appeared that under Lee Teng-hui and Chen Shui-bian Taiwan might take actions that China perceived as separatist, requiring Beijing to respond with force and therefore, perhaps, requiring U.S. intervention. That concern only grew as the PRC built military capabilities to deter Taipei from mounting a challenge to China's fundamental interests and to punish it if deterrence failed. It was to reduce the risk of conflict through miscalculation by Beijing and Taipei that the U.S. defense commitment to Taiwan evolved from one known as "strategic ambiguity" (remaining vague on what Washington would do in the event of a conflict) to an approach that I have called "dual deterrence." Under the latter, the United States implicitly warned Beijing that it would defend Taiwan in the event of an unprovoked attack and implicitly warned Taipei that U.S. support would be in doubt if it provoked the conflict.[7] The clear implication was that the United States would respond to an unprovoked Chinese attack. Dual deterrence and actions by both the Clinton and Bush administrations ensured a measure of stability in the U.S.-China-Taiwan triangle during this period.

In the second decade of the twenty-first century, Washington can no longer readily assume that the cross-Strait future will be just like the past. On the one hand, there is now a greater possibility than ever before that the two sides will find a way to resolve their fundamental dispute and end one of the longest-running post–World War II disputes. Even though stabilization is not yet complete, progress is still possible, given the right kind of creativity. However, any movement toward resolution would test the principles of U.S. policy. Is the resolution truly peaceful and voluntary on Taiwan's part, without any hint of PRC intimidation? Is Washington's stated, exclusive emphasis on process sincere, or does it really care about the substance as well? On the other hand, in the early 1970s it was the perceived rise of the Soviet Union that created a strategic dilemma for the United States, leading it to align with China and reduce its commitment to Taiwan. Now the rising power is China, and the United States is again faced with a strategic dilemma. Does it accommodate China's rise—really, its revival? Or does it seek to block it or shape it? Whatever option it picks, will it have to make new concessions concerning its relations with Taiwan?

U.S.-Taiwan Relations during Ma Ying-jeou's First Term

After Ma Ying-jeou's election in March 2008, the general belief in the United States was that it was good for the United States. Both the Bush administration and presidential candidate Barack Obama expressed the hope that Ma's policies would bring about more peaceful and stable cross-Strait relations. Scholars like me spoke of the "strategic" or "historic" opportunity available to Beijing and Taipei to reverse the situation of mutual fear that had existed since the late 1990s. Moreover, Obama signaled even before his election that U.S. relations with Taiwan would improve in tandem with the improvement of cross-Strait relations. On the basis of Washington's traditional one-China policy, he said that his administration would strengthen channels of communication with Taipei, provide the arms "necessary for Taiwan to deter possible aggression," and support Ma's efforts to improve cross-Strait relations.[8]

By and large, the United States adjusted its Taiwan policy to take positive account of the progress that had occurred between Beijing and Taipei. The most significant step was probably the decision, announced in December 2011, to include Taiwan in the U.S. visa waiver program. Given the number of Taiwan people who travel to the United States and the cost and inconvenience of securing a visa, this step is a broad benefit for the island's people. Washington also resumed the visit to Taiwan of American officials up to the level of deputy secretary. The conduct of day-to-day interactions was reportedly smooth. And arms sales continued, episodically but in large volumes: $6.5 billion in 2008; $6.4 billion in 2010; and $5.9 billion in 2011.[9] China's opposition to those sales affected the timing of Washington's decision to officially notify Congress that contracts were imminent but not whether sales would occur.[10] The Obama administration continued to endorse the improving cross-Strait relationship, most notably in joint statements at the time of summits between President Hu Jintao of the PRC and President Obama. For example, the statement released during the January 2011 summit said: "The United States supports the peaceful development of relations across the Taiwan Strait and looks forward to efforts by both sides to increase dialogues and interactions in economic, political, and other fields, and to develop more positive and stable cross-Strait relations." It also "applauded" the Economic Cooperation Framework Agreement (ECFA) signed seven months before.[11]

One exception to the improving bilateral relationship concerned economic ties. The Obama administration had sought to resume discussions with Taipei on economic issues under the Trade and Investment Framework Agreement (TIFA) concluded in 1994. U.S. trade negotiators insisted that before that could happen, Taiwan had to address some specific barriers, particularly market access for beef. In part because of the political clout of U.S. cattle interests and their defenders in Congress, the Obama administration made a satisfactory outcome on beef exports a precondition for holding a TIFA meeting. The two sides had good intentions, and they reached a market access agreement in the second half of 2009. Unwisely, the Ma administration decided to publicly sign the understanding right before elections for county magistrates and mayors. In the public uproar that followed, fueled in part by unsubstantiated concerns about food safety, Taiwan's legislature imposed restrictions that had the effect of reneging on the agreement, despite the fact that the KMT caucus had a large majority in the Legislative Yuan. However, its members were unhappy with Ma's performance in other areas.

After that setback, the Obama administration's enthusiasm for TIFA waned temporarily, but it made a new effort, and talks were scheduled for early 2011. Then, Taiwan's health minister, without adequately consulting the rest of government, decided to enforce a legal ban on ractopamine, a chemical added to livestock feed to increase the protein content of meat. He did so in a manner designed to secure maximum publicity and in spite of an understanding between the two governments that Taiwan would somehow adjust the ban to ensure continued imports of foreign beef. The TIFA meetings were again canceled. In both cases, politicians readily played on public concerns about food safety. A senior U.S. official indicated that in Washington's view the stakes were greater than what type of meats Taiwan consumers ate: "Taiwan has taken a series of actions in recent years on agricultural trade issues that have damaged its credibility as a reliable trading partner and have proved to be a serious impediment" to improving economic relations.[12] There was a positive turn in the latter part of 2012, after Ma had secured reelection. In July, he got the legislature to approve modest levels of ractopamine in beef, and by the fall it appeared that TIFA talks would soon resume.

Overall, however, U.S.-Taiwan relations between 2008 and 2012 were positive and better than over the previous fifteen years. The positive U.S. steps cited above caused some in Taiwan, particularly Ma's opponents, to charge that Washington was taking sides in the island's elections. Strengthening those charges was an on-background statement of a U.S. official in September 2011 that expressed "doubts" about whether Tsai Ing-wen, if elected, was "willing and able to continue the stability in cross-Strait relations the region has enjoyed in recent years."[13] Indeed, for Taiwan presidential elections from 2000 on, the United States adopted a two-sided—and some would say contradictory—approach. On the one hand, it publicly eschewed any preference for one candidate over another, a stance that it takes with all democratic countries. On the other, it signaled that U.S.-Taiwan relations would be a function of Taipei's future policies, especially its China policies, and how they affected American interests. In the run-up to the 2000 contest, in my capacity as chairman of the

American Institute in Taiwan, I stated that relationship matter of factly, and some in the KMT thought that we were siding with the DPP. President George W. Bush criticized Chen Shui-bian publicly and fairly directly in December 2003. Thomas C. Christensen, as deputy assistant secretary of state, did so publicly, explicitly, and at length in September 2007. Without question, the United States faces a dilemma here, but it cannot suspend the pursuit of its interests in order to prove a rigid neutrality. Indeed, if Washington had *not* taken favorable policy steps between 2008 and 2012, even though it believed that Ma Ying-jeou's policies toward China accorded with U.S. interests, in effect it would have been siding with the DPP.

The "Abandonment" Debate

The other possible exception to the generally favorable trend in U.S.-Taiwan relations was "new thinking" in America about the costs and benefits of the U.S. commitment to the island. Most distressing to Taipei was the view of some American strategists that the shifting balance of power between the United States and China meant that support for Taiwan was no longer in U.S. interests. But the discussion was more complex than that.

It was Nancy Bernkopf Tucker of Georgetown University who presciently first warned that new realities might alter the U.S.-Taiwan-China triangle and negate the prior assumptions of U.S. policy. She argued that Washington could no longer presume that Taipei would *not* agree to unification with China, even though the odds of that happening were not great. Consequently, it was time for the United States to consider whether and how it should prudently recalibrate its interests. On the one hand, she reaffirmed past U.S. policy of peaceful resolution and "respect for the choices made by Taiwan's people" as well as opposition to imposing a solution to the cross-Strait dispute. On the other hand, she held that the United States should not oppose a resolution that was truly peaceful and voluntary on the part of Taiwan. To challenge such an outcome on the grounds that "unification would not be in the U.S. interest or that Taiwan's actions were [ipso facto] involuntary" would meet with resistance from the American public, puzzlement on the part of the people of Taiwan, and a likely armed conflict with China.[14] In effect, Tucker was suggesting that Taiwan, in pursuit of its own interests, might "abandon" the United States and that there were significant limits on what Washington might or should do to stop it.[15]

Yet Tucker's article was ahead of its time, appearing in the summer of 2002, when cross-Strait relations were deteriorating and the chance of voluntary unification was miniscule. In addition, the gap between U.S. and PRC power was still large. So no one chose to respond. The arrival of the Ma Ying-jeou administration in May 2008 reshuffled the deck of assumptions about the status quo. PRC power was growing and unification seemed more likely. Not surprisingly, new American voices were heard, and in one way or another they were all variations on the theme of abandonment. Some continued in the Tucker vein, asking whether Taipei might abandon America, but they disagreed on what it meant.

In 2010, Bruce Gilley, a political scientist at Portland State University, presented a new version of Tucker's scenario. He offered the European historical example of "Finlandization," referring to Finland's accommodation of the Soviet Union in 1948 after having been invaded by the USSR at the beginning of World War II. Helsinki made three policy commitments to Moscow. First, it would not join alliances challenging Moscow or serve as a base for any country challenging Soviet interests. Second, in return, Moscow agreed to uphold Finnish "autonomy" and respect Finland's democratic system. And third, from 1956 to 1981, "Finland pursued a policy of strategic appeasement and neutrality on U.S.-Soviet issues and limited domestic criticism of the Soviet Union," a policy that the Finnish public supported.[16] Gilley argued that what China and Taiwan have attempted since 2008 bears a striking resemblance to Soviet-Finnish relations during the cold war:

> [They] are now approaching their relationship using completely different assumptions. . . . Whereas they previously saw the relationship as a military dispute, today both sides have embraced a view of security that is premised on high-level contact, trust, and reduced threats of force, [and] placed global [economic] integration and competitiveness ahead of nationalist protectionism.[17]

In his view, strategic appeasement was a calculated and rational response on Taiwan's part to a situation of power asymmetry.

Gilley argues that if Taiwan were to reposition itself as a "neutral power, rather than a U.S. strategic ally"—and, in effect, abandon the United States (my formulation, not his)—it would be a boon for U.S. interests. "Finlandization" by Taiwan would "moderat[e] the security dilemma that haunts the Washington-Beijing relationship." As he defines it, Taiwan's approach would be "a godsend for a U.S. administration that increasingly needs China's cooperation in . . . maintaining the peaceful international liberal order." Grand strategy would dictate U.S. Taiwan policy rather than the parochial agendas of "narrow lobbies." Keeping Taiwan in America's "strategic orbit" is not necessary, given deployments elsewhere in the region.[18]

Other Americans were not so sanguine about where Taiwan was going or what it meant. The most negative view was that of a conservative American analyst who predicted early in Ma Ying-jeou's term that by 2012 Taiwan would become a special administrative region of the PRC—in his view, a disaster for both the United States and the people of Taiwan. Representative Dana Rohrabacher, a conservative Republican from California and a long-time advocate for Taiwan, made a similar analysis of the Ma administration's policies. In his view, Taiwan was now working with an "autocratic China," and since he opposed autocracy, his goals and Taiwan's were diverging and the island's government no longer deserved his support.[19]

Yet other Americans began to argue the United States should abandon Taiwan to protect its strategic interests, which, of course, intensified Taipei's fears. For Charles Glaser, a George Washington University political scientist, it is the United States that should abandon Taiwan, for a variety of reasons: the nontrivial possibility that leaders in Taipei might entrap the United States in a war; improvements in Chinese conventional and strategic forces, which reduce the effectiveness of U.S. deterrence; the danger of an arms race if the United States seeks to enhance deterrence by acquiring capabilities that will make China more vulnerable; and the impact that removing "the most obvious and contentious flash point between the United States and China" would have on Beijing's perceptions of U.S. intentions and Chinese actions that stem from that assessment. Washington should, he argues, execute disengagement gradually, but do so all the same. In essence, Taiwan has become a strategic liability that Washington can no longer afford as it seeks to avoid long-term hostility with an increasingly powerful China.[20] In a similar vein, Chas Freeman asserts that

> the kind of long-term relationship of friendship and cooperation China and America want with each other is incompatible with our emotionally fraught difference over the Taiwan issue. . . . We are coming to a point at which we can no longer finesse our differences. . . . We must either resolve them [by U.S. accommodation of Taiwan's unification] or live with the increasingly adverse consequences of our failure to do so.[21]

A panel organized by the Miller Center of the University of Virginia concluded that domestic politics in Taiwan plus U.S. and PRC policies were driving a vicious circle of militarization of what is essentially a political conflict and that a rethinking of U.S. policy was therefore necessary.[22] Retired admiral Bill Owens argued that halting arms sales to Taiwan is a necessary and sufficient condition for the United States to have a friendly and productive relationship with China.[23] Michael Swaine believes that the United States cannot sustain its past support for Taiwan's security and so should try to negotiate an understanding with China whereby Washington will limit arms sales and Beijing will restrain its weapons acquisition and deployments. The United States would consult with Taipei concerning this bargain, but it should still attempt it.[24] Zbigniew Brzezinski, Jimmy Carter's national security adviser, goes further. He fears that in an era when America is declining and needs to foster strategic cooperation with China, arms sales to Taiwan will foster only unnecessary Chinese hostility. So he suggests that in view of U.S. weakness, Taiwan should just accept some undefined elaboration of Beijing's one-country, two-systems formula for unification (Brzezinski suggests "one country, several systems"), which would end the island's security dependence on the United States.[25] Finally, it has been argued in a more operational vein that Washington should reduce its Taiwan commitment because the PLA's capacity to complicate or even block any U.S. intervention is improving, so that even if it wanted to intervene, success would be far from certain.[26]

Robert Sutter of George Washington University has a more subtle argument. According to Sutter, a kind of "dual abandonment" is at play. The United States is doing less and less to help Taiwan and keep it safe because it wishes to preserve constructive relations with China. Taiwan under Ma Ying-jeou has emphasized cooperation with the Mainland in ways that have increased Beijing's leverage over the island but has ignored the simultaneous need to strengthen itself. To the extent that Taiwan is misguided in its calculation of its own interests, Sutter might say that it is "abandoning itself" while setting a trajectory that will undermine American equities. Because Sutter believes that these trends have received little or no attention, he seeks to alert stakeholders before it is too late to do anything about them.[27]

What, for its part, is the United States government's view on its relationship with Taiwan? For those who feared that the Obama administration agreed with recommendations to abandon Taiwan, an episode concerning China's "core interests" might provide one piece of confirming evidence.[28] This term became current in late 2008, as Beijing sought to specify its top policy priorities in the hope that other powers would not challenge China on what it saw as most important. As of July 2009, three items had been authoritatively identified as core interests: preserving China's basic state system and national security; national sovereignty and territorial integrity; and the continued stable development of China's economy and society.[29] Within the second item, Taiwan, Tibet, and Xinjiang were definitely included.

As part of its effort to constrain U.S. policy, Beijing then sought to get the Obama administration to agree to the concept of respecting core interests, particularly in regard to sovereignty and territorial integrity and their concrete implications. The Taiwan section of the joint statement issued by the two governments at the November 2009 Obama–Hu Jintao summit read: "The United States and China underscored the importance of the Taiwan issue in U.S.-China relations. China emphasized that the Taiwan issue concerns China's *sovereignty and territorial integrity*, and expressed the hope that the United States will honor its relevant commitments and appreciate and support the Chinese side's position on this issue. The United States stated that it follows its one-China policy and abides by the *principles* of the three U.S.-China joint communiqués." The U.S. side also praised the recent progress in cross-Strait relations. Then, in a new paragraph, the statement continued: "The two countries reiterated that *the fundamental principle of respect for each other's sovereignty and territorial integrity* is at the *core* of the three U.S.-China joint communiqués which guide U.S.-China relations. Neither side supports any attempts by any force to undermine this principle. The two sides agreed that *respecting each other's core interests* is extremely important to ensure steady progress in U.S.-China relations."[30]

In briefings after the summit, the administration made the case that the treatment of the Taiwan issue had been deliberately separated in the text from the more general discussion of core interests, that the latter did not necessarily apply to the former, and that Taiwan policy had not changed. Chinese commentators rejected that interpretation, and Beijing could argue that because phrases like "sovereignty and territorial integrity" and "principles" were present in both paragraphs, the Taiwan discussion was effectively linked to the more general one on core interests.[31] Whatever the interpretation, the words "core interests" did not appear in the joint statement for the second Hu–Obama summit in January 2011. The omission is certainly significant: once Beijing has secured such a commitment in one authoritative document, it usually seeks to repeat it in subsequent ones. Michael Swaine suggests that the silence in 2011 "most likely reflects . . . a U.S. desire to avoid the controversy that followed the inclusion of the term in the 2009 joint statement."[32]

Subsequently, U.S. officials refuted the idea that the United States might abandon Taiwan. Testifying before the House Foreign Affairs Committee in October 2011, Kurt Campbell, the assistant secretary of state for East Asian and Pacific affairs, reaffirmed a "strong and enduring commitment to the maintenance of peace and stability across the Taiwan Strait." The United States would not sacrifice Taiwan as it built relations with China. Indeed, relations between Beijing and Washington, Beijing and Taipei, and Taipei and Washington—whether positive or negative—were mutually reinforcing. Thus, Campbell reaffirmed the Obama administration's approval of the progress in cross-Strait relations under Ma Ying-jeou, because it was consistent with U.S. interests, not detrimental. On the premise that Taiwan must be "confident that it has the capacity to resist intimidation and coercion as it continues to engage with the mainland," Campbell reiterated the U.S. intention to provide it with "carefully selected defense articles and services." Arms sales and interaction with the island's armed forces would "contribute to the maintenance of peace and to a durable deterrent." The fact that China's military buildup relevant to Taiwan had continued despite the improvement in political and economic relations only justified continuity in U.S.-Taiwan security ties.[33]

Scenarios, Interests, and Implications

U.S. policy regarding the Taiwan Strait issue has been a function of what happens in cross-Strait relations. When those ties deteriorated after the mid-1990s, Washington concluded that its own interest in peace and stability was at risk and moved toward a dual-deterrence approach. When Beijing and Taipei improved relations after 2008, Washington shifted. It had less reason to take proactive measures to guard against conflict. Ties with Taiwan improved and U.S.-China relations were not dominated by what was happening between the two sides of the Strait.

How will the evolution of cross-Strait relations affect U.S. interests and policy? As a point of departure, chapter 6 outlined several scenarios for the evolution of Taiwan-China ties in the medium term. What are the implications of each of those for U.S. interests and how Washington might respond?[34]

A continuation of the stabilization that occurred during Ma Ying-jeou's first term would be positive for U.S. interests. It reduces further the likelihood that cross-Strait relations will be a security problem for the United States; Taiwan therefore will recede as an issue in U.S.-China relations and in American politics. If Taipei decided that negotiating a peace accord would support its interests, the U.S. relationship with the island's armed forces, particularly involving arms sales, would likely be an issue that would require coordination between Washington and Taipei. But on balance continuation of stabilization would not challenge fundamental interests.

If stabilization were to stall, it would not be terrible for the United States. It would not require a return to the exercise of dual deterrence as in the 1995–2008 period and may actually give the United States more leverage if the two sides look to it for help on issues that they cannot address themselves. A key question would be which side—Taiwan or the PRC—was more responsible for the stall. The analysis of chapter 5 suggests that Taiwan would have good reason to worry about PRC terms for a political framework and peace accord, terms that would undermine its position in any negotiations to resolve the fundamental dispute. A stall would also raise the prospect that the PLA buildup would continue unabated, rendering Taiwan more vulnerable and making it easier over time for Beijing to intimidate the island to do its bidding.[35]

Accelerated movement toward unification might well pose serious challenges to American interests, but it would depend on the terms of unification. A significant Chinese concession to Taiwan on the sovereignty issue would be welcome generally and would be a positive sign of its fundamental approach to the domestic political order. That would not be a bad outcome. If Taiwan made a voluntary choice for unification, even on the PRC's terms, and negotiated an agreement with Beijing that excluded the basing of PLA air and naval forces on Taiwan, the security implications for the United States would be modest, since Washington has long since abandoned the idea that Taiwan is a useful platform against China. In that regard, former PRC president Jiang Zemin pledged in 1995 that under China's one-country, two-systems formula, Taiwan "may also retain its armed forces and administer its party, governmental and military systems by itself. The Central Government will not station troops or send administrative personnel there."[36]

If, on the other hand, Beijing reneged on that commitment but Taiwan accepted its terms for political unification *and* a PLA presence on the island, it would complicate U.S. defense strategy within the East Asian region. PLA surface ships and submarines based at Taiwan naval bases would have easier access to the open waters of the Pacific. Aircraft flying out of Taiwan airbases would have greater range. The security of Okinawa would be in question. Beijing might challenge the American stance on freedom of navigation. U.S. friends in East Asia, particularly Japan, would no doubt conclude that the postwar structure of power in the region, based on the unfettered forward deployment of U.S. forces, was coming to an end. Washington would be rather hard pressed to devise a strategy to maintain its influence. At the same time, if Taiwan chose unification through a political process that somehow ignored or distorted the wishes of the broad majority of the people, it would confirm the old fear that their fate would be decided against their will.

In absolutely the worst case, Beijing would lose patience with Taiwan and use or threaten to use its military forces to bring Taiwan to heel. That would pose a serious challenge to the United States, which has long been the provider of security in East Asia. If Beijing's exercise of coercion were to succeed, it would represent a failure of the long-term American strategy to shape China into a constructive member of the international community and the domestic political bargain made at the time that the United States established diplo-matic relations with China: that a coercive outcome concerning Taiwan was unacceptable. Even if PRC coercion failed, U.S.-China relations would remain hostile for decades—again a failure for the policy pursued since Richard Nixon.

A more likely but still bad case would be Chinese intimidation to get Taipei to capitulate to unification under the one-country, two-systems formula. Tai-wan would face a huge dilemma, and the politics of its response would be fraught with fear and division. Inevitably, the island's leaders would look to the United States for help. Washington's sympathies would be with Taiwan, particularly if it believed that Taipei had had good reason to eschew negotia-tions with Beijing. Yet sympathy might be outweighed by a desire to protect U.S. economic and political interests with China.

The varying implications for U.S. interests that these different scenarios yield in turn demand different policy responses.

—If Beijing and Taipei can continue the current, positive process at a pace that the Taiwan public can accept, Washington has the comfortable option of confining itself to supporting the process and doing what it can to create a context for it to persist. Yet it still faces several questions. What balance should the United States strike between its relations with Beijing and its ties with Taipei? If Taiwan continues economic liberalization with the Mainland, should Washington intensify liberalization with Taiwan? Might Beijing mod-erate its military buildup vis-à-vis Taiwan, and if it does, will Taiwan adjust its arms procurement requests of the United States?

—If the process stagnates, there may be things that the United States can do quietly to foster movement. It might offer its good offices in some way to help remove the reasons for the stalemate. One question is whether to adjust its relations with each of the two parties accordingly, depending on which side is deemed more responsible for the stagnation. If that happens, the United States should continue support for Taiwan on security issues. Taipei should make sure that the U.S. government and opinion makers understand the rea-sons for its reluctance in order to ensure that proposals for American aban-donment of Taiwan do not gain broader appeal.

—If the current process begins to accelerate toward unification on terms that allow China to project military power from Taiwan or threaten freedom of navigation, Washington would have to consider quietly shaping the negotiations—for example, by urging Taipei to block any PLA presence on Taiwan. If unification resulted in the PLA's deployment to the island, Wash-ington would face the challenge of fundamentally adjusting U.S. security pol-icy in Asia and the Pacific.

—If China chooses to exert pressure on or even to coerce Taiwan, the United States would face the choice of whether to assist Taiwan in standing up to the PRC challenge or whether to accommodate Taiwan's demise as a separate entity. A Chinese pressure strategy would expose the vagueness in the U.S. rhetorical insistence on peaceful resolution of the Taiwan Strait issue. The explicit point of peaceful resolution is that the dispute be resolved nonviolently. But implicitly, it also suggests that any Taiwan decision to cede to Beijing should be purely voluntary.[37] The possibility that Taiwan, in circumstances that make a purely voluntary choice impossible, would concede to Beijing anyway would further complicate any U.S. response.

Power Transition in East Asia

Yet teasing out U.S. policy implications from cross-Strait developments is only part of the story. Rapid economic growth has expanded Beijing's diplomatic influence and provided the budgetary and technological resources it needs to modernize the People's Liberation Army, and the speed at which China is accumulating power complicates U.S. calculations about Taiwan policy. That is, the evolution of U.S.-China relations in an era of power transition affects cross-Strait relations and U.S. ties with Taiwan. One view, described earlier in this chapter, is that Washington should end its security commitment to Taiwan because it has become a strategic liability. But there is another logic: precisely because a power transition is under way, it is all the more important to preserve that commitment.

It is a long-standing idea in the field of international relations that conflict is likely when regional and global power balances shift quickly.[38] Managing those transitions is one of the most difficult challenges that any international system will face. Rising powers tend to have sharp elbows and a temptation to expand their presence and influence. As they do so, they impinge on the interests of established powers. Complicating this interaction is the reality that the major established power is usually uncertain about the intentions of the rising power. Will it accommodate the existing system or seek to overturn it? Whether the rising power is cautious or reckless only confuses the established power's calculations. In theory, its response should be appropriate to the goals and tactics of the rising power. The different options are familiar: appeasement, engagement, bandwagoning, binding, engagement through strength, balancing, containment, or preventive war. A mixed strategy—most commonly engagement and balancing—is also possible and appropriate in a situation of uncertainty. Perceptions matter here. If the established power is wrong in its evaluation of the rising power's aims, it is liable to overreact or underreact, making conflict more likely.[39] (The rising power must cope with similar uncertainty about the intentions and tactics of the major established power in fashioning an appropriate response.)

So far and on balance, the mainstream scholarly consensus has been that a rising China has played a cooperative and accommodative role in the international system as a whole and vis-à-vis the United States, the system's key actor. It seems as though China's aims are limited and that its cooperative stance can continue for a long time. Yet the pattern of behavior that is cited to justify this conclusion is also consistent with a China that has revisionist goals but takes a very cautious approach to risk. That is, it would make little sense for China to challenge the United States when the latter still has the power advantage. Other scholars predict, however, that such a Chinese challenge to the U.S.-dominated international system or East Asian regional order is inevitable.[40] PRC behavior in recent years in the East and South China seas suggests to some at least that the challenge already has begun.

China and the United States continually repeat the mantra of their "commitment to building a positive, cooperative, and comprehensive U.S.–China relationship for the 21st century, which serves the interests of the American and Chinese peoples and of the global community."[41] Yet this rhetorical consensus may mask doubts in each capital about the intentions of the other. A recent study by Brookings China scholar Kenneth Lieberthal and Peking University professor Wang Jisi revealed that the perceptions that policy officials on each side have regarding the long-term intentions of the other are not encouraging. U.S. officials focus on China's mercantilist and even predatory economic policies, its tolerance or direction of cyber attacks, the PRC's authoritarian system, and, most worrisome, the PLA's acquisition of capabilities that seem designed to constrain power projection by U.S. armed forces. From those trends, the American side concludes that "the Chinese side thinks in terms of a long-term zero-sum game" that "requires that America prepare to defend its interests."[42] According to Wang, Chinese officials believe China's power is growing and American power is receding. In spite of that purported trend—or because of it—they believe that "the ultimate goal of the U.S . . . is to maintain its global hegemony" by, among other things, seeking to "constrain or even upset China's rise." In Chinese eyes, Washington's emphasis on democracy and human rights, the sale of weapons to Taiwan, military surveillance activities off China's coast, American economic policies, and the approach to third countries like Iran and North Korea are all elements of this containment plot.[43]

One limitation of power transition theory is that it blurs the global international system with its regional subsystems and overlooks key questions.[44] Jack Levy of Rutgers University asks: "How does a global power balance threats to its global interests and threats to its regional interests? How does the regional threat environment of a rising regional state affect its behavior to the global power and the global power's behavior toward the rising challenger?"[45] Those questions are especially germane when a global power has significant interests in the home region of the rising power. It may be comforting to conclude, accurately in my view, that China is unlikely for many decades to have the kind of power and influence to seriously challenge the dominant position of the United States in regions *other* than East Asia. But that is also irrelevant, because since World War II Washington has believed that its global dominance is a function of its position in East Asia. That is not only the region where China's power is greatest and its interests are fundamental, it is also the region where other countries that have depended on the United States for their security are warily watching China's rise. As Thomas Christensen put it, China may not be catching up with the United States globally, but it will pose problems for America in China's home region.[46]

To add to the complexity, there has been an evolution among specialists on how to think about the interaction between the rising and established powers and the security dilemmas that emerge between them. Originally, the focus was on the material power of parties who had objective reasons to cooperate but who ended up as rivals because each regarded the other's power accumulation as evidence of hostile intent and so increased its own power ("self-help"), thus creating a vicious circle. Also important in understanding this dynamic were issues such as the intensity of the perception-response interaction and whether the perceptions that trigger the response were accurate or not.[47] A security dilemma in which the perception of hostile intent reflects misunderstanding is easier to mitigate than one driven by a conflict of goals. A situation in which the parties rely on defensive measures is less intense and more easily managed than one in which they make offensive preparations to cope with insecurity. Yet the basic focus is on material power, and even here it is not clear what elements of power are most relevant (economic, political, military, and so forth.)[48]

Yet a narrow version of the security dilemma concept—a downward spiral of mutual fear regarding material power—is only moderately helpful in understanding bilateral tensions.[49] Also important are interactions for good or ill on specific points of tension. The lessons learned in those areas inform conclusions about broader trends. In the context of general insecurity, specific spirals also occur that cause each side to become more suspicious of the other's intentions. Each side interprets today's relations more negatively because of the lessons learned cumulatively from past interactions regarding sensitive issues.[50] Just as important as the amount of power that each party possesses is how each uses that power and "socializes" the other about its character and goals.

So, relations between the United States and a resurgent China will likely be marked by a series of specific test cases in which their respective interests collide and friction is as likely as (or more likely than) mutual accommodation. If frictions predominate, the "socialization" in the specific cases will be negative and will foster broader perceptions of hostile intent. The list of test cases is not short. In early 2012, it included the North Korean nuclear program; maritime East Asia; Iran's nuclear program; civil conflict in countries like Egypt, Libya, and Syria; the future of Pakistan; the global economy; climate change; and so on. In light of the previous discussion, the test cases in East Asia will be most consequential for the long-term U.S.-China relationship.

Taiwan is another test case. Particularly in Chinese perceptions, Taiwan has been an integral part of the U.S. hedge against China's rise. Material power is certainly at play: the United States maintains security cooperation with Taiwan to mitigate its fear of PRC intentions and to strengthen deterrence. China is developing capabilities to complicate U.S. intervention in a Taiwan conflict. In addition to this material power spiral, Taiwan is the issue on which mutual learning by the United States and the PRC has lasted the longest and has been most intense. For China especially, the lessons learned have been negative. The conventional lesson that China has learned is that America has used Taiwan to check and contain China's rise.

Americans who favor ending the U.S. security commitment to Taiwan believe that doing so is the only way to socialize China in a positive direction and that it will mitigate the broader bilateral security dilemma. As of late 2011, the last time that an Obama administration official spoke at length on Taiwan policy, it still took the opposite position: that Taiwan remained a significant element in America's effort to address the rise of China. Kurt Campbell's October 2011 testimony before the House Foreign Affairs Committee began with the premise that retreat from East Asia was not an option ("the region is a center of gravity for U.S. security and prosperity. . . . As Asia rises, so too must America's role in it."). Moreover, how China dealt with Taiwan was critical: "A peaceful future for cross-Strait relations is central to the stability and prosperity of the entire region and is therefore of *vital importance* to the United States. . . . Our management of U.S.-Taiwan relations will have a great impact on the way our partners view us across the Asia-Pacific region."[51] Yet the longer-term questions about where Taiwan fits in U.S. strategy for coping with a resurgent China remain.

Will Taiwan "Abandon" the United States?

Of course, U.S. choices would be simplified if, hypothetically, Taiwan made a judgment similar to the one that Bruce Gilley believes is animating the Ma administration's policy. Such a judgment would have several elements. First of all, Taipei gains increasing confidence that its political equities can be sufficiently protected during the stabilization phase and even if the time comes to conduct negotiations on the fundamental dispute. Second, the expansion of cross-Strait cooperation and interdependence gives China an overwhelming and growing stake in peace. Third, as a partial result, Taipei concludes that the danger of PLA coercion had declined to a very low level. Assuming broad political support for such a judgment, acquiring American arms and relying on a U.S. security commitment would no longer be necessary and the festering sore in U.S.-China relations could finally heal.

Certainly, conservative "friends of Taiwan" like Representative Rohrabacher, who likely do want to use Taiwan to contain China, would be dismayed at such a choice. Other Americans, such as those who believe that Taiwan has become a strategic liability for the United States with respect to China, would be pleased to be rid of the responsibility. And, as Tucker cogently argued in 2002, it would be difficult for Washington to oppose such an outcome if Taiwan chose it voluntarily. Taiwan's leaders and public are the best judges of the island's interests. Just because they chose to promote those interests for six decades by aligning with the United States does not mean they will choose to do so forever. There is, of course, the possibility that a Taiwan decision to adopt a policy of accommodation of Beijing would be flawed because it was made through a political system that distorted the wishes of the people in some significant way. But it is not clear that the United States should seek to intervene under those circumstances to reverse that choice—if only because America is not exactly an example of a system that effectively reflects public preferences.

Yet the thrust of the analysis in previous chapters is that Taiwan is unlikely to make a voluntary decision along those lines, at least in the foreseeable future. The first Ma administration's encounter with China produced two cautionary lessons. On the one hand, confidence about Beijing's political and military intentions is still hard to come by. On the other, domestic support for a policy of extensive accommodation does not yet exist. Taiwan, therefore, will be extremely reluctant to conclude that it would be a *good* choice to "abandon" the United States. Hence the suggestion in the last chapter that Taipei strengthen its relationship with Washington.

Nonetheless, it is conceivable that the island might conclude that accommodating or appeasing China was its *only* choice because the power imbalance between them was becoming so extreme. Taiwan would still have reason to fear China's intentions, but, hypothetically, it would still be exclusively dependent economically on the Mainland; unable to ensure adequate deterrence of the PLA; more marginalized from the international community; confused about its political identity; and plagued by psychological despair. Those factors might cause leaders and the public to collectively decide that settling on Beijing's terms was the most prudent course of action. And one of those terms would be cutting the security cord to the United States. Such an outcome might seem impossible in 2012, but the previous chapters suggest that it could become more likely if Taiwan itself does not take steps to strengthen its economic, security, and political capacity. If Taiwan were to concede to China under pressure, it would no doubt provoke debates in the United States about "who lost Taiwan," reminiscent of the poisonous discourse of the early 1950s about the "loss" of China. As with that episode, those who argued that the result was a blessing in disguise would be on the defensive. But, as in the case of voluntary accommodation, it is hard to see how the United States can help Taiwan if it is unwilling or unable to help itself.

Should the United States Abandon Taiwan?

China, of course, would be very pleased if the United States abandoned Taiwan or Taiwan abandoned the United States (or both). It has long believed that Taiwan would be more likely to essentially accept its terms if Taipei no longer had U.S. support. But American analysts have offered several reasons why the United States should not dissociate itself from Taiwan as long as Taiwan desires American support:[52]

—Although Taiwan has at times been the most important source of U.S.-China conflict, it is not the only one. For example, Beijing's goals in East Asia are not limited to bringing the island back into the PRC fold. In addition, it is expanding its security perimeter away from its eastern and southern coast, where it has been for decades. That in turn has meant that the PLA navy and air force are operating increasingly in the traditional domain of U.S. and Japanese forces. Removing Taiwan as a problem would in no way end or reduce this mutual impingement; it would only change its location. Taiwan aside, Beijing would still regard American "socialization" as negative.

—U.S. allies and partners—Japan, the Republic of Korea, and others not necessarily in the Asian region—have much at stake in Washington's future approach to Taiwan. Simply put, if the United States would abandon Taiwan, it could abandon them. Of course, there may be hypothetical reasons why America might withdraw support that stem from Taiwan's policies rather than its own commitment. So the reasons for any abandonment would be important. But the fear remains.

These are valid arguments. Moreover, there is the simple reality that U.S. security support for Taiwan is not the reason that China has failed to achieve its political goals regarding Taiwan. Unification has not occurred on China's terms simply because its approach to resolving the fundamental dispute is not acceptable to the island's government and public. Ending U.S. arms sales is not the panacea that some suggest.

As argued above, there is another reason for America to support Taiwan if it has no intention of challenging China's fundamental interests and seeks to broaden the scope of cross-Strait cooperation yet remains skeptical of Beijing's unification formula: that is, the larger dynamic of the revival of China and the U.S. response and how U.S.-Taiwan relations fit within that dynamic. It is one of the test cases that, over time, that will shape how Beijing and Washington evaluate each other's fundamental intentions.

Should the United States concede to Beijing on Taiwan, the lessons that China would learn about the intentions of the region's dominant power would likely discourage moderation and accommodation on other issues like Korea or maritime East Asia; in that respect, America's friends and allies are right. Continuity of U.S. policy toward Taiwan will not guarantee that China's actions in other areas will support the status quo, but it increases the likelihood that it will. Conversely, if China addresses its Taiwan problem with creativity and due regard for the views on the island, that will say something positive about what kind of great power the PRC will be. A more aggressive approach, one that relies on pressure and intimidation, signals reason for concern about its broader intentions. In this regard, Taiwan is the canary in the East Asian mineshaft.

The dynamic of power transition is connected with how the two sides of the Strait address their differences. Remaining in the domain of mutual persuasion would serve the interest of regional stability and of Taiwan itself. If the leaders and people of the island chose to resolve the fundamental dispute through that process, there is no reason for the United States to object, as its long-time declaratory policy implies. The burden of persuasion will be on China to convince Taiwan that its approach is in Taiwan's interests. If, on the other hand, the two sides were trapped in the domain of power asymmetry and PRC pressure in spite of Taiwan views, that would not bode well for the island or for East Asia. In that case, regional stability and a peaceful Taiwan Strait should incline Washington to weigh in on Taiwan's behalf—particularly if Taiwan is working to strengthen itself.

What Should the United States Do?

If it is in the U.S. interest to increase the chances that cross-Strait relations stay in the paradigm of mutual persuasion and that the attendant interaction between the U.S. and China on the Taiwan "test case" is positive, what should Washington do? What should it do about arms sales to Taiwan? What should it do to help strengthen Taiwan? Should it somehow seek to shape cross-Strait negotiations?

Arms Sales

The U.S. security relationship with Taiwan involves both arms sales and institutional interactions, and it seeks to strengthen Taiwan's political confidence as well as its military capacity. A senior State Department official said in October 2011 that the U.S. military relationship with Taiwan's defense forces "can ensure that it develops a well-trained, motivated, effectively equipped and modernized fighting force that will contribute to the maintenance of peace and to a durable deterrent."[53] A Pentagon official asserted at the same time:

> A Taiwan that is strong, confident, and free from threats or intimidation, in our view, is best postured to discuss and adhere to whatever future arrangements the two sides of the Taiwan Strait may peaceably agree upon. In contrast, a Taiwan that is vulnerable, isolated, and under threat would not be in a position to discuss its future with the mainland and might invite the very aggression we would seek to deter.[54]

Taipei also believes that U.S. arms have both a military and political purpose. They can improve Taiwan's military deterrent against PLA coercion, and they can also fortify Taipei's political resolve to resist Chinese intimidation and so avoid PRC pressure for "preemptive capitulation to the inexorable in response to an offer Taiwan cannot refuse."[55] In effect, both militarily and politically, arms sales can keep cross-Strait interaction within the domain of mutual persuasion and out of the domain of power asymmetry.

China, of course, rejects U.S. arms sales to Taiwan and claims that they only increase PRC mistrust toward the United States. It believes that the United

States strengthens Taiwan to contain China, to maintain credibility with allies, and to stimulate jobs. It also asserts that U.S. arms sales constrain the positive development of Chinese relations with the United States. In the view of Zheng Bijian, a senior PRC spokesperson, U.S.-China cooperation to maintain stability in the Taiwan Strait was "far from sufficient." Indeed, "the U.S. arms sales to Taiwan have long been a problem that has seriously hampered the development of our bilateral ties."[56] Interestingly, Beijing criticizes the United States for its arms sales but is silent toward Taipei. Yet the most effective "socialization" of Beijing must combine a relatively strong and confident Taiwan and firm U.S. policy with openness on Taipei's part to the right kind of political reconciliation.

But recall that there is something of a contradiction between the two "uses" of American military equipment. What some Americans think Taiwan most needs for military deterrence (see chapter 8 for examples) may have only modest symbolic, psychological, and political value (which has been important to Taiwan), but the systems that have the most potent political value may have only marginal military utility. Advanced aircraft like the C/D model of the F-16 fighter may give Taipei the confidence that it needs to resist PRC intimidation, but as the PLA becomes more able to disable the runways on which Taiwan's air force depends and to use surface-to-air missiles to attack any planes that get off the ground, the military value of those aircraft declines. Whether, given Taiwan's finite defense budget resources, such advanced systems yield defense capabilities that are commensurate with the cost is an open question that is already being discussed.[57] As Peter Lavoy, the Pentagon official responsible for Taiwan, put it in October 2011: "Taiwan defense spending cannot match the Mainland's, nor can it develop the same type of military the Mainland is developing. Taiwan needs to focus its planning and procurement efforts on non-traditional innovative and asymmetric approaches."[58]

At a minimum, the United States and Taiwan need to facilitate a more robust discussion of how to strike a sensible balance between the political and military purposes of U.S. weapons systems. Clearly, Taiwan gains most when a system has both political and military value and not as much when symbolism outweighs enhanced deterrence. When Washington faces decisions about transferring arms to Taiwan, it is more likely to accept the harm to U.S.-China relations if it believes that the items in question have a military as well as political value. But the cost of advanced systems means that Taiwan must be careful in its choices. On the other hand, public education can increase the perceived psychological value of systems that contribute a lot to deterrence and are relatively cheap but that do not seem at first glance to be that "useful."

Other subjects are worthy of attention and discussion. First is Taiwan's ongoing, independent acquisition of systems, such as cruise missiles, that can hit targets on the Mainland. Such systems certainly make tactical military sense, since they increase the vulnerability of the PLA's missile, air, and naval bases. However, American military planners have consistently worried that independent Taiwan attacks on Mainland targets would create difficulties in limiting the scope of a conflict and maintaining escalation control.[59] To the extent that Taiwan's entire defense strategy is based on the premise of U.S. intervention, U.S. doubts about such capabilities do not serve Taiwan's fundamental interest. There also are reports that the United States has denied certain sophisticated components for Taiwan's cruise missiles because it does not support the island's military having offensive weapons and because of limits imposed by the Missile Technology Control Regime.[60] Despite these points of divergence in this area, it would be worthwhile for Washington and Taipei to see if they can reduce the gap. It is China's ballistic and cruise missiles that create Taiwan's greatest vulnerability, and there is a limit to what Taiwan can do to counter such offensive capabilities with defensive ones. Giving Taiwan the ability to put China's missile capabilities at risk would enhance the island's confidence and cross-Strait deterrence.

Second is the "dual-use" character of U.S. arms sales to Taiwan, which raises a question. If it is the American political commitment that Taiwan needs most in order to sustain its psychological confidence as it seeks to persuade Beijing at the negotiating table and to resist any PRC pressure, then the most effective thing that Washington can do to promote Taipei's confidence is to articulate regularly and more precisely the PRC actions that it will not accept. The current formulation is not bad. Here is what Kurt Campbell said in October 2011: "We insist that cross-Strait differences be resolved peacefully and according to the wishes of the people on both sides of the Strait. We do not support Taiwan independence. We are opposed to unilateral attempts by either side to change the status quo. We welcome efforts on both sides to engage in a dialogue that reduces tensions and increases contacts across the Strait. And we are committed to preserving the peace and stability in the Taiwan Strait that has prevailed in recent years."[61] Still, the possibility that Beijing might someday shift from mutual persuasion to pressuring Taipei to accept an outcome that is not totally voluntary but is still "peaceful" (that is, nonviolent) suggests the need for a stronger warning against intimidation. A good place to start is with one of the policy statements in the Taiwan Relations Act—it is U.S. policy to "consider any effort to determine the future of Taiwan by other than peaceful means, including by boycotts or embargoes, a threat to the peace and security of the Western Pacific area and of grave concern to the United States."[62]

Third is the possibility of a cross-Strait peace accord. Washington and Taipei should understand that even if an accord would be difficult to negotiate and seems unlikely now, it is not out of the question. Taiwan may decide that an accord is in its interest. If that is the case, the two capitals should assume that at some point Beijing would raise the issue of U.S. arms sales to and security cooperation with Taipei. That PRC scholar Sun Zhe suggested that even the discussion of confidence-building measures would require a credible declaration from Taiwan concerning this issue indicates that it would certainly be on the agenda for a peace accord.[63] To be sure, a PRC effort to limit Taiwan's acquisition of capabilities without restraining its own would likely make a draft agreement politically unacceptable on the island. Yet, given the possibility of cross-Strait security negotiations, Taipei and Washington should be prepared to discuss privately the many implications for their defense relationship.

Finally, there have been some proposals that the United States should rethink its arms sales policy altogether, either to promote positive relations with China or to demilitarize what is deemed to be a political dispute. The most extensive recommendation comes from Michael Swaine of the Carnegie Endowment for International Peace. Essentially, he believes that the United States is losing a race over China concerning Taiwan's security. As the PLA has built capabilities relevant to a Taiwan conflict, Washington has responded so far by providing Taipei with some advanced systems, urged restraint on the PRC, and intensified surveillance activities and naval and air deployments against China. The race could be suspended if there were sufficient domestic consensus in Taiwan to reach a political understanding with Beijing, but Swaine believes that is unlikely. Rather, he argues, the relative shift in the balance of resources and power between the United States and the PRC will place Washington at a growing disadvantage, and it will be less able to resist opposition to future arms sales. Deterrence as it has existed will weaken, and Taiwan will become an even more toxic issue in U.S.-China relations.[64] In order to stabilize cross-Strait security relations, Swaine proposes a U.S.-China understanding:

> Washington policymakers should consider negotiating directly with Beijing, in consultation with Taipei, a set of mutual assurances regarding PLA force levels and deployments on the one hand, and major U.S. arms sales and defense assistance to Taiwan on the other hand, that are linked to the opening of a cross-Strait political dialogue.[65]

Swaine's idea is similar to suggestions from PRC officials that the United States and China should enter into talks regarding U.S. arms sales. For example, they raised it during the March 2010 Beijing visit of James Steinberg, deputy secretary of state, and Jeffrey Bader, National Security Council senior director for Asia in March 2010, after the Obama administration's first major arms sale to Taiwan. According to Bader's account, "the Chinese proposed 'consultations with China on future sales and for limitations of various kinds of sales.'"[66] The Obama administration deflected the Chinese idea but not without some difficulty. It has itself sought discussions with Beijing on sensitive security issues such as nuclear weapons, outer space, cyberspace, and so on. During the March 2010 Steinberg-Bader visit, they acknowledged the reality that in such a dialogue, "the Chinese . . . could raise subjects of concern to them . . . including the Taiwan Strait. Steinberg made it clear, however, that any discussions touching on the Taiwan Strait could not take U.S. arms sales to Taiwan as their focus but could deal with the balance of forces in the region generally and ways to lower tensions *through acts by all*, not just by the United States."[67]

Even if a U.S. administration agreed to new negotiations on Taiwan arms sales, the prospects for success would be doubtful from the outset. China would likely try to base the talks on the premise that the United States had violated the terms of the U.S.-China communiqué of 1982—specifically its pledges to limit the quality and quantity of the weapons that it transferred to Taiwan—and that the purpose of the talks was to bring Washington into compliance. Beijing's likely goal would be to secure what it failed to achieve in the 1982 negotiations—a date certain for the end of arms sales. Washington would reject such framing by saying that its pledges were premised on China's commitment to resolve differences with Taiwan issue peacefully, a commitment that two decades of military buildup call into question. It would also stress the fundamental logic of U.S. policy: U.S. arms sales to Taiwan are a response to Taipei's sense of vulnerability, which in turn is a function of China's own military capabilities and deployments. Therefore, the best way for Beijing to reduce or end Taiwan's requests for advanced American equipment would be to alter Taiwan's threat assessment in a positive direction.

Even if these conceptual minefields could be bypassed, Swaine properly identifies three potential problems. First, Washington would be accused both at home and in Taiwan of "selling out" Taiwan and damaging American credibility with allies. Second, the United States and China might find it hard to come up with a mutually acceptable package of Chinese forces and deployments and U.S. arms sales. Third, the United States might subject itself to manipulation by the other two parties, thus increasing the danger of miscalculation. But Swaine argues that none of these problems is as serious as it seems.[68]

Another potential objection is that this would violate the "six assurances" that the United States conveyed to Taiwan at the time that it was negotiating the 1982 arms sales communiqué with China. The assurances that are most relevant here are that Washington would not mediate the cross-Strait dispute or pressure Taiwan to negotiate. Those assurances were important to Taipei at the time and have continued to be, but one cannot rule out the possibility that Taipei might decide under different circumstances in the future that it was in Taiwan's interests to relax those restraints on U.S. action. And Swaine is careful to specify that consultation with Taipei would accompany negotiations with Beijing.

Yet Swaine's solutions to his first problem—enhancing the U.S. security presence in East Asia and siding with Taipei somewhat on cross-Strait political issues—do not really solve the problem. Washington has been reluctant to be an intermediary between the PRC and the ROC precisely because taking such a role requires domestic support in the United States from beginning to end. And Washington certainly cannot be assured of sustained political support in Taiwan for such negotiations, if only because it is in no position to shape opinion there. If Taipei agreed to U.S.-PRC negotiations, it would become public knowledge in both Taiwan and the United States sooner or later. Political opposition would no doubt follow. The political firestorm that erupted when Ma Ying-jeou simply talked about the possibility of a peace accord should demonstrate the difficulty—impossibility, perhaps—of negotiating on Taipei's behalf. The Taiwan public would likely assume, rightly or wrongly, that any such exercise would end badly, in part because it would fear that the United States had too much to gain in other aspects of its relationship with China by satisfying Beijing on the Taiwan issue. No government would risk entrusting the island's future to the United States in the face of such opposition.

On the second point, Swaine is correct that the main PRC assets at issue here are its ballistic missiles, because they are relevant only for a Taiwan contingency. That might reduce the substantive complexity of such an arrangement, but he is too quick to assume that Beijing would agree to the verification measures that would be necessary. Indeed, even if China were to allow destruction of those missiles, with outside monitoring (a questionable assumption given the likely sovereignty objections), it is probably impossible to verify that the PLA was not rebuilding its missile arsenal in secret. At the same time, Swaine ignores the possibility that Beijing could seek other restraints on the United States besides arms sales. The at least implicit American commitment to Taiwan's defense, the Pentagon's institutional links to the Taiwan armed forces, and U.S. surveillance activities against the PLA all come to mind.

A point of serious vagueness in Swaine's proposal is the linking of the military discussion to the opening of a cross-Strait political dialogue. The idea is that the United States might get China to grant more favorable terms to Taiwan in return for its limiting arms sales.[69] But that is different from a guarantee that those terms will meet Taiwan's interests, and there is no certainty of a consensus on the island of what the terms should be. The stalemate in cross-Strait political relations stems less from the lack of political consensus on Taiwan than on Beijing's unwillingness to make an offer to Taipei that it can take seriously. Indeed, if there is one issue on Taiwan on which a broad consensus exists, it is that the PRC's one-country, two-systems approach is fundamentally flawed. Its unwillingness to accept the Republic of China in some way is a major case in point. The danger is that American intrusion into cross-Strait political issues at the same time that it is limiting arms sales will make it easier for Beijing to intimidate Taipei, not less.

Economic Ties

Since the initial cross-Strait opening in the mid-1980s, successive U.S. administrations have supported cross-Strait dialogue and the expansion of economic cooperation.[70] By implication, Washington has not been concerned that such trends might result in the island's growing economic dependence on the Mainland. On the other hand, there is the broader question of whether it is in the U.S. interest to be excluded or to exclude itself from the process of trade and economic liberalization in the East Asian region. In that respect, Washington has supported the widest circle of trade liberalization, advocating, for example, an Asia-Pacific free trade area based on the Asia-Pacific Economic Cooperation (APEC) forum as an alternative to an intra-Asian free trade area. From the U.S. point of view, it is the depth of business relationships that should define the scope of liberalization, not geography. Moreover, Washington has advocated "high-quality" free trade agreements (FTAs) that are comprehensive in their coverage and that address trade barriers within economies (like failure to protect intellectual property rights) in addition to those that occur at borders.[71]

There is the subsidiary question here of whether Taiwan should be included in such liberalizing arrangements. Where possible, the United States has worked quietly to increase the chances for Taiwan's inclusion. When China sought to enter APEC in 1991, the George H.W. Bush administration insisted that "Chinese Taipei" enter at the same time. Similarly, the United States worked in the 1990s to craft the provisions of the World Trade Organization so that Taiwan would be included as a "special customs territory" and that such entities had the right to enter into free trade agreements. In the U.S. view, Taiwan is a major trading economy, particularly in East Asia and across the Pacific, so it should be included in new rounds of liberalization. That is consistent with the position voiced by a senior official of the Obama administration: "The United States has long been a vocal supporter of Taiwan's meaningful participation in international organizations."[72]

Taiwan has long seen the political value of being included in multilateral trade groups, whether global, like the World Trade Organization, or regional. Moreover, it sees the economic harm of being excluded, because that would distort trade and investment away from Taiwan. In part because of its marginalization, it has hoped to compensate by negotiating free trade arrangements on a bilateral basis, particularly with the United States. The Ma administration recognized that even trying such bilateral liberalization would require China's tacit consent, so it was prepared to formalize the ECFA with China first and then approach other trading partners. It also understood that it would have to be flexible on what to call Taiwan (not the Republic of China or Taiwan) and what to call the agreement (not "free trade agreement" since China rejects the idea that Taiwan as a member of the WTO has the right to conclude understandings under that name).

Although negations between Taiwan and the United States under the Trade and Investment Framework Agreement have been a start-and-stop affair, it is in the two countries' mutual interest to liberalize economic relations. For Taiwan, liberalization would complement the ECFA process under way with the Mainland and further stimulate the structural adjustment of the domestic economy. For the United States, market opening with Taiwan is one way of getting itself "back in the game" of East Asian economic regionalism. Washington would certainly prefer to do economic liberalization on a global or Asia-Pacific basis, but neither the global Doha round nor an FTA based on APEC, which would include Taiwan, seems likely in the foreseeable future. Next best would be to include Taiwan in the Trans-Pacific Partnership (TPP), a group of like-minded Asia-Pacific economies that seek high-quality liberalization.[73] After that would be a bilateral free-trade arrangement, which could take the form of a single agreement or a set of understandings that would add up to an FTA. The TIFA process can complement TPP and serve as the venue for the bilateral talks.

For Taiwan to be included in TPP or to merit some sort of bilateral free trade process with the United States, several things must happen. First, Taiwan will have to address to some degree the outstanding issues with the United States and other trading partners. Key here for the United States are agriculture, including beef; pharmaceuticals; and medical devices.[74] That in turn will require the government to build the political case that balanced liberalization and the structural adjustment that it will induce will be good for the entire population and outweigh the parochial interests of specific groups like farmers and doctors (particularly farmers who continue to produce legacy crops like rice). Second, the United States should abandon its practice of withholding the *beginning* of serious trade negotiations in order to extract concessions from Taiwan on outstanding disputes. That in turn will require the administration to make the case to American vested interests that their concerns can be satisfied at the negotiating table. Third, Washington will have to be prepared to face down China's likely objections to either venture on the grounds that only sovereign states may conclude trade liberalization agreements and that Taiwan is not a sovereign state. The U.S. response should be that as a member of the WTO, the special customs territory of Taiwan, Penghu, Jinmen, and Matsu (as Taiwan is referred to) has every right to conclude such agreements, but that the United States will ensure flexibility when it comes to nomenclature. To facilitate a firm administration response, it will be necessary to secure stronger support from business and Congress for such efforts— from business because Beijing may seek to pressure American companies active in China to oppose them; from Congress because at least some agreements will require some sort of legislative approval. Taiwan should join the administration in building that support.

Assisting Cross-Strait Negotiations

Some might make a case that the obstacles to truly stabilizing cross-Strait relations or even resolving the fundamental dispute are so daunting that the only way to remove those impediments is for the United States to help the two sides remove them—and that doing so would in fact promote U.S. interests. In the abstract, there are a variety of ways that the United States could play an intermediary role between China and Taiwan. What Chinese leaders have suggested is that Washington "support the peaceful development of the relations across the Taiwan Strait with concrete action."[75] Presumably, that means limiting arms sales and pressing Taipei to discuss with Beijing subjects about which it is reluctant to talk. But for the United States to adopt such a course would be to end the neutral stance on the substance of cross-Strait relations to which it has adhered for decades. It would also likely make it more difficult for Taiwan to hew to the mode of mutual persuasion and make it easier for China to manipulate power asymmetry.

There are other ways in which Washington could play a more active role in cross-Strait relations but still maintain its neutral stance. It could act simply as a messenger between Beijing and Taipei. It could provide what is called intellectual facilitation. Here, the United States would transmit the views of one capital to the other and in addition offer its analysis of what those views meant in order to elicit a fuller response, but it would not offer any views of its own. More intrusively, it could provide process facilitation, by offering a venue where the two sides might talk with each other. Beyond that, it could mediate between the two parties on the substance of the dispute. These four are basically mutually exclusive, for they entail different modes of facilitating communication. A fifth, which could supplement any one of the four, is to serve as a guarantor for whatever settlement the two sides concluded.

Hitherto the United States has eschewed any serious role as a mediator between Taipei and Beijing. Several factors have encouraged its restraint, which is unusual in American foreign policy:

—Historically, the United States was badly burned in the late 1940s when General George Marshall tried to mediate between the ROC government under Chiang Kai-shek and the Chinese Communist Party under Mao Zedong.

—Beijing has always defined the dispute as a Chinese internal affair and so resists U.S. diplomatic involvement.

—Standing policy dictates that the dispute should be settled by the two parties themselves; that Washington worries only about process, not substance; that it will neither pressure Taiwan to negotiate with Beijing nor seek to play the role of mediator itself.[76]

—Any American administration that considered an intermediation effort would worry about whether it could sustain Congress's and Taiwan's support for its mediation throughout the process, no matter how willing they were at the outset.

—The United States is a party to the dispute since it is the sole external source of Taiwan's security. That support would likely become a subject of negotiations and seriously complicate any U.S. effort to be an honest broker.[77]

What has transpired since 2008 has changed the context surrounding any decision by the United States to insert itself. Before then, the priority was simply getting the two sides to talk with each other—an objective that something like intellectual facilitation might have achieved. But Beijing and Taipei have found a way to address their differences themselves and have made some progress, so any American attempt to facilitate further progress would target the tough substantive issues that still divide Taiwan and China. In such an attempt, Washington would become inextricably enmeshed in the details of the issues and become an object of manipulation by Beijing or Taipei or both. If Washington sought to limit its role to an appropriate scope, it would probably fail. Wherever it drew the line, either side or both would seek to pull it over the line in ways that expanded the American role. It would become the umpire of disputes that occurred as the negotiations proceeded. It would become responsible for the outcome of the negotiations and so be blamed for any breakdown.

Moreover, there is an intriguing asymmetry in the cross-Strait dispute that not only complicates the efforts by the two sides to stabilize it but also any effort by an outside mediator. That has to do with which side is more reluctant at different stages of the negotiation process. The PRC, I have argued elsewhere, is the main obstacle to getting to an agreement that makes substantive sense for Taiwan while Taipei is the main obstacle to actually getting any draft accord adopted. In negotiations on a hypothetical peace accord, for example, Beijing would likely seek a restriction on U.S. arms sales to Taiwan but refuse to place any limits on its own military capabilities. But if a draft agreement were actually reached, Taiwan's government would face strong political resistance to getting it approved. This asymmetry would complicate any effort of the United States to play a significant intermediation role. On a peace accord, it would likely side with Taipei on the need for Beijing to reduce Taiwan's sense of vulnerability, a stance that Beijing would likely resist in part because it is the United States that provides Taiwan with weaponry. On the other hand, Washington would have to take the side of those on Taiwan favoring adoption of an accord, which might be perceived as exerting pressure and would be inconsistent with U.S. democratic values as well.

This analysis strongly suggests that generally there are too many factors constraining the United States to permit a major intermediation role. A central premise of U.S. policy remains sound: any agreements between Taiwan and China will be more enduring if they themselves create the agreements and are responsible for their implementation.

11 | *Epilogue*

It was rainy in Taipei on May 20, 2012, the day that Ma Ying-jeou was sworn in for a second term as Taiwan's president. It was typical weather for northern Taiwan in late spring and a sharp contrast to the sparkling blue skies of four years before.

As was the weather, Taiwan politics was reverting to the norm. In 2008, Ma won an easy victory because voters were dissatisfied with the outcome of Chen Shui-bian's presidency. In 2012, the election was a referendum on Ma's policies. His pursuit of engagement with China may have made sense for Taiwan as a whole, but it did not necessarily make sense for every individual and firm, although that is the nature of economic liberalization anywhere. For Taiwan, China was not just another trading partner. China had its own ideas about Taiwan's future, and it had increasingly robust military capabilities. To make matters worse for Ma, the global economic crisis exploded not long after he took office and his government did not respond well to a serious natural disaster in August 2009. And then there was the Democratic Progressive Party, which rebounded from its loss in 2008 to mount a serious challenge during the 2012 campaign. Even the inauguration ceremony did not bring a time-out from politics, as legislators and the media debated administration proposals to raise taxes and energy costs and the Green forces mounted large demonstrations.

Ma's second inauguration differed in other ways from both his first inauguration and those of his three predecessors.[1] It was purposefully low key. Ma dispensed with a large, semi-public event attended by thousands of people. This time, the only ceremony took place in the auditorium of the Office of the President. It was televised throughout the island, allowing the public to participate, but only in a virtual way. More significant was that the 2012 inauguration lacked the sense of nervous anticipation that surrounded the inaugurations of 1996, 2000, 2004, and 2008. On those occasions, a cloud of tension and uncertainty hung over the presidential campaigns and the transition period that followed. Questions swirled before the swearing-in—in China, the United States, the East Asian region, and Taiwan itself. In which direction would Taiwan's newly elected or reelected leader take policy? How would China and other interested parties respond? What would the United States do? How would the lifestyle of Taiwan's people change? In those four years, observers looked to the inaugural address to provide clarity in uncertain times and hope that the future would be better than the recent past, so the media subjected the addresses of Lee Teng-hui in 1996, Chen Shui-bian in 2000 and 2004, and Ma Ying-jeou in 2008 to microscopic examination.

Ma's address in 2012 was different. His general policy direction was already well known, and he had provided substantial detail about a second term before the election. The previous four years had been stable by cross-Strait standards, and Beijing and Washington were relatively confident that continuity would prevail. Ma's words therefore were not the touchstone that observers had sought on previous occasions. As was appropriate for someone in the middle of his presidency, informing the public about the serious task of governing was more important than rhetorical flourishes.

Much of Ma's speech dwelt on several things that Taiwan has to do to remain internationally competitive. Domestically, that required reforming the education system in order to ensure human resources of high quality. Externally, it meant continuing a policy of liberalization—not just with China but with all its major trading partners. That in turn required removing protectionist barriers that raise doubts about Taiwan's commitment to free trade. Doing so was especially important for liberalization with the United States, and in June 2012 the Legislative Yuan liberalized access for American beef, a long-standing stumbling block.

Ma also used his inaugural address to restate the various elements of his policies on relations with China. He affirmed the 1992 consensus, "whereby each side acknowledges the existence of 'one China,' but maintains its own interpretation of what that means." And he was explicit on what it meant for Taiwan: the Republic of China. He made a bow to Beijing's view that Taiwan and the Mainland constituted the "sovereign territory" of China but then defined "China" as the Republic of China. He reasserted the need to maintain the "status quo of 'no unification, no independence, and no use of force.'" He suggested that the two sides establish a consensus of "mutual nonrecognition" when it came to sovereignty and "mutual nondenial" when it came to jurisdiction (the "authority to govern"). The implication was that theretofore

Beijing had been unwilling to tolerate Taipei's position on either issue.[2] What Ma advocated for the next four years was that "the two sides of the Strait . . . open up new areas of cooperation and continue working to consolidate peace, expand prosperity and deepen mutual trust." That modest agenda was an echo of that in his first inaugural address, but it lacked what he had said in 2008 about consultation with Beijing on international space and a possible peace accord, suggesting that he had set those aside. Instead, he cited Taiwan's own independent steps to expand its international presence, implying that no prior discussion with Beijing was necessary. On defense, he quoted an ancient Chinese saying: "Though the world may be at peace, being unprepared to fight invites danger." Finally, he noted the need to be transparent and accountable to the public and opposition parties in formulating cross-Strait policy and suggested that the peoples on the two sides of the Strait would have a mutual feeling of "otherness" as long as democracy was absent in the People's Republic of China.[3] In short, Ma broke little new ground and sought to lower expectations about the future.

Ma's stance accords with the conclusions of this volume. In his first term, the two sides of the Taiwan Strait had taken certain risks to bring some stability to a relationship that had been rather tense and fractious for more than a decade. Each had sought to reassure the other that its long-term intentions were benign while setting boundaries on what was possible in the near term. Together, they availed themselves of opportunities for cooperation when the benefits appeared to outweigh the risks. The Taiwan public was satisfied enough with the results of economic stabilization that it endorsed Ma for another term and sustained his party's control of the Legislative Yuan—with a diminished majority, but a majority all the same. The election seemed to reflect the balance of sentiment in Taiwan society toward China: around 55 percent were in favor of Ma's policies and around 45 percent were against. And when spokesmen for China's Taiwan policy assessed Ma's first term and the 2012 elections, on balance they were positive.[4]

Ma's second inaugural address reflected the caution that he now shows regarding stabilization in areas other than economics and business. Domestic politics was a major constraint. From his first inauguration to the second, he repeatedly confronted the limits of engaging Beijing on political and security issues before the Taiwan public was ready for him to do so. But internal opposition was not the only obstacle to further stabilization. Beijing has not figured out how to address Taipei's strong adherence to the Republic of China and its implications for cross-Strait relations and international society or how to reconcile China's claim of peaceful intentions with its continuing preparation for war. In that context, perhaps all that can reasonably happen during Ma's second term is to consolidate the gains of the first and to make sober preparation for advances into new arenas, stage by stage.

If the momentum of cross-Strait stabilization slows—something that Beijing appears to accept—then the chances of any progress toward resolution of the fundamental dispute will remain low to nil. Ma has explicitly ruled out any discussion of unification during his term, and Hu Jintao has long since made gradualism a hallmark of his policy. During Ma's first term Taipei did not negotiate issues of stabilization in a way or with a result that undermines its position in any future discussions on resolution. In the meantime, each side must find ways to assure the other that this very gradual process does not put its long-term goals at risk. The challenge to Taipei on this score is more complex because of the tendency of opposition forces and the media to read the worst into its assurances to Beijing. The most recent example of this tendency was the firestorm that occurred in April 2012 when a former chairman of the KMT reportedly told Hu Jintao that Taiwan and the Mainland constituted "one country, two areas." Ma tried to use his inaugural address to put the matter to rest, saying as noted above that the country under discussion was the Republic of China.

If there is a danger, it is that the PRC leadership will lose patience with the current mode of interaction with the Ma administration—mutual persuasion—and take advantage of the power asymmetry that exists between the two sides of the Strait to advance its goal of unification. There is certainly no objective reason for it to do so. If sentiment on Taiwan continues to favor some degree of engagement with China and if the Kuomintang is able to reflect that sentiment at election time, as it did in 2012 under less-than-optimal circumstances, then the possibility of any serious move by the Green forces toward independence is low to nonexistent. No doubt the DPP will regain the presidency at some point and perhaps the legislature. But at that point, generational change within society and the party, plus the discipline of election defeats, will incline DPP candidates and a new DPP president toward more moderate policies and practices than Chen Shui-bian pursued. What should be important for China are the policies that a future DPP administration pursues, not its past association with Taiwan independence.

Moreover, Beijing really has no reason to lose patience and resort to pressure, since its own policies are the reason that progress does not occur on political and security stabilization in the near term and ultimate resolution in the longer term. On unification, there has never been a market in Taiwan for Beijing's one-country, two-systems formula. The fundamental reason is the attachment of the island's political elite and a majority of the population to the Republic of China. If there were absolutely no way for China to reconcile its own goal of a political union that includes Taiwan with Taiwan's claim that it is a sovereign entity, then there might be reason for impatience. But dual sovereignty arrangements exist in modern political systems, and there are creative people on both sides of the Strait who might design a new arrangement "with Chinese characteristics." It is a mark of progress that some PRC scholars understand that their government must address the issue of the ROC if it wishes to achieve its fundamental goal.

For now, it appears that those in charge of Beijing's Taiwan policy are prepared to stick to the gradualism inherent in Hu Jintao's "peaceful development" policy. But Hu began the withdrawal from his paramount positions in November 2012, and his successors have the option, at least hypothetically, of insisting that Taipei accommodate their objectives more quickly. They also have the hypothetical option of accommodating Taipei in some way. There is no evidence that Xi Jinping and his colleagues will change policy, but in any case, they would not provide such evidence in the early stage of their rise to the very top. Once they get there, much will depend on their assessment of what they will gain by forcing the pace, the costs of not doing so, and the tolerance of the Taiwan public for yielding to Beijing. What they do will also depend on how they choose to use the growing power at their disposal, for good or ill. Regrettably, China does not have a good record of evaluating situations that are not to its liking, both generally and regarding Taiwan, and it has a tendency to blame others for the deficiencies of its own policies. Moreover, Beijing is only beginning to learn how to employ its new power. What would be best for all concerned would be for China to eschew leverage and pressure and, perhaps, meet Taipei halfway on the issues that fundamentally divide the two sides of the Strait.

Whatever the course of Chinese policy—and because there is a chance that Beijing will lose patience—it is in Taiwan's interest to strengthen itself. The objective should be to reduce the PRC's incentives to apply pressure on Taipei. The obvious areas of focus are economic competitiveness, military deterrence, relations with the United States, and political reform. None on its own is easy; doing all at the same time will be extremely hard. But a stronger Taiwan will be a more confident Taiwan, one that is better able to shape China's trajectory in its favor.

Because the Taiwan Strait remains uncharted, there is all the more reason for the United States to adhere to long-standing policy. It is in Washington's interest (to say nothing of Taiwan's) that China remain in the mode of mutual persuasion and reject any temptation to exploit its growing power asymmetry with the island. The United States can raise the odds of continuity rather than radical change by maintaining a robust presence in the Western Pacific and by insisting, as it has for decades, that China resolve the cross-Strait dispute peacefully—that is, without violence and without intimidation. It should quietly remind Beijing that the one-country, two-systems approach is the obstacle to the unification that it seeks, not Taiwan independence or U.S. meddling. Of course, such a policy will be more successful if Taiwan is prepared to help itself in appropriate ways. But much is at stake in whether and how the United States chooses to use its power here—not just the fate of the people of a fellow democracy, as if that were not enough, but also Washington's ability to shape the choices that China makes as it works to return to the ranks of the great powers.

Notes

Chapter One

1. "Full Text of Statement by Chen Yunlin, Director of CPC Central Committee Taiwan Work Office and of State Council Taiwan Affairs Office, on Current Cross-Strait Relations," Xinhua Domestic Service, May 22, 2008 (Open Source Center [hereafter OSC] CPP20080522705001).

2. "CNA: U.S. State Department Congratulates President Ma Ying-jeou on Inauguration," Central News Agency, May 21, 2008 (OSC CPP20080521968129).

3. Barack Obama letter to Ma Ying-jeou, May 20, 2008; on file with author.

4. China's own recent policy had facilitated this transition. Under President Hu Jintao, Beijing's goal had shifted from promoting unification to opposing independence, and China clarified the benefits that would flow to Taiwan if the island's leaders eschewed the objective of independence.

5. Since the early 1990s, officially there had been only indirect contact between Beijing and Taipei. At that time, neither regarded the other as a legal government. Taiwan relaxed its position somewhat early on; the PRC regime has stuck to its position that the government of the Republic of China ceased to exist at the time that the PRC was established on October 1, 1949, and that the rulers in Taipei were subnational "authorities." The two sides set up semi-official organizations to conduct negotiations on behalf of the two governments.

6. Those agreements had been virtually completed under the Chen Shui-bian administration, but Beijing had not wished to conclude them because doing so might have boosted the popularity of Ma's DPP opponent in the presidential election.

7. This digest is drawn from items that appeared between May 13 and May 27 in the Open Source Center's series of article summaries under the titles "Taiwan-China Highlights: Taishang News" and "Highlights: Cross-Strait News"; on file with author.

8. For an early DPP statement of skepticism concerning Ma's policies, see "Policy Briefing Session for Diplomats and Foreign Representatives," September 26, 2008 (www.dpp.org.tw/index_en).

9. "Lu Urges Close Scrutiny of China's Political Motives," *Taipei Times*, July 15, 2010 (OSC CPP20100715968004).

10. On the theme in Taiwan political culture of "traitors in our midst," see Richard C. Bush, *Untying the Knot: Making Peace in the Taiwan Strait* (Brookings, 2005), p. 149.

11. Alan D. Romberg, "Cross-Strait Relations: Weathering the Storm," *China Leadership Monitor*, no. 30 (Fall 2009) (http://media.hoover.org/documents/CLM30AR.pdf). In response to those calls, the Ma administration sent the message to Beijing that they were undermining Ma's domestic political standing.

12. U.S.-China Economic and Security Review Commission, Hearing, "China-Taiwan: Recent Economic, Political, and Military Developments across the Strait and Implications for the United States," March 18, 2010 (www.uscc.gov/hearings/2010hearings/hr10_03_18.php).

13. "Full Text: China's Peaceful Development," Xinhua English, September 6, 2011 (OSC CPP20110906968009).

14. On competing historical definitions of the Taiwan problem in U.S. policy, see Richard C. Bush, "The Status of the ROC and Taiwan, 1950–72: Explorations in United States Policy," in *At Cross Purposes: U.S.-Taiwan Relations since 1942* (Armonk, N.Y.: M.E. Sharpe, 2004), pp. 85–123.

15. See Bush, *Untying the Knot*, particularly pp. 27–107.

16. See Shelley Rigger, "The Unfinished Business of Taiwan's Democratization," in *Dangerous Strait: The U.S.-Taiwan-China Crisis*, edited by Nancy Bernkopf Tucker (Columbia University Press, 2005), pp. 16–43.

17. Richard C. Bush, "The Revival of China as a Great Power and What It Means for the United States," talk at Towson State University, November 17, 2008 (www.brookings.edu/speeches/2008/1117_china_bush.aspx).

Chapter Two

1. Richard C. Bush, *Untying the Knot: Making Peace in the Taiwan Strait* (Brookings, 2005). See also Denny Roy, *Taiwan: A Political History* (Cornell University Press, 2003); Nancy Bernkopf Tucker, *Taiwan, Hong Kong, and the United States, 1945–1992: Uncertain Friendship* (New York: Twayne Publishers, 1994); Jay Taylor, *The Generalissimo's Son: Chiang Ching-kuo and the Revolutions in China and Taiwan* (Harvard University Press, 2000); and Shelley Rigger, *Why Taiwan Matters: Small Island, Global Powerhouse* (New York: Rowman and Littlefield Publishers, 2011).

2. Deng Xiaoping stated that belief most stridently in the negotiations that resulted in China and the United States recognizing each other and establishing diplomatic relations; see Patrick Tyler, *A Great Wall: Six Presidents and China: An Investigative History* (New York: Public Affairs, 1999), p. 263.

3. Lee became president after Chiang Ching-kuo died in January 1988. He was selected again on an indirect basis in 1990. It was not until 1996 that Taiwan had direct presidential elections. On China's anxiety about Lee Teng-hui simply because he was Taiwanese, see Bush, *Untying the Knot*, pp. 205–06.

4. Shelley Rigger, *From Opposition to Power: Taiwan's Democratic Progressive Party* (Boulder, Colo.: Lynne Rienner, 2001), p. 125.

5. Thus, the first meeting of the leaders of SEF and ARATS achieved less than had been expected; see Steven Goldstein, "The Rest of the Story: The Impact of Domestic Politics on Taiwan's Mainland Policy," *Harvard Studies on Taiwan*, vol. 2 (1998), pp. 62–90.

6. Michael D. Swaine, "Chinese Decision-Making Regarding Taiwan: 1979–2000," in *The Making of Chinese Foreign and Security Policy in the Era of Reform*, edited by David Michael Lampton (Stanford University Press, 2001), pp. 289–336.

7. Lee restated past Taipei policy, called on Beijing to renounce the use of force, and generally blamed Beijing for the lack of progress; see Bush, *Untying the Knot*, p. 51.

8. Robert L. Suettinger, *Beyond Tiananmen: The Politics of U.S.-China Relations, 1989–2000* (Brookings, 2003), pp. 219–20. But Lee's speech was no different from what he had been saying on Taiwan.

9. David M. Finkelstein, "China's National Military Strategy: An Overview of the 'Military Strategic Guidelines,'" in *Right-Sizing the People's Liberation Army: Exploring the Contours of China's Military*, edited by Roy Kamphausen and Andrew Scobell (Carlisle, Pa.: Strategic Studies Institute, U.S. Army War College, 2007), pp. 69–140, especially pp. 115–17. The cited sections concerning Taiwan (on pp. 115–16) are from a 1993 speech by Jiang Zemin. The emphasis on Taiwan would take concrete form later in the decade as China purchased significant amounts of advanced military equipment abroad, especially from Russia.

10. In January 1995, Chinese president Jiang Zemin said: "Adhering to the principle of one China is the basis and prerequisite for peaceful reunification. China's sovereignty and territorial integrity must never be allowed to suffer division. We must resolutely oppose any statement and action . . . which are contrary to the principle of one China." See Taiwan Affairs Office, "Jiang Zemin's Eight-Point Proposal," January 30, 1995 (www.gwytb.gov.cn:8088/detail.asp?table=JiangEP&title=Jiang+Zemin%27s+Eight%2Dpoint+Proposal&m_id=3).

11. Bush, *Untying the Knot*, pp. 55–57.

12. This is one theme of Richard C. Bush and Michael E. O'Hanlon, *A War Like No Other: The Truth about China's Challenge to America* (New York: John Wiley and Sons, 2007).

13. On China's misunderstanding of Lee, see Richard Bush, "Lee Teng-hui and 'Separatism,'" in *Dangerous Strait: The U.S.-Taiwan-China Crisis*, edited by Nancy Bernkopf Tucker (Columbia University Press, 2005), pp. 70–92.

14. Taiwan also had its misunderstandings, and domestic politics were at play in China as well as Taiwan.

15. The resolution read: "Taiwan is a sovereign and independent country. . . . Taiwan, although named the Republic of China under its current constitution, is not subject to the jurisdiction of the People's Republic of China. Any change in the independent status quo must be decided by all residents of Taiwan by means of plebiscite"; see Rigger, *From Opposition to Power*, pp. 131–32.

16. That was ambiguous. The Chinese character "guo" can mean country or state, and he could have been referring to the PRC and the ROC.

17. On dual deterrence, see Richard Bush, "The U.S. Policy of Dual Deterrence," in *If China Attacks Taiwan: Military Strategy, Politics, and Economics*, edited by Steve Tsang (New York: Routledge, 2006), pp. 35–53; and Timothy Crawford, "Pivotal Deterrence and the Kosovo War: Why the Holbrooke Agreement Failed," *Political Science Quarterly*, vol. 116 (Winter 2001–02), pp. 499–523.

18. I and others have used the concept of "security dilemma" to explain the negative security spiral that occurred between China and Taiwan; see Bush, *Untying the Knot*, pp. 107–41; and Thomas J. Christensen, "The Contemporary Security Dilemma: Deterring a Taiwan Conflict," *Washington Quarterly*, vol. 25 (Autumn 2002), pp. 7–21. On the concept of the security dilemma generally, see Ken Booth and Nicholas J. Wheeler, *The Security Dilemma: Fear, Cooperation, and Trust in World Politics* (New York: Palgrave Macmillan, 2008).

19. "Taiwan Affairs Office of CPC Central Committee, Taiwan Affairs Office of State Council Are Authorized to Issue Statement on Current Cross-Strait Relations," Xinhua News Agency, May 17, 2004 (Open Source Center [hereafter OSC] CPP20040511600076); emphasis added.

20. "Full Text of Anti-Secession Law," *People's Daily*, March 14, 2005 (http://english.peopledaily.com.cn/200503/14/print20050314_176746.html).

21. "PRC's Hu Jintao, KMT's Lien Chan Issue Press Communiqué on 'Peaceful Cross-Strait Development,'" Xinhua, April 29, 2005 (OSC FEA20050429002897).

22. Qian Qichen, "Adhere to the Basic Policy of 'One Country, Two Systems' and Strive to Promote the Development of Cross-Strait Relations," Xinhua News Service, January 24, 2002 (OSC CPP20020124000121).

23. The "Mainland and Taiwan belong" clause was also worrisome, because it referred to geographic entities, not political ones. In addition, the PRC had a different formulation for purposes of the international system, one part of which was that Taiwan was a part of China. For more on Taiwan skepticism regarding the one-China principle, see Bush, *Untying the Knot*, pp. 287–88.

24. "Taiwan's Renaissance," Ma Ying-jeou inaugural address, May 20, 2008 (http://english.president.gov.tw/Default.aspx?tabid=491&itemid=16304&rmid=2355). For a comparison of Ma's performance relative to his inauguration proposals, see Alan D. Romberg, "Ma at Mid-Term: Challenges for Cross-Strait Relations," *China Leadership Monitor*, no. 33 (Summer 2010) (http://media.hoover.org/sites/default/files/documents/CLM33AR.pdf).

25. Richard C. Bush, "The Status of the ROC and Taiwan: Explorations in United States Policy," in *At Cross Purposes*, pp. 85–123; Bush, *Untying the Knot*, pp. 82–91.

26. Why was Ma ambiguous on these issues? Different observers had different answers. DPP partisans worried that he had a secret unification agenda and was not being honest with the Taiwan public. Some in China thought that Ma wanted to fortify the ROC as a second China, contrary to the one-China principle. Ma would say that it was only through deferring discussion of these issues ("mutual nondenial") that the two sides could achieve even the most basic progress.

27. Romberg, "Ma at Mid-Term."

28. "Blue" and "Green" refer to the main colors of the flags of the two parties.

29. In one television network poll done in early 2011, 50 percent of those surveyed said that they were Taiwanese, 3 percent said that they were Chinese, and 43 percent said that they were both Taiwanese and Chinese; see "TVBS on Identity and Independence," from "The View from Taiwan," the blog of Michael Turton, February 5, 2011 (http://michaelturton.blogspot.com/2011/02/tvbs-on-identity-and-independence.html).

30. Strangely, there has been no systematic polling on Taiwan to estimate the size of these blocs, which are the common categories for political discourse. I arrive at my rough estimate by assuming that the Deep Greens are those who tell pollsters that they want independence either immediately or later and that the Deep Blues are those who say that they want unification either right away or in the future. The "Light" blocs are composed of those who prefer the status quo. The figure for the Light Blues is the share of Ma Ying-jeou's supporters in late 2011 who favored the status quo while the figure for Light Greens is the analogous share of Tsai Ying-wen's supporters. See "Opinion Poll on Taiwan's Future," *United Daily News*, November 17, 2011 (OSC CPP20111117427010).

31. For a graph of recent trends, see "Party Identification Tracking Analysis," Global Views Survey Research Center, March 2010 (www.taiwansecurity.org/2010/GVSRC_PID_201002_Eng.pdf); see also Dafydd Fell, *Government and Politics in Taiwan* (New York: Routledge, 2012), p. 106.

32. Communication from Ho Szu-yin, November 2011.

33. Alan M. Wachman, *Taiwan: National Identity and Democratization* (Armonk, N.Y.: M. E. Sharpe, 1994).

34. Shelley Rigger, "Disaggregating the Concept of National Identity," *Asia Program Special Report* 114 (Washington: Woodrow Wilson International Center for Scholars, August 2003), pp. 17–21. This was originally presented at the Woodrow Wilson International Center for Scholars at an Asia Program event entitled "The Evolution of a Taiwanese Identity."

35. Similarly, American colonists came to define their identity through opposition to an imperial political order, in spite of the fact that most of them were of British origin.

36. For the multi-year trend, see Mainland Affairs Council, "The Pace of Cross-Strait Exchanges" (www.mac.gov.tw/public/Attachment/16914254123.gif). For the September 2011 poll, see Mainland Affairs Council, "MAC: The Public Highly Affirms

the Operation of the Mechanism for Institutionalized Cross-Strait Negotiations," press release 69, September 25, 2011 (www.mac.gov.tw/public/Data/1102614225371.pdf).

37. "2010 National Condition," *CommonWealth*, December 15, 2009 (http://www.cw.com.tw/article/index.jsp?id=39740).

38. Mainland Affairs Council, "Percentage Distribution of the Questionnaire for the Routine Survey on 'the Public's View on Current Cross-Strait Relations,'" February 2, 2012. The survey was conducted by the Election Study Center of National Chengchi University from November 26 to 30, 2011 (www.mac.gov.tw/ct.asp?xItem= 101204&ctNode=7280&mp=3).

39. Shelley Rigger, "Taiwan's Rising Rationalism: Generations, Politics, and 'Taiwanese Nationalism,'" *Policy Studies* no. 26, East-West Center, 2006; cited passage is on p. viii.

40. Zhang Nianchi, "My Humble Opinion on Some Important Issues on Current Cross-Strait Relations," *Zhongguo Pinglun*, October 2011 (OSC CPP20111003787012).

41. That dynamic appears to have been at work in the 2012 election; see the discussion on the 2012 election below.

42. Communication with Taiwan resident, August 14, 2011.

43. Kenneth G. Lieberthal, *Governing China: From Revolution through Reform*, 2nd ed. (New York: W.W. Norton, 2004); Andrew J. Nathan and Bruce Gilley, *China's New Rulers: The Secret Files*, 2nd rev. ed. (New York: New York Review of Books, 2003).

44. Suettinger, *Beyond Tiananmen*, pp. 224–25, 245–46, 262–63.

45. Linda Jakobson and Dean Knox, *New Actors Shape China's Foreign Policy* (Stockholm: Stockholm International Peace Research Institute, 2010).

46. Alice L. Miller, "The CCP Central Committee's Leading Small Groups," *China Leadership Monitor*, no. 28 (Fall 2008), pp. 11–12. On the proliferation of domestic interests involved in external affairs, see Jakobson and Knox, *New Actors Shape China's Foreign Policy*.

47. The most detailed account appears in Michael D. Swaine, "Chinese Decision-Making Regarding Taiwan." See also Andrew Scobell, *China's Use of Military Force: Beyond the Great Wall and the Long March* (Cambridge University Press, 2003), pp. 171–91.

48. Joseph Fewsmith and Stanley Rosen, "The Domestic Context of Chinese Foreign Policy: Does Public Opinion Matter?" in *The Making of Chinese Foreign and Security Policy*, edited by Lampton, pp. 158–69; cited passage is on p. 153.

49. Richard C. Bush, *The Perils of Proximity: China-Japan Security Relations* (Brookings, 2010), pp. 191–210.

50. Peter Hayes Gries, *China's New Nationalism: Pride, Politics, and Diplomacy* (University of California Press, 2004). Reliance on nationalism to promote legitimacy grew after Tiananmen.

Chapter Three

1. "Chinese, Taiwanese View Each Other Differently: Poll," Central News Agency, June 30, 2009 (Open Source Center [hereafter OSC] CPP20090630968242).

2. Note that in order to avoid prejudging the issue, I use the term "resolution of the fundamental dispute" rather than choose any specific form of resolution (for example, unification).

3. Richard C. Bush, *Untying the Knot: Making Peace in the Taiwan Strait* (Brookings, 2005), pp. 107-41.

4. Ibid., pp. 81–106.

5. Stephen D. Krasner, *Sovereignty: Organized Hypocrisy* (Princeton University Press, 1999), pp. 4, 11–25. See also Allen Carlson, *Unifying China, Integrating with the World: Securing Chinese Sovereignty in the Reform Era* (Stanford University Press, 2007).

6. "Join Hands to Promote Peaceful Development of Cross-Strait Relations; Strive with Unity of Purpose for the Great Rejuvenation of the Chinese Nation," Xinhua Domestic Service, December 31, 2008 (OSC CPP20081231005002). This address, which was given on the thirtieth anniversary of another key policy statement, certainly conveyed the outcome of a deliberative interagency process, on which see Richard C. Bush, *The Perils of Proximity: China-Japan Security Relations* (Brookings, 2010), pp. 149–55.

7. Alan Romberg concludes that Hu's policy is based on the "realization that it would take a long time to move to unification, and that in the meantime, the two sides needed to weave a fabric of relationships that could serve as the basis for ultimate 'reunification' on terms acceptable to both." See Alan D. Romberg, "Ma at Mid-Term: Challenges for Cross-Strait Relations," *China Leadership Monitor*, no. 33 (Summer 2010), p. 10 (http://media.hoover.org/sites/default/files/documents/CLM33AR.pdf).

8. Huang Jiashu, "Huang Jiashu: The Two Sides Should Not Deliberately Seek or Play Up Hostility," Zhongguo Pinglun Tongxunshe, November 14, 2009 (OSC CPP20091116710010).

9. Zhang Nianchi, "The Phase of Peaceful Development Needing Extra Care," *Zhongguo Pinglun*, no. 139 (July 2009) (OSC CPP20090709710011).

10. Li Peng, "Further Analysis on the Construction of the Framework for the Peaceful Development of Cross-Strait Relations," *Taiwan Yanjiu*, August 2009 (OSC CPP20091028671003).

11. "President Ma: More Time Sought for Deeper Cross-Strait Exchanges," *China Times*, September 1, 2010 (CPP20100901427002).

12. "Growing amid Challenges, Progressing amid Reconstruction," Ma Ying-jeou's 2009 National Day Speech, Central News Agency, October 10, 2009 (OSC CPP20091010968043).

13. "President Ma Tells *Washington Post* PRC, Taiwan Reached 'Workable Status Quo,'" Kuomintang, May 10, 2010 (OSC CPP20100410427003).

14. Yun-han Chu, "Rapprochement in the Taiwan Strait: The Opportunities and Challenges for Taipei," on file with author; cited passage is on pp. 99–110.

15. Bih-jaw Lin, "Taiwan: Why It Is Necessary to Consolidate Democracy and Enhance Governance under the New Status Quo," on file with author; cited passages are on pp. 6, 7.

16. Mark Landler, "Israel and Palestinian Leader Extend Egypt Talks," September 14, 2010 (www.nytimes.com/2010/09/15/world/middleeast/15mideast.html?_r= 1&ref=middleeast).

17. In developing this distinction, I was aided greatly by the ideas of Phillip C. Saunders of National Defense University; see his "Three Logics of Chinese Policy toward Taiwan and Taiwan's Strategic Responses," draft paper presented at the conference "A New Strategy for a New Era: Revisiting Taiwan's National Security Strategy," Taipei, August 27–28, 2011 (cited by permission). Saunders presents three logics: persuasion, leverage, and united front. I would argue that leverage and united front are each a part of the exploitation of power asymmetry.

18. "Taiwan's Ma Ying-jeou Delivers Victory Speech, Touches on Cross-Strait Ties," China Television Company, January 14, 2012 (OSC CPP20120114004001).

19. During Chen Shui-bian's administration, Chen suggested an integration model for bringing China and Taiwan together. The opposition Kuomintang then floated a proposal for a Chinese confederation, which it thought was a formula wherein both China's desire for unification and Taiwan's need to preserve a sovereign status could be accommodated. Beijing rejected both ideas. See Bush, *Untying the Knot*, pp. 272–76.

20. Alan D. Romberg, "After the Taiwan Election: Restoring Dialogue while Reserving Options," *China Leadership Monitor*, no. 25 (Summer 2008) (http://media. hoover.org/sites/default/files/documents/CLM25AR.pdf), p. 13. The Chinese for Siew's formulation is 正视现实，开创未来，搁置争议，追求双赢 (*zhengshi xianshi, kaichuang weilai, gezhizhengyi, chuiqiu shuangying*); for Hu's, it is 建立互信，搁置争议，求同存异，共创双赢 (*jianli huxin, gezhi zhengyi, qiutong cunyi, kongchuang shuangying*).

21. Thomas Powers, "He Got the Big Things Right," *New York Review of Books*, April 26, 2012, p. 35.

22. On the potential of leverage, see Robert Sutter, "Taiwan's Future: Narrowing Straits," NBR Analysis, National Bureau of Asian Research, May 2011 (http://csis.org/files/media/csis/pubs/pac0917.pdf).

23. Yan Anlin, "Building a Framework for Peaceful Development Is a Task for Both Sides of the Strait: A Pondering on the Future of Cross-Strait Relations after Ma Ying-jeou's Reelection," *Zhongguo Pinglun*, April 2012 (OSC CPP20120403787001).

24. Office of the Secretary of Defense, "Annual Report to Congress: Military and Security Developments Involving the People's Republic of China 2010," released August 2011, p. 1 (www.defense.gov/pubs/pdfs/2011_CMPR_Final.pdf).

25. See, for example, Chas W. Freeman Jr., "The Taiwan Problem and China's Strategy for Resolving It," remarks at the Center for Naval Analysis, September 14, 2011 (www.mepc.org/articles-commentary/speeches/taiwan-problem-and-chinas-strategy-resolving-it).

Chapter Four

1. Jay Taylor, *The Generalissimo's Son: Chiang Ching-kuo and the Revolutions in China and Taiwan* (Harvard University Press, 2000), pp. 369–70.

2. Daniel H. Rosen and Zhi Wang, *The Implications of China-Taiwan Economic Liberalization*, Policy Analysis in International Economics 93 (Washington: Peterson Institute for International Economics, January 2011), p. 32.

3. For an in-depth examination of Taiwan's place in global supply chains in the information technology sector, see Merritt T. Cooke, "The Politics of Greater China's Integration into the Global Info Tech (IT) Supply Chain," *Journal of Contemporary China*, vol. 13 (August 2004), pp. 491–506.

4. On the division of labor in the Taiwan shoe industry, see You-tien Hsing, *Making Capitalism in China: The Taiwan Connection* (Oxford University Press, 1998).

5. Douglas Fuller draws an important contrast between companies in Taiwan's integrated-circuit sector and the systems manufacturers that manage supply chains on behalf of major multinational corporations. The former are technologically strong and hold their own vis-à-vis leading global firms, but the latter are in a dependent position that has subjected them to pressures to cut costs. See Douglas B. Fuller, "The Changing Limits and the Limits of Change: The State, Private Firms, International Industry, and China in the Evolution of Taiwan's Electronics Industry," *Journal of Contemporary China*, vol. 14 (August 2005), pp. 483–506.

6. American Chamber of Commerce in Taipei, "2012 Taiwan White Paper," *Taiwan Business Topics*, vol. 42 (May 2011), p. WP14.

7. Philip Liu, "ECFA: A Shot in the Arm for Taiwan's Economy," *Taiwan Economic News*, July 6, 2010 (Open Source Center [hereafter OSC] CPP20100706968113); "CNA: Taiwan Service Sector May Face Boycott after ECFA Signing," Central News Agency, June 25, 2010 (OSC CPP20100625968182).

8. "Taiwan Releases English Version of ECFA Text," Ministry of Economic Affairs, September 21, 2010 (OSC CPP20100921312005). The committee was established on January 6, 2011; see "Cross-Strait Trade Committee Launched," *China Post*, January 7, 2011 (OSC CPP20110107968057).

9. Mo Yan-chih, "SEF and ARATS Review Previous Talks in Taipei," *Taipei Times*, June 9, 2011 (OSC CPP 20110609968002).

10. Lin Shu-yuan and Ann Chen, "CNA: Taiwan, China to Exchange Trade Representative Offices," Central News Agency, January 10, 2012 (OSC CPP20120110968209).

11. Qiang Xin, "Beyond Power Politics: Institution-building and Mainland China's Taiwan Policy Transition," *Journal of Contemporary China*, vol. 19 (June 2010), p. 534.

12. Ho Meng-kui, Chiu Kuo-chiang, and Bear Lee, "CNA: Taipei Urged to Stand Firm on International Arbitration in China Pact," Central News Agency, September 21, 2011 (OSC CPP20110921968178); "Secret Detention Is Top Fear for Taiwan's Businessmen in China," *Want China Times*, September 27, 2011 (OSC CPP20110927968106).

13. Shu-ling Ko, "Cross-Strait Obstacles Still Remain: Ma," *Taipei Times*, April 12, 2011 (www.taipeitimes.com/News/taiwan/archives/2011/04/12/2003500542).

14. Shalendra D. Sharma, "Taiwan Takes on China . . . and Wins," *Global Asia*, vol. 5 (Winter 2010), p. 71. On the short-term nature of the forecast, see Rosen and Wang, *Implications of China-Taiwan Economic Liberalization*, p. 70.

15. Rosen and Wang, *Implications of China-Taiwan Economic Liberalization*, pp. 68–70.

16. Ibid., pp. 73–75.

17. Sharma, "Taiwan Takes on China . . . and Wins," p. 71.

18. Rosen and Wang, *Implications of China-Taiwan Economic Liberalization*, p. 70.

19. Chen-yuan Tung, "The East Asian Economic Integration Regime and Taiwan," *Asian Perspective*, vol. 34 (2010), pp. 83–112.

20. "Excerpts of Taiwan President Ma's 1 July Statement on Signing ECFA," Office of the President of the ROC, July 1, 2010 (OSC 20100706427001). In China, Wang Yi, head of China's Taiwan Affairs Office, called the signing "a 'milestone' in the peaceful development of cross-Strait relations." See "Mainland's Taiwan Affairs Chief Hails Economic Pacts," Xinhua English, June 29, 2010 (OSC CPP20100629968163).

21. Ching-Hsuan Huang, "2010 Top 1000 CEO Survey: Optimism on the Upswing," *CommonWealth*, no. 463 (December 30, 2010) (http://english.cw.com.tw/article.do?action=show&id=12533); "2011 Business Climate Survey," *Taiwan Business Topics*, vol. 40, no. 12 (December 2010) (www.amcham.com.tw/content/blogcategory/273/477/), p. 42.

22. Li Hanfang, "Cross-Strait Scholars: Signing of ECFS Helps Establish a New Cross-Strait Economic Cooperation Model," Xinhua Domestic, June 29, 2010 (OSC CPP20100629318004).

23. Chih-Cheng Lo and Tien-Wang Tsaur, *Deconstructing ECFA: Challenges and Opportunities* (Taipei: Taiwan Brain Trust, 2010). For the core-periphery prediction, see Tien-Lin Huang, "ECFA and the Core-Periphery Effect," in *Deconstructing ECFA*, edited by Lo and Tsaur, pp. 75–89; cited passage is on p.78.

24. "Taiwan Should Avoid Excessive Economic Reliance on China," *Want China Times*, January 31, 2011 (www.wantchinatimes.com/news-print-cnt.aspx?id=20110130000037&cid=1701).

25. T. J. Cheng, "China-Taiwan Economic Linkage: Between Insulation and Superconductivity," in *Dangerous Strait: The U.S.-Taiwan-China Crisis*, edited by Nancy Bernkopf Tucker (Columbia University Press, 2005), pp. 104–16.

26. Tsai Ing-wen, "Taiwan and Globalization: An Island Nation Perspective," Democratic Progressive Party, January 2010 (OSC CPP20100503427001).

27. Chen-yuan Tung, "A Closer Look at the Elections," *Taipei Times*, December 3, 2010 (OSC CPP2010120396822).

28. "Results of Implementing Provisions of the Cross-Straits Economic Cooperation Framework Agreement's Early Harvest Program," *Taiwan in Depth*, March 16, 2012 (OSC CPP20120316312002).

29. Jacques deLisle, "Taiwan: Elections at Home, Economic Relations with the Mainland, and U.S.-China-Taiwan Relations: An FPRI Symposium Report," *E-Notes*, Foreign Policy Research Institute, January 2011 (www.fpri.org/enotes/ 201101.delisle.taiwanelection.html).

30. James Lee, "ECFA's Early Harvest Program Successful: MOEA," Central News Agency, July 29, 2011 (OSC CPP20110729968186); Vincent Y. Chao, "ECFA Impact Should Be Reassessed: Academics," *Taipei Times*, June 28, 2011 (OSC CPP20110630968124); Kwangyin Liu, "ECFA Delivers Record Growth in Taiwan Investment," *Taiwan Today*, June 7, 2011 (www.taiwantoday.tw/ct.asp?xItem= 166785&ctNode=445). For a detailed review of results for 2011, see "Results of Implementing Provisions."

31. Hung-Mao Tien and Chen-Yuan Tung, "Taiwan in 2010: Mapping for a New Political Landscape and Economic Outlook," *Asian Survey*, vol. 51 (January-February 2011), p. 82; Chen Hsiu-lan, "One Year Later, Taiwanese Officials Assess Cross-Strait ECFA," *Want China Times*, September 17, 2011 (OSC CPP20110917968083); "Results of Implementing Provisions."

32. Mainland Affairs Council, "Opening Up and Guarding the Country: Benefits of 15 Cross-Strait Agreements," July 2011 (www.mac.gov.tw/public/Data/ 181811155971.pdf), pp. 5, 9, 10, 11, 12, 25.

33. Liu Chien-pang and Elizabeth Hsu, "CNA: 3 Million Chinese Visit Taiwan in Tour Groups since May 2008," Central News Agency, January 4, 2012 (OSC CPP20120104968180).

34. Jane Rickards, "Gauging the Cross-Strait Economic Impact," *Taiwan Business Topics*, vol. 41, no. 12 (December 2011), pp. 18–26.

35. Chen-yuan Tung, "ECFA Not a Free Ride for Taiwan," *Taipei Times*, July 4, 2010 (www.taipeitimes.com/News/editorials/archives/2010/07/04/2003477063/2).

36. Ibid.; Rosen and Wang, *Implications of China-Taiwan Economic Liberalization*, pp. 78–92.

37. Rosen and Wang, *Implications of China-Taiwan Economic Liberalization*, pp. 102–03.

38. Hsiao-Wen Wang, "Taiwan's Fast-Growing Enterprises: China: A Giant Stage for Small Enterprises," *CommonWealth*, no. 451, July 15, 2010 (http://english.cw.com.tw/ article.do?action=show&id=12111).

39. Shu-ren Koo, "Taiwan's Trade Strategy: The Dangers of ECFA Obsession," *CommonWealth*, no. 434, November 12, 2009 (http://english.cw.com.tw/article.do?action= show&id=11504).

40. Peter Tzeng, "The Lost Paradigm: Taiwan's SME Sector," *Taiwan Business Topics*, vol. 39, no. 9 (September 2009), pp. 16–24.

41. Rosen and Wang, *Implications of China-Taiwan Economic Liberalization*, p. 96.

42. Hsiu-chuan Shih, "Little Support for Ma's China Policy: Poll," *Taipei Times*, October 25, 2011 (OSC CPP20111025968012).

43. "President Ma Ying-jeou's Approval and Trust Ratings," Kuomintang, August 19, 2011 (www.kmt.org.tw/english/page.aspx?type=article&mnum=114&anum=10024). The ratings were based on polls done by the Global Views Survey Research Center, which is no longer in operation. The conclusion that Ma's approval rating tracked the ups and downs of the global economy and so forth is based on research done by Jennifer Mason.

44. Kevin Tze Wai Wong, "The Emergence of Class Cleavage in Taiwan in the Twenty-First Century: The Impact of Cross-Strait Economic Integration," *Issues and Studies*, vol. 46 (June 2010), pp. 127–72.

45. To-Far Wang, "ECFA Beijing Possessed," in *Deconstructing ECFA: Challenges and Opportunities*, edited by Lo and Tsaur, pp. 98–99.

46. Specifically, it said that agreements were signed by semi-official organizations (SEF and ARATS) and that the Ma administration had not treated ECFA as an agreement under the aegis of the World Trade Organization, which would have given it a more interstate character. See I-chung Lai, "Examination of Cross-strait Agreements that Weaken Taiwan's Sovereignty, Circumvent Reality, and Build on Illusions," *Taiwan Brain Trust Newsletter*, no. 16, June 2011 (OSC CPP20110804312001).

47. "Chinese Mainland Reiterates Importance of 1992 Consensus for Cross-Strait Ties," Xinhua English, December 29, 2010 (OSC CPP20101229968081).

48. From the summary of Yue-chien Lai, "1992 Consensus Favorable," *Lien-ho Pao*, January 6, 2010 (OSC CPP20110107086002).

49. "Establishment and History of the SEF," Straits Exchange Foundation (www.sef.org.tw/ct.asp?xItem=48843&CtNode=3987&mp=300).

50. I was chairman of AIT and head of its Washington office from 1997 to 2002.

51. Mignonne M. J. Chen, "Implications of Economic Cooperation Framework Agreement (ECFA) for Taiwan, Cross-Strait Development, and Regional Integration," *Prospects and Perspectives*, no. 13 [Prospect Foundation newsletter] (September 2010) (www.pf.org.tw/).

52. "Cross-Strait Trade Committee Launched," *China Post*, January 7, 2011 (OSC CPP20110107968057).

53. "Cross-Strait Economic Cooperation Committee Established," *Want China Times*, January 6, 2011 (www.wantchinatimes.com/news-subclass-cnt.aspx?cid=1102&MainCatID=&id=20110106000147). The information about meeting venues and phone contact was revealed in my interviews with Taiwan officials.

54. All references to the financial cooperation agreement are to Mainland Affairs Council, "The Third Round of the Chiang-Chen Talks: Economic and Trade Matters," April 2009 (www.mac.gov.tw/public/Data/972210564271.pdf), pp. 17–21.

55. In this context, "supply" refers to one side providing some of its currency to the other so that its banks can conduct business in that currency. "Flowback" refers to a bank's selling its excess supply of the other's currency back to the other side. Supply and flowback are especially necessary in the absence of fully open foreign exchange markets.

56. Peter T. Y. Cheung, "Intergovernmental Relations between Mainland China and the Hong Kong SAR," in *Public Administration in Southeast Asia: Thailand, Philippines, Malaysia, Hong Kong, and Macao*, edited by Evan M. Berman (Boca Raton, Fla.: CRC Press, 2011), pp. 255–81.

57. "MAC Confirms Delays to Cross-Strait Investment Protection Pact Talks," *China Post*, June 21, 2012 (OSC CPP 20120621968219). The other unresolved issue was how quickly local Chinese authorities who detained a Taiwan business person were required to notify his or her family.

58. Jason Tan and Lisa Wang, "Minister Downplays Impact of U.S.-S. Korea FTA," *Taipei Times*, October 15, 2011 (OSC CPP 20111015968015); Angela Tsai and Ann Chen, "CNA: Taiwan to Resume Export Tax Rebates to Battle South Korea," Central News Agency, October 6, 2011 (OSC CPP20111009968098); Sherry Tang and others, "CNA: U.S.-South Korea FTA Forecast to Cost Taiwan US$3 Billion," Central News Agency, March 15, 2012 (OSC CPP20120315968237).

59. Sophia Wu, "CNA: Taiwan, Japan Investment Pact Symbolizes Major Progress in Bilateral Ties," Central News Agency, September 22, 2011 (OSC CPP20110922968153).

60. Democratic Progressive Party, "National Security Strategy," August 2011 (www.scribd.com/doc/62902537/National-Security-Strategy-2011).

61. "Lu Urges Close Scrutiny of China's Political Motives," *Taipei Times*, July 15, 2010 (OSC CPP20100715968004).

62. "The Outline of the 12th Five-Year Program for National Economic and Social Development of the People's Republic of China," Xinhua Domestic, March 16, 2011 (OSC CPP20110316047002).

63. Zhao Liqing, "ECFA hou liangan heping fazhan chincheng: xianjun houzheng shixian Hu-Ma hui [The Course of the Peaceful Development of Cross-Strait Relations after ECFA: Do Military Issues First and Political Ones Later and So Realize a Hu-Ma Summit]," *Zhongguo Pinglun*, July 2010, p. 4.

64. "Political Issues Can No Longer Be Avoided Following the ECFA Signing between the Two Sides," Zhongguo Pinglun Tongxunshe, July 2, 2010 (OSC 2010070216306).

65. Zhang Nianchi, "ECFA, Cross-Strait Relations," *Zhongguo Pinglun*, September 2010 (OSC CPP20100907707001).

66. Office of the President of the Republic of China, "President Chen Shui-bian's New Year Message," December 31, 2000 (OSC CPP20001231000031). The Taiwan scholar who most clearly applied the concept of functional integration to Taiwan was the late Yung Wei. See, for example, Wei Yung, "From Functional Integration to Structural Readjustment: Taipei-Beijing Relations and the Role of the United States," *Journal of Contemporary China*, vol. 13 (August 2004), pp. 427–60.

67. David Huang, "Integration's the Key to Strait Woes," *Taipei Times*, February 13, 2001 (www.taipeitimes.com/News/edit/archives/2001/02/23/73496).

68. Christopher M. Dent, "The International Political Economy of Northeast Asian Economic Integration," in *Northeast Asian Regionalism: Lessons from the European*

Experience, edited by Christopher M. Dent and David W. F. Huang (New York: Routledge, 2002), pp. 81–82.

69. Michael O'Neill, *The Politics of European Integration: A Reader* (New York: Routledge, 1996), pp. 81–121.

70. Andrew Moravcsik, *The Choice for Europe: Social Purpose and State Power from Messina to Maastricht* (Cornell University Press, 1998), pp. 1–17; cited passage is on pp. 15–16.

71. Interview with a former Taiwan official, October 2010.

72. Chen, "One Year Later, Taiwanese Officials Assess Cross-Strait ECFA."

Chapter Five

1. "Wang Yi: Give Precedence to Handling Economic Affairs and Proceed Gradually in an Orderly Manner; Place Emphasis on Developing Mutual Trust and Act Gradually to Address Difficult Problems," Xinhua Domestic, April 26, 2009 (Open Source Center [hereafter OSC] CPP20090426072017).

2. Alan D. Romberg, "Cross-Strait Relations: Weathering the Storm," *China Leadership Monitor*, no. 30 (Fall 2009) (http://media.hoover.org/documents/CLM30AR.pdf), p. 12.

3. Yu Keli, "The Two Sides of the Strait Should Look Squarely at the Issue of Ending the State of Hostility and Signing a Peace Agreement," *Zhongguo Pinglun*, August 2009 (OSC CPP20090805710007); Wang Ping and Liu Xiaodan, "Researcher Guo Zhenyuan Says Cross-Strait Peaceful Development Needs to be Secured by an Agreement," Zhongguo Pinglun Tongxunshe, August 14, 2009 (OSC CPP 20090814710001). Both Yu and Guo used the bottleneck metaphor to argue specifically for an early conclusion of a peace accord, but they were making a broader point as well.

4. Huang Jiashu, "Guanyu liangan zhengzhi tanpan di sikao [Pondering Cross-Strait Political Talks]," *Zhongguo Pinglun*, no. 155 (December 2010), p. 4.

5. Chang Ya-chung, "Liangan zhuquan gongxiang yu teshu guanxi [Shared Sovereignty and the Special Relationship in Cross-Strait Relations]," *Zhongguo Pinglun* (February 2010), p. 11.

6. Chen Binhua and Ying Jian, "Zheng Bijian: The Path to Peaceful Development of Cross-Strait Relations Will Open Up Wider," Xinhua Domestic, November 13, 2009 (OSC CPP20091113062012). On the DPP reaction, see Wen Kuei-hsiang and Bear Lee, "CNA: Taiwan's Opposition Camp Angry at Beijing Scholar's Remarks," Central News Agency, November 14, 2009 (OSC CPP20091114968164).

7. Liu Chen-ching, Chang Ming-kun, and Bear Lee, "CNA: Taiwan Scholar Urges Latitude in Cross-Strait Peace Pact," Central News Agency, November 14, 2009 (OSC CPP20091014681165).

8. Alan D. Romberg, "2010: The Winter of PRC Discontent," *China Leadership Monitor*, no. 31 (Winter 2010) (http://media.hoover.org/documents/CLM31AR.pdf), p. 2.

9. "Beijing Does Not Have a Timetable for Political Talks with Taiwan," *Yazhou Zhoukan*, April 4, 2010 (OSC CPP20100330710006); the official cited in this article was Taiwan Affairs Office director Wang Yi.

10. "Editorial: Let Them Come, Let Them Speak," *Taipei Times*, November 17, 2009 (OSC CPP20091117968006).

11. Romberg, "Cross-Strait Relations: Weathering the Storm," p. 13.

12. For example, see Ma Ying-jeou, remarks at "Taiwan's Role in Peace and Stability in East Asia: A Discussion with Dr. Ma Ying-jeou," Brookings, March 23, 2006 (www.brookings.edu/~/media/events/2006/3/23taiwan/20060323.pdf).

13. Ma Ying-jeou, "Taiwan's Renaissance," inaugural address, Office of the President, May 20, 2008 (http://english.president.gov.tw/Default.aspx?tabid=491&itemid=16304&rmid=2355).

14. Hu Jintao, "Join Hands to Promote Peaceful Development of Cross-Strait Relations; Strive with Unity of Purpose for the Great Rejuvenation of the Chinese Nation," speech at the Forum Marking the 30th Anniversary of the Issuance of the "Message to Compatriots in Taiwan," Xinhua Domestic Service, December 31, 2008 (OSC CPP20081231005002).

15. "Taiwan Defense White Paper Includes Confidence-Building Measures with China," *Taiwan News*, October 20, 2009 (OSC CPP20091020968201); "Full Text: China's National Defense in 2010," Xinhua English, March 31, 2011 (OSC CPP20110331968049).

16. "How to Develop Cross-Strait Military Confidence-Building Measures?" *KMT Policy Committee Biweekly on Mainland Situation*, no. 1561 (October 14, 2009), pp. 1–5 (OSC CPP20091016312003).

17. Yu, "The Two Sides of the Strait Should Look Squarely at the Issue of Ending the State of Hostility and Signing a Peace Agreement." Wang Weixing, a scholar with the PLA's Academy of Military Sciences used the same "bottleneck" metaphor. See Wang Weixing, "Soldiers on Both Sides of the Strait Should Join Hands in Building Military Security Trust," *Zhongguo Pinglun*, February 2009 (OSC CPP20090204710006).

18. Yu Keli, "Promoting Political Relations Is the Only Way for the Two Sides," *Zhongguo Pinglun*, December 2009 (CPP20091230710007).

19. "Benqi Huitan: Chuli Liangan Zhengzhi Nanti You Xinjie [The Motosu Meeting: A New Understanding of Managing the Difficult Cross-Strait Political Issue]," Zhongguo Pinglunshe, April 9, 2002 (www.chinareviewnews.com/crn-webapp/search/allDetail.jsp?id=101310736&sw=%E6%9C%AC%E6%A0%96%E4%BC%9A%E8%B0%88). For more on the dynamics of negotiations, see Richard C. Bush, *Untying the Knot: Making Peace in the Taiwan Strait* (Brookings, 2005), pp. 270–96.

20. Mainland Affairs Council, "The Third Round of Chiang-Chen Talks: Joint Crime-Fighting and Judicial Assistance," June 6, 2009 (www.mac.gov.tw/public/Data/97221050871.pdf), pp. 6–12.

21. "China Vice Security Minister Visited Taiwan, Report Says," *Taipei Times*, September 28, 2010 (OSC CPP20100928055001); "NPA Director-General Returns from

Historic Mainland Visit for Police Cooperation," Kuomintang, November 4, 2010 (OSC CPP20101104427005); "Taiwan's Top Prosecutor Leads Delegation to Beijing," *China Post,* June 8, 2011 (OSC CPP20110608968286).

22. "Cross-Strait Cooperation Cited as Key in Fight against Crime: Police," *China Post,* March 3, 2011 (OSC CPP20110303968095); Michael Wines, "Nearly 600 Arrested in Asian Swindling Ring," *New York Times,* June 10, 2011, p. 7.

23. Drew Thompson, "The Geopolitics of Cross-Strait Disaster Relief," *China Brief,* vol. 9, September 10, 2009 (www.jamestown.org/programs/chinabrief/single/?tx_ ttnews%5Btt_news%5D=35470&tx_ttnews%5BbackPid%5D=25&cHash=4d33f614ab); "Tzu Chi Establishes Foundation in Mainland China," Kuomintang, August 23, 2010 (OSC CPP20100823427001).

24. Bush, *Untying the Knot,* pp. 226–29. For a 2011 inventory of Taiwan's international participation, see T. Y. Wang, Wei-Chin Lee, and Ching-Hsin Yu, "Taiwan's Expansion of International Space: Opportunities and Challenges," *Journal of Contemporary China,* vol. 20 (March 2011), pp. 249–67.

25. Bonnie S. Glaser, remarks at "International Organizations and Taiwan," Brookings, March 14, 2011 (www.brookings.edu/~/media/events/2011/3/14%20taiwan/20110314_taiwan.pdf), pp. 19–20.

26. "Taiwan to Take Part in UN Women's Session," *Taiwan Today,* February 24, 2012 (OSC CPP20120224968150). The Commission on the Status of Women is a functional commission of the UN Economic and Social Council.

27. Glaser, remarks at "International Organizations and Taiwan"; cited passage is on p. 20. See also Alan D. Romberg, "Cross-Strait Relations: Setting the Stage for 2012," *China Leadership Monitor,* no. 34 (Winter 2011) (http://media.hoover.org/sites/default/files/documents/CLM34AR.pdf), p. 14. For another careful analysis of Taiwan's mixed record in expanding international space since 2008, see Sigrid Winkler, "Taiwan's UN Dilemma: To Be or Not to Be," June 2012, Brookings Center for Northeast Asian Policy Studies, *Taiwan-U.S. Quarterly Analysis* 1 (www.brookings.edu/research/opinions/2012/06/20-taiwan-un-winkler).

28. Romberg, "Cross-Strait Relations: Setting the State for 2012," p. 12.

29. Ching-Hsuan Huang, "2009 Top 1000 CEO Survey: Both Optimism and Concern for Cross-strait Ties," *CommonWealth,* no. 421, May 5, 2009 (http://english.cw.com.tw/article.do?action=show&id=11000); Mainland Affairs Council, "Minister Lai Shin-yuan Meets with ARATS Chairman Chen Yunlin in Taichung This Afternoon," December 22, 2009 (http://www.mac.gov.tw/ct.asp?xItem=72181&ctNode=6665&mp=203); Nancy Liu, "CNA: Sovereignty Persists as a Challenge In Reelection: President," Central News Agency, May 13, 2011 (OSC CPP20110513968116).

30. Hu, "Join Hands to Promote Peaceful Development of Cross-Strait Relations." The Hu Jintao–Lien Chan joint statement of April 2005 asserted that "carrying forward together Chinese culture help[s] to eliminate alienation, increase mutual trust, and accumulate consensus"; see "'Full text' of 'Press Communiqué on Talks Between CPC

General Secretary Hu Jintao and KMT Chairman Lien Chan on 29 April 2005,'" Xinhua Domestic Service, April 29, 2005 (OSC CPP20050429000169).

31. On the reasons for the growing salience of identity politics, see chapter 4; Bush, *Untying the Knot*, pp. 142–55; and Alan M. Wachman, *Taiwan: National Identity and Democratization* (Armonk, N.Y.: M.E. Sharpe, 1994), pp. 119–24.

32. "2010 State of the Nation Survey: Income Gap of People's Minds," *Common-Wealth*, no. 437, December 15, 2009 (http://english.cw.com.tw/article.do?action=show&id=11589&offset=3), pp. 4–5. Syaru Shirley Lin demonstrates that the marginalization of the Chinese-only identity occurred as Taiwan gradually converged around more centrist and pragmatic economic policies; see her "National Identity, Economic Interdependence, and Taiwan's Cross-Strait Policy: The Case of ECFA," in *New Dynamics in Cross-Taiwan Straits Relations: How Far Can the Rapprochement Go*? edited by Richard Weixing Hu (London: Routledge, 2013, forthcoming).

33. Hu, "Join Hands to Promote Peaceful Development of Cross-Strait Relations."

34. Ma Ying-jeou, "Building Up Taiwan, Invigorating Chinese Heritage," New Year's Day Message, Office of the President, January 1, 2011 (http://english.president.gov.tw/Default.aspx?tabid=491&itemid=23186&rmid=2355).

35. "About 270 People from Taiwan to Attend Cross-Strait Forum: KMT," Xinhua English, July 8, 2009 (OSC PP20090708968280).

36. "Text of Joint Proposition of the Cross-Strait Economic and Cultural Forum," Xinhua Domestic, July 12, 2009 (OSC CPP20090712005001).

37. "Cross-Strait Cultural Exchanges Two-Way, Reciprocal: Chinese Official," Central News Agency, September 7, 2010 (CPP20100907968146); "Cool Response in Taiwan to Proposal of China Culture Minister for Cultural Agreement," *Taiwan News*, September 6, 2010 (CPP20100906968145); "Taiwan Prepared to Negotiate Cultural Pact with China: Official," Central News Agency, December 18, 2010 (CPP20101218968072).

38. "Chinese United by Cultural Ties," *China Daily*, January 19, 2011 (OSC CPP20110119968021); "Different Views on Chinese Cultural Identity Exchanged at Cross-Strait Conference," *United Daily News*, January 19, 2011 (OSC CPP20110119312012). Cited passage is from "MAC Minister Questions Need for Cultural Pact," *Taiwan Today*, January 19, 2011 (OSC CPP20110119968222). In an article later in January, Wang Yi called for the two sides to "continuously accumulate a consensus for signing an agreement on cultural and educational exchanges"; see Wang Yi, "The Cultural Realm and Cross-Strait Pursuits," *People's Daily*, January 31, 2011 (OSC CPP20110126787005).

39. David G. Brown, "China-Taiwan Relations: Economic Cooperation Framework Agreement Signed," *Comparative Connections*, vol. 12 (July 2010), n.p. (http://csis.org/files/publication/1002qchina_taiwan.pdf); "Draft Cross-Strait Education ECFA Ready for MAC Review," Central News Agency, August 29, 2010 (OSC CPP20100829968050).

40. Andrew Jacobs, "A Reunified Painting Stirs Big Thoughts in China and Taiwan," *New York Times*, July 6, 2011, p. 7.

41. Zhao Lingmin, "Taiwan: Impression and Thoughts," *Nanfang Chuang,* July 18, 2011 (OSC CPP20110801787004); Andrew Jacobs, "As Chinese Visit Taiwan, the Cultural Influence Is Subdued," *New York Times,* August 10, 2011, p. 4. It is worth noting that the sort of public behavior that the journalist describes on the Mainland today was fairly common on Taiwan in the mid-1970s. For a sophisticated PRC treatment of the commonalities and difference between Taiwan and Mainland culture, see Yu Xintian, "Liangan wenhua youyitong: ying bingqi qujieh" [Culture on the Two Sides of the Strait Has Similarities and Differences; It's Necessary to Eliminate Distortions], *Zhongguo Pinglun,* July 2010, pp. 10–14.

42. Han Han, "Discovering in Taiwan What Has Been Lost on the Mainland," *South China Morning Post,* May 19, 2012 (OSC CPP20120519704013).

43. Jean-Pierre Cabestan, "Reactions on the Mainland to the Taiwanese Election," *China Analysis,* April 2012, pp. 3–5 (http://ecfr.eu/page/-/China_Analysis_Taiwan_after_the_election_April2012.pdf).

44. Zhou Zhihuai, "Exploration of Several Issues in Process of Peaceful Development of Cross-Strait Ties," *Zhongguo Pinglun,* May 2012, pp. 4–7 (OSC CPP20120504787017).

45. Hu, "Join Hands to Promote Peaceful Development of Cross-Strait Relations."

46. On this point, see Lin Hsiu-chi, "Consensus Must be Reached on Connotation of 'One China,'" *Ta Kung Pao,* February 24, 2010 (OSC CPP20100224710005).

47. Li Peng, "Further Analysis on the Construction of the Framework for the Peaceful Development of Cross-Strait Relations," *Taiwan Yanjiu,* August 2009 (OSC CPP20091028671003).

48. Communication to the author from Cheng Li, June 26, 2012.

49. "President Ma: Mutual Non-Recognition of Sovereignty and Mutual Non-Denial of Jurisdiction in Cross-Strait Relations," Kuomintang, May 31, 2011 (OSC CPP20110531427002).

50. "Beijing Does Not Have a Timetable for Political Talks with Taiwan."

51. "Liangan xuezhe Yantao Liangan Guanxi Heping Fazhan Lujing [Scholars from the Two Sides of the Strait Discuss the Path of Cross-Strait Peaceful Development]," *Zhongguo Pinglunshe,* September 14, 2009 (www.chinareviewnews.com/doc/1010/7/5/9/101075949.html?coluid=7&kindid=0&docid=101075949&mdate=0914231956).

52. Li Weinuo, "Enhancing Political Mutual Trust, Tackling Tricky Political Affairs Are Important Issues That Both Sides of the Strait Have to Ponder at the Moment," *Renmin Ribao,* June 3, 2010 (OSC CPP20100603710002).

53. "Taiwan's DPP Members Attend Hong Kong Seminar on Cross-Strait Relations," *Yazhou Zhoukan,* June 20, 2010, pp. 18–19 (OSC CPP20100617702003).

54. Zhu Junzhe, "Taiwan, Mainland Need to Launch Political Dialogue, Scholars Say," *Want China Times,* October 29, 2010 (OSC CPP20101029312002).

55. Chris Wang, "CNA: Start Cross-Strait Political Talks at Academic Level: Scholars," Central News Agency, November 2, 2010 (OSC CPP20101102968183).

56. Chen Bihua and others, "Guo Shengkun and Wang Yi Meet with Taiwan Scholars Attending the Ninth Seminar on Cross-Strait Relations," Xinhua Domestic, Janu-

ary 17, 2011 (OSC CPP20110119071003). The National Committee on American Foreign Policy also facilitates dialogue among specialists from the United States, China, and Taiwan and occasionally publishes reports. See, for example, its "Making Peace in the Taiwan Strait," May 2009. (www.ncafp.org/articles/09%20Making%20Peace%20in%20the%20Taiwan%20Strait%20-%20May.pdf).

57. Yu, "The Two Sides of the Strait Should Look Squarely at the Issue of Ending the State of Hostility and Signing a Peace Agreement."

58. Yu Keli, "Some Thoughts on Advancing Cross-Strait Relations and Their Peaceful Development," *Taiwan Yanjiu*, December 2008 (OSC CPP200090514671003). The article was published in the same month as Hu Jintao's speech, but as a key adviser in the policy process, Yu certainly knew of the speech's content.

59. Li Zhongwei, "Yu Keli: Two Sides of the Strait Should Strive to Resolve Political Issues," Zhongguo Pinglun Tongxunshe, July 2, 2010 (OSC CPP20100702788002).

60. Yu, "Promoting Political Relations Is the Only Way for the Two Sides." Yu's warning was issued in the context of discussing a peace accord, but it applies to broader political negotiations as well.

61. Zhang Nianchi, "The Phase of Peaceful Development Needing Extra Care," *Zhongguo Pinglun*, July 2009 (OSC CPP20090709710011).

62. Wang Jianmin, "Cross-Strait Political Antagonism Remains Serious," *Shijie Zhishi*, November 1, 2010 (OSC CPP20101122671002).

63. Huang Jiashu, "Huang Jiashu: The Two Sides Should Not Deliberately Seek or Play Up Hostility," Zhongguo Pinglun Tongxunshe, November 14, 2009 (OSC CPP20091116710010).

64. Chu Shulong, "Communication for Better Understanding and Improvement of Cross-Taiwan Strait Relations," Brookings Northeast Asia Commentary 50 (June 2011) (www.brookings.edu/articles/2011/06_cross_strait_shulong.aspx).

65. Chen Qimao, "The Taiwan Straits Situation since Ma Came to Office and Conditions for Cross-Straits Political Negotiations: A View from Shanghai," *Journal of Contemporary China*, vol. 20 (January 2011), pp. 153–60; cited passage is on p. 156.

66. Ibid., p. 158.

67. Zhang Huangmin, "Shared Interpretation of One China: New Coordinates for Cross-Strait Mutual Political Trust in the Future," Zhongguo Pinglun Tongxunshe, February 7, 2011 (OSC CPP20110207312002).

68. Liu Guoshen, "Liangan Guanxi Zhengzhi Huxin ABC [The ABCs of Mutual Trust in Cross-Strait Relations]," *Zhongguo Pinglun*, December 2009, pp. 19–20.

69. Romberg, "Cross-Strait Relations: Setting the Stage for 2012," p. 13.

70. Zhang, "Shared Interpretation of One China."

71. Chang Hsien-chao, "Liangan heping tanpan di zhengzhi kunnan yu daiti xuanze [The Political Difficulties of Cross-Strait Peace Negotiations and Alternative Options]"; draft on file with author.

72. Chang Ya-chung, "A Modest Proposal for a Basic Agreement on Peaceful Cross-Strait Development," *Journal of Current Chinese Affairs*, vol. 39, no. 1 (2010), pp. 137;

Chang Ya-chung, "Cross-Strait Integration, Peace, and Development: On a Stable Path Leading to Win-Win Mutual Benefits," 2010, p. 16 (on file with author). For the white paper, Sun Chen, former president of National Taiwan University (NTU), was chief convener of the group; retired ambassador Raymond Tai and NTU professor Hwang Kwang-kuo were co-conveners.

73. Chang, "A Modest Proposal for a Basic Agreement," pp. 133–48; Chang, "Cross-Strait Integration, Peace, and Development."

74. Chang, "A Modest Proposal for a Basic Agreement," p. 138.

75. Ibid., pp. 138–39.

76. Ibid., p. 140.

77. Chang, "Cross-strait Integration, Peace, and Development," p. 24–25. The Chinese for *constitutional order subject* is 宪法秩序主体 (*xianfa zhixu zhuti*).

78. Chang, "A Modest Proposal for a Basic Agreement," pp. 142–44; cited passages are on pp. 142 and 143 respectively.

79. Ibid., pp. 144–45; cited passage is on p. 144.

80. Cited passage is from "ARATS Vice Chairman Zhang Mingqing Responds to Taiwan Scholar Chang Ya-chung's Cross-Strait Integration Proposal," *Central Daily News*, June 7–8, 2010 (OSC CPP20100608569001). Zhang, "Shared Interpretation of One China."

81. Communications to the author from two prominent mainstream Taiwan scholars, August 24, 2011.

82. Author's communication with a scholar who wished to remain anonymous, August 23, 2011. On Chen Shui-bian's "integration" overture, see Bush, *Untying the Knot*, p. 66–67. Foreign scholars have weighed in. Jean Pierre Cabestan argues that the two sides must recognize each other's sovereignty, something that China especially has refused to do. Christopher Hughes believes that Chang overestimates Taiwan's weakness. Each says that China must accept Taiwan's distinctive, democratic character. See Jean Pierre Cabestan, "Commentary on 'A Modest Proposal for a Basic Agreement on Peaceful Cross-Strait Development,'" *Journal of Current Chinese Affairs*, vol. 39, no. 1 (2010), p. 163; and Christopher R. Hughes, "Commentary on 'A Modest Proposal for a Basic Agreement on Peaceful Cross-Strait Development,'" *Journal of Current Chinese Affairs*, vol. 39, no. 1 (2010), p. 142.

83. Chang, "Cross-Strait Integration, Peace, and Development," pp. 23, 25.

84. Ibid., pp. 25–26.

85. Chang, "A Modest Proposal for a Basic Agreement," pp. 141–42; cited passage is on p. 141.

86. DPP individuals attended at least one conference that was attended by Mainland academics, but it was held in Hong Kong, not China itself, and the DPP people were not in the party's mainstream; see "Taiwan's DPP Members Attend Hong Kong Seminar on Cross-Strait Relations."

87. Zhu, "Taiwan, Mainland Need to Launch Political Dialogue, Scholars Say."

88. Zhang, "Shared Interpretation of One China."

89. "Benqi Huitan" [The Motosu Meeting].

90. Huang, "Guanyu liangan zhengzhi tanpan di sikao [Pondering Cross-Strait Political Talks]," pp. 7–8. This focus on formulas extends to names of the key entities. Xia Liping reported formulas that different scholars had offered on the cross-Strait political relationship before unification in descending order of preference: China (Beijing) and Chinese Taipei; China (Beijing) and China (Taipei); Chinese government and Taiwan authorities. See Xia Liping, "Several Considerations in Cross-Strait Negotiations of Political, Military Issues," *Zhongguo Pinglun,* no. 162 (June 2011) (OSC CPP20110608787007), pp. 27, 29.

91. Zhang Nianchi, "China Will Certainly Move toward Final Unification: Commenting on Cao Xingcheng's 'Cross-Strait Peaceful Co-existence Act,'" *Zhongguo Pinglun,* May 16, 2010 (OSC CPP20100518710013).

92. Zhang states clearly that "a country in a country" is not a confederacy or federation.

93. For a discussion of competing metaphors, see "CNA: Opinions Differ on What Metaphors to Use for Cross-Strait Relations," Central News Agency, April 10, 2010 (OSC CPP20100410968028).

94. For a more extensive historical discussion of this distinction, see Richard C. Bush, "The Significance of the Republic of China for Cross-Strait Relations," presentation at the symposium "The Dawn of Modern China: The 100th Anniversary of the 1911 Revolution and the Significance of the Republic of China," Brookings, Washington, May 20, 2011 (www.brookings.edu/speeches/2011/0520_china_bush.aspx). See also Richard C. Bush, "The Status of the ROC and Taiwan, 1950–1972," in *At Cross Purposes: U.S.-Taiwan Relations since 1942* (Armonk, N.Y.: M.E. Sharpe, 2004), pp. 85–123.

95. Hendrik Spruyt, *The Sovereign State and Its Competitors: An Analysis of Systems Change* (Princeton University Press, 1994).

96. Thus Xia Liping of Tongji University in Shanghai suggested that Taiwan put in writing that the two sides are "one country, two regions" and that their relationship is a special one but not one between two countries. See Xia Liping, "Several Considerations in Cross-Strait Negotiations of Political, Military Issues," *Zhongguo Pinglun,* no. 162 (June 2011), p. 27 (OSC CPP20110608787007).

97. Note that the United States has a repertoire of legal and political statuses for its various subnational units—state, territory, federal district, commonwealth, and so on—each with different authority and powers.

98. Author's conversation with a Taiwan scholar, May 2010.

99. Xia, "Several Considerations in Cross-Strait Negotiations of Political, Military Issues," pp. 28, 31.

100. Ibid., p. 29.

101. Ibid., p. 30.

102. Ma Ying-jeou approaches the issue from two perspectives. Politically and historically, he stresses the alignment between the ROC government and Taiwan, the

only territory that the ROC government has ruled since 1949. As he said on the ROC's National Day in 2010: "Today, we continue to grow and develop on this land. We share a collective destiny and embrace a common dream. We cherish Taiwan and identify with the Republic of China. We wish the best for Taiwan and want the ROC to flourish." Yet constitutionally, he asserts that the Republic of China is the government of all of China, and that it is a sovereign state. See "CNA: 'Full Text' of Taiwan President Ma Ying-jeou's 2010 National Day Address," Central News Agency, October 10, 2010 (OSC CPP20101010968038); Office of the President, "Transcript of President Ma Ying-jeou's Recent Interview with Mario Vazquez Rana, Chairman of Mexico's El Sol de Mexico Newspaper Group," September 3, 2008 (OSC CPP20080903312001); "CNA: Taiwan President Ma Ying-jeou's 2011 New Year's Day Message," Central News Agency, January 1, 2011 (OSC CPP20110101968035); "MAC: Government Refers to Other Side of Strait as 'Mainland China' as Stipulated in Constitution," Kuomintang, February 25, 2011 (OSC CPP20110225427004).

103. Bush, *Untying the Knot*, pp. 91–99; 230–33.

104. Yang Chao-chung, "Hong Kong Media Criticize Harsh Measures during Li Visit," *Want China Times*, August 27, 2011 (OSC CPP20110827968047).

105. Bush, *Untying the Knot*, pp. 233–38.

106. Yu, "Promoting Political Relations Is the Only Way for the Two Sides."

107. Chen, "The Taiwan Straits Situation since Ma came to Office," p. 160.

108. Elizabeth Hsu, "CNA: Talk of the Day: Fewer Taiwanese Fear Cross-strait Conflict," Central News Agency, September 11, 2010 (OSC CPP20100911968088).

109. Mainland Affairs Council, "Percentage Distribution of the Questionnaire for the Routine Survey on 'the Public's View on Current Cross-Strait Relations,'" February 2, 2012 (www.mac.gov.tw/ct.asp?xItem=101204&ctNode=7280&mp=3). The survey was conducted by the Election Study Center of National Chengchi University, November 26–30, 2011.

110. Charles Glaser, "Will China's Rise Lead to War: Why Realism Does Not Mean Pessimism," *Foreign Affairs*, vol. 90 (March-April 2011), pp. 80–83; cited passages is on p. 82.

111. "Message to Taiwan Compatriots," *Beijing Review*, January 5, 1979, pp. 16–17.

112. Jiang Zemin, "Continue to Promote the Reunification of the Motherland," speech made at Spring Festival, January 30, 1995 (www.fmprc.gov.cn/eng/ljzg/3568/t17784.htm).

113. "Inaugural Address, Lee Teng-hui, President, Republic of China," May 20, 1996 (http://newcongress.yam.org.tw/taiwan_sino/leespeec.html).

114. "4th Ld [Fourth Lead]: Do Best to Seek Peaceful Reunification, but Never Tolerate 'Taiwan Independence': President Hu," Xinhua English, March 4, 2005 (OSC CPP20050304000166) ("Fourth lead" refers to one of a series of stories on the same subject that are put out in sequence over a short period of time. The later versions add information and correct errors.); "Full Text of Anti-Secession Law," *People's Daily*, March 14, 2005 (http://english.peopledaily.com.cn/200503/14/print20050314_176746.html).

115. "Press Communiqué on Talks between CPC General Secretary Hu Jintao and KMT Chairman Lien Chan on 29 April 2005," Xinhua Domestic, April 29, 2005 (OSC CPP2005042900016).

116. Phillip C. Saunders and Scott L. Kastner, "Bridge over Troubled Water? Envisioning a China-Taiwan Peace Agreement," *International Security*, vol. 33 (Spring 2009), pp. 87–114.

117. Ibid., pp. 91–92.

118. "Before Signing Any Peace Agreement, First Identify the Signatories," *United Daily News*, February 22, 2011 (OOSC 20110222427009).

119. Saunders and Kastner, "Bridge over Troubled Water?" pp. 92–98.

120. See Sun Zhe, *Houweiji Shijie yu Zhongmei Zhanlue Jingzheng* [Strategic Readjustment of U.S.-China Relations in the Post-Crisis World] (Beijing: Shishi chubanshe, 2011), pp. 397–406; cited passages are from a draft of the essay on file with the author.

121. "Beijing Scholar Sun Zhe Says Taiwan's 'No Request for Arms Sales' Key to Making Breakthrough in Cross-Strait Relations," *Zhongguo Shibao*, February 29, 2012 (OSC CPP20120229569001).

122. Chang Hsien-chao, "Liangan heping xieyi di zhengzhi kunnan yu daian xuanze [The Political Difficulties of a Cross-Strait Peace Accord and Alternative Options]," paper prepared for a June 2010 conference; on file with author.

123. Wang, "Soldiers on Both Sides of the Strait Should Join Hands in Building Military Security Trust." Consistent with PRC practice, Wang does not use the term CBMs. Chinese use euphemisms like Hu Jintao's formulation: "mechanism of mutual trust for military security." For the views of another military intellectual, see "TKP Exclusive Interview with PRC Expert Peng Guangqian on ECFA," *Ta Kung Pao,* July 19, 2010 (OSC 20100719788005).

124. Liu Guofen, "Issues to Note Before Concluding a Cross-Strait Peace Agreement," Zhongguo Pinglun Tongxunshe, February 17, 2010 (OSC CPP20100217710009).

125. Sun, *Houweiji Shijie yu Zhongmei Zhanlue Jingzheng* [Strategic Readjustment of U.S.-China Relations in the Post-Crisis World].

126. Wang Ping, Liu Hsiao-tan, and Huang Cheng, "Luo Yuan: Cross-Strait Military Mutual Trust Needs to Analyze and Solve Three Mysterious Ideas," Zhongguo Pinglun Tongxunshe, August 12, 2009 (OSC CPP20090817707001).

127. Chen Ming-tong, "Taiwan Qianshu 'Liangan Hoping Xieyi' di Fengxian Guanli" [On Taiwan's Signing a Cross-Strait Peace Accord], conference paper, November 2009; used with permission of the author.

128. This discussion is drawn from Andrew Yang Nien-tzu, "Study of Current Promotion of Cross-Strait Military Confidence Building," in *Ma Zontgong Zhizhenghou di Liangan Xinju: Lun Liangan Guanxi Hsinluxiang* [The New Cross-Strait Relations after President Ma Took Office: On the New Direction in Cross-Strait Relations], edited by Cai Zhaoming (Taipei: Cross-Strait Interflow Prospect Foundation, 2009), pp. 175–88.

129. Liu, Chang, and Lee, "CNA: Taiwan Scholar Urges Latitude in Cross-Strait Peace Pact." See also the policy paper of the ruling Kuomintang, "How to Develop Cross-Strait Military Confidence-Building Measures?"

130. Lin Bih-jaw, "Peace-Building under Trust and Self-Defense," *Prospects and Perspectives*, no. 16 (November 2011) (OSC CPP20120313312001).

131. Lin Bih-jaw, "Taiwan: Why It Is Necessary to Consolidate Democracy and Enhance Governance under the New Status Quo," manuscript provided by Lin to author in 2009, pp. 13–15, 21.

132. Bonnie S. Glaser, "Cross-Strait Confidence Building: The Case for Military Confidence-Building Measures," in *Breaking the China-Taiwan Impasse*, edited by Donald S. Zagoria (Westport, Conn.: Praeger, 2003), pp. 155–72.

133. Kwei-Bo Huang, "Cross-Strait CBMs: Taiwan's Views on Opportunities, Obstacles, and Challenges," in *New Opportunities and Challenges for Taiwan's Security*, edited by Roger Cliff, Phillip C. Saunders, and Scott Harold (Santa Monica, Cal.: RAND Corporation, 2011), table 4.1, p. 26; "CBM Tools" from "Confidence Building Measures in South Asia," South Asia Program, Henry L. Stimson Center (www.stimson.org/research-pages/confidence-building-measures-in-south-asia-/).

134. On this issue, Bonnie Glaser of the Center on Strategic and International Studies has done the most careful and exhaustive work. See her "Cross-Strait Confidence Building" and periodic CSIS reports.

135. Ken Allen and Bernard Cole discuss how moderately tense situations can spin out of control because of weaknesses in command and control (Allen for the air force and Cole for the navy) in Kenneth W. Allen, "Air Force Deterrence and Escalation Calculations for a Taiwan Strait Conflict: China, Taiwan, and the United States," and Bernard D. Cole, "The Military Instrument of Statecraft at Sea: Naval Options in an Escalatory Scenario Involving Taiwan, 2007–2016," both in *Assessing the Threat: The Chinese Military and Taiwan's Security*, edited by Michael D. Swaine, Andrew N. D. Yang, and Evan S. Medeiros, with Oriana Skylar Mastro (Washington: Carnegie Endowment for International Peace, 2007), pp. 153–83 and 185–211, respectively.

136. "Former Army Commander's Memoirs Disclose CBMs Drafted during DPP Administration," OSC Summary, December 8, 2011 (OSC CPP20111208569001); J. Michael Cole, "Task Force Working on Cross-Strait CBM: Source," *Taipei Times*, November 24, 2011 (OSC CPP20111124968006).

137. "Taiwan Defense White Paper Includes Confidence-Building Measures with China."

138. Bonnie S. Glaser, "China's Approach to CBMs with Taiwan: Lessons from China's CBMs with Neighboring Countries," in *New Opportunities and Challenges for Taiwan's Security*, edited by Roger Cliff, Phillip C. Saunders, and Scott Harold (Santa Monica, Cal: RAND Corporation, 2011), p. 16.

139. Steven M. Goldstein, "Cross-Strait CBMs: Like a Fish Needs a Bicycle," in *New Opportunities and Challenges for Taiwan's Security*, edited by Cliff, Saunders, and Harold, p. 44; Liu Chang, Zhao Bo, and Li Hanfang, "Mainland, Taiwan Will Launch

First Joint All-Directional Sea-Land-Air Three-Dimensional Search and Rescue Exercise," Xinhua Domestic Service, September 15, 2010 (OSC CPP20110915005007). Note that the participants in the exercise were civilian, not military, agencies.

140. "In Search of Military Consensus," *Taipei Times,* December 26, 2010 (OSC CPP20101226968006).

141. Toshinao Ishii and Kenichi Yoshida, "President Ma Gives Exclusive Interview to *Yomiuri Shimbun:* 'Removal of Missiles Prerequisite for Peace with China,'" *Yomiuri Shimbun,* June 4, 2008 (OSC JPP20080604043001).

142. "Exclusive: Taiwan's Ma Urges China to Scrap Missiles," Reuters, October 19, 2009 (www.reuters.com/article/2009/10/19/us-taiwan-president-exclusive-idUS-TRE59I0NV20091019?feedType=RSS&virtualBrandChannel=11563).

143. A more consequential PRC step would be to eliminate the bases from which the missiles would be fired.

144. Saunders and Kastner, "Bridge over Troubled Water?" pp. 99–107.

145. Ibid., pp. 107–10.

146. Ibid., pp. 110–12.

147. Yu, "The Two Sides of the Strait Should Look Squarely at the Issue of Ending the State of Hostility and Signing a Peace Agreement."

148. Liu, "Issues to Note before Concluding a Cross-Strait Peace Agreement."

149. Communication to the author from a Chinese scholar, December 2012.

150. "China Asks Taiwan Leave Small Island in Return for Missile Withdrawal: Reports," *Taiwan News,* June 21, 2010 (OSC CPP20110621968134); Wang, Liu, and Huang, "Luo Yuan: Cross-Strait Military Mutual Trust Needs to Analyze and Solve Three Mysterious Ideas"; We Guo'an, "Taiwan Authorities Are the Key to a PRC Withdrawal of Missiles," *Huanqiu Shibao,* March 17, 2009 (OSC CPP20090325710008).

151. Shih Ping, "ECFA Lights Up the Direction of Peaceful Development across the Strait," *Ta Kung Pao,* July 19, 2010 (OSC CPP20100719788005).

152. Bonnie Glaser, "Cross-Strait Confidence Building," p. 164; Bonnie Glaser and Brad Glosserman, "Promoting Confidence Building across the Taiwan Strait," Report of the CSIS International Security Program and Pacific Forum CSIS, September 2008 (http://csis.org/files/media/csis/pubs/080910_glaser_promotingconfidence_web.pdf), pp. 9–10.

153. Bonnie Glaser, "China's Approach to CBMs with Taiwan."

154. Eric A. McVadon, "The Reckless and the Resolute: Confrontations in the South China Sea," *China Security,* vol. 5 (Spring 2009), p. 7. In the ASEAN Regional Forum (ARF), the longest-running multilateral "regime" in East Asia, China has resisted Japanese efforts to use the forum to develop tools for serious objectives like preventive diplomacy or conflict resolution; see Takeshi Yuzawa, "The Evolution of Preventive Diplomacy in the ASEAN Regional Forum: Problems and Prospects," *Asian Survey,* vol. 46 (October-November 2006), pp. 785–804.

155. Tsai Ming-yen, "Taiwan dui Liangan junshi huxin di yanjiu yu weilai zuofa [Research and Future Methods on Taiwan and Military Confidence]," paper prepared

for "Symposium on Prospects for Taiwan Strait Security and Mutual Trust," sponsored by the Center for Asia-Pacific Region Research of Academia Sinica, June 29, 2010. See also Ding Shufan, "Zhongguo liangan junshi huxin zhengce: jianchi yige Zhongguo yuanze he zuizhong tongyi [China's Policy toward Cross-Strait Military Trust: Adhering to the One-China Principle and Ultimate Unification]," paper prepared for the same symposium. Both papers were provided to the author by Dr. Lin Cheng-yi.

156. Office of the Secretary of Defense, "Annual Report to Congress: Military and Security Developments Involving the People's Republic of China 2012" (hereafter "2012 Report"), released May 2012, pp. 2–3, 18.

157. Office of the Secretary of Defense, "2012 Report," p. 3.

158. Office of the Secretary of Defense, "Annual Report to Congress: Military and Security Developments Involving the People's Republic of China 2011" (hereafter "2011 Report"), released August 2011, p. 28.

159. Ibid., p. 29.

160. For more on anti-access and area denial capability, see Thomas G. Mahnken, "China's Anti-Access Strategy in Historical and Theoretical Perspective," *Journal of Strategic Studies*, vol. 34 (June 2011), pp. 299–323; and Michael S. Chase, "Not in Our Backyard: China's Emerging Anti-Access Strategy," Policy Memo (Washington: Progressive Policy Institute, October 7, 2010).

161. "Prepared Statement of Dr. Peter Lavoy, Acting Assistant Secretary of Defense for Asian and Pacific Security Affairs," testimony before House Foreign Affairs Committee, October 4, 2011 (http://foreignaffairs.house.gov/112/lav100411.pdf); Chen Hung-chin and Sofia Wu, "CNA: No Letup in Chinese Drills Simulating Taiwan Attack: Ex-Official," Central News Agency, August 25, 2011 (OSC CPP20110825968210). The PLA has not carried out those exercises in areas close to Taiwan to avoid provocation, but it has conducted them all the same.

162. Office of the Secretary of Defense, "2012 Report," pp. 18–19.

163. On Taiwan's concern about cyber attacks, see "Chinese Cyber-Attacks Worse Than Feared: NSB," *China Post*, September 27, 2012 (OSC CPP20120927968281).

164. There is a risk, the DOD report notes, that Beijing would underestimate the degree to which any attempt to limit maritime traffic to and from Taiwan would trigger countervailing international pressure and military escalation.

165. Office of the Secretary of Defense, "2012 Report," p. 17.

166. Office of the Secretary of Defense, "2011 Report," p. 50.

167. "Full Text: China's National Defense in 2010," Xinhua English, March 31, 2011 (OSC CPP20110331968049).

168. "Full Text of Anti-Secession Law," Xinhua English, March 14, 2005 (OSC CPP20050314000022). The essence of the third criterion—that Beijing's patience is not unlimited—has a long history; Deng Xiaoping told Jimmy Carter that China might use force if Taiwan refused to negotiate over a long period of time. See Alan D. Romberg, *Rein In at the Brink of the Precipice: American Policy toward Taiwan and U.S.-PRC Relations* (Washington: Henry L. Stimson Center, 2003), p. 98.

169. Office of the Secretary of Defense, "2011 Report," p. 47.

170. "President Ma Holds Discussions with Experts on PRC Military Affairs," Office of the President, October 28, 2010 (http://english.president.gov.tw/Default.aspx?tabid=491&itemid=22660&rmid=2355); Elaine Hou, "President Ma Eyes Defense Upgrade for Taiwan," *Taiwan Today*, April 8, 2011 (OSC CPP20110408968112).

171. Ministry of National Defense R.O.C., "[PRC] Military Strategy against Taiwan," in *2011 National Defense Report*, p.55.

172. Goldstein, "Cross-Strait CBMs: Like a Fish Needs a Bicycle," pp. 43–44.

173. Huang Kwei-Bo of Taiwan's National Chengchi University notes the lack of public understanding on Taiwan of how CBMs might improve its security when China's intentions are in doubt. See Huang, "Cross-Strait CBMs: Taiwan's Views on Opportunities, Obstacles, and Challenges," pp. 27, 29–30; cited passage is on p. 27.

174. "President Ma Holds Press Conference to Mark Third Anniversary of His Inauguration," Office of the President, May 19, 2011 (http://english.president.gov.tw/Default.aspx?tabid=491&itemid=24428&rmid=2355).

175. "President Ma Attends Ceremony to Inaugurate New Navy Vessels and Equipment for Hai Chiao ("Sea Dragon") Squadron," Office of the President, April 7, 2011 (http://english.president.gov.tw/Default.aspx?tabid=491&itemid=23954&rmid=2355).

176. Chen Luwei and Li Mingxian, "Taiwan as a Land King Can Prosper through Doing a Good Job in its Relations with the U.S., China, and Japan," *Lien Ho Pao*, May 16, 2010 (OSC CPP20100517312002).

177. Lee Shu-hua and S.C. Chang, "CNA: Existing Cross-strait Accords Part of 'Peace Pact': President," Central News Agency, February 8, 2012 (OSC CPP20120208968220).

178. "The Liberty Times Editorial: Ma Acting as China's Trojan Horse," *Taipei Times* (reprinted from *Liberty Times*), July 27, 2011 (OSC CPP20110727968011); and "The Liberty Times Editorial: A Vote for Ma Is a Vote for China," *Taipei Times* (reprinted from *Liberty Times*), July 29, 2011 (OSC CPP20110729968011).

179. "Xia Yingzhou Says Nation Can Benefit From Retired Military Generals' Discussion of Security Issues in China," *Lien Ho Pao*, June 9, 2011 (OSC 20110610312001).

180. "Ma: Cross-Strait Peace Agreement Possible if Three Conditions Met," Kuomintang, October 18, 2011 (OSC CPP20111018427003).

181. Lin Shen-hsu and Jamie Wang, "CNA: Ma's Peace Accord with China Is a Step toward Unification: DPP," Central News Agency, October 17, 2011 (OSC CPP20111017968178); Lai Yi-chung, "Peace Pact Will Lead to De Jure Annexation," *Tzu-yu Shih-pao*, October 19, 2011 (OSC CPP20111019986001); Chris Wang, "Peace Proposal Puts Taiwan at Risk: Tsai," *Taipei Times*, October 20, 2011 (OSC CPP20111020968002).

182. "The President Offers 10 Major Guarantees for 'Cross-Straits Peace Agreement,'" Office of the President, October 24, 2011 (OSC CPP20111024312001).

183. "People" is singular in Chang's English translation; could be either singular or plural in Chinese.

Chapter Six

1. T'ien Hsi-ju, "Qualities of a Leader: What Qualities Should the President of Taiwan Possess? Leadership Ability Comparison among Ma, Ts'ai, and Soong," *Ts'ai Hsun,* September 29–October 12, 2011 (OSC CPP20110930312002), pp. 76–81.

2. Zoher Abdoolcarim, "Neither Independence nor Unification," *Time,* Jan 12, 2012 (www.time.com/time/magazine/article/0,9171,2103707-1,00.html).

3. The main administrative units within Taiwan are counties and municipalities. A "Taiwan provincial government" was set up in 1949 to enhance the fiction that the Taipei government was the government of all of China—that is, to indicate that there were other provinces, "temporarily" in communist hands. But except for some KMT-held islands near the Chinese coast, the territorial scope of the government in Taipei was the same as that of the "Taiwan provincial government."

4. "Local KMT Factions Decline after New Municipalities Formed," *Want China Times,* November 1, 2011 (OSC CPP20111101968168). Generally, machines, or factions, remain a significant factor only in elections at the lowest political level; see Wang Ye-li, "Voters Determine Future of Political Factions," *Yuan-ching 2030: Yung-pao Meng-hsiang Yin-hsiang Wei-lai* [Embracing 2030] (Taipei: Yuanjian Publishing, 2011), pp. 82–83 (OSC CPP20120316312007).

5. Chai Ssu-chia, "Maintain Open Cooperation, Rather than Call for Stop Abruptly: Don't Let Faction Division Lead to a Lose-Lose Situation," *Hsin Hsin Wen,* December 23, 2010 (OSC CPP20110316329001); "Central News Agency: Talk of the Day—Hopefuls Eying Presidential Election," Central News Agency, February 27, 2001 (OSC CPP20110227968134).

6. Lin Ting-yao, "Battle for Taishang Votes in Presidential Election: Blue Camp Snatches China Votes, Green Fights for Southeast Asia," *Shibao Zhoukan,* July 8, 2011 (OSC CPP20110811397002); "Ma Ying-jeou Must Address Loss of Corporate Voter Base," *Want China Times,* September 8, 2011 (OSC CPP20110908968124).

7. "AFP: More Than 200,000 Taiwan Businessmen Head Home from China to Vote," Agence France-Presse, January 10, 2012 (OSC CPP20120110968188).

8. Yun-han Chu, "How to Size Up Taiwan's 2012 Election," presentation at a symposium on the election sponsored by the Brookings Institution and the Center for Strategic and International Studies, January 17, 2012 (www.brookings.edu/~/media/Files/events/2012/0117_taiwan_elections/0117_chuy_powerpoint.pdf).

9. Mainland Affairs Council, "Percentage Distribution of the Questionnaire for the Routine Survey on 'the Public's View on Current Cross-Strait Relations,'" February 2, 2012. The survey was conducted by the Election Study Center of National Chengchi University from November 26 to 30, 2011 (www.mac.gov.tw/ct.asp?xItem=101204&ctNode=7280&mp=3).

10. For Ma's defense of his policies, see "Century of Struggle: A Democratic Taiwan," Ma Ying-jeou's 2011 National Day address, Central News Agency, October 10, 2011 (OSC CPP20111010968054). On the DPP approach to the economy, see "Tai-

wan's Next: Decide the Future Now: DPP 2012 Campaign Platform," *Democracy and Progress*, DPP newsletter, July 2011 (OSC CPP20110808312003); "DPP Is Willing to Accept ROC Identity: Tsai," *China Post*, October 10, 2011 (OSC CPP20111010968044).

11. T'ien Hsi-ju: "Qualities of a Leader."

12. James Lee, "Central News Agency: DPP Chief Denies '92 Consensus,' Calls for New Mechanism," Central News Agency, August 23, 2011 (OSC CPP20110823968063).

13. Hermia Lin, Kelven Huang, and Deborah Kuo, "CNA: President Makes '1992 Consensus' Cross-Strait Ties Bible," Central News Agency, August 23, 2011 (OSC CPP20110823968087).

14. Chen Chang-wen, "Whether It is Called 1992 Consensus Not [the] Point," *Chung-kuo Shi-pao*, August 29, 2011 (OSC CPP20110829086001).

15. "China's Swift Response to Tsai Leaves No Room for Doubt," *Want China Times*, August 25, 2011

16. "Chinese Mainland Expects Progress in Steady Development of Cross-Strait Relations: Senior Official," Xinhua English, July 28, 2011 (OSC CPP20110728968166). At least one Chinese scholar warned that a President Tsai might take a set of steps that Beijing would oppose: pardoning Chen Shui-bian, promoting constitutional revision, resuming a zero-sum competition in the international arena, and so on; see Wang Jianmin, "What If Tsai Ing-wen Was to Take Office?" *Zhongguo Pinglun*, July 2011 (OSC CPP20110720671022).

17. Tsai Ing-wen, "Taiwan: Policy Challenges, Choices, and Democratic Governance," speech at Harvard University, September 15, 2011 (OSC CPP20110916427003).

18. "Soong Says PRC against Him Making Presidential Bid," *Taipei Times*, September 29, 2011 (OSC CPP20110929968217).

19. "Taiwan Must 'Choose Correctly' in Elections: Jia Qinglin," *Want China Times* (reprinted from *Liberty Times*), May 7, 2011 (www.wantchinatimes.com/news-sub-class-cnt.aspx?cid=1101&MainCatID=&id=20110507000125); "Liberty Times Editorial: Taiwan Must Get Off China Drug," *Taipei Times*, August 4, 2011 (OSC CPP20110804968010).

20. Wang Jianmin, "Ruhe Gailiang Nantaiwan yu Dalu di Hudong Guanxi [How to Improve the Interactive Relationship between Southern Taiwan and the Mainland]," *Zhongguo Pinglun*, October 2010, pp. 35–41.

21. "Liberty Times Editorial: A Vote for Ma Is a Vote for China," *Taipei Times*, July 29, 2011 (OSC CPP CPP20110729968011). See also Edward Friedman, "China's Influence on Taiwanese Politics," *Ballots and Bullets*, January 6, 2012 (http://nottspolitics.org/2012/01/06/chinas-influence-on-taiwanese-politics).

22. "Tsai Ing-wen's Remarks at the American Enterprise Institute (AEI) Sept. 13, 2011," Minchu Chinpu Tang (Democratic Progressive Party), September 14, 2011 (OSC CPP20110914427001); Chris Wang, "Tsai Clarifies 'Unification' Comments," *Taipei Times*, September 19, 2011 (OSC CPP20110919968005); "Tsai Ing-wen Comments on Unification with PRC, Taiwan Consensus," Formosa Television, September 18, 2011 (OSC CPP20110919427002); "Consensus Must First Be Reached in Taiwan: Tsai," *China Post*, September 14, 2011 (OSC CPP20110914968249).

23. For one such suggestion, see David Brown, "DPP Must Clarify Its China Policy," *Taipei Times*, August 19, 2011 (OSC CPP20110819968007).

24. "Second-Generation DPP Members Express Reservations about Tsai Ing-wen," editorial, *Lien Ho Pao*, August 17, 2011 (OSC CPP20110822427007).

25. "Editorial: Tsai Ing-wen Throws in the Towel," *Taipei Times*, December 17, 2010 (OSC CPP20101217968006).

26. Chris Wang, "Tsai's Recognition of ROC 'Dangerous,' Activist Koo Says," *Taipei Times*, October 14, 2011 (OSC CPP20111014968017).

27. Chris Wang, "Peace Proposal Puts Taiwan at Risk: Tsai," *Taipei Times*, October 20, 2011 (OSC CPP20111020968002).

28. Denny Roy, "Taiwan: Crisis Deferred, but Maybe Not for Long," *Asia Pacific Bulletin*, no. 145, January 19, 2012 (www.eastwestcenter.org/publications/taiwan-crisis-deferred-maybe-not-long).

29. Chu, "How to Size Up Taiwan's 2012 Election"; Alan D. Romberg, "After the Taiwan Elections: Planning for the Future," *China Leadership Monitor*, no. 34, Spring 2012, p. 4 (http://media.hoover.org/sites/default/files/documents/CLM37AR.pdf).

30. Romberg, "After the Taiwan Elections," p. 3.

31. Chou Yung-chieh and Elizabeth Hsu, "Central News Agency: U.S. Scholar Surprised by Taiwan Solidarity Union's Vote Gain," Central News Agency, January 21, 2012 (OSC CPP20120121968101).

32. These observations are from Nathan F. Batto, "The Presidential and Legislative Election Dynamics: 2012 vs. 2008," draft paper prepared for the conference "Taiwan: A Tentative Balance Sheet of Ma Ying-jeou's First Term," Hong Kong Baptist University, May 24–25 2012; used with the author's permission.

33. For more, see Richard C. Bush, The Perils of Proximity: China-Japan Security Relations (Brookings, 2010), pp.125–26.

34. Cheng Li, "China's Midterm Jockeying: Gearing Up for 2012 (Part 1: Provincial Chiefs)," *China Leadership Monitor*, no. 31 (Winter 2010) (http://media.hoover.org/sites/default/files/documents/CLM31CL.pdf), p. 6.

35. Cheng Li, "China's Midterm Jockeying: Gearing Up for 2012 (Part 2: Cabinet Ministers)," *China Leadership Monitor*, no. 32 (Spring 2010) (http://media.hoover.org/sites/default/files/documents/CLM32CL.pdf), pp. 14–16.

36. Cheng Li, "China's Midterm Jockeying: Gearing Up for 2012 (Part 3: Military Leaders)," *China Leadership Monitor*, no. 33 (Summer 2010) (http://media.hoover.org/sites/default/files/documents/CLM33CL.pdf), p. 2.

37. The new premier of the state council is announced at an even-numbered National People's Congress. Wen Jiabao became premier in March 2003, and Li Keqiang is expected to replace him in 2013. But the premier has a less significant role in Taiwan policy than the party general secretary and PRC president.

38. The numerical estimate is from Kenneth G. Lieberthal, *Governing China: From Revolution through Reform*, 2nd ed. (New York: W.W. Norton, 2004), pp. 207–12.

39. Richard C. Bush, *Untying the Knot: Making Peace in the Taiwan Strait* (Brookings, 2005), pp. 184–85.

40. Keith B. Richburg, "Xi Jinping, Likely China's Next Leader, Called Pragmatic, Low Key," *Washington Post*, August 15, 2011 (www.washingtonpost.com/world/asia-pacific/xi-jinping-likely-chinas-next-leader-called-pragmatic-low-key/2011/08/15/gIQA5W83GJ).

41. Wu Ming, *Xi Jinping Zhuan: Zhongguo Xin Lingxiu* [Biography of Xi Jinping: China's New Leader] (Hong Kong: Xianggang wenhua yishu chobanshe, 2010), pp. 212–13.

42. Zhao Hong and Liang Ruobing, "Economic Zone on the West Coast of Taiwan Strait," Background Brief 458, East Asian Institute, National University of Singapore, June 18, 2009 (www.eai.nus.edu.sg/BB458.pdf); Liu Xinlian, "Bridging the Straits," *Beijing Review*, April 2, 2011 (OSC CPP20110412707004).

43. Jacques deLisle, "Strait Ahead? China's Fifth Generation Leaders and Beijing's Taiwan Policy," *E-Notes*, Foreign Policy Research Institute, July 2011, pp. 3–4 (www.fpri.org/enotes/2011/201107.delisle.chinatransition.pdf).

44. The head of Taiwan's chief intelligence agency expressed skepticism in March 2012 that Xi Jinping would bring a significant change in policy: "Xi Jinping may be the CPC leader with the best understanding of Taiwan in history, but he will still fall short of Taiwan people's expectations, because the CPC is unlikely to compromise on issues involving its core interests." See "NSB Chief Interviewed on Xi Jinping, Cross-Strait Exchanges, Intelligence Work," Central News Agency, March 10, 2012 (OSC CPP20120310569001); Chen Pei-huang and Elizabeth Hsu, "Central News Agency: Ties with China Could Shift Next Year: Security Chief," Central News Agency, October 24, 2011 (OSC CPP20111024968172).

45. deLisle, "Strait Ahead?" p. 4.

46. "4th Ld [Fourth Lead]: Do Best to Seek Peaceful Reunification, but Never Tolerate 'Taiwan Independence': President Hu," Xinhua English, March 4, 2005 (OSC CPP20050304000166). ("Fourth lead" refers to one of a series of stories on the same subject that are put out in sequence over a short period of time. The later versions add information and correct errors.)

47. This discussion concerns policymaking in noncrisis situations. On crisis decisionmaking, see Bush, *Perils of Proximity*, pp. 233–37, 249–56; Michael D. Swaine, Zhang Tuosheng, and Danielle F. S. Cohen, *Managing Sino-American Crises: Case Studies and Analysis* (Washington: Carnegie Endowment for International Peace, 2006).

48. Zhang Nianchi, "My Humble Opinion on Some Important Issues on Current Cross-Strait Relations," *Zhongguo Pinglun*, October 2011 (OSC CPP20111003787012).

49. "Full Text of PRC Premier Wen Jiabao's Live News Conference," CCTV-1, March 14, 2012 (OSC CPP20120314047001).

50. Wang Yi, "A 2012 New Year's Message from Wang Yi: Carrying on and Forging Ahead, Writing a New Chapter," *Liang'an Guanxi*, January 30, 2012 (OSC CPP20120210329001).

51. Wang Yi, "Speech Delivered by Wang Yi during 10th Seminar on Cross-Strait Relations [Full Text]," Taiwan Affairs Office, March 15, 2012 (OSC CPP20120329329001).

52. Liu Shuling, "Chen Yunlin Says ARATS Begins to Study the Establishment of a Comprehensive Office between ARATS and SEF on Their Respective Side," *Zhongguo Xinwen She,* March 10, 2012 (OSC CPP20120310075026).

53. Chiu Kuo-chiang, Huang Chi-kuang, and Lilian Wu, "CNA: Cross-Strait Peace Accord Worth Discussing if Time Is Ripe: Arats Head," Central News Agency, March 10, 2012 (OSC CPP20120310968164).

54. Sui Hsiao-chiao, "Li Jiaquan: Ma Should Consider Political Contacts," *Ta Kung Pao,* January 16, 2012 (OSC CPP20120216718010). See also Zhu Songling, "New Opportunity for Peaceful Development of Cross-Strait Relations," *Liaowang,* January 30, 2012 (OSC CPP20120214787003).

55. "PLA Major General Luo Yuan Calls for Stepping Up Unification Progress," *Wang Pao,* March 7, 2012 (OSC CPP20120307569001).

56. Guo Zhenyuan, "The Mainstream Public Opinion That Underscores the Island's Opposition to 'Taiwan Opposition' and Approval of the '1992 Consensus': The Two Sides Should Work Together in Making Good Use of the Mainstream Public Opinion in Creating a New Situation of Peaceful Development in Cross-Strait Relations," *Liaowang,* January 30, 2012 (OSC CPP20120214787002).

57. Yan Anlin, "Looking at the Direction and Focus of Developments in Cross-Strait Relations over the Next Four Years as Viewed from Ma Ying-jeou's 'Inaugural Address,'" *Zhongguo Pinglun,* July 2012 (OSC CPP20120712787019).

58. "Mainland's Top Taiwan Affairs Official Stresses New Chances for Cross-Strait Relations Based on '1992 Consensus,'" Xinhua English, January 30, 2012 (OSC CPP20120130968173); Xu Shiquan, "How the Taiwan Election Will Affect China-U.S. Relations," January 22, 2012 (http://chinausfocus.com/slider/how-the-taiwan-election-will-affect-china-us-relations/).

59. Wang Yi, "Consolidating and Deepening Cross-Strait Relations: Opening Up New Prospects for Peaceful Development," *Qiushi,* April 2012 (OSC CPP20120416787011).

60. I am grateful to friends in Taiwan for helping me identify consolidation as one possibility.

61. Wang Yi, "Speech Delivered by Wang Yi during 10th Seminar on Cross-Strait Relations."

62. "Cross-Strait Trade Barriers Persist Despite ECFA," *Want China Times,* February 4, 2012 (OSC CPP20120204968081).

63. Chinese National Federation of Industries [Taiwan], "'2011 nian Quanguo Gongyeh Zonghui Baipishu' Yiti Banli Qinging [Status of Actions on Issues in the 2011 Chinese Federation of Industries White Paper]," February 2012 (www.cnfi.org.tw/cnfi/2011-3.pdf), p. 8-6.

64. Yun-han Chu, "How to Size Up Taiwan's 2012 Election," Brookings-Center for Strategic and International Studies Symposium, January 17, 2012 (www.brookings.edu/~/media/Files/events/2012/0117_taiwan_elections/0117_chuy_powerpoint.pdf).

65. Taipei Forum Foundation, "Summary: Cross-Strait Relations," March 2012 (OSC CPP20120405312004). I am a member of the board of the Taipei Forum Foundation.

66. Wang, "A 2012 New Year's Message from Wang Yi."

67. "Taiwan Chooses 8 Sectors for Cross-Strait Cooperation This Year," *Want China Times*, February 4, 2012 (OSC CPP20120204968034).

68. Wei Shen, "Cultivating the Cross-Straits Generation," *China Daily*, February 4, 2012 (www.chinadaily.com.cn/cndy/2012-02/04/content_14536119).

69. Mainland Affairs Council, "Explanation on the Signing of the Cross-Strait Investment Protection Agreement," August 16, 2012 (www.mac.gov.tw/ct.asp?xItem=102792&ctNode=6256&mp=3); Mainland Affairs Council, "Reference Materials on the Signing of the Cross-Strait Customs Cooperation Agreement," July 2, 2012 (www.mac.gov.tw/ct.asp?xItem=102515&ctNode=6256&mp=3); Lee Hsin-Yin, "CNA: Statement on Safety of Taiwan Investors Is Binding: China Official," Central News Agency, August 9, 2012 (OSC CPP20120809968232); Tsai Su-jung and others, "CNA: Implementation of Cross-strait Agreement Is Key: Businessmen," Central News Agency, August 9, 2012 (OSC CPP20120809968256); Lee Hsin-Yin, "CNA: Execution of Taiwan-China Pact More Crucial Than Actual Text: Scholars," Central News Agency, August 8, 2012 (OSC CPP20120808968092); "Xinhua: Chinese Mainland, Taiwan Sign Memorandum on Currency Clearing," Xinhua, August 31, 2012 (OSC CPP20120831968129); Sofia Wu, "CNA: Talk of the Day: Both Applause, Doubts Greet Investment Pact," Central News Agency, August 8, 2012 (OSC CPP20120809968259). The cited passage is from the last item. On skepticism about the PRC's commitment to fulfilling the spirit of the agreement, see Lu Hsing-chou, "Think the Taiwan Affairs Office Is on Our Side? What a Joke!" *Ts'ai Hsun*, September 2012 (OSC CPP20120924397001).

70. "Mainland Urges Countries Not to Develop Official Ties with Taiwan," Xinhua English, February 22, 2012 (OSC CPP20120222968199); "MOFA, MAC, DPP Respond to Beijing's Opposition to Taiwan's Official Exchanges with International Community," Central News Agency, February 23, 2012 (OSC CPP20120223569001).

Chapter Seven

1. See, for example, Aaron L. Friedberg, *A Contest for Supremacy: China, America, and the Struggle for Mastery in Asia* (New York: W.W. Norton, 2011).

2. Clues about how it might seek to achieve its Taiwan goals through pressure may be available in the history of the Chinese Communist Party's manipulation of its dominant position *domestically* since 1949. That is, CCP's policies toward intellectuals, religious groups, and other groups that seek a degree of autonomy from the state may be relevant here. The classic work on the united front is Lyman P. Van Slyke, *Enemies and Friends: The United Front in Chinese Communist History* (Stanford University Press, 1967).

3. Robert Sutter, "Taiwan's Future: Narrowing Straits," NBR Analysis (Seattle, Wash.: National Bureau of Asian Research, May 2011), p. 18.

4. In the human rights episode, the United States sought to exert leverage on China and China exerted counter-leverage.

5. Andreas Fuchs and Nils-Hendrick Klann, "Paying a Visit: The 'Dalai Lama Effect' on International Trade," Discussion Paper 113, Center for European Governance and Economic Development Research, Georg-August University, Goettingen, October 2011 (www.uni-goettingen.de/en60920.html).

6. Andrew Higgins, "Philippine Banana Growers Bear Brunt of China's Displeasure," *Washington Post*, June 11, 2012, pp. 1, 7.

7. "2011 Taiwan White Paper Issue," *Taiwan Business Topics*, vol. 41 (May 2011), p. 8. The organization's concern sparked a riposte from officials of the Ministry of Economic Affairs; see "CNA: MOEA Rebuts AmCham Claim of Overreliance on Trade with China," Central News Agency, June 8, 2011 (OSC CPP20110609968100).

8. Li Zitong, "Taiwan's Security Official Admits China's Buying Deals Aimed at Promoting Unification," *Want China Times*, October 21, 2010 (OSC CPP20101021312007).

9. Gary Clyde Hufbauer and others, *Economic Sanctions Reconsidered*, 3rd ed. (Washington: Peterson Institute for International Economics, 2007), p. 165. For a broader treatment of the use of economic tools in external policy that considers both incentives and sanctions, see David A. Baldwin, *Economic Statecraft* (Princeton University Press, 1985).

10. Daniel H. Rosen and Zhi Wang, *Implications of China-Taiwan Economic Liberalization* (Washington: Peterson Institute of International Economics, 2011), pp. 12–14, 31–32.

11. Jane Rickards, "Gauging the Cross-Strait Economic Impact," *Taiwan Business Topics*, vol. 41 (December 2011), p. 24.

12. T. J. Cheng, "China-Taiwan Economic Linkage: Between Insulation and Superconductivity," in *Dangerous Strait: The U.S.-Taiwan-China Crisis*, edited by Nancy Bernkopf Tucker (Columbia University Press, 2005), pp. 104–16. See also Denny Roy, "Cross-Strait Economic Relations: Opportunities Outweigh Risks," Asia-Pacific Center for Security Studies Occasional Papers Series, April 2004 (www.apcss.org/wp-content/uploads/2010/PDFs/Ocasional%20Papers/Cross-StraitEconomicRelations.pdf).

13. Robert Keohane and Joseph Nye, *Power and Interdependence*, 2nd ed. (New York: HarperCollins Publishing, 1989), pp. 10–11.

14. Murray Scot Tanner, *Chinese Economic Coercion against Taiwan: A Tricky Weapon to Use* (Santa Monica, Calif.: RAND Corporation, 2007), p. 102

15. According to surveys, the greatest concern of Taiwan business people who work on the Mainland is being detained without charge and without any notification of family or others; see "Secret Detention Is Top Fear for Taiwan's Businessmen in China," *Want China Times*, September 27, 2011 (OSC CPP20110927968106).

16. Tanner, *Chinese Economic Coercion against Taiwan*, pp. 135–43; quoted passage is on p. 139. Shu Keng and Gunter Shubert reach the same conclusion in their "Agents

of China-Taiwan Unification? The Political Role of Taiwan Business People in Cross-Strait Economic Integration," *Asian Survey*, vol. 50 (March-April 2010), pp. 298–303. On the global impact of economic disruptions, see Steve Lohr, "Stress Test for the Global Supply Chain," *New York Times*, March 19, 2011 (www.nytimes.com/2011/03/20/business/20supply.html?scp=1&sq=Stress%20Test%20for%20the%20Global%20Supply%20Chain&st=cse).

17. See, for example, Jean-Marc F. Blanchard and Norrin M. Ripsman, "Asking the Right Question: When Do Economic Sanctions Work Best?" *Security Studies*, vol. 9, no. 1–2 (1999).

18. Chen-yuan Tung, "Cross-Strait Economic Relations: China's Leverage and Taiwan's Vulnerability," *Issues and Studies*, vol. 39 (September 2003), pp. 137–75; cited passage is on p. 137. Also on Taiwan, see Steve Chan, "The Politics of Economic Exchange: Carrots and Sticks in Taiwan-China-U.S. Relations," *Issues and Studies*, vol. 42 (June 2006), pp. 1–22.

19. Tanner, *Chinese Economic Coercion against Taiwan*, p. 135.

20. Shelley Rigger and Toy Reid, "Taiwanese Investors in Mainland China: Creating a Context for Peace," in *Cross-Strait at the Turning Point: Institution, Identity, and Democracy*, edited by I Yuan (Taipei: National Chengchi University, Institute of International Relations, 2008), pp. 78–111; cited passage is on p. 110.

21. This discussion draws from Sherry Lee, David Huang, and Shu-ren Koo, "Chinese Wolves at Taiwan's Door," *CommonWealth Magazine*, no. 469, April 7, 2011 (OSC CPP20110407427009).

22. Rigger and Reid, "Taiwanese Investors in Mainland China," pp. 78–111; cited passage is on p. 110.

23. Roy, "Cross-Strait Economic Relations."

24. Hufbauer and others, *Economic Sanctions Reconsidered*, pp. 89–90; Central Intelligence Agency, "Country Comparison: GDP (Purchasing Power Parity)," *World Factbook* (www.cia.gov/library/publications/the-world-factbook/rankorder/2001rank.html [May 3, 2012]).

25. Hufbauer and others, *Economic Sanctions Reconsidered*, pp. 90–91.

26. Note that this discussion of the success rate of sanctions has been confined to securing a "major policy change." Hufbauer and his colleagues found that sanctions were successful half the time in achieving "modest policy changes." See Hufbauer and others, *Economic Sanctions Reconsidered*, pp. 158–60. And, indeed, in the run-up to the 2012 presidential election, Beijing engaged in a not-so-subtle effort to encourage Taiwan voters to reelect Ma Ying-jeou (see chapter 4). In cases of modest policy changes, the degree of trade linkage associated with success was only 23 percent (about Taiwan's linkage with China), but the linkage associated with failure was only 5 percent less; see Hufabuer and others, *Economic Sanctions Reconsidered*, p. 90. In a different vein, Daniel Drezner argues that most studies of the effectiveness of sanctions have looked only at cases in which sanctions were imposed and not at those in which they were just threatened. If threats are included, the success rate goes up and so alters the assessment of

effectiveness. See Daniel W. Drezner, "The Hidden Hand of Economic Coercion," *International Organization*, vol. 57 (Summer 2003), pp. 643–59.

27. Albert O. Hirschman, *National Power and the Structure of Foreign Trade* (University of California Press, 1945), pp. 34–35.

28. "Dangqian Guoji Guanxi Yanjiuzhong de Ruogan Zhongdian Wenti [Certain Major Issues in Studying Current International Relations]," *Guoji Zhanwang*, February 15, 2001, p. 7.

29. M. Taylor Fravel, "China's Search for Military Power," *Washington Quarterly*, vol. 31 (Summer 2008), pp. 125–41.

30. "Chinese Cyber-Attacks Worse Than Feared: NSB," *China Post*, September 27, 2012 (OSC CPP20120927968281).

31. Shirley Kan, "Taiwan: Major U.S. Arms Sales since 1990," Congressional Research Service Report RL30957, October 21, 2011, pp. 33–34.

32. Richard A. Bitzinger, "China's New Defence Budget: What Does It Tell Us?" RSIS Commentaries 0602012, April 12, 2012 (www.rsis.edu.sg/publications/Perspective/ RSIS0602012.pdf).

33. Office of the Secretary of Defense, "Annual Report to Congress: Military and Security Developments Involving the People's Republic of China 2010" (hereafter "2010 Report"), p. 45. For surface combatants, "modern" is defined as multi-mission platforms with significant capabilities in at least two warfare areas. "Modern" for submarines is defined as those platforms capable of firing an anti-ship cruise missile. For air forces, "modern" is defined as fourth-generation platforms (Su-27, Su-30, F-10) and platforms with fourth generation–like capabilities (FB-7). "Modern" surface-to-air missiles are defined as advanced Russian systems (SA-10, SA-20) and their PRC indigenous equivalents (HQ-9).

34. Ministry of National Defense R.O.C., "Figure 6-3: Defense Budget Allocations from 2002 to 2011," *2011 National Defense Report* (http://2011mndreport.mnd.gov.tw/ en/pdf/100report_english.pdf), p. 177.

35. This difference has relevance for the intensity of the China-Taiwan security dilemma, increasing Taiwan's sense of vulnerability. See Charles Glaser, "Will China's Rise Lead to War? Why Realism Does Not Mean Pessimism," *Foreign Affairs*, vol. 90 (March-April 2011), pp. 82–83.

36. Ministry of National Defense R.O.C., *Quadrennial Defense Review* (Taipei: Ministry of National Defense, 2009), pp. 8, 27.

37. Office of the Secretary of Defense, "Annual Report to Congress: Military and Security Developments Involving the People's Republic of China 2012" (hereafter "2012 Report"), released May 2012, p. 17.

38. Thomas J. Christensen, *Worse than a Monolith: Alliance Politics and Problems of Coercive Diplomacy in Asia* (Princeton University Press, 2011), p. 1. The classic work on coercive diplomacy is Thomas C. Schelling, *Arms and Influence* (Yale University Press, 1966). A more recent application of the concept is James W. Davis Jr., *Threats and Promises: The Pursuit of International Influence* (Johns Hopkins University Press, 2000).

39. Christensen, *Worse than a Monolith*, p. 3.

40. "2012 Report," pp. 6–8.

41. For a discussion of civil-military relations, see Richard C. Bush, *The Perils of Proximity: China-Japan Security Relations* (Brookings, 2010), pp. 87–123.

42. On the PLA budget process, see Dennis J. Blasko and others, "Defense-Related Spending in China: A Preliminary Analysis and Comparison with American Equivalents," United States–China Policy Foundation, 2007, pp. 31–45.

43. Office of the Secretary of Defense, "Annual Report to Congress: Military and Security Developments Involving the People's Republic of China 2011" (hereafter "2011 Report"), released August 2011, p. 78; "2012 Report," p. 29.

44. "2012 Report," p. 21.

45. "Full Text: China's National Defense in 2010," Xinhua English, March 31, 2011 (OSC CPP20110331968049).

46. "2010 Report," p. 50.

47. 2011 Report,", p. 47.

48. "Full Text of Anti-Secession Law," Xinhua English, March 14, 2005 (OSC CPP20050314000022). For historical background on the limits of Beijing's patience, see Alan D. Romberg, *Rein In at the Brink of the Precipice: American Policy toward Taiwan and U.S.-PRC Relations* (Washington: Henry L. Stimson Center, 2003), p. 98.

49. Roger Cliff and others, *Shaking the Heavens and Splitting the Earth: Chinese Air Force Employment Concepts in the 21st Century* (Santa Monica, Calif.: RAND Corporation, 2011), pp. 227–37. The same capabilities would reduce the ability of U.S. forces to intervene on Taiwan's behalf.

50. David A. Shlapak, "The Rockets' Red Glare: Implications of Improvements in PRC Air and Missile Strike Capabilities," in *New Opportunities and Challenges for Taiwan's Security*, edited by Roger Cliff, Phillip C. Saunders, and Scott Harold (Santa Monica, Calif.: RAND Corporation, 2011), pp. 75. This judgment is based on a 2009 RAND study, David A. Shlapak and others, *A Question of Balance: Political Context and Military Aspects of the China-Taiwan Dispute* (Santa Monica, Calif.: RAND Corporation, 2009), especially pp. 53–90.

51. Hirschman, *National Power and the Structure of Foreign Trade*, p. 29.

52. Scott L. Kastner, *Political Conflict and Economic Interdependence across the Taiwan Strait and Beyond* (Stanford University Press, 2009).

53. Cheng, "China-Taiwan Economic Linkage," pp. 104–16.

54. "Searching for a Way Out, Chinese Brides Look across Taiwan Strait," *Washington Post*, October 14, 2004, p. A26.

55. Tse-Kang Leng, "Economic Globalization and IT Talent Flows across the Taiwan Strait," *Asian Survey*, vol. 42 (March-April 2002), pp. 230–50.

56. Others have argued that these contacts can themselves reduce tensions; see Ralph N. Clough, *Cooperation or Conflict in the Taiwan Strait?* (Lanham, Md.: Rowman & Littlefield Publishers, 1999); and Keng and Shubert, "Agents of China-Taiwan Unification?" pp. 304–06.

57. "Control Yuan Details Money Donated in '10 to KMT, DPP," *China Post*, August 26, 2011 (OSC CPP20110826968219); Keng and Shubert, "Agents of China-Taiwan Unification?" pp. 303–04, 309; cited passage is on p. 309.

58. Gunter Schubert, "The Political Thinking of Mainland *Taishang*: Some Preliminary Observations from the Field," *Journal of Current Chinese Affairs*, vol. 39, no. 1 (2010), pp. 93–97.

59. Richard Bush and Alan Romberg, "'Cross-Strait Moderation and the United States': A Response to Robert Sutter," *PacNet*, no. 17A (March 2009) (http://csis.org/files/media/csis/pubs/pac0917a.pdf).

60. Lai Shin-yuan, "Taiwan's Mainland Policy: Borrowing the Opponent's Force and Using It as One's Own—Turning the Threat of War into Peace and Prosperity," speech at American Enterprise Institute, August 5, 2010 (http://www.mac.gov.tw/ct.asp?xItem=86790&ctNode=6256&mp=3).

61. On prospect theory and the domains of losses and gains, see Jack S. Levy, "Prospect Theory, Rational Choice, and International Relations," *International Studies Quarterly*, vol. 41 (March 1997), pp. 87–112.

62. Chong-pin Lin, "Beijing's New Grand Strategy: An Offensive with Extra-Military Instruments," *China Brief*, vol. 6 (December 6, 2006), p. 3.

63. Lin Chong-pin, "Taiwan's Position in Future U.S.-China Relations," *Yuanjing 2030: Yongbao Mengxiang Yinxiang Weilai* [Embracing 2030] (Taipei: Yuan-chien Publishing, 2011), pp. 38–39.

64. Alastair Iain Johnston, *Cultural Realism: Strategic Culture, and Grand Strategy in Chinese History* (Princeton University Press, 1995).

65. Sun Tzu, *The Art of War*, translated with an introduction by Samuel B. Griffith (Oxford University Press, 1963). Sun Tzu and Sun Zi refer to the same person; the names have been transliterated differently, according to the transliteration system in use at the time.

66. Francois Jullien, *The Propensity of Things: Toward a History of Efficacy in China*, translated by Janet Lloyd (New York: Urzone, 1995), pp. 25–57.

67. M. Taylor Fravel, "China's Strategy in the South China Sea," *Contemporary Southeast Asia*, vol. 33 (December 2011), pp. 292–319.

68. Scott A. Boorman, *The Protracted Game: A Wei-ch'i Interpretation of Maoist Revolutionary Strategy* (Oxford University Press, 1969).

69. For an illuminating discussion, see David Lai, *Learning from the Stones: A Go Approach to Mastering China's Strategic Concept, Shi* (Carlisle, Pa.: Strategic Studies Institute, U.S. Army War College, May 2004).

70. Su Chi, "'Looking for a Balancing Point in the Taiwan-U.S.-China Triangle," *Yuanjing 2030*, pp. 42–43.

71. John Pomfret, "U.S. Takes a Tougher Tone with China," *Washington Post*, July 30, 2010 (www.washingtonpost.com/wp-dyn/content/article/2010/07/29/AR2010072906416_pf.html).

72. Denny Roy, "South China Sea: Not Just about 'Free Trade,'" *Asia-Pacific Bulletin,* no. 177, August 14, 2012 (www.eastwestcenter.org/sites/default/files/private/apb177_0.pdf). On China's behavior in the South China Sea, see also Bonnie S. Glaser, "Statement before the House Foreign Affairs Committee," *Hearing on Beijing as an Emerging Power in the South China Sea,* September 12, 2012 (http://foreignaffairs.house.gov/112/HHRG-112-FA00-WState-GlaserB-20120912.pdf).

73. Chas W. Freeman Jr., "The Taiwan Problem and China's Strategy for Resolving It," remarks at the Center for Naval Analysis, September 14, 2011 (www.mepc.org/articles-commentary/speeches/taiwan-problem-and-chinas-strategy-resolving-it).

74. Ibid.

75. On the struggle over Hong Kong reversion, see Christine Loh, *Underground Front: The Chinese Communist Party in Hong Kong* (Hong Kong University Press, 2010); and Ezra F. Vogel, *Deng Xiaoping and the Transformation of China* (Harvard University Press, 2011), pp. 477–511. On Beijing's post-reversion united front tactics, see Bush, *Untying the Knot,* pp. 229–33.

76. On the use of dependence to constrain workers, see Andrew G. Walder, *Communist Neo-Traditionalism: Work and Authority in Chinese Industry* (University of California Press, 1986). On the treatment of intellectuals in general, see Edward Gu, "Social Capital, Institutional Change and the Development of Nongovernmental Intellectual Organizations in China," in *Chinese Intellectuals between State and Market,* edited by Edward Gu and Merle Goldman (New York: Routledge, 2004), pp. 21–42. On natural scientists in particular, see H. Lyman Miller, *Science and Dissent in Post-Mao China: The Politics of Knowledge* (University of Washington Press, 1996). On minor political parties, see Gerry Groot, *Managing Transitions: The Chinese Communist Party, United Front Work, Corporatism, and Hegemony* (New York: Routledge, 2004).

77. See Bush, *Untying the Knot,* 199–217; Bush, *Perils of Proximity,* pp. 137–144.

78. Hirschman, *National Power and the Structure of Foreign Trade,* pp. 34–41. Actually, during the Great Depression, Germany's share of Czechoslovakia's total trade declined, but that did not diminish Germany's desire to increase dependence. B. R. Mitchell, *International Historical Statistics Europe, 1750–2000,* 5th ed. (New York: Palgrave Macmillan, 2004), pp. 576, 597.

79. Paul Wilson, "The Dilemma of Madeleine Albright," *New York Review of Books,* June 7, 2012, pp. 35–37; cited passage is on p. 37; communication to the author from Vanda Felbab-Brown, June 7, 2012.

Chapter Eight

1. Similarly, Phillip Saunders of National Defense University argues that Taiwan must take steps of its own to mitigate the effect of PRC attempts to use economic and coercive leverage against Taiwan and of its united front tactics to reshape political attitudes; see his "Three Logics of Chinese Policy toward Taiwan and Taiwan's Strate-

gic Responses," draft paper presented at the conference "A New Strategy for a New Era: Revisiting Taiwan's National Security Strategy," Taipei, August 27–28, 2011 (cited with permission).

2. "Taiwan Report on Low Birth Rate—Part 2," Formosa Television, October 3, 2010 (Open Source Center [hereafter OSC] CPP20101004427002). See also Fuyuan Hsiao, "Taiwan's Shrinking Population: The 1.5 Million Baby Challenge," *Common-Wealth*, no. 444, April 7, 2010 (http://english.cw.com.tw/article.do?action=show&id=11861).

3. Directorate General of Budget, Accounting, and Statistics (DGBAS), "Table 104. Disposable Income, Consumption Expenditure, and Savings of Households," *Statistical Yearbook of National Economics: The Republic of China 2010* (Executive Yuan, R.O.C., October 2011) (http://eng.dgbas.gov.tw/public/data/dgbas03/bs2/yearbook_eng/y104.pdf), p. 168–69; DGBAS, "Table 22. Important Indicators of Labor Force Status," *Statistical Yearbook of National Economics 2010* (http://eng.dgbas.gov.tw/public/data/dgbas03/bs2/yearbook_eng/y022.pdf), p. 44.

4. For details, see Richard C. Bush, "The Social Foundation of Taiwan's Future: Guns, Wheelchairs, and Shark's Fin Soup," talk presented at the Columbia University symposium "Taiwan in the Twenty-First Century: Politics, Economy, and Society," Taipei, June 13, 2010 (www.brookings.edu/speeches/2010/0613_taiwan_bush.aspx). On government debt, see "Economy: Taiwan," *World Factbook 2012* (www.cia.gov/library/publications/the-world-factbook/geos/tw.html); and "National Debt per Capita Sees Fourth Straight Rise," *China Post,* March 7, 2012 (OSC CPP20120307968321).

5. Yi-Shan Chen, "Tax System on the Skids: Who Is Stealing Taiwan's Future?" *CommonWealth*, no. 406, September 25, 2008 (http://english.cw.com.tw/article.do?action=show&id=10471); Rebecca Lin, "Statute for Industrial Innovation: A Lose-Lose Proposition?" *CommonWealth*, no. 445, April 22, 2010 (http://english.cw.com.tw/article.do?action=show&id=11897).

6. For more on this subject, see Bush, "The Social Foundation of Taiwan's Future."

7. "Join Hands to Promote Peaceful Development of Cross-Strait Relations; Strive with Unity of Purpose for the Great Rejuvenation of the Chinese Nation," Xinhua Domestic Service, December 31, 2008 (OSC CPP20081231005002).

8. Su Chi has regretted the lack of confidence that Taiwan's people have in "the ROC as the name of the government"; see Chai Ssu-chia and Elizabeth Hsu, "CNA: Taiwan Lacks Confidence in Cross-Strait Relations: Scholar," Central News Agency, March 26, 2012 (OSC CPP20120326968225).

9. Stephen D. Krasner, *Sovereignty: Organized Hypocrisy* (Princeton University Press, 1999), pp. 4, 11–25.

10. Yu Keli, "Promoting Political Relations Is the Only Way for the Two Sides," *Zhongguo Pinglun*, December 2009 (CPP20091230710007). Yu's warning was issued in the context of discussing a peace accord, but it applies to broader political negotiations as well.

11. "NSB Confirms 169 Taiwan Citizens Holding Government, Military Positions in China," *Liberty Times*, March 27, 2012 (OSC CPP20120327569001); "Taiwanese Political Engagement on Mainland Helpful," Xinhua News Agency, English, March 28, 2012 (OSC CPP20120328968173); communication to the author from Cheng Li, April 22, 2012.

12. "CNA: Ex-NSC Head Calls for 'Taiwan Consensus,' Cross-Strait Dialogue," Central News Agency, December 6, 2010 (OSC CPP20101207968137); "Su Chi Urges DPP to Talk with KMT," *Taipei Times*, December 7, 2010 (OSC CPP20101207968008).

13. Tung Chen-yuan, "Recalibrating DPP China Policy," *Taipei Times*, February 22, 2011 (OSC CPP20110222968008). See also Tung's *Taiwan di Zhongguo Zhanlue: Cong Hucong dao Pinghen* [Taiwan's China Strategy: From Accommodation to Equality] (Taipei: Xiuwei Information, 2011), especially pp. 189–215.

14. Chris Wang, "DPP Cites Six Main Reasons for Loss," *Taipei Times*, February 16, 2012 (OSC CPP20120216968057).

15. "DPP Legislator: Cross-Strait Issue Led to Tsai's Loss," Kuomintang, February 16, 2012 (OSC CPP20120216312003). Frank Hsieh Chang-ting is the only senior DPP leader who has consistently advocated grounding the DPP position in the ROC constitution, which would reduce the existing gap with the KMT (see "Frank Hsieh: Protecting Taiwan Is Protecting ROC," *Lien Ho Pao*, June 13, 2012 (OSC CPP20120613569001). But because he is outside the DPP mainstream, his idea has never gained traction.

16. "Su Chi Urges DPP to Talk with KMT," *Taipei Times*, December 7, 2010 (OSC CPP20101207968008); Lin T'ing-yao and Weng Yu-lan, "Su Chi Presents Ma with Seven Words of Truth: Make Toughness and Tenderness Work in Concert," *Shih-pao Chou-k'an*, January 20–February 2, 2012 (OSC CPP20120120397001), pp. 30–33.

17. "CNA: Think Tank Offers to Mediate Cross-Party Talks on China Issues," Central News Agency, August 14, 2011 (OSC CPP20110814968054). For Tung Chen-yuan's commentary on Su's effort, see his "How to Resolve Domestic Conflicts," *Taipei Times*, August 22, 2011 (OSC CPP20110822968010). Lee Shu-hua and Bear Lee, "CNA: Official Group Needed to Manage Peaceful Cross-Strait Development," Central News Agency, March 20, 2012 (OSC CPP20120320968214). I am a board member of the Taipei Forum.

18. "Taiwan at Risk of Losing China market: TAITRA Head," *Want China Times*, July 3, 2011 (OSC CPP20110705968004).

19. On the options for Japanese firms that face similar competitive pressures, see Claes G. Alvstam, Patrik Strom, and Naoyuki Yoshino, "On the Economic Interdependence between China and Japan: Challenges and Possibilities," *Asia Pacific Viewpoint*, vol. 50 (August 2009), especially pp. 212–13.

20. Jau-Yi Wu, "Major Challenges in a New Year: Taiwanese Businesses in China Face New Barriers," *CommonWealth*, no. 388, January 2, 2008 (http://english.cw.com.tw/article.do?action=show&id=3417); Jimmy Hsiung and Elaine Huang, "Taiwanese

Enterprises in China: Failure—and How to Avoid It," *CommonWealth*, no. 442, March 10, 2010 (http://english.cw.com.tw/article.do?action=show&id=11795).

21. Song Bing-zhong, "Taiwanese Firms in China Struggle with Changing Times," *Want China Times*, June 27, 2011 (OSC CPP20110630968270). See also "Taiwanese Businesses in China Need Support to Survive," *Want China Times*, June 15, 2011 (OSC CPP20110617968099); Benjamin Chiang, "Taiwanese Enterprises in China Entrepreneurs Turn Landlords," *CommonWealth*, no.490, February 16, 2012 (OSC CPP20120229312001).

22. Flor Wang, "CNA: Economic Daily News—New Warnings for Taiwan's Businesses in China," Central News Agency, April 2, 2011 (OSC CPP20110402968077); Chen Man-nug, "China Remains Leading Destination for Taiwanese Conglomerates," *Want China Times*, October 27, 2011 (OSC CPP20111027968225). In August 2011, a delegation of officials from Taiwan's Ministry of Economic Affairs traveled to China to investigate ways to help such firms; Lin Shu-yuan and Scully Hsia, "CNA: MOEA Delegation to Visit China to Help Taiwanese Firms," Central News Agency, August 26, 2011 (OSC CPP20110826968175).

23. James McGregor, "China's Drive for 'Indigenous Innovation': A Web of Industrial Policies," July 28, 2010, pp. 3–8 (www.uschamber.com/sites/default/files/international/asia/files/100728chinareport_0.pdf).

24. Kenneth G. Lieberthal, *Managing the China Challenge: How to Achieve Corporate Success in the People's Republic* (Brookings, 2011).

25. Fuyuan Hsiao, "Global Technology Paradigm Shift: Big Upheavals—New Opportunities," *CommonWealth*, no. 418, March 25, 2009 (http://english.cw.com.tw/article.do?action=show&id=10902).

26. Benjamin Chiang, "China's Unfair Playing Field: Will Taiwan Be Left Nibbling the Giant's Crumbs?" *CommonWealth*, no. 456, September 22, 2010 (http://english.cw.com.tw/article.do?action=show&id=12286).

27. Elaine Huang, "The Industrial Standards Battle: China Sets the Rules: How to Win the Game," *CommonWealth*, no. 463, December 30, 2010 (http://english.cw.com.tw/article.do?action=show&id=12535).

28. Hong Kai-ying and Lin Shang-tso, "Brain Drain in Taiwan as Chinese Headhunters Target Experts," *Want China Times*, September 11, 2011 (OSC CPP20110911968036). See also David Huang, Benjamin Chiang, and Jerry Lai, "2011 Most Admired Company Survey: Taiwan Makes a Stand in the Talent War," *CommonWealth*, no. 482, October 6, 2011 (OSC CPO20111027312003).

29. On China's weak rule of law, see the *New York Times* series of articles on "China's Legal System: Rule by Law," most of which were published in the fall of 2005; for example, Joseph Kahn, "Deep Flaws, and Little Justice, in China's Court System," *New York Times*, September 21, 2005 (www.nytimes.com/2005/09/21/international/asia/21confess.html?ex=1172466000&en=7c4614ffb44d4110&ei=5070). On the impact on the investment protection agreement, see "MAC Confirms Delays to Cross-Strait Investment Protection Pact Talks," *China Post*, June 21, 2012 (OSC CPP 20120621968219).

30. See Marcus Noland and Howard Pack, *Industrial Policy in an Era of Globalization: Lessons from Asia* (Washington: Peterson Institute for International Economics, 2003).

31. Sara Wu and Jin Chen, "Keeping 'Made in Taiwan' in Taiwan: Manufacturing Scrambles for a Future," *CommonWealth*, no. 476, July 14, 2011 (OSC CPP20110809312004).

32. Michael E. Porter, "Creating an Economic Strategy for Taiwan," presentation at Global Leaders Forum, Taipei, April 8, 2010 (www.isc.hbs.edu/pdf/2010-0408_Taiwan.pdf).

33. Denis Fred Simon, "The Orbital Mechanics of Taiwan's Emerging Technology Trajectory," presentation at the Columbia University symposium "Taiwan in the Twenty-First Century: Politics, Economy, and Society," Taipei, June 13, 2010.

34. "President and Vice President Hold Press Conference on Second Anniversary of Inauguration," Office of the President, May 19, 2010 (OSC CPP20100519046002).

35. "CNA: Taiwan President Ma Ying-jeou's 2011 New Year's Day Message," Central News Agency, January 1, 2011 (OSC CPP20110101968035). Innovation is also prescribed as a way out for Hong Kong firms, which are facing similar competitive pressures; see Naubahar Sharif, "Innovation and Survival in Guangdong: How Hong Kong Companies Can Succeed," *Hong Kong Journal* (January 2011) (www.hkjournal.org/PDF/2011_spring/5.pdf). For a similar argument concerning the United States, see Martin Neil Baily, "Adjusting to China: A Challenge to the U.S. Manufacturing Sector," *Policy Brief* 179 (January 2011), Brookings (www.brookings.edu/papers/2011/01_china_challenge_baily.aspx).

36. Wu and Chen, "Keeping 'Made in Taiwan' in Taiwan."

37. "Statute for Industrial Innovation," Ministry of Economic Affairs, May 12, 2010 (www.moeaidb.gov.tw/external/ctlr?lang=1&PRO=law.LawView&id=4643); "Text of Vice President Siew's Remarks on Taiwan in 21st Century," Office of the President, June 13, 2010 (OSC CPP20100614427001).

38. "CNA: Taiwan President Ma Ying-jeou's 2011 New Year's Day Message."

39. "Hybrid Vigour; IT in Taiwan and China," *The Economist*, May 29, 2010, p. 66.

40. Douglas B. Fuller, "The Changing Limits and the Limits of Change: The State, Private Firms, International Industry and China in the Evolution of Taiwan's Electronics Industry," *Journal of Contemporary China*, vol. 14 (August 2005), pp. 505–06.

41. "Post-ECFA Measures to Help SMEs on the Way," *Taiwan Today*, July 9, 2010 (OSC CPP20100709681148).

42. Ching-Hsuan Huang, "2009 Top 1000 CEO Survey: Both Optimism and Concern for Cross-Strait Ties," *CommonWealth*, no. 421, May 5, 2009 (http://english.cw.com.tw/article.do?action=show&id=11000).

43. "Report on ARATS-SEF Talks in Chongqing: Full Text of Agreement on Cross-Strait Cooperation on Protection of Intellectual Property Rights," Xinhua Domestic, June 29, 2010 (OSC CPP20100629005002).

44. For the latest U.S. government report, see Office of the U.S. Trade Representative, "2011 Special 301 Report," April 2011 (www.ustr.gov/sites/default/files/2012%20Special%20301%20Report_0.pdf), pp. 19–25.

45. Lieberthal, *Managing the China Challenge*, pp. 16–31.

46. "President and Vice President Hold 'New Inflection Point for Taiwan, New Era for Asia: Choosing Correctly at a Critical Juncture' Press Conference," Office of the President, July 1, 2010 (OSC CPP20100713312003).

47. Alice Yang, "Taiwan's Civil Service: Rising out of the Mire," *CommonWealth*, no. 403, August 14, 2008 (http://english.cw.com.tw/article.do?action=show&id=10360).

48. American Chamber of Commerce in Taipei, "2011 Taiwan White Paper," *Taiwan Business Topics*, vol. 41 (May 2011), pp. WP6–WP7; cited passage is on p. WP6.

49. American Chamber of Commerce in Taipei, "2012 Taiwan White Paper," *Taiwan Business Topics*, vol. 42 (May 2012), p. WP8.

50. "Raising the Bar for Taiwan's Higher Education," *Taiwan Business Topics*, vol. 40 (August 2010), pp. 34–36.

51. Sherry Lee, "Solutions to Taiwan's Education Woes," *CommonWealth*, no. 395, April 23, 2008 (http://english.cw.com.tw/article.do?action=show&id=10069); Ming-ling Hsieh, "Taiwan's Higher Education: Out of Sync with the Real World," *CommonWealth*, no. 410, November 19, 2008 (http://english.cw.com.tw/article.do?action=show&id=10619); Yi-Shan Chen, "Taiwanese Higher Education in Crisis: My University Has Disappeared!" *CommonWealth*, no. 444, April 7, 2010 (http://english.cw.com.tw/article.do?action=show&id=11879); Ting-feng Wu, "Education Survey: Science Losing Luster among Taiwan's Students," *CommonWealth*, no. 460, November 17, 2010 (http://english.cw.com.tw/article.do?action=show&id=12425).

52. Jennifer Huang and C.J. Lin, "CNA: Taiwan Universities Tumble in Recent World University Rankings," Central News Agency, October 6, 2011 (OSC CPP20111006968097).

53. "Ma: National Security Cannot Depend on Beijing's Goodwill," Kuomintang, April 19, 2012 (OSC CPP20120420312001).

54. Thomas G. Mahnken and others, "Asia in the Balance: Transforming U.S. Military Strategy in Asia," American Enterprise Institute, June 2012, p. 11 (www.aei.org/files/2012/05/31/-asia-in-the-balance-transforming-us-military-strategy-in-asia_134736206767).

55. "President Ma holds Discussions with Experts on PRC Military Affairs," Office of the President, October 28, 2010 (http://english.president.gov.tw/Default.aspx?tabid=491&itemid=22660&rmid=2355); Elaine Hou, "President Ma Eyes Defense Upgrade for Taiwan," *Taiwan Today*, April 8, 2011 (OSC CPP20110408968112).

56. Ma Ying-jeou, "Vision for a Golden Decade Ahead," remarks at the American Chamber of Commerce in Taipei, November 22, 2011, Office of the President (OSC CPP20111123427001).

57. Office of the Secretary of Defense, "Annual Report to Congress: Military and Security Developments Involving the People's Republic of China 2012," May 2012, p. 17.

58. "Kurt M. Campbell, Assistant Secretary, Bureau of East Asian and Pacific Affairs, Testimony before the House Foreign Affairs Committee, Washington, October 4, 2011," October 5, 2011 (http://ait.org.tw/en/officialtext-ot1116.html).

59. Ma Ying-jeou, "Building National Security for the Republic of China," speech by video conference at the Center for Strategic and International Studies, May 12, 2011 (http://english.president.gov.tw/Default.aspx?tabid=491&itemid=24284&rmid =2355).

60. Ministry of National Defense R.O.C., *Quadrennial Defense Review 2009* (Taipei: 2009) (www.mnd.gov.tw/qdr/file/ec1.pdf); cited passage is on p. 28.

61. Mainland Affairs Council, "Beijing's Hostility toward ROC," April 24, 2012 (www.mac.gov.tw/public/Attachment/24249412649.gif).

62. For conceptual background, see Evan S. Medeiros, "Strategic Hedging and the Future of Asia-Pacific Security," *Washington Quarterly*, vol. 29 (Winter 2005–06), pp. 145–67; Randall Schweller, "Managing the Rise of Great Powers: History and Theory," in *Engaging China: The Management of an Emerging Power*, edited by Alastair Iain Johnston and Robert S. Ross (New York: Routledge, 1999), pp. 1–31; Thomas J. Christensen, "The Contemporary Security Dilemma: Deterring a Taiwan Conflict," *Washington Quarterly*, vol. 25 (Autumn 2002), pp. 12–13. Some scholars stress that deterrence includes both reassurance and strengthening capabilities, all for the purpose of reducing an adversary's need and ability to use force; see Christensen, "The Contemporary Security Dilemma." In this discussion, I use the term "deterrence" to refer only to an actor's strengthening its capabilities in order to raise the cost of coercion.

63. For a description of how decisionmakers in the Obama administration started with a revised U.S. defense strategy that sought to close the gap between the threat environment and resources, with implications (ultimately) for the equipment procured for the military, see Scott Wilson and Greg Jaffe, "A Strong Defense for Obama, Military's Support for His Budget May Outflank Congress," *Washington Post*, January 8, 2012, pp. A1, 10.

64. Ministry of National Defense R.O.C., "National Defense Strategic Guidance," in *Quadrennial Defense Review 2009* (www.mnd.gov.tw/qdr/file/ec2.pdf), pp. 64–65.

65. Ministry of National Defense R.O.C., "Military Strategic Concepts," *2011 National Defense Report*, p.108 (http://2011mndreport.mnd.gov.tw/en/pdf/100report_ english.pdf). Taiwan's first *Quadrennial Defense Review*, released in 2009, stated this defense strategy in identical language.

66. Ibid., p. 109.

67. Ministry of National Defense R.O.C., "National Defense Strategic Guidance," p. 72.

68. Ibid.

69. Ibid., p. 73.

70. Nancy Bernkopf Tucker, "Strategic Ambiguity or Strategic Clarity?" in *Dangerous Strait: The U.S.-Taiwan-China Crisis*, edited by Nancy Bernkopf Tucker (Columbia University Press, 2005), pp. 186–212; Richard Bush, "The U.S. Policy of Dual Deterrence," in *If China Attacks Taiwan: Military Strategy, Politics, and Economics*, edited by Steve Tsang (New York: Routledge, 2005), pp. 35–53. On area denial, see M. Taylor Fravel, "China's Search for Military Power," *Washington Quarterly*, vol. 31 (Summer 2008), pp. 125–41; Michael McDevitt, "The Strategic and Operational Context

Driving PLA Navy Building," in *Right-Sizing the People's Liberation Army: Exploring the Contours of China's Military*, edited by Roy Kamphausen and Andrew Scobell (Carlisle, Pa.: Strategic Studies Institute, U.S. Army War College, 2007), pp. 481–522.

71. Bernard D. Cole, *Taiwan's Security: History and Prospects* (New York: Routledge, 2006), pp. 50–51; William S. Murray, "Revisiting Taiwan's Defense Strategy," *Naval War College Review,* vol. 61 (Summer 2008), p. 15.

72. Murray, "Revisiting Taiwan's Defense Strategy," p. 14.

73. Ibid., p. 24.

74. Cited passages from, respectively, Cole, *Taiwan's Security*, p. 169, and Alexander Chieh-cheng Huang, "A Midterm Assessment of Taiwan's First Quadrennial Defense Review," *Taiwan-U.S. Quarterly Analysis* 5, Brookings Institution Center for Northeast Asian Policy Studies, February 2011 (www.brookings.edu/papers/2011/02_taiwan_huang.aspx).

75. Murray, "Revisiting Taiwan's Defense Strategy," p. 15.

76. Cole, *Taiwan's Security*, pp. 169.

77. Fu S. Mei, "Taiwan's Defense White Paper Shows New Candor on Challenges Ahead," *China Brief,* vol. 11 (September 2, 2011) (www.jamestown.org/single/?no_cache=1&tx_ttnews%5Btt_news%5D=38360&tx_ttnews%5BbackPid%5D=517).

78. Andrew N. D. Yang, "Taiwan's Defense Preparation against the Chinese Military Threat," in *Assessing the Threat: The Chinese Military and Taiwan's Security*, edited by Michael D. Swaine, Andrew N. D. Yang, and Evan S. Medeiros (Washington: Carnegie Endowment for International Peace, 2007), pp. 268–75.

79. Mei, "Taiwan's Defense White Paper Shows New Candor on Challenges Ahead."

80. J. Michael Cole, "Ministry Mum on HF-2E's on Penghu," *Taipei Times*, September 14, 2011, p. 3 (www.taipeitimes.com/News/taiwan/print/2011/09/14/2003513241).

81. Ibid.

82. David A. Shlapak, "The Rockets' Red Glare: Implications of Improvements in PRC Air and Missile Strike Capabilities," in *New Opportunities and Challenges for Taiwan's Security*, edited by Roger Cliff, Phillip C. Saunders, and Scott Harold (Santa Monica, Calif.: RAND Corporation, 2011), pp. 76–77; Ed Ross, "Taiwan's Ballistic-Missile Deterrence and Defense Capabilities," *China Brief,* vol. 11 (February 10, 2011) (www.jamestown.org/single/?no_cache=1&tx_ttnews%5Btt_news%5D=37489&tx_ttnews%5BbackPid%5D=517); Mahnken and others, "Asia in the Balance," p. 19.

83. Michael J. Lustumbo, "A New Taiwan Strategy to Adapt to PLA Precision Strike Capabilities," in *New Opportunities and Challenges for Taiwan's Security*, edited by Cliff, Saunders, and Harold, pp. 127–36.

84. One American analyst has gone so far as to suggest that a conventional defense of Taiwan is becoming so difficult that the only way to ensure Taiwan's security in extremis would be for Washington to make an extended nuclear deterrence commitment to Taiwan; see Shlapak, "The Rockets' Red Glare," p. 79.

85. Emmanuelle Tzeng and Elizabeth Hsu, "CNA: Nearly 80% of Taiwanese Will Voluntarily Defend Country: Poll," Central News Agency, December 27, 2010 (OSC

CPP20101227968071). The significance of the poll results is diluted somewhat by the finding that those who were forty to fifty-nine years of age were the most willing to fight and that blue-collar workers were more willing than white-collar workers.

86. "Prepared Statement of Dr. Peter Lavoy, Acting Assistant Secretary of Defense for Asian and Pacific Security Affairs," Testimony before House Foreign Affairs Committee, October 4, 2011 (http://foreignaffairs.house.gov/112/lav100411.pdf).

87. Lustumbo, "A New Taiwan Strategy to Adapt to PLA Precision Strike Capabilities," p. 135.

88. Murray, "Revisiting Taiwan's Defense Strategy," pp. 26–28; Lustumbo, "A New Taiwan Strategy to Adapt to PLA Precision Strike Capabilities," p. 133.

89. Murray, "Revisiting Taiwan's Defense Strategy," pp. 28–29.

90. Ibid., pp. 25–28.

91. Ibid., p. 30.

92. Jimmy Chuang, "MND Says It Is Amenable To 'New' Ideas on Defense," *Taipei Times,* December 3, 2008 (OSC CPP20081203968043).

93. Shelley Rigger, "The Unfinished Business of Taiwan's Democratization," in *Dangerous Strait: The U.S.-Taiwan-China Crisis,* edited by Tucker, p. 43.

94. "Su Chi's Advice May Grate on the Ears, but Reforms Must Not Be Delayed," *China Times,* May 25, 2012 (OSC CPP20120605312003).

95. Jerry Lai, "Four Little Dragons—Taiwan: Model Student, Back of the Class," *CommonWealth,* no. 488, December 29, 2011 (OSC CPP20111229427007).

96. Larry Diamond, "How Good a Democracy Has the Republic of China Become? Taiwan's Democracy in Comparative Perspective," *A Spectacular Century: The Republic of China Centennial Democracy Forums: Conference Manual,* June 2001, p. 174. These data are from the Asian Barometer survey.

97. Opposition parties criticized the KMT's using its majority on the procedure committee to block LY consideration of their proposals; see Yen Ruo-jin, "KMT Blocks Proposals Despite New Procedure," *Taipei Times,* April 11, 2012 (OSC CPP20120411968017).

98. "Su Chi's Advice May Grate on the Ears."

99. Shiouw-duan Hawang, "Legislative Structure and Reform," paper presented at the Brookings Institution and Center on Strategic and International Studies conference "Consolidating Taiwan's Democracy: Challenges, Opportunities, and Prospects," March 22, 2006 (on file with author); Shih Hsiao-kuang, "KMT May Get Only Half of Legislative Convener Seats," *Taipei Times,* February 28, 2012 (OSC CPP20120228968009); Lee Yu-hsin, "DPP Sets Sights on Procedure Committee," *Taipei Times,* February 6, 2012 (OSC CPP20120206968003); Jacques de Lisle, "Taiwan's 2012 Presidential and Legislative Elections," *E-Notes,* Foreign Policy Research Institute, January 2012 (www.fpri.org/enotes/2012/201201.delisle.taiwan.html). LY Speaker Wang Jin-pyng sought to create a central role for himself in the review of the ECFA and did not cooperate with the Ma administration to secure approval for the agreement, even though the Kuomintang controlled both the executive and legislative branches. See Alan D. Romberg, "Cross-Strait Relations: Setting the Stage for 2012," *China Leader-*

ship Monitor, no. 34 (Winter 2011) (http://media.hoover.org/sites/default/files/documents/CLM34AR.pdf), p. 4. On the rule of law, Jacques de Lisle has confirmed the public perception that the politically powerful tend to win in sensitive cases. Moreover, access to the system can be a problem and judges and prosecutors are not always up to handling complex economic cases. See "Judiciary System," paper for the March 2006 conference "Consolidating Taiwan's Democracy" (on file with author).

100. Yu-chung Shen, "Semi-Presidentialism in Taiwan: A Shadow of the Constitution of the Weimar Republic," *Taiwan Journal of Democracy*, vol. 7 (July 2011), pp. 135–52; cited passage is on p. 152.

101. "Editorial: Blue-Green Fault Line Weakens Taiwan," *Taipei Times*, June 15, 2012 (OSC CPP20120615968010).

102. Gary D. Rawnsley, "The Media and Democracy in China and Taiwan," *Taiwan Journal of Democracy*, vol. 3 (July 2007), pp. 66–67.

103. Ibid., pp. 73–74.

104. Ibid., p. 75; Freedom House, "Taiwan (2011)," *Freedom of the Press*, 2011 (www.freedomhouse.org/template.cfm?page=251&year=2011). One Taiwan commentator asserted that ownership by corporations was the cause of the decline in professional ethics; Chiu Hei-yuan, "Taiwan Is in Need of a Brand New Media Order," *Taipei Times*, November 7, 2011 (OSC CPP20111107968003).

105. Rawnsley, "The Media and Democracy in China and Taiwan," pp. 64, 74–75.

106. While working in Congress, I fielded such ideas proposed by Taiwanese activists.

107. Shelley Rigger, *From Opposition to Power: Taiwan's Democratic Progressive Party* (Boulder, Colo.: Lynne Rienner, 2001), p. 131.

108. On the politics of referendum legislation, see Shelley Rigger, *Why Taiwan Matters: Small Island, Global Powerhouse* (Lanham, Md.: Rowman and Littlefield, 2011), pp. 82–84.

109. Indeed, the principal question in 2004 concerned China's military threat and the question in 2008 was on Taiwan's international participation. On each question the public's views were well known.

110. Lin Cho-shui, "End the Political Chaos at Its Systemic Source," *Yuanjing 2030: Yuanbao Mengxiang Yinxiang Weilai* [Embracing 2030] (Taipei: Yuan-chien Publishing, 2011), pp. 84–85.

111. Tsai Ing-wen, "Taiwan: Policy Challenges, Choices, and Democratic Governance," speech at Harvard University, September 15, 2011, (OSC CPP20110916427003).

112. Mainland Affairs Council, "Opening Up and Guarding the Country: Benefits of 15 Cross-Strait Agreements, July 2011" (www.mac.gov.tw/public/Data/181811155971.pdf), p. 8. On the LY consideration of ECFA, see Alan D. Romberg, "Cross-Strait Relations: Setting the Stage for 2012," *China Leadership Monitor*, no. 34 (Winter 2011) (http://media.hoover.org/sites/default/files/documents/CLM34AR.pdf), pp. 4–5.

113. "Act Governing Relations between the People of the Taiwan Area and the Mainland Area," originally passed in 1992 and subsequently amended (www.mac.gov.tw/ct.asp?xItem=90541&ctNode=5914&mp=3).

114. Shih-chan Dai and Chung-li Wu, "The Role of the Legislative Yuan under Ma Ying-jeou: The Case of China Policy Legislation and Agreements," draft paper prepared for the conference "Taiwan: A Tentative Balance Sheet of Ma Ying-jeou's First Term," Hong Kong Baptist University, May 24–25 2012; used with the authors' permission.

115. Robert D. Putnam, "Diplomacy and Domestic Politics: The Logic of Two-Level Games," *International Organization*, vol. 42 (Summer 1988), pp. 427–60. For an application of Putnam's approach to cross-Strait interactions in the 1990s, see Steven Goldstein, "The Rest of the Story: The Impact of Domestic Politics on Taiwan's Mainland Policy," *Harvard Studies on Taiwan*, vol. 2 (1998), pp. 62–90.

116. Jay Chou and Lillian Wu, "CNA: Taiwan's Talks with China to Get More Difficult: Official," Central News Agency, October 7, 2011 (OSC CPP20111007968085).

117. Rawnsley, "The Media and Democracy in China and Taiwan," pp. 75–78; Freedom House, "Taiwan (2011)."

118. Huang Ching-lung, "The Changing Roles of the Media in Taiwan's Democratization Process," working paper, Brookings Institution Center for Northeast Asian Policy Studies, July 2009 (www.brookings.edu/papers/2009/07_taiwan_huang.aspx); Gary D. Rawnsley and Ming-yeh Rawnsley, "The Media in Democratic Taiwan," in *Taiwan since Martial Law: Society, Culture, Politics, Economy* (2013, forthcoming), p. 395 (draft essay provided to the author).

119. Rawnsley and Rawnsley, "The Media in Democratic Taiwan," p. 396.

120. Communication from Dafydd Fell to the author, November 13, 2011.

121. A total of seventy legislators are picked from geographic districts. Thirty-four come from the party lists, and six are reserved for aborigine representatives.

122. The current system replaced one that had a stronger element of proportional representation, which led to greater fragmentation and polarization.

123. One Taiwan scholar associated with the DPP, Liu Shih-chung, concluded that the United States was not completely happy with Ma Ying-jeou's efforts to stabilize relations with Beijing while simultaneously reassuring Washington that he was not moving too fast; see "Think Tank Scholar Says U.S. Does Not Want Taiwan, China Going to Negotiating Table Too Soon," *China Review News*, April 7, 2012 (OSC CPP20120407569001); communication to the author from Liu Shih-chung, April 17, 2012.

124. Rigger, *Why Taiwan Matters*.

125. Nancy Liu, "CNA: Ait Chairman Presses Further on U.S. Beef Issue," Central News Agency, January 31, 2012 (OSC CPP20120131968204).

126. Lee Shu-hua and Elizabeth Hsu, "CNA: Ma Acknowledges Beef Issue Key to Trade Talks with U.S.," Central News Agency, March 21 2012 (OSC CPP20120321968224).

127. "Prepared Statement of Dr. Peter Lavoy."

Chapter Nine

1. See, for example, Yan Anlin, "Building a Framework for Peaceful Development Is a Task for Both Sides of the Strait: A Pondering on the Future of Cross-Strait Relations after Ma Ying-jeou's Reelection," *Zhongguo Pinglun*, April 2012 (Open Source Center [hereafter OSC] CPP20120403787001).

2. Taiwan Affairs Office, "Speech Delivered by Wang Yi during 10th Seminar on Cross-Strait Relations," March 15, 2012 (OSC CPP20120329329001).

3. On the difficulties of implementation, see Dov S. Zakheim, *A Vulcan's Tale: How the Bush Administration Mismanaged the Reconstruction of Afghanistan* (Washington: Brookings, 2011).

4. Shelley Rigger, "Disaggregating the Concept of National Identity," *Asia Program Special Report* 114 (Washington: Woodrow Wilson International Center for Scholars, August 2003), pp. 17–21; originally presented at the Woodrow Wilson International Center for Scholars Asia Program event "The Evolution of a Taiwanese Identity."

5. "TVBS on Identity and Independence," from *The View from Taiwan*, the blog of Michael Turton, February 5, 2011 (http://michaelturton.blogspot.com/2011/02/tvbs-on-identity-and-independence.html).

6. Shelley Rigger, *Taiwan's Rising Rationalism: Generations, Politics, and Taiwanese Nationalism*, Policy Study 26 (Washington: East-West Center, 2006).

7. Wang Jianmin, "'Taiwan zhuti yishih' dui daonei zhengzhi yu liangan guanxi di yingxiang shengri yanjun [The Influence of 'Taiwan Subjective Consciousness' on Domestic Politics and Cross-Strait Relations Is Becoming Increasingly Grim]," *Zhongguo Pinglun*, April 2012, p. 29.

8. See Richard C. Bush, *Untying the Knot: Making Peace in the Taiwan Strait* (Brookings, 2005), pp. 229–38.

9. Alan D. Romberg, "The 2012 Taiwan Election: Off and Running," *China Leadership Monitor*, no. 30 (Summer 2011) (http://media.hoover.org/documents/CLM35AR.pdf).

10. Frank Hsieh, "Protecting Taiwan Is Protecting the Republic of China," *Lien Ho Pao*, June 12, 2012 (OSC CPP20120613569001).

11. Xu Shiquan, "DPP Transformation and Constitutional One China," *American Foreign Policy Interests*, vol. 34 (July-August 2011), pp. 216–19.

12. For one example of such skepticism, see Wang Jianmin, "Democratic Progressive Party: Figuring Out Cross-Strait Policy Adjustments," *Shijie Zhishi* (April 2012), pp. 54–55 (OSC CPP20120522671005).

13. Zhang Nianchi, "Zailun Liangan Guanxi Daqushih [Addressing Again the Big Trend in Cross-Strait Relations]," *Zhongguo Pinglun*, March 2012, pp 4-6.

14. "Join Hands to Promote Peaceful Development of Cross-Strait Relations; Strive with Unity of Purpose for the Great Rejuvenation of the Chinese Nation," Xinhua Domestic Service, December 31, 2008 (OSC CPP20081231005002).

15. Even the small Taiwan groups that favor unification began with the premise that it would occur under the aegis of the ROC; see "Pro-Unification Parties, Groups in Taiwan Set Up New Organization Headed by Hsu Li-nong," *China Times*, March 10, 2012 (OSC CPP20120310569001).

16. Wang Yi, "Speech Delivered by Wang Yi during 10th Seminar on Cross-Strait Relations (Full Text)," Taiwan Affairs Office, March 15, 2012 (OSC CPP20120329329001).

17. On this point, Chinese make a play on words. They use the term *Taidu* to refer to efforts to create a Republic of Taiwan and *Dutai* to refer to a permanent situation of one China and one Taiwan; Lu Yimin, "Ma Ying-jeou bei Beijing Shiwei Dutai [Beijing Regards Ma Ying-jeou as Promoting a Separate Taiwan]," *Pingguo Ribao*, February 29, 2009 (www.appledaily.com.tw/appledaily/article/property/20090225/31420761).

18. "Beijing Scholar Sun Zhe Says Taiwan's 'No Request for Arms Sales' Key to Making Breakthrough in Cross-Strait Relations," *Chung-kuo Shih-pao*, February 29, 2012 (OSC CPP20120229569001); Alan D. Romberg, "Cross-Strait Relations: Setting the Stage for 2012," *China Leadership Monitor*, no. 34 (Winter 2011) (http://media.hoover.org/sites/default/files/documents/CLM34AR.pdf), p. 12.

19. Bush, *Untying the Knot*, pp. 275–76.

20. Zhang Huangmin, "Share Interpretation of One China: New Coordinates for Cross-Strait Mutual Political Trust in the Future," Zhongguo Pinglun Tongxunshe, February 7, 2011 (OSC CPP20110207312002).

21. Chen Qimao, "The Taiwan Straits Situation since Ma came to Office and Conditions for Cross-Straits Political Negotiations: A View from Shanghai," *Journal of Contemporary China*, vol. 20 (January 2011), pp. 153–60; cited passage is on pp. 155–56. An article in the journal of the PRC Foreign Ministry's think tank provided a basically factual description of the way terms like "Taiwan" and "the Republic of China" are used in different contexts but did not address, as Chen does, Taipei's claim that the ROC is a sovereign entity; see Zhou Gongye and Wang Jianmin, "Political Interpretation of the Name 'Taiwan,'" *Shijie Zhishi*, August 2011 (OSC CPP20111007671010), pp. 46–48.

22. Chu Shulong, "Communication for Better Understanding and Improvement of Cross-Taiwan Strait Relations," Brookings Northeast Asia Commentary 50, June 2011 (www.brookings.edu/articles/2011/06_cross_strait_shulong.aspx).

23. Zhang Nianchi, "Create a Condition for Solving the 'Republic of China' Issue," *Zhongguo Pinglun*, May 2010 (OSC CPP20100518710013). See also Jean-Pierre Cabestan, "Reactions on the Mainland to the Taiwanese Election," *China Analysis*, April 2012, pp. 3-5 (http://ecfr.eu/page/-/China_Analysis_Taiwan_after_the_election_April2012.pdf).

24. On dual sovereignty in the Atlantic world, see Bernard Bailyn, *To Begin the World Anew: The Genius and Ambiguities of the American Founders* (New York: Alfred A. Knopf, 2003), pp. 3–36.

25. Mainland Affairs Council, "Unification or Independence" (line graph) (www.mac.gov.tw/public/Attachment/24249404071.gif).

26. Rigger, *Taiwan's Rising Rationalism,* p. viii.

27. Zhang Nianchi, "Staying out of Blind Spots in Cross-Strait Relations," *Zhongguo Pinglun,* April 2010 (OSC CPP20100409710008).

28. Wang Weixing, "The United States and Taiwan Start a Quasi-Military Alliance," *Shijie Zhishi,* July 1, 2002 (OSC CCP20020717000147); Xi Yang, "An Exercise of the Taiwan Military to 'Defend Independence' by Force," *Ta Kung Pao,* May 27, 2002 (OSC CPP20020527000018).

29. Wang Jianmin, "U.S. Is Biggest Obstacle to Cross-Strait Peace Accord," Zhongping She, April 19, 2012 (OSC CPP20120419569001).

30. "U.S.-China Joint Statement," White House, Office of the Press Secretary, January 19, 2011 (www.whitehouse.gov/the-press-office/2011/01/19/us-china-joint-statement); emphasis added.

31. Yun-han Chu, "Taiwan's National Identity Politics and the Prospect of Cross-Strait Relations," *Asian Survey,* vol. 44 (July-August 2004), pp. 503–06.

32. Edward D. Mansfield and Jack Snyder, *Electing to Fight: Why Emerging Democracies Go to War* (MIT Press, 2005).

33. Ma Ying-jeou, "Upholding Ideals, Working Together for Reform and Creating Greater Well-Being for Taiwan," inaugural address, May 20, 2012 (http://english.president.gov.tw/Default.aspx?tabid=491&itemid=27199&rmid=2355).

Chapter Ten

1. See Richard Halloran, "The U.S.-Taiwan Military Charade," *Taipei Times,* April 27, 2012 (Open Source Center [hereafter OSC] CPP20120427968005).

2. On the diplomacy of U.S.-PRC rapprochement, see Richard C. Bush, "The 'Sacred Texts' of United States–China–Taiwan Relations," in *At Cross Purposes: U.S.-Taiwan Relations since 1942* (Armonk, N.Y.: M.E. Sharpe, 2004), pp. 124–78. Some believe that the Taiwan Relations Act requires the United States to come to the defense of Taiwan, but it does not; see ibid., pp. 152–60.

3. For a thorough review of this history, see Nancy Bernkopf Tucker, *Strait Talk: United States–Taiwan Relations and the Crisis with China* (Harvard University Press, 2010).

4. Guo Zhenyuan, "The Impact of the Taiwan Issue on the Sino-U.S. Relationship over the Next Four Years," *Zhongguo Pinglun,* March 2009, p. 41.

5. "Join Hands to Promote Peaceful Development of Cross-Strait Relations; Strive with Unity of Purpose for the Great Rejuvenation of the Chinese Nation," Xinhua Domestic Service, December 31, 2008 (OSC CPP20081231005002).

6. More recently, Washington offered two elaborations: the Christopher warning that neither side should unilaterally change the status quo and the idea that the dispute should be addressed in a manner acceptable to the people of Taiwan. But those

emendations are consistent with an exclusive focus on process. The second elaboration did not mean that the United States would necessarily agree with what Taiwan leaders asserted was acceptable to the people of the island. For American warnings against letting Taiwan leaders define U.S. interests, see Robert S. Ross, "The 1995–96 Taiwan Strait Confrontation: Coercion, Credibility, and the Use of Force," *International Security,* vol. 25 (Fall 2000), p. 123; Chas W. Freeman Jr., "Preventing War in the Taiwan Strait," *Foreign Affairs,* vol. 77 (July-August 1998), p. 7.

7. On strategic ambiguity, see Nancy Bernkopf Tucker, "Strategic Ambiguity or Strategic Clarity?" in *Dangerous Strait: The U.S.-Taiwan-China Crisis,* edited by Nancy Bernkopf Tucker (Columbia University Press, 2005), pp. 186–212. On dual deterrence, see Richard Bush, "The U.S. Policy of Dual Deterrence," in *If China Attacks Taiwan: Military Strategy, Politics, and Economics,* edited by Steve Tsang (New York: Routledge, 2005), pp. 35–53.

8. "CNA: U.S. State Department Congratulates President Ma Ying-jeou on Inauguration," Central News Agency, May 21, 2008 (OSC CPP20080521968129); Barack Obama Letter to Ma Ying-jeou, May 20, 2008 (on file with author).

9. Shirley Kan, "Taiwan: Major U.S. Arms Sales since 1990," Congressional Research Service Report RL30957, October 21, 2011.

10. For example, on the delay of the 2010 announcement until after Barack Obama's November 2009 visit to China, see Jeffrey A. Bader, *Obama and China's Rise: An Insider's Account of America's Asia Strategy* (Brookings, 2012), pp. 54, 71–74.

11. "U.S.-China Joint Statement," White House, Office of the Press Secretary, January 19, 2011 (www.whitehouse.gov/the-press-office/2011/01/19/us-china-joint-statement).

12. Kurt M. Campbell, testimony, *Hearing on Why Taiwan Matters, Part II, before the House Foreign Affairs Committee,* October 4, 2011 (http://foreignaffairs.house.gov/112/cam100411.pdf).

13. Anna Fifield, Robin Kwong, and Kathrin Hille, "U.S. Concerned about Taiwan Candidate," *Financial Times,* September 15, 2011 (www.ft.com/intl/cms/s/0/f926fd14-df93-11e0-845a-00144feabdc0.html#axzz1Y84rkxY1).

14. Nancy Bernkopf Tucker, "If Taiwan Chooses Unification, Should the United States Care?" *Washington Quarterly,* vol. 25 (Summer 2002), pp. 15–28; cited passages are from p. 27 and p. 26.

15. The seminal discussion of abandonment and entrapment as the two fears that bedevil any alliance relationship is found in Glenn Snyder, *Alliance Politics* (Cornell University Press, 2007).

16. Bruce Gilley, "Not So Dire Straits: How the Finlandization of Taiwan Benefits U.S. Security," *Foreign Affairs,* vol. 89, no. 1 (January-February 2010), pp. 44–60.

17. Ibid., p. 48.

18. Ibid., p. 58.

19. Nadia Tsao, "Rohrabacher to Leave Taiwan Caucus Position," *Taipei Times,* March 15, 2009 (OSC CPP20090315968003).

20. Charles Glaser, "Will China's Rise Lead to War? Why Realism Does Not Mean Pessimism," *Foreign Affairs* 90, no. 2 (March-April 2011), p. 80–91.

21. Chas W. Freeman, Jr., "Beijing, Washington, and the Shifting Balance of Prestige," remarks to the China Maritime Studies Institute, Newport, R.I., May 10, 2011 (www.mepc.org/articles-commentary/speeches/beijing-washington-and-shifting-balance-prestige).

22. "A Way Ahead with China: Steering the Right Course with the Middle Kingdom," recommendations from the Miller Center of Public Affairs Roundtable, Miller Center of Public Affairs, University of Virginia, March 2011 (millercenter.org/policy/chinaroundtable), pp. 24–25.

23. Bill Owens, "America Must Start Treating China as a Friend," *Financial Times*, November 17, 2009.

24. Michael D. Swaine, *America's Challenge: Engaging a Rising China in the Twenty-First Century* (Washington: Carnegie Endowment for International Peace, 2011).

25. Zbigniew Brzezinski, "Balancing the East, Upgrading the West: U.S. Grand Strategy in an Age of Upheaval," *Foreign Affairs*, vol. 91 (January-February 2012), pp. 91–92, 177–78.

26. William Lowther, "U.S. Expert Poses 'Dramatic Question' about Taiwan," *Taipei Times*, April 20, 2012 (OSC CPP20120420968013). The U.S. expert cited was my colleague Michael O'Hanlon.

27. Robert Sutter, "Taiwan's Future: Narrowing Strait," *NBR Analysis* 96 (Seattle, Wash.: National Bureau of Asian Research, May 2011).

28. On "core interests" generally, see Michael D. Swaine, "China's Assertive Behavior, Part One: On 'Core Interests,'" *China Leadership Monitor*, no. 34 (Winter 2011) (http://media.hoover.org/sites/default/files/documents/CLM34MS.pdf).

29. Dai Bingguo, "Closing Remarks for U.S.-China Strategic and Economic Dialogue," Washington, July 28, 2009 (www.state.gov/secretary/rm/2009a/july/126599.htm).

30. "U.S.-China Joint Statement," White House, Office of the Press Secretary, January 19, 2011 (www.whitehouse.gov/the-press-office/2011/01/19/us-china-joint-statement); emphasis added.

31. Ma Hao-liang, "Obama's Cross-Strait Policy Inclined to Favor the Mainland," *Ta Kung Pao*, November 27, 2009 (OSC CPP20091127710003).

32. Swaine, "China's Assertive Behavior, Part One," p. 7.

33. Kurt M. Campbell, testimony.

34. I first developed these ideas in my essay, "Taiwan and East Asian Security," *Orbis*, vol. 55 (March 2011), pp. 285–88.

35. Note that if the DPP had returned to power in 2012, it would not necessarily have pursued a provocative approach and created problems for U.S. policy, even if Beijing imposed a stall, which would have been likely. If a new DPP government *had* undertaken provocative policies, it would not have been a good outcome for the United States, because it would raise the chances of a cross-Strait conflict, at least

through miscalculation. In that case, Washington would probably resume dual deterrence, maintaining a delicate balance between its warnings and reassurances to each side of the Strait. But China could be less willing to heed U.S. warnings because its relative power has grown, and it could become more willing to consider intimidation or coercion against Taiwan.

36. Jiang Zemin, "Continue to Promote the Reunification of the Motherland," speech, January 30, 1995 (www.fmprc.gov.cn/eng/ljzg/3568/t17784.htm).

37. Obama administration officials have signaled an awareness of this problem in noting that "intimidation" is one threat that Taiwan might face.

38. See, for example, Aaron L. Friedberg, *A Contest for Supremacy: China and America and the Struggle for Mastery in Asia* (New York: W.W. Norton, 2011); and Glaser, "Will China's Rise Lead to War?" For my own discussion of these issues, see Richard C. Bush, "The Revival of China as a Great Power and What It Means for the United States," speech at Towson State University, November 17, 2008 (www.brookings.edu/~/media/Files/rc/speeches/2008/1117_china_bush/1117_china_bush.pdf).

39. See Randall Schweller, "Managing the Rise of Great Powers: History and Theory," in *Engaging China: The Management of an Emerging Power*, edited by Alastair Iain Johnston and Robert Ross (New York: Routledge, 1999), pp. 1–31.

40. Friedberg, *A Contest for Supremacy*; Swaine, *America's Challenge*. Power transitions are relevant to the discussion in previous chapters of the concepts of security dilemma and hedging since a rapid power transition can complicate the dynamics of a security dilemma, leading established powers to read the worst into the intentions of the rising power and to take countering actions.

41. White House, Office of the Press Secretary, "U.S. - China Joint Statement."

42. Kenneth Lieberthal and Wang Jisi, *Addressing U.S.-China Strategic Distrust*, Monograph 4 (Brookings, John L. Thornton China Center, 2012), pp. x–xi.

43. Ibid., pp. viii–ix.

44. This paragraph draws on Jack S. Levy, "Power Transition Theory and the Rise of China," in *China's Ascent: Power, Security, and the Future of International Politics*, edited by Robert S. Ross and Zhu Feng (Cornell University Press, 2008), pp. 11–33.

45. Ibid., p. 32.

46. Thomas J. Christensen, "Posing Problems without Catching Up: China's Rise and Challenges for U.S. Security Policy," *International Security*, vol. 25 (Spring 2001), pp. 5–40.

47. Glaser, "Will China's Rise Lead to War?"; Robert Jervis, "Cooperation under the Security Dilemma," *World Politics*, vol. 30 (January 1978), pp. 186–214; Robert Jervis, *Perception and Misperception in International Politics* (Princeton University Press, 1976); Alastair Iain Johnston, "Beijing's Security Behavior in the Asia-Pacific: Is China a Dissatisfied Power?" in *Rethinking Security in East Asia: Identity, Power, and Efficiency*, edited by J. J. Suh, Peter J. Katzenstein, and Allen Carlson (Stanford University Press, 2004), pp. 34–96.

48. On why China's imminent emergence as the world's largest economy in and of itself is irrelevant to an evaluation of its power, see Richard Bush, "As Number One, China to Face Hour of Choice," *YaleGlobal Online*, June 30, 2011 (http://yaleglobal. yale.edu/content/number-one-china-face-hour-choice).

49. See Richard C. Bush, "China-Japan Tensions, 1995–2006: Why They Happened, What to Do," Brookings Institution Foreign Policy Program Policy Paper 16 (June 2009) (www.brookings.edu/papers/2009/06_china_japan_bush.aspx).

50. Another factor that can drive a security dilemma is historical memory. For a multifaceted approach, see Richard C. Bush, *The Perils of Proximity: China-Japan Security Relations* (Brookings, 2010), pp. 23–40.

51. Kurt M. Campbell, testimony; emphasis added.

52. See, for example, Nancy Bernkopf Tucker and Bonnie Glaser, "Should the United States Abandon Taiwan?" *Washington Quarterly*, vol. 34 (Fall 2011), pp. 23–37; and Shelley Rigger, *Why Taiwan Matters: Small Island, Global Powerhouse* (Lanham, Md.: Rowman & Littlefield, 2011), especially pp. 187–98.

53. Kurt M. Campbell, testimony.

54. Dr. Peter Lavoy, Acting Assistant Secretary of Defense for Asian and Pacific Security Affairs, testimony before the House Foreign Affairs Committee, October 4, 2011 (http://foreignaffairs.house.gov/112/lav100411.pdf).

55. Chas W. Freeman Jr., "The Taiwan Problem and China's Strategy for Resolving It," remarks at the Center for Naval Analysis, September 14, 2011 (www.mepc.org/articles-commentary/speeches/taiwan-problem-and-chinas-strategy-resolving-it).

56. "Taking Account of 'Two Situations,' Expand 'Convergence of Interests,' and Build 'Communities of Interests' between China and the United States"; "Five-Point Suggestion Made by Mr. Zheng Bijian on Sino-U.S. Relations," October 2011, unpublished papers on file with author.

57. William Lowther, "U.S.-Sino Ties Can Rebound from Sale: Glaser," *Taipei Times*, May 23, 2012, p. 3.

58. Dr. Peter Lavoy, testimony.

59. For a discussion of the U.S. aversion to Taiwan offensive capabilities, see J. Michael Cole, "Faulty Logic behind U.S. Arms Sales," *Taipei Times*, March 2, 2012 (OSC CPP20120302968003).

60. J. Michael Cole, "Taiwan Needs to Go Asymmetrical," *Taipei Times*, September 23, 2011 (OSC CPP20110923968038). The Missile Technology Control Regime prohibits members from transferring full missile systems or components if the resulting missiles would have a range of greater than 300 kilometers; see "MTCR Guidelines and the Equipment, Software, and Technology Annex" (www.mtcr.infor/english/guidelines.html). Taiwan's Hsiung-Feng 2E surface-to-surface cruise missile has a range of 600 kilometers (see Cole, "Faulty Logic behind U.S. Arms Sales").

61. Kurt M. Campbell, testimony. It was the Clinton administration that first said that any resolution should, aside from being peaceful, receive the assent of the people of Taiwan. That reflected a realistic recognition that Taiwan had a democratic system. The Bush administration broadened that formula to include the people of the Main-

land but without saying how the citizens of an authoritarian system would register their preferences.

62. Taiwan Relations Act, Public Law 96-8, 96th Congress (1979) (www.scribd.com/doc/20385/Taiwan-Relations-Act).

63. Sun Zhe, *Houweiji Shijie yu Zhongmei Zhanlue Jingzheng* [Strategic Readjustment of U.S.-China Relations in the Post-Crisis World] (Beijing: Shishi chubanshe, 2011).

64. Swaine, *America's Challenge*, pp. 359–60.

65. Ibid., p. 360.

66. Bader, *Obama and China's Rise*, pp. 76–77. In October 2011, Zheng Bijian told an American audience, "It is crucial that the U.S. government carries out its commitment [under the August 1982 communiqué] and takes actions to support the improvement and development of cross-Straits relations. This is in the interest of all parties concerned, including the United States. . . . The two sides should seek consensus through consultation on a timetable for the United States to honor its commitment made in the August 17 communiqué, i.e. gradually reduce and finally terminate its arms sales to Taiwan." See "Taking Account of 'Two Situations.'"

67. Bader, *Obama and China's Rise*, pp. 76–77; emphasis added.

68. Ibid., pp. 360–62.

69. Ibid., p. 361.

70. The first to do so publicly was George Shultz, who in remarks in Shanghai in February 1987 said that Washington "welcome[d] developments, including indirect trade and increasing people-to-people interchange, which have contributed to a relaxation of tensions in the Taiwan Strait." See Nancy Bernkopf Tucker, *Strait Talk: United States Taiwan Relations and the Crisis with China* (Harvard University Press, 2009), p. 167. The Obama administration praised ECFA among other post-2008 steps; see the White House, Office of the Press Secretary, "U.S. - China Joint Statement," January 19, 2011 (www.whitehouse.gov/the-press-office/2011/01/19/us-china-joint-statement).

71. C. Fred Bergston, "Toward a Free Trade Area of the Asia Pacific," Peterson Institute for International Economics, Policy Brief 07-2, February 2007 (www.piie.com/publications/interstitial.cfm?ResearchID=710).

72. Kurt M. Campbell, testimony.

73. Claude Barfield and Phillip Levy, "Tales of the South Pacific: President Obama and the Transpacific Partnership," American Enterprise Institute, December 18, 2009 (www.aei.org/outlook/100927); letters from Ronald Kirk, U.S. Trade Representative, to Nancy Pelosi, Speaker of the House of Representatives, and Robert C. Byrd, President Pro-Tempore of the U.S. Senate, December 14, 2009 (www.ustr.gov/webfm_send/1559); Joshua Meltzer, "The Trans-Pacific Partnership: Its Economic and Strategic Implications," Brookings Institution, September 30, 2011 (www.brookings.edu/opinions/2011/0930_trans_pacific_partnership_meltzer.aspx).

74. Office of the U.S. Trade Representative, "2011 National Trade Estimate Report on Foreign Trade Barriers," March 2011, pp. 337–43 (www.ustr.gov/webfm_send/2740).

75. "3rd Ld Writethru: Chinese, U.S. Presidents Meet on Bilateral Ties," Xinhua English, June 20, 2012 (OSC CPP20120620968156).

76. The latter point on pressure and mediation were two of the "six assurances" that the Reagan administration conveyed to Taipei in 1982.

77. For more details on these points, see Richard C. Bush, *Untying the Knot: Making Peace in the Taiwan Strait* (Brookings, 2005), pp. 296–303.

Chapter Eleven

1. "Upholding Ideals, Working Together for Reform, and Creating Greater Well-Being for Taiwan," Central News Agency, May 20, 2012 (Open Source Center [hereafter OSC] CPP20120520968035). Also available at http://english.president.gov.tw/Default.aspx?tabid=491&itemid=27199&rmid=2355.

2. Ma highlighted the importance of the concept of the "two mutuals" later in May when speaking to an international law conference. He said that it "was inspired by Germany's experience" between 1972 and 1990, when hostility declined but the prospects for unification were uncertain; see "President Ma Attends Opening of the 2012 Thematic Congress of the International Academy of Comparative Law," Office of the President, May 24, 2012 (http://english.president.gov.tw/Default.aspx?tabid=491&itemid=27531&rmid=2355). When Taiwan reporters suggested that Ma had intimated that Germany might be a model for China-Taiwan unification, the spokesman for China's Taiwan Affairs Office shot down the idea on the grounds that "the circumstances of the two Germanys were different from the circumstances on the two sides of the Taiwan Strait"; see Mao Leilei and Lin Su, "State Council Taiwan Affairs Office Comments on Ma Ying-jeou's 20 May Speech: Compatible with China's Propositions and of Positive Significance," Xinhua Domestic Service, May 30, 2012 (OSC CPP20120530047002).

3. Ma Ying-jeou, "Upholding Ideals, Working Together for Reform, and Creating Greater Well-Being for Taiwan."

4. For the authoritative statement, see Wang Yi, "Speech Delivered by Wang Yi during 10th Seminar on Cross-Strait Relations [Full Text]," Taiwan Affairs Office, March 15, 2012 (OSC CPP20120329329001).

Index